P9-DCX-642

FIFTY KEY FIGURES IN MANAGEMENT

Fifty Key Figures in Management presents the lives and ideas of influential people who have helped redefine the way we think about management. The book covers well-known and controversial figures from around the world and from the Renaissance onwards, including:

- Edward Cadbury
- Peter Drucker
- Henry Ford
- Bill Gates
- Henry J. Heinz
- Philip Kotler
- Machiavelli
- Matsushita Konosuke
- Cosimo dei Medici
- Jack Welch.

This highly readable and informative guide is essential reading for all those with an interest in the key personalities involved in the development of management as we know it today.

Morgen Witzel is a historian of management and writer on business.

ROUTLEDGE KEY GUIDES

Routledge Key Guides are accessible, informative and lucid handbooks, which define and discuss the central concepts, thinkers and debates in a broad range of academic disciplines. All are written by noted experts in their respective subjects. Clear, concise exposition of complex and stimulating issues and ideas makes *Routledge Key Guides* the ultimate reference resources for students, teachers, researchers and the interested lay person.

Ancient History: Key Themes and Approaches
Neville Morley

Business: The Key Concepts
Mark Vernon

Cinema Studies: The Key Concepts (Second edition)
Susan Hayward

Communication, Cultural and Media Studies:
The Key Concepts (Third edition)
John Hartley

Cultural Theory: The Key Concepts
Edited by Andrew Edgar and Peter Sedgwick

Cultural Theory: The Key Thinkers
Andrew Edgar and Peter Sedgwick

Eastern Philosophy: Key Readings
Oliver Leaman

Fifty Contemporary Choreographers
Edited by Martha Bremser

Fifty Contemporary Filmmakers
Edited by Yvonne Tasker

Fifty Eastern Thinkers
Diané Collinson, Kathryn Plant and
Robert Wilkinson

Fifty Key Classical Authors
Alison Sharrock and Rhiannon Ash

Fifty Key Contemporary Thinkers
John Lechte

Fifty Key Figures in Management
Morgen Witzel

Fifty Key Figures in Twentieth Century British
Politics
Keith Laybourn

Fifty Key Jewish Thinkers
Dan Cohn-Sherbok

Fifty Key Thinkers on the Environment
Edited by Joy Palmer with
Peter Blaze Corcoran and David A. Cooper

Fifty Key Thinkers on History
Marnie Hughes-Warrington

Fifty Key Thinkers in International Relations
Martin Griffiths

Fifty Major Economists
Steven Pressman

Fifty Major Philosophers
Diané Collinson

Fifty Major Thinkers on Education
Joy Palmer

Fifty Modern Thinkers on Education
Joy Palmer

Gurdjieff: The Key Concepts
Sophia Wellbeloved

International Relations: The Key Concepts
Martin Griffiths and Terry O'Callaghan

Key Concepts in Eastern Philosophy
Oliver Leaman

Key Concepts in Language and Linguistics
R. L. Trask

Key Concepts in the Philosophy of Education
John Gingell and Christopher Winch

Key Writers on Art: From Antiquity to the
Nineteenth Century
Edited by Chris Murray

Key Writers on Art: The Twentieth Century
Edited by Chris Murray

Popular Music: The Key Concepts
Roy Shuker

Post-Colonial Studies: The Key Concepts
Bill Ashcroft, Gareth Griffiths and
Helen Tiffin

Social and Cultural Anthropology:
The Key Concepts
Nigel Rapport and Joanna Overing

Sport and Physical Education: The Key Concepts
Timothy Chandler, Mike Cronin and
Wray Vamplew

Sport Psychology: The Key Concepts
Ellis Cashmore

Television Studies: The Key Concepts
Neil Casey, Bernadette Casey, Justin Lewis,
Ben Calvert and Liam French

FIFTY KEY FIGURES IN MANAGEMENT

Morgen Witzel

Routledge
Taylor & Francis Group

LONDON AND NEW YORK

First published 2003
by Routledge
11 New Fetter Lane, London EC4P 4EE

Simultaneously published in the USA and Canada
by Routledge
29 West 35th Street, New York, NY 10001

Routledge is an imprint of the Taylor & Francis Group

© 2003 Morgen Witzel

Typeset in Bembo by Taylor & Francis Books Ltd
Printed and bound in Great Britain by
TJ International Ltd, Padstow, Cornwall

British Library Cataloguing in Publication Data
A catalogue record for this book is available from the British Library

Library of Congress Cataloging in Publication Data
Witzel, Morgen.
Fifty key figures in Management/Morgen Witzel
p.c.m. Includes bibliographical references and index.
1. Management. 2. Executives–Biography. 3. Industrialists–Biography. 4.
Management–Study and teaching. I. Title.
HD31.W585 2003
658'0092'2–dc21   2002031933

ISBN 0–415–36977–0 (hbk)
ISBN 0–415–36978–9 (pbk)

ALPHABETICAL LIST OF
CONTENTS

Chronological list of contents   viii
Preface   xi
Management themes   xvi

Chris Argyris (1923–)   3

Richard Arkwright (1732–92)   9

Charles Babbage (1792–1871)   17

Tomás Bat'a (1876–1932)   23

Max Boisot (1943–)   30

James Burnham (1905–87)   36

Edward Cadbury (1873–1948)   43

Herbert N. Casson (1869–1951)   48

Alfred D. Chandler (1918–)   56

Arie de Geus (1930–)   63

W. Edwards Deming (1900–93)   66

Peter Drucker (1909–)   73

Pierre du Pont (1870–1954)   81

Harrington Emerson (1853–1931)   87

Henri Fayol (1841–1925)   96

Mary Parker Follett (1868–1933)   102

Henry Ford (1863–1947)   109

Jay Wright Forrester (1918–)   118

Fukuzawa Yukichi (1835–1901)   122

Bill Gates (1955–)   129

Edwin Gay (1867–1946)   136

Frank Bunker Gilbreth (1868–1924) and
Lillian Gilbreth (1878–1972)   142

Andrew Grove (1936–)   149

Charles Handy (1932–)   155

Henry J. Heinz (1844–1919)   162

Geert Hofstede (1928–)   169

Ibuka Masaru (1908–1997)   173

Philip Kotler (1931–)   177

Laozi (Lao Tzu) (6th century BC)   184

William Lever (1851–1925)   188

Niccolò Machiavelli (1469–1527)   194

Marshall McLuhan (1911–80)   198

Abraham Maslow (1908–70)   203

Matsushita Konosuke (1894–1989)   208

Cosimo dei Medici (1389–1464)   213

Henry Mintzberg (1939–)   219

James D. Mooney (1884–1957)   225

Gareth Morgan (1943–)   232

J.P. Morgan (1837–1913)   239

Nonaka Ikujiro (1935–)   247

Ohmae Kenichi (1943–)   253

Robert Owen (1771–1858)   258

Tom Peters (1942–)   266

Michael Porter (1947–)   272

Herbert Simon (1916–2001)   277

Sunzi (Sun Tzu) (*c.* 4th century BC)   282

Frederick Winslow Taylor (1856–1915)   286

Toyoda Kiichiro (1894–1952)   294

Lyndall Fownes Urwick (1891–1983)   299

Jack Welch (1935–)   306

Further reading   311
Index   313

CHRONOLOGICAL LIST OF CONTENTS

Laozi (Lao Tzu) (6th century BC)   184

Sunzi (Sun Tzu) (c. 4th century BC)   282

Cosimo dei Medici (1389–1464)   213

Niccolò Machiavelli (1469–1527)   199

Richard Arkwright (1732–92)   9

Robert Owen (1771–1858)   258

Charles Babbage (1792–1871)   17

Fukuzawa Yukichi (1835–1901)   122

J.P. Morgan (1837–1913)   239

Henri Fayol (1841–1925)   96

Henry J. Heinz (1844–1919)   162

William Lever (1851–1925)   188

Harrington Emerson (1853–1931)   87

Frederick Winslow Taylor (1856–1915)   286

Henry Ford (1863–1947)   109

Edwin Gay (1867–1946)   136

Mary Parker Follett (1868–1933)   102

Frank Bunker Gilbreth (1868–1924) and
    Lillian Gilbreth (1878–1972)   142

Herbert N. Casson (1869–1951)   48

Pierre du Pont (1870–1954)   81

Edward Cadbury (1873–1948)   43

Tomás Bat'a (1876–1932)   23

James D. Mooney (1884–1957)   225

Lyndall Fownes Urwick (1891–1983)   299

Matsushita Konosuke (1894–1989)   208

Toyoda Kiichiro (1894–1952)   294

W. Edwards Deming (1900–93)   66

James Burnham (1905–87)   36

Ibuka Masaru (1908–97)   173

Abraham Maslow (1908–70)   203

Peter Drucker (1909–)   73

Marshall McLuhan (1911–80)   194

Herbert Simon (1916–2001)   277

Alfred D. Chandler (1918–)   56

Jay Wright Forrester (1918–)   118

Chris Argyris (1923–)   3

Geert Hofstede (1928–)   169

Arie de Geus (1930–)   63

Philip Kotler (1931–)   177

Charles Handy (1932–)   155

Nonaka Ikujiro (1935–)   247

Jack Welch (1935–)   306

Andrew Grove (1936–)   149

Henry Mintzberg (1939–)   219

Tom Peters (1942–)   266

Max Boisot (1943–)   30

Gareth Morgan (1943–)   232

Ohmae Kenichi (1943–)   253

Michael Porter (1947–)   272

Bill Gates (1955–)   129

Further reading   311
Index   313

PREFACE

The title of this book, *Fifty Key Figures in Management*, immediately poses two questions: first, what is 'management', and second, what is a 'key figure'?

Management is one of the most important phenomena of modern civilisation. Andrew Thomson and Roger Young, writing in the preface to the first volume of *The Evolution of Modern Management* (2002), Edward Brech's monumental work on British management history, sum up the case: 'Management is the means by which organisations set and carry through their objectives; without it, modern civilisation and its processes of wealth creation would not exist.'[1] Yet for all its importance and omnipresence, absolute definitions of what 'management' is are difficult to find. Many of the figures cited in this book have quite firm ideas about what management is, but these definitions do not always coincide: consider, for example, the differing concepts of management that appear in the works of F.W. Taylor, Peter Drucker and Tom Peters.

One useful way of approaching the concept is to consider the origins of the term. 'Management' and its associated words, 'manager', 'manage', etc., first appear in English in the late sixteenth century, in the time of Shakespeare. They derive ultimately from the Latin word *manus*, literally meaning 'hand' but also with connotations of 'power' and 'jurisdiction'. In the late Middle Ages we find the Italian word *maneggiare* gradually supplanting the older *factore* as the term for an official in charge of a trading or manufacturing enterprise (our word 'factory', originally used to mean a trading post as well as a place of production, comes from this root). The French term *manegerie* begins to appear in the sixteenth century as well. In English, the term 'management' for a long time referred in general terms to the controlling or direction of affairs, whether one's own or those of other people, and from the seventeenth century on there were literally hundreds of books published with the word 'management' in their titles, referring to everything from agriculture and forestry to health care, children's education and prisons. And by the middle of the seventeenth century, the word was being applied to business and financial matters as well.

Management in its original meaning, then, meant 'to do' and, more importantly, 'to cause to be done'. Looking at management today and the activities which are associated with it – guiding, leading, planning, controlling, directing, coordinating, and so on – one can see that this idea still broadly holds true. The works of all of the figures cited in this volume, and indeed of most influential writers on management, rest on the implicit assumption that management is concerned with guiding/directing/coordinating the work of other people with the requisite resources.

A 'key figure' is usually perceived as someone who has been of more than usual importance in their field. The fifty key figures[2] we have included here are people who, through their ideas or by practice and example, have made a major contribution to how management is understood and done. They are by no means always the most famous people in their field, or the ones who have sold the most books. Along with major names like Peter Drucker, Charles Handy, Henry Mintzberg, Bill Gates and Jack Welch, we have included less high-profile figures such as Charles Babbage, Mary Parker Follett, Jay Wright Forrester, Matsushita Konosuke and Herbert Simon. The inclusion of some, such as Marshall McLuhan, Andrew Grove and Laozi, will probably come as a surprise. But this book is not intended as a catalogue of the great and the good: it is a collection of people who, as individuals, changed our perception of management and helped, even if only in subtle ways, to improve managerial practice around the world.

Their backgrounds are highly diverse. Today we tend to think of management as being a separate discipline, existing in its own little compartment. This was not always the case. A century ago, when the first fully fledged theories of management were being constructed in the aftermath of the Victorian scientific revolution, managers and management academics borrowed as widely as possible, from engineering and the natural sciences, military science, politics, law, economics, sociology, psychology and even literature and the fine arts. Harrington Emerson, the first efficiency guru, once claimed that his ideas on management had been drawn from the study of three things: the conducting of symphony orchestras, the breeding of racehorses and railway timetables.

When we look at the people who have made and continue to make real breakthroughs in management education and practice, we see that they have often been exposed to a wide variety of influences. The ideas about management expressed in these pages are drawn from many different sources: anthropology and electronics, psychology and politics, philosophy and personal religious belief, experiences of battle and of manual labour. Before entering management, Herbert Casson had been a socialist agitator; Richard Arkwright had been a barber and wigmaker; Lyndall Urwick had served in the British army. Others have had more conventional academic or business backgrounds, but none can be said to be conventional thinkers. They looked at management as currently practised, challenged its existing assumptions, and sought out fundamental principles that would lead to improvement.

It is important to note that we are not just considering management in the present day. Too many people fall into the trap of thinking that management has no past, or at least that nothing can be learned about management today by studying the past. Whereas scientists, lawyers, philosophers, artists, political leaders and many other professionals see themselves as part of a long tradition and make reference to the past, managers perversely refuse to acknowledge their own heritage. In so doing, they miss out on the origins of their discipline and the rich diversity of influences that has helped make management what it is today. F.W. Taylor, Harrington Emerson, Frank and Lillian Gilbreth, Henri Fayol and others like them developed seminal ideas that continue to form part of the core of management thinking and practice. Whether we like it or not, we owe at least part of our present knowledge to these past pioneers. It seems only right, when considering key figures in management, to go back and look at those people who set the paradigm within which we continue to work today.

A third question may arise at this point: why only fifty figures? Why not 500, or 5,000? Admittedly, the number 'fifty' has been chosen arbitrarily; we could as easily have had forty-nine or fifty-one key figures. But our purpose here is to introduce a selection of the most important figures in management, and not to include every last figure of note. A final figure had to be chosen, and the round number 'fifty' has several attractions: enough to give a broad coverage of the subject and to include some minor but nonetheless important figures, but few enough to force us to be rigorous in considering who was a 'key figure' and who was not.

The final choice of fifty key figures has necessarily been a subjective one, and has been influenced by my own view of what management is, how it has developed and where it may be going in the future.

Management is – or should be – a holistic discipline; managers should draw their inspiration and ideas from a broad variety of sources, past as well as present and from outside the field of management as well as within it. Key figures, therefore, are those who have influenced the development of management *as a whole*, not just some function or aspect of it. As a result, readers may be as surprised by some of the omissions in this book as by some of the figures included. There is, for example, no place for Ted Levitt, Chester Barnard or H. Igor Ansoff, figures who normally appear in collections of great management thinkers due to their major contributions in their particular fields. Some usually regarded as disciplinary specialists have been included, such as Henry Mintzberg (strategy) and Philip Kotler (marketing), but these are people whose importance is such that it has transcended their own discipline and influenced the entire body of thinking about the purpose and nature of management.

I admit also to a particular bias. To my way of thinking, knowledge is *the* single most important ingredient in successful management, and the new writers on the role of knowledge in management and organization are opening doors to a fresh approach to management which is holistic rather than functional, and which treats knowledge as the organization's most important source of capital. In so doing, these writers are making explicit concepts that have been embedded in management for a very long time, but which until now have been poorly understood. The inclusion of Chris Argyris, Max Boisot, Arie de Geus and Nonaka Ikujiro is justified on the grounds that their work is changing the way we think about and do management, even as this book is being written.

That is my own interpretation. In fact, every reader of this book should be able to think of people whom they would consider to be 'key figures' who have been left out of this collection. That is well and good. If readers are encouraged to sit down and work out who they consider their own 'key figures' to be, and why, then they will learn a great deal about management, including why it is important and what its objectives and functions are. The purpose of this book is not didactic; I do not offer these fifty examples with the idea that the reader should learn from them by copying and imitating their efforts. Rather, it is my hope that consideration of their ideas and works will show that there are many different ways to think about and examine management, all of which can be valid and all of which can be conducive to learning.

The challenge of managing for success in today's turbulent business environment is an immense one. I hope that this book will help students of management and others to broaden their horizons and to think more deeply about what management is, where it came from and where it is going.

My thinking on this subject was considerably developed and refined during two years when I was editor of the *Biographical Dictionary of Management*, published in 2001, and I owe a great deal to my colleagues on the editorial board and my fellow authors on that project, notably Karl Moore, David Lewis, Daniel Wren, Sasaki Tsuneo and Sawai Minoru. I owe thanks also to Malcolm Warner, with whom I first worked on the *International Encyclopedia of Business and Management*, and who has been a good colleague and friend ever since. Edward Brech's heroic efforts to promote the study of management history have been a source of inspiration. Gay Haskins introduced me to the works of Max Boisot; Peter Starbuck, one of the world's leading authorities on Drucker, has always been generous with his ideas; and virtually everything I know about Tomas Bat'a comes from Milan Zeleny.

I want to particularly thank Roger Thorp, formerly of Routledge, who encouraged and supported this project from the very beginning. His successor, Rosie Waters, has also been a warm supporter and a pleasure to work with. Milon Nagi, ever courteous and reliable, has managed the nuts and bolts of the project from the publisher's end and made my task much easier. To them, and to the many others in the profession of management with whom I have worked over the years and who have helped to shape my thinking, go my grateful thanks. Thanks go also to Vanessa Winch and Matt Beard for producing and copy-editing the final text so carefully and efficiently.

Morgen Witzel
Northlew, Devon
18 March 2002

Notes

1 A. Thomson and R. Young, 'Preface', in E.F.L. Brech, *The Evolution of Modern Management*, Bristol: Thoemmes Press, 2002, vol. 1, p. xiii.
2 To be strictly accurate there are fifty-one key figures here, as the contributions of Frank and Lillian Gilbreth are discussed conjointly.

MANAGEMENT THEMES

The following chart shows some of the major 'themes' or issues of importance within management that are discussed in this book, and indicates in which entries these themes are discussed. This chart is meant as a general guide only, and should not be taken as all-embracing. The chart can be used to find entries which will provide discussion of particular themes; within each entry, the internal cross-references can be used to navigate to other subjects of interest.

	Management systems and principles	Managerial and national culture	Globalisation/ localisation	Organisation and structure	Markets and marketing	Strategy and planning	Ethics and corporate governance	Knowledge and education	Innovation and technology
Chris Argyris (1923–)		X		X				X	
Richard Arkwright (1732–92)			X	X	X				X
Charles Babbage (1792–1871)			X		X			X	X
Tomás Bat'a (1876–1932)	X	X		X	X		X		X
Max Boisot (1943–)		X	X					X	
James Burnham (1905–87)		X	X				X		
Edward Cadbury (1873–1948)	X			X	X		X	X	
Herbert N. Casson (1869–1951)	X			X				X	X
Alfred D. Chandler (1918–)			X	X		X			
Arie de Geus (1930–)			X	X		X		X	X
W. Edwards Deming (1900–93)			X		X			X	X
Peter Drucker (1909–)	X			X		X		X	X
Pierre du Pont (1870–1954)				X		X		X	X

Name						
Harrington Emerson (1853–1931)	X					X X
Henri Fayol (1841–1925)	X	X		X		X X
Mary Parker Follett (1868–1933)	X	X		X		X
Henry Ford (1863–1947)			X	X	X	X X
Jay Wright Forrester (1918–)			X	X		X X
Fukuzawa Yukichi (1835–1901)	X		X	X		X
Bill Gates (1955–)			X	X	X	
Edwin Gay (1867–1946)			X		X	X
Frank Bunker Gilbreth (1868–1924) and Lillian Gilbreth (1878–1972)			X	X		X
Andrew Grove (1936–)	X		X	X	X	X
Charles Handy (1932–)	X	X	X	X	X	X
Henry J. Heinz (1844–1919)			X	X	X	
Geert Hofstede (1928–)	X		X	X		X
Ibuka Masaru (1908–1997)	X		X	X		X X
Philip Kotler (1931–)			X	X		
Laozi (Lao Tzu) (6th century BC)	X		X	X	X	
William Lever (1851–1925)			X	X	X	
Niccolò Machiavelli (1469–1527)	X	X	X	X		
Marshall McLuhan (1911–80)			X	X	X	
Abraham Maslow (1908–70)	X			X		
Matsushita Konosuke (1894–1989)	X		X	X		X
Cosimo dei Medici (1389–1464)			X	X		

(Continued over)

	Management systems and principles	Managerial and national culture	Globalisa-tion/localisation	Organisation and structure	Markets and marketing	Strategy and planning	Ethics and corporate governance	Knowledge and education	Innovation and technology
Henry Mintzberg (1939–)	X	X		X		X			
James D. Mooney (1884–1957)	X	X		X		X	X		
Gareth Morgan (1943–)	X	X		X				X	
J.P. Morgan (1837–1913)			X				X		
Nonaka Ikujiro (1935–)		X	X	X		X		X	X
Ohmae Kenichi (1943–)		X	X	X		X			X
Robert Owen (1771–1858)				X			X	X	
Tom Peters (1942–)	X	X		X	X			X	X
Michael Porter (1947–)			X			X			
Herbert Simon (1916–2001)				X		X		X	
Sunzi (Sun Tzu) (c. 4th century BC)		X				X			
Frederick Winslow Taylor (1856–1915)	X			X			X	X	
Toyoda Kiichiro (1894–1952)		X		X				X	X
Lyndall Fownes Urwick (1891–1983)	X			X	X				
Jack Welch (1935–)	X			X				X	

FIFTY KEY FIGURES IN MANAGEMENT

CHRIS ARGYRIS (1923–)

Chris Argyris is best known for his work, with his long-time collaborator Donald Schön, in developing the theory of 'action science' and its application to business situations. Action science is a process of scientific research and analysis which is closely connected to the process it studies and continuously feeds back knowledge into that process, rather than trying to remain objective and impartial as does 'normal' science. A recognition of the role of knowledge in breaking down barriers and driving forward organisational change and innovation lies at the heart of Argyris's later theories on organisation. His work on action science in the 1970s laid the groundwork for many of the theories of 'knowledge management' that emerged in the 1990s.

The son of Greek immigrants, Argyris was born in Newark, New Jersey on 16 July 1923. Part of his early childhood was spent in Greece, and by the time he first attended school he still had only a limited command of English. This, and more generally the fact that he came from a minority group, set him apart from the other children at school and instilled in him a tendency to reflection and introspection.[1] During the Second World War he served as an officer in the US Army Corps of Signals, going on to university after the war. He took his PhD from the School of Industrial and Labor Relations at Cornell University in 1951. His first academic post was at Yale University, as director of research in labour; by 1960 he was a professor of business administration and one of the rising stars in business education. In 1971 he moved to Harvard where he was appointed James Bryant Conant Professor of Education and Organizational Behavior, a post he continues to hold.

Argyris's writings can be divided roughly into three stages, although there is considerable overlap and books in the later stages always refer heavily to earlier work. In the first stage, in the late 1950s and early 1960s, Argyris considers the problems of organisation and the 'fit' between the needs of organisations and those of individuals. In the second stage, he looks at the problems of organisational change and the use of action science as a change tool. In the third stage, he moves beyond the specific problems of change to consider the role of organisational knowledge more widely. In so doing, he helped pioneer the field of knowledge management.

Reflective by nature, Argyris's wartime role and his subsequent academic career had developed his ability to analyse problems and look for long-term solutions. His first concern was with what he termed

3

the lack of congruence between the needs and goals of organisations on the one hand, and the needs and goals of those people who are part of organisations on the other.[2] In particular, he criticised the 'machine bureaucracy' that characterised (and continues to characterise) so many business organisations. Hierarchical and rigidly structured, machine bureaucracies are managed from the top downward: communication is nearly always from the upper levels to the lower levels of the hierarchy, and when communication does flow upwards it is usually at a time and in a format specified by senior management. The need for managerial control leads top management to impose limitations on the actions of their subordinates: while on the one hand, top management specifies to junior managers and workers what their roles and duties *are*, it also tends, even if only implicitly, to prohibit or at least discourage many activities that *are not* part of those duties. An individual is given a job specification: the elements of that specification are required to help meet the organisation's goals, while any activity not specifically mentioned is considered a distraction from that goal and should be prohibited.

Managers manage, in other words, by controlling and limiting the efforts of those below them. This approach to management has two problems. First, it takes no account of individuals' own goals, which could be at variance with those of the organisation. If employees do not share the organisation's goals, they will not be motivated to pursue them: inefficiency, disharmony and conflict will result. More seriously, it takes no account of people's ability to grow and change with experience. Employees are not cogs in a machine, they are independent, self-aware entities. As they grow older and gain experience, they become more independent and active; therefore, to keep them 'in line' and focused on the needs of the organisation, the limitations and controls on them grow correspondingly greater. To give a simple example, a young graduate placed in a junior management job will have much to learn and will probably be satisfied with the responsibilities placed on him or her; but a 40-year-old manager in the same position will see much more potential for growth and change and is likely to be frustrated by the restrictions imposed on his or her job.

Companies try to get around this problem by promoting people with potential into more responsible positions, widening their scope of activities and increasing personal freedom. However, by failing to understand the fit between organisations and people, they create problems of a different kind. In the late 1960s the Canadian psychologist Laurence Peter developed the Peter Principle, commonly expressed as: 'in a hierarchy, every employee tends to rise to the level of his [sic] own incompetence'.[3] According to Peter, although organisations promote employees to senior positions on the basis of merit, they tend to do so on the basis of how well an employee is doing his or her current job. Less important, if considered at all, is whether the employee will be able to do the job into which he or she is being promoted. In other words, promotion is a reward for past success, and bears little or no relation to future needs of the organisation, or indeed of the employee. This becomes a problem when, as is often the case, employees and managers are promoted into positions for which they are not suited. At this point the 'level of incompetence' is reached. The employee is not capable of doing the job into which he or she has been promoted, and stops being successful. Further promotions are not forthcoming, and the organisation is stuck with a dissatisfied employee doing a job poorly.

Organisations limit the actions of their members, and this leads to resistance on the part of the latter. Sometimes this can lead to conflict and obstruction, or gold-bricking (giving the appearance of working while actually doing as little as possible), or even criminal behaviour such as theft in the office. Sometimes the dissatisfied employees simply leave. Most commonly, however, employees opt for an easy life, doing their jobs with little involvement and trying to keep the organisation from interfering with their lives as much as possible. For these employees, any change in the organisation is perceived as a threat. To counteract change, employees adopt what Argyris describes as 'defensive routines', actions which can inhibit or slow down change, or even block it altogether. Some employees will employ defensive routines for negative reasons, purely because they do not wish to upset the status quo. More dangerous, says Argyris, are those who seek to block change for what they feel are positive reasons: they may be seeking to protect colleagues who are threatened by change, for example, or they may genuinely believe that the proposed changes are harmful and will damage the organisation.[4] Many of these defensive routines become deeply embedded in the organisation's culture, so that even new employees brought in to promote change become 'infected' and thus part of the problem.

In the next phase of his work, Argyris began to look at how to overcome the problem of resistance to change. In the 1970s, after two decades of prosperity, American business was beginning to feel the pinch: the oil shocks, the end of international currency agreements and the challenge of imported goods, especially from Japan, were beginning to make themselves felt. Consultants and other observers were calling for radical change in the way American business was organised and run. In 1982, Tom **Peters** and Robert Waterman would publish their manifesto for radical change, *In Search of Excellence*, based on their experiences at McKinsey & Co. in the 1970s and their observations of the best and worst of American business. The need for change offered a challenge to Argyris: how to defeat defensive routines and make change management itself into an integral part of the organisation.

This led at the same time to a change in Argyris's own methodological approach. Up until then, like most social scientists, he conducted his research through observing the behaviour of people in groups. Now, in partnership with the sociologist Donald Schön, he switched his attention from behaviour *per se* to studying the reasons behind behaviour. What causes organisations and people to behave as they do? To get at the answers to this question, Argyris realised it was necessary to get away from the standard model of scientific research in which people and groups were observed objectively by neutral observers. Despite all precautions, this kind of research led inevitably to bias. This phenomenon had been observed in the 1920s and 1930s during research at Western Electric's Hawthorne plant, near Chicago, where the research team led by Harvard University scholars Fritz Roethlisberger and Elton Mayo were puzzled as to why the sample of employees they were studying and interviewing were performing consistently better than the average across the firm. After a number of experiments with environment, lighting and so on, the researchers reached the startling conclusion that the group being studied performed better *because they were being studied*. The presence of the researchers and the attention being paid to their own work gave the workers in the sample group a stronger sense of self-worth and motivated them to do better.[5]

For Argyris and Schön, it was time that scientific research came down out of its ivory tower and integrated itself into the organisation. The term 'action research' was intended to denote a new kind of research, conducted by managers and workers themselves on a continuous basis and constantly feeding back into their work.[6] The purpose of action research was to create 'actionable knowledge', 'the knowledge that people use to create the world',[7] rather than knowledge that was irrelevant to everyday use, no matter how excellent the methods of acquiring it might be. In his ideal world, businesses do not call in outside experts to observe and make recommendations; they do their own scientific research, on the job, as they go along, and make the gathering of knowledge and its utilisation a part of the manager's daily task.

Argyris's method of integrating knowledge into the organisation is called by him 'double loop learning'. Single loop learning is a simple process whereby feedback from previous actions is used to alter future actions. This can be effective in limited situations, but does place management in a largely reactive situation. Double loop learning, on the other hand, uses feedback from past actions to question not only the nature of future actions, but all the underlying assumptions on which future decisions are to be made. When considering feedback, managers need to ask not only, 'what should we do next?', but also, 'why are we doing it?', and even more importantly, 'what else ought we to be doing?' Only by asking these questions can organisational learning become deep-rooted and truly effective.

Again, there will be resistance in the organisation to double loop learning, as it necessarily involves challenging existing assumptions and, in turn, throwing out some of those assumptions if they are proved to be no longer valid. The response to new knowledge, especially if that knowledge is threatening, can often be, 'I don't want to know that'. This phenomenon has been observed elsewhere; back in the early years of the century, Herbert **Casson** had remarked with exasperation on the unwillingness of many executives to learn. But Argyris argues that the knowledge generated by double loop learning can be so powerful and so persuasive that it can break down even the strongest defensive routines. Action science is by no means a panacea; overcoming defensive routines also requires patience and persuasion. But in the long run, persuading people by sharing knowledge with them is bound to be more effective than issuing directives and orders that will be ignored or circumvented.

Action science and double loop learning entail the continuous generation of new knowledge, and also the diffusion of that knowledge widely throughout the firm. In his later works, Argyris has been concerned with how firms acquire and use knowledge. *Knowledge for Action* (1993) considers how managers should employ knowledge in their work, while *Flawed Advice and the Management Trap* (2000) suggests means by which managers can judge whether the advice they are getting from 'independent experts' is likely to be of practical value to them. In the last book there are echoes of Mary Parker **Follett**, questioning whether experts are indeed custodians of truth. Both would agree that the knowledge we gain for ourselves is superior to that which we acquire second-hand from others: independent experts and advisors do have a role to play, but their ideas should not necessarily be accepted at face value, and in the end nothing can substitute for knowledge generated within, and specific to, the organisation. The need to create knowledge, and how to do it, is one of the central issues in current theories of knowledge management.

Argyris's books can be difficult reads. Newcomers to the field of management, particularly to organisation behaviour, are likely to find his books densely written and the central ideas not always easy to tease out. One criticism which has been levelled against him, with some fairness, is that, ironically, he is too concerned with the concept of action science and has not done enough to explain how it can be put into practice (some of his later books attempt to redress this problem). Against this, Argyris attempts to show how knowledge can be used to break down the monolithic structure of organisations and make them more fluid and adaptable and at the same time happier and better places to work. Less of an overt revolutionary than Tom Peters, less prescriptive than the likes of **Porter** and **Deming**, Argyris's nearest equivalents as a management thinker are probably Charles **Handy** and Henry **Mintzberg**, two others who, from vastly different perspectives, believe there are few hard and fast answers in an activity that is ultimately about human agency, and that it is what we know and how we employ that knowledge that ultimately determines managerial success or failure.

See also: **Boisot, de Geus, Follett, Forrester, Handy, Maslow, Morgan, Nonaka, Simon**

Major works

Personality and Organization, New York: Harper, 1957.
Integrating the Individual and the Organization, New York: Wiley, 1964.
Organization and Innovation, Chicago: Wiley, 1965.
Intervention Theory and Method, Reading, MA: Addison-Wesley, 1970
Management and Organizational Development, New York: McGraw-Hill, 1971.
(With D. Schön) Theory in Practice, San Francisco: Jossey-Bass, 1974.
Increasing Leadership Effectiveness, New York: Wiley, 1976.
(With D. Schön) Organizational Learning, Reading, MA: Addison-Wesley, 1978.
Inner Contradictions of Rigorous Research, New York: Academic Press, 1980.
Reasoning, Learning and Action, San Francisco: Jossey-Bass, 1982.
On Organizational Learning, Oxford: Blackwell, 1993.
Knowledge for Action: A Guide to Overcoming Barriers to Organizational Change, San Francisco: Jossey-Bass, 1993.
Flawed Advice and the Management Trap: How Managers Can Know When They're Getting Good Advice and When They're Not, Oxford: Oxford University Press, 2000.

Further reading

After looking at Argyris's theories, it is useful to compare them to other theories of organisational learning. Recommended are the following:

Buzan, T., *Use Your Head*, London: BBC Books, 1974.
De Geus, A., *The Living Company: Habits for Survival in a Turbulent Environment*, 1997.
Follett, M.P., *Creative Experience*, New York: Longmans Green, 1924.
Hickman, J.R. (ed.), *Leading Organizations: Perspectives for a New Era*, Thousand Oaks, CA: Sage, 1998
Nonaka, I. and Takeuchi, H., *The Knowledge-Creating Company*, Oxford: Oxford University Press, 1995.
Schön, D., *The Reflective Practitioner*, New York: Basic Books, 1983.
Senge, P.M., *The Fifth Discipline: The Art and Practice of the Learning Organisation*, New York: Doubleday, 1990.

Notes

1   This is the conclusion of one important biographer; see C. Lundberg, 'Argyris, Chris', in M. Warner (ed.), *International Encyclopedia of Business and Management*, London: International Thomson Business Press, 1998, vol. 1, p. 18.
2   C. Argyris, *Personality and Organization*, New York: Harper, 1957.
3   L.J. Peters, *The Peter Principle*, London: Pan, 1969.
4   For a more detailed description of the concept of 'defensive routines', see especially C. Argyris, *Management and Organizational Development*, New York: McGraw-Hill, 1971.
5   See F. Roethlisberger and W.J. Dickson, *Management and the Worker*, Cambridge, MA: Harvard University Press, 1939.
6   Argyris and Schön coined the term 'action research' to indicate a contrast with 'normal research', the standard objective, rigorous research methods used by social scientists. 'Normal research' is the term used, slightly pejoratively, by T.S. Kuhn to denote the standard scientific paradigm of the day. 'Action science' is a broader term including action research and related analysis and application.
7   C. Argyris, *Knowledge for Action*, San Francisco: Jossey-Bass, 1993, p. 1.

RICHARD ARKWRIGHT (1732–92)

Richard Arkwright is one of the central figures of the Industrial Revolution, and is often credited with the founding of the factory system. A controversial figure in his own time, Arkwright is most often considered for his achievements as a production engineer. However, he was also an entrepreneurial genius of the first order, who played an important role in the diffusion of new manufacturing technology. In developing methods for mechanised, large-scale production, Arkwright laid the foundations for mass production and its necessary counterpart, mass marketing.

Arkwright was born on 23 December 1732 in Preston, Lancashire, the thirteenth child of a tailor. He grew up in a family that was constantly on the brink of poverty. Although he later became one of the richest men in Britain, he never forgot his humble background and used to joke that his family could trace its ancestry back to Noah, 'the first ark wright'. He was taught to read and write at home and was then apprenticed to a local barber. Barbers in the early eighteenth century still doubled as surgeons, and it is here that Arkwright received his first, albeit rudimentary, education in science.

Completing his apprenticeship when he was eighteen, Arkwright moved to the nearby town of Bolton and set up his own barbershop. The practice went well, and Arkwright was able to accumulate enough capital to branch out, first into wig-making and then later into inn-keeping, although the latter venture appears to have been less successful. By the early 1760s he was a moderately prosperous small businessman, and had probably already exceeded any expectations his family may have had for him.

The eighteenth-century Enlightenment in Britain was a time not only of great advances in science, but also of tremendous popular interest in the subject. Most towns of any size had a 'philosophical society' or similar body which met frequently and allowed amateur enthusiasts an opportunity to dabble in science and mechanics and compare the results of their work with those of other like-minded people. A plethora of journals, often of very small circulation, offered would-be scientists and inventors the chance to put their ideas and theories into print. By the second half of the century, most educated people had at least a passing interest in science, and across the country there were literally thousands of people in attic rooms and small workshops tinkering with new ideas and new devices.

One area which had attracted attention early was the mechanical production of cloth. Some advances had been made; in 1725, for example, the Lombe brothers, Thomas and Joseph, had developed a system for the machine spinning of silk thread and had set up a small factory in Derby.[1] However, it was the spinning of cotton yarn which received the most attention, as it was widely perceived that the potential market for cotton textiles would be very large. At the time, cotton textiles were nearly all imported from India and were correspondingly expensive. Arkwright, coming as he did from an area in which textile production was already an important part of the economy, understood both the technical problems and the potential market if those problems could be solved. By the mid-1760s, he had worked out a rough design for a spinning frame, a powered machine which would spin cotton into thread using a series of rollers. However, he lacked the technical ability to put the design into practice.

The turning point came in 1767, when Arkwright met and registered a partnership with John Kay, a clockmaker from Bury in Lancashire. Kay was also an inventor, and had indeed already registered several patents. The role of clockmakers in the Industrial Revolution is often forgotten. To understand this role, we need to go back to the late seventeenth century when the Royal Navy launched its search for a reliable marine chronometer. That search took a century, and although it culminated in the now-famous work of John Harrison, clockmakers and watchmakers around the country had been involved in experimenting and developing new skills, particularly the art of making precision gears for machines. By the 1760s, Britain led the world in this particular branch of engineering. The mechanical production plants of the Industrial Revolution required gears for power transmission, as well as other precision parts such as rollers and slides, and the clockmakers and watchmakers were the only people with the requisite skills to make these. By the 1780s, when new factories were being built at a rapid rate, well-to-do Londoners were complaining that it was impossible to get their clocks serviced or repaired; all the capital's clockmakers had gone north to build cotton mills.

The partnership with Kay also landed Arkwright in controversy for the first time. Before joining Arkwright, Kay had worked with another Lancashire inventor, Thomas Highs. There seems to have been a dispute between the two, quite possibly over ownership of the ideas they had been working on, and it seems that when Kay joined Arkwright he took with him several designs from the previous partnership. Kay and Arkwright claimed these were Kay's work; Highs claimed they were his own, and that Arkwright and Kay had stolen them from him. Highs's case was never proven, but accusations of theft of intellectual property followed Arkwright for the rest of his career.[2]

By 1768 Arkwright, with Kay's technical assistance, had completed the design for the spinning frame. The final stages of the work were carried out in great secrecy in a room over Arkwright's inn, where to deflect attention from their real purpose they let it be known that they were planning a campaign for a local election. Arkwright then took his design and his small reserves of capital and moved to Nottingham, then a leading centre of cotton textiles production. He found two partners, John Smalley and David Thornley, and together they set up a small spinning mill worked by horse-power. This was an important stage in prototyping; technical adjustments were made to increase efficiency, and Arkwright also became convinced that horse-power was insufficient. He turned instead to the use of water power. By now some of Nottingham's leading businessmen were interested and two of them, Jedediah Strutt and Samuel Need, offered to back Arkwright in the production of a large-scale water-powered mill; their interest was in securing a supply of inexpensive cotton yarn to use in their own business, the making of hosiery. A suitable site was found at Cromford in Derbyshire, and the spinning frame, now known as the 'water frame' due to its adaptation to water power, went into full production.

During the first half of the 1770s Arkwright devoted himself to building up and improving the Cromford factory. With Need and Strutt, he was involved in lobbying government to remove duties on imports of raw Indian cotton, a necessary step in bringing costs down still further and growing the market. Most of his time, however, was spent in the factory. Before raw cotton could be spun into yarn, a number of preparatory processes such as carding, drawing and roving were required, and Arkwright's idea was to mechanise these as well. Regrettably, he left us no written account of how he went about this; he seems to have carried many of his designs in his head, any sketches there might have been have now been destroyed. As before, he recruited clockmakers and others with technical expertise to put his ideas into practice, and as before, outraged accusations of theft of intellectual property arose from various quarters. Quite how much of the result was due to Arkwright's own ingenuity and how much to ideas 'borrowed' from other quarters is impossible to determine. By 1775, however, Arkwright had established a complete production line for the manufacture of cotton yarn from raw cotton through all his stages. This was the true heart of the factory system: a single machine process, capable of continuous production through multiple stages of the product's life, driven by a permanent supply of power and capable of being worked in shifts.

In 1775, Arkwright patented this system and then set about exploiting it. Already a wealthy man, he used his own capital to finance new mills such as that at Chorley in Lancashire. But he had recognised early on that the real potential of the new system lay in its diffusion. As well as cotton yarn, he began selling the technology to make it. He sold licenses to other entrepreneurs who wished to use the technology, sometimes directly investing in these new ventures as well; he even on occasion provided consultancy advice, for example to David Dale when the latter was setting up his factory at New Lanark in

Scotland. By 1780, fifteen Arkwright-patent mills were in operation, employing about 5,000 people.

By 1780, Arkwright was facing the problem that always confronts the owners of intellectual property – how to stop pirates. Providing one could find the necessary skilled workmen, the Arkwright system was easy to imitate, and mills using unlicensed versions of the technology began springing up across the north of England. In 1781, Arkwright took several of the pirates to court, and lost. His patent had always been a shaky one, and it was argued successfully that, as some of the components of the system were not Arkwright's own patent, he could not claim patent rights over the system as a whole. The patent was declared null and void and Arkwright's factory technology was effectively placed in the public domain.

His response was typically robust. The six years, 1775–81, had given him a huge competitive advantage, putting him far ahead of his rivals in terms of both technological development and skilled labour. He had always recognised that the market was far too large for one person or one firm to dominate. Now, as new factories were being established at an ever-accelerating rate, Arkwright turned from selling licenses to build his system to selling actual system components such as water frames. By 1784, he was earning £60,000 a year from original equipment sales alone, in addition to profits from his factories.[3]

Arkwright continued to back new entrepreneurs, and provided financial support for Samuel Oldknow early in the latter's meteoric career. His business interests by 1790 were an elaborate web of cross-investments, both incoming and outgoing. Arkwright used business partnerships to establish networks of relationships with both suppliers and customers. Although he was now, by some calculations, one of the five richest men in Britain and certainly had no need of new capital, he often invited his principal customers in textile manufacturing to take up partnerships in new ventures, as a way of building and maintaining good relationships. Arkwright was never reluctant to enrich others, so long as he enriched himself at the same time.

Arkwright also continued to refine his manufacturing technology, and was particularly interested in power generation. In the late 1780s he began to experiment with steam engines, and this brought him to the attention of James Watt and Matthew Boulton, who were then in the process of improving the original steam engine designed by Thomas Newcomen decades before. A lengthy correspondence ensued, and Arkwright was still working on methods of using steam power in factories at the time of his death.

Arkwright was knighted in 1786, and soon thereafter began work on a grand manor house near Cromford. A compulsive workaholic, he worked every day at his desk from 5 a.m. to 9 p.m. Unsurprisingly, the pace began to tell, and he developed heart problems. He died at Cromford on 3 August, 1792.

Assessing Arkwright's impact on modern management is difficult in a short space. There is, first of all, his work as a production engineer. Richard Fitton, author of one of the few reliable biographies of Arkwright,[4] calls him the founder of the modern factory system, and most commentators seem to agree. Although it is important to remember that prototype factories had been in existence for some time, it was Arkwright who first turned this method of production into a *system*: that is, an organisation that could be replicated and widely diffused regardless of place and product. Power looms were introduced to mechanise the weaving of cloth in the first years of the nineteenth century. It was not long before the system began to be applied to other textiles such as wool; in the 1840s, Titus Salt made his fortune in Bradford by developing factories for producing alpaca. The nineteenth century saw the factory system gradually spreading into the production of metal goods and machinery, notably weapons and, eventually and most famously, automobiles.

Mass production, of course, meant mass markets. Arkwright never articulated this idea clearly (not in the same way that Henry **Ford**, for example, was to do with his vision of cheap motor car production opening up a huge new market for cars in middle–class America), but he seems to have understood it, and this principle lay behind his support for the lifting of import duties on raw cotton. Cheaper cotton meant lower production costs; this in turn meant the chance to bring down the price of finished goods, which in turn meant more customers. Driving down the price meant lower unit profits, but this was more than offset by the increased volume of sales. And the mass market was found not only in Britain, of course, but also overseas. British textile exports contributed immeasurably to Britain's balance of trade over the succeeding century.

Of vital importance too is the diffusion of technology and skills that came out of Arkwright's establishment. To succeed, the Industrial Revolution needed both requisite technology and a supply of skilled labour. As noted above, Arkwright himself was an important diffuser of production technology, first through licensing and then through original equipment sales. His senior managerial and technical staff were also in great demand, and these men would often hop from job to job wherever the best pay and conditions were on offer, not unlike top-flight bankers and management consultants today. As they did so, they transferred their own skills and knowledge to other establishments. Most famous perhaps of these roving managers is Thomas Marshall, a former Arkwright superintendent who emigrated to the USA in 1791 and founded the US textile industry in New England.

The economic impact of the factory system continues to be the subject of considerable debate. Karl Marx and Friedrich Engels (the latter a factory owner himself) believed that the factory system was a means of concentrating capital; its net impact was to upset the balance between capital and labour in favour of the former, and make greater exploitation of labour possible. And, of course, this did happen: the factory system saw an almost immediate rise in the level of labour conflict and unrest. Arkwright himself seems to have learned an early lesson in this field when rioting workers burned down his factory at Chorley in 1779; he recognised that the mechanical system required cooperative workers if it was to function efficiently. Accordingly, he paid well, better than many of his competitors, and provided bonuses and free entertainments for his workers; in some cases he also awarded prizes to top-performing workers.[5] But the factory system had nonetheless created a new dynamic in the field of capital–labour relations, one with long-lasting consequences.

More intriguing is the recent analysis of the factory system by transaction costs theorists. Their view is that the factory system introduced greater economic efficiency by reducing transaction costs; whereas formerly the spinning of yarn, for example, had consisted of a number of separate stages each carried out at different establishments, now all those stages had been collapsed into a single process. This lowered the costs of coordination, and also permitted the monitoring of quality. One recent commentator believes that the real revolution of the factory system lay in the switch of emphasis from product to process. In contracting or putting-out systems, the most common method of manufacturing prior to the Industrial Revolution, the entrepreneur could only monitor the end product, accepting or rejecting goods delivered according to whether they met quality standards; there was no control over the process. By bringing the process of production under direct managerial control, Arkwright and his successors could concentrate on engineering the process so as to produce a higher quality of product at a lower cost.[6]

Routinised production led to the division of labour on the one hand, and to the commoditisation of many goods on the other. The social consequences of both have been enormous, and one of the most lasting consequences of Arkwright's innovations has been a renewal and intensification of the scrutiny of the role of business and management in society. The factory system led directly to the rising power and concentration of capital, and this in turn put the ethical aspects of business under the spotlight. Business practices which had seemed normative, such as child labour (Arkwright employed children as young as eight in his factories, though his son later stopped this practice), were suddenly reconsidered. The idea that the increasing power of the employer brought with it increasing responsibility to employees was articulated forcibly by the mill owner Robert **Owen** in the next century, who strongly advocated reform of the labour laws and the provision of education, welfare, housing and other benefits by employers. The arguments over the nature and extent of the ethical dimension of management that began in the late eighteenth century are still with us today.

See also: **Babbage, Cadbury, Ford, Lever, Owen**

Major works

Arkwright left behind no written work bar a small amount of correspondence. See bibliography in Fitton, *The Arkwrights: Spinners of Fortune* (below) for more details.

Further reading

In the 1820s and 1830s a number of books were published on the history of the cotton industry and these give details of Arkwright's career drawn from interviews with people who had known him; however, many of these are unreliable. William Radcliffe, himself a factory owner who played a leading role in the introduction of the power loom, is one of the best writers of such works and is worth reading. In our own time, given Arkwright's importance, there has been surprisingly little good work done on him; Richard Fitton's biography, which is both scholarly and readable, is recommended.

Berg, M., *The Age of Manufactures: Industry, Innovation and Work in Britain, 1720–1800*, Oxford: Berg, 1985.
Chapman, S., *Merchant Enterprise in Britain*, Cambridge: Cambridge University Press, 1992.
Fitton, R.S., *The Arkwrights: Spinners of Fortune*, Manchester: Manchester University Press, 1989.
Fitton, R.S. and Wadsworth, A.K., *The Strutts and the Arkwrights 1758–1830: A Study of the Early Factory System*, Manchester: Manchester University Press, 1958.
Pollard, S., *The Genesis of Modern Management*, Harmondsworth: Penguin, 1965.
Radcliffe, William, *Origin of the New System of Manufacture*, Manchester, 1828.
Unwin, G., *Samuel Oldknow and the Arkwrights*, Manchester: Manchester University Press, 1968.

Notes

1   As noted in the preface, the word 'factory' could at this point mean any trading or production facility; the fur-trading posts of the Hudson's Bay Company in the Canadian north, for example, were also known as 'factories'. The word 'mill', which also appears in this entry, is often synonymous with 'factory'.

2   See for a summary of Highs's claim, R. Guest, *A Compendious History of the Cotton Manufacture*, Manchester: Joseph Pratt, 1823.

3   R.S. Fitton, *The Arkwrights: Spinners of Fortune*, Manchester: Manchester University Press, 1989, p. 91.

4   *Ibid*.

5   Sydney Pollard, *The Genesis of Modern Management*, Harmondsworth: Penguin, 1965, p. 225.

6   R.N. Langlois, 'The Coevolution of Technology and Organisation in the Transition to the Factory System', in P.L. Robertson (ed.), *Authority and Control in Modern Industry*, London: Routledge, 1999, pp. 36–55.

CHARLES BABBAGE (1792–1871)

Mathematician, scientist and economist, Charles Babbage is hailed as the inventor of the modern computer. That alone has earned him a place in the management hall of fame. Much of what we now do in management relies utterly on Babbage's invention, so much so that often we cannot remember how things were done in the pre-computer age. But also, far ahead of his time, Babbage argued that business should be conducted according to scientifically based principles, and that science had an important role to play in the management of business enterprises. Thus historians of management consider him to be a forerunner of the scientific management movement, which began in the USA two decades after Babbage's death.

Babbage was born on 26 December 1792. There is some dispute over the place of birth, with the village of Teignmouth in Devon being most commonly cited; though the nearby town of Totnes is sometimes mentioned, and the London suburb of Walworth is also cited in some sources. His father was a prominent banker who maintained homes in both Devon and London. (To complete the confusion, his date of birth is also sometimes given as 1791.) Babbage himself was educated at schools in Devon and then in the London area. He had a natural facility for mathematics, and it is said that he taught himself algebra at an early age. In 1811 he went to the University of Cambridge, where he excelled at mathematics to the point where by the end of the first year he had exhausted the knowledge of tutors, and from then on pursued his own researches.

Graduating from Peterhouse College in 1814, Babbage moved to London where he became prominent in scientific circles. He was elected a fellow of the Royal Society in 1816, and in 1820 with a university friend, John Herschel, founded the Astronomical Society; he served as an officer of the society for some years thereafter. He also helped to found the London Statistical Society, one of the most important associations of scientists and political economists in the early nineteenth century, and it is likely that Babbage's own interest in economics stems from this point. In 1828, Babbage became Lucasian Professor of Mathematics at Cambridge, a highly prestigious appointment whose previous holders had included Isaac Newton and the blind Nicholas Saunderson who, coincidentally, had also made experiments with calculating machines. Babbage held the post for eleven years, although it is not known whether he ever actually gave a lecture at Cambridge.

Babbage's own interest in calculating machines had begun while he was at university. The idea for such machines was not new. In the sixteenth century, the French philosopher Blaise Pascal had designed one, and other versions had been developed since, and even sold commercially. Babbage studied the previous models, which were comparatively simple – not much more advanced than the abacus in some cases – and became convinced of their potential. Originally he saw them as being useful in astronomy and navigation, and he seems to have toyed with the idea of calculating machines which could be installed on board ships; but as time went on he realised that the implications were much broader. His idea was for a calculating engine that would be both faster and more accurate than human calculations, with applications not only in navigation but more generally in commerce, industry and government.

In 1820, Babbage began working on a prototype that he called a 'difference engine' (the name stems from the fundamental principle of calculation involved, the method of finite differences). The difference engine was basically an advance, albeit a major one, on previous calculating machines, and was intended to provide rapid, accurate calculations for a variety of purposes. The prototype was completed in 1822 and was a success, leading Babbage to press on with the construction of a far larger and more complex model. He received financial support from the government and also from a number of private individuals.

The second difference engine was never completed. Now in his early thirties, Babbage was already showing signs of the irascibility and bad temper that were to be major features of his later life. Possibly the strain of the enormous enterprise had begun to tell on him. Lacking some of the technical skills for construction of the larger machine, he brought into partnership an engineer, Joseph Clement, who set about correcting Babbage's blueprints and making the machine's working parts. At first the relationship was amicable, but the tempers of both men soon began to fray and work sometimes stopped for long periods while Babbage and Clement tried to patch up their differences. In 1828 they quarrelled for a final time, and this time Clement broke the partnership, taking with him all the parts and all the blueprints and designs for the machine. Although he himself seems never to have worked on the machine again, Clement refused to return any of the designs to Babbage.

By this time Babbage himself was already considering a far more radical invention, which he called the 'analytical engine'. Unlike the difference engine, the primary purpose of which was to make calculations and lay them out in tables, the analytical engine was in effect a programmable calculator which could take instructions and perform a variety of different functions. Instructions and data were fed in using series of punched cards, originally developed for Jacquard power looms (it is worth noting that punched cards were still being used by IBM and other computer makers well over a century later). Calculations were then printed out, in a variety of forms. Most important of all, the machine was designed to be capable of storing data in memory.

When Babbage first proposed the idea and began soliciting funds, he was astonished to find himself the object of widespread criticism and ridicule. Fellow scientists, especially his rivals, claimed the project was impossible. The government, mindful of the money it had lost when backing the second difference engine, refused support. A few private individuals did provide money – notably the Duke of Wellington, who gave £5,000 – but funds were never enough to see the project through. Babbage also lacked technical expertise, though he did have invaluable assistance from Ada, Countess of Lovelace, daughter of Lord Byron and a mathematician whose genius exceeded even Babbage's own. The Countess corrected a number of his calculations, and together they succeeded by 1840 in getting a part of the analytical engine built, but then funds ran out.

Babbage and the Countess then devised a scheme for winning large sums of money by gambling on racehorses, using mathematical calculations of bets and odds. Inevitably, this scheme failed and this cost yet more money. Ada Lovelace died in 1852, further souring Babbage, who in his final years devoted much of his energy to a campaign to rid London's streets of organ-grinders and other street musicians, who he claimed were ruining his health. He died in 1871, bitter and alone.

In 1872, a committee from the Royal Astronomical Society examined his designs for the analytical engine and concluded that, if the design had been carried out, the result might have been the beginning of a new epoch in mathematics, astronomy and science at large, so great were the possibilities. Nevertheless, no one could be found to provide the money to take the designs forward. In the end, it took a war for Babbage's dream to be finally realised. In the 1940s, the British scientist Alan Turing and his colleagues, engaged in developing computers for breaking German radio signal codes, realised that Babbage had already effectively invented the programmable computer and consulted his notes and designs. The second half of the twentieth century saw a great upsurge of interest in Babbage's work, and he is now generally recognised as the 'father of the computer'.

A prolific writer, Babbage wrote more than eighty books and pamphlets. Most concerned scientific and technical subjects, but several were on economics and business. *The Exposition of 1851*, for example, discusses the links between scientific and technical progress on the one hand and economic prosperity on the other. Most famous, however, is *The Economy of Machinery and Manufactures*, now regarded not only as a classic work of political economy but also as one of the founding texts of modern management.

Babbage argued that business could and should be conducted according to scientific principles. He equated rationalism with prosperity and order, not only at the macroeconomic level but also at the level of individual business concerns. A believer in a rational society, Babbage felt that the links between business and society were very strong, and that businesses likewise should conduct themselves in a rational manner. Science, meaning not only the employment of technology but the application of scientific methods of study, was the key to establishing that rationalism. While he stops short of actually listing scientific principles of management, it is clear that Babbage believed such principles existed.

Technology, said Babbage, had the power to revolutionise production. This had already happened in the previous century, when Richard Arkwright had led the way in developing the factory system for textiles manufacture, but Babbage felt that this was only the first step. Technology could and should spread to every branch of industry. It was here that he felt his computers, especially the analytical engine, had a valuable role to play. By speeding up the process and increasing accuracy of calculations, businesses and their owners and managers would have more and better information available and could make accurate decisions based on a rational consideration of all the facts.

Likewise, technology could be used to improve the lot of workers by reducing the amount of manual labour required and making work less strenuous. Like the early writers on scientific management such as Taylor and Emerson, he believed that mechanisation could improve working conditions. However, he also recognised that mechanisation would bring problems in terms of labour relations, especially if the wages of the workers failed to keep pace with the profits of the owners of capital. Babbage believed that a rational society was also a just and equitable one, in which people had the right to profit from their own work. He called for profit sharing, so that workers as well as capitalists could benefit:

> It would be of great importance if, in every large establish-ment the mode of payment could be so arranged, that every person employed should derive advantage from the success of the whole; and that the profits of each individual, as the factory itself produced profit, [increased] without the necessity of making any change in wages.[1]

The benefits of profit sharing would be fourfold:

1 That every person engaged [in the factory] would have a *direct* interest in its prosperity . . .
2 Every person concerned in the factory would have an immediate interest in preventing any waste or mismanage-ment in all departments.
3 The talents of all connected with it would be strongly connected to its improvement in every department.
4 None but workmen of high character and qualifications could obtain admission into such establishments.[2]

Profit-sharing schemes were widely adopted in the late nineteenth and early twentieth centuries, and some of these schemes, notably that of the British retailer John Lewis, are still in existence. John Lewis himself, writing 120 years after Babbage, argued for profit sharing and worker participation in management for many of the same reasons advanced by Babbage: worker participation, said Lewis, gave employees access to knowledge and a greater degree of control over their own lives, thus increasing personal happiness, as well as a vested interest in the prosperity of the firm.[3]

Again well in advance of his time, Babbage goes beyond issues relating to simple production and consumption to discuss marketing and selling. Another benefit of the introduction of technology, Babbage believed, was an improvement in the quality of goods sold to consumers. In two chapters in *The Economy of Machinery and Manufactures* (1835) – 'On the Influence of Verification on Price' and 'On the Influence of Durability on Price' – Babbage shows how product quality affects the price that goods can command in the market. This means not only actual product quality, but also the *perception* of product quality by customers. Babbage argued that the latter can, when assessing the quality of goods before purchase, incur *costs*, in terms of time and sometimes also of money. The level of cost varies according to the good. The quality of loaf sugar, for example, can be verified quickly, usually on sight. The quality of tea takes longer to ascertain, and verification usually requires consumption of some portion of the product. Manufacturers can help to overcome this problem by sending quality signals to the customer, the most common of which is the maker's mark or trade mark (ancestor of the modern brand name). So long as this mark is backed up by consistent product quality, manufacturers will be able to charge a premium price and thus make greater profits – or, at least, maintain profitability in the face of increasing competition. Babbage was thus the first writer on management to make explicit the connections between product quality, price and profit, and he had also begun to explore issues relating to branding and customer loyalty. Exactly this same link between quality, branding and customer loyalty was made by the first great brand marketers of the modern era, William **Lever** and Henry **Heinz**.

Babbage's influence today is primarily in the scientific and technical field, and his work on economics and business is all but forgotten; he is rarely cited in modern business bibliographies. Yet his influence was immense. John Stuart Mill and Karl Marx both read and cited him with approval in their later work. Herbert **Casson** and Lyndall **Urwick** both note that Babbage had anticipated much of the thinking behind the scientific management movement, and Urwick and Edward Brech believe him to be one of the most important management thinkers of all time. As the technology that he dreamed of becomes ever more central to everyday managerial work, it is time to reassess Babbage's contribution and ideas, and to see what others of his nearly forgotten theories might be applicable today.

See also: **Arkwright, Emerson, Gates, Ibuka, Taylor, Urwick**

Major works

As well as his work on computing and other subjects, Babbage wrote the following books which remain relevant to management.

Reflections on the Decline of Science in England and Some of Its Causes, London: B. Fellowes, 1830.
The Economy of Machinery and Manufactures, London: Charles Knight, 1835.
The Exposition of 1851, London: John Murray, 1852.

Further reading

Most books on Babbage concentrate on his work on the computer, and discussions of his ideas on economics and management are scarce. A rounded biography and assessment of his career is long overdue. Some of the works which do cover this aspect of his career include the following:

Kyman, A., *Charles Babbage: Pioneer of the Computer,* Oxford: Oxford University Press, 1985.
Morrison, A. and Morrison, P. (eds), *Charles Babbage and His Calculating Engines,* New York: Dover, 1961.
Moseley, M., *Irascible Genius: A Life of Charles Babbage, Inventor,* London: Hutchinson, 1964.
Urwick, L.F. and Brech, E.F.L., *The Making of Scientific Management,* vol. 1, *Thirteen Pioneers,* London: Management Publications Trust, 1947; repr. Bristol: Thoemmes Press, 1994.

Notes

1   C. Babbage, *The Economy of Machinery and Manufactures,* London: Charles Knight, 1835, p. 251.
2   *Ibid.,* p. 257.
3   J.S. Lewis, *Fairer Shares,* London: Staples Press, 1954.

TOMÁS BAT'A (1876–1932)

In the 1920s, Tomás Bat'a built up a large international business using a unique blend of the techniques of scientific management on the one hand and innovative human resources policies on the other. His management methods have become known as the 'Bat'a system of management', and are the subject of increasing scholarly interest. Bat'a anticipated many modern management movements such as workplace autonomy, decentralisation, flexible manufacturing and industrial democracy. His slogan, 'Every worker a capitalist!', which expressed his views on employee participation and the right to share in profits, earned him the admiration of many but the hatred of many others.

Bat'a was born on 3 March 1876 in the town of Zlín in Moravia, then a province of the Austro-Hungarian empire. His family had been shoemakers for many generations, and Bat'a himself apprenticed as a cobbler. In 1891 he moved to Vienna to start his own business, which quickly failed. Undeterred, he returned to Zlín and founded another business in partnership with his brother and sister in 1894; this business too ran into difficulties and the Bat'as were threatened with bankruptcy. Bat'a later claimed this event changed the course of his life.[1] He applied himself to his work, introduced some innovative new products and paid off the company's debts. By 1900 he had accumulated enough capital to move into volume production, and established his first factory in Zlín with fifty employees. His enterprise was still on a fairly small scale, however, and when at the start of the First World War he won an order for 50,000 pairs of shoes for the army, he could not handle the full production. Instead, he set up a cooperative arrangement with other shoe-makers in the town, and the order was filled on time.

The business grew rapidly, and by the end of the war the Bat'a company was employing 5,000 people. Trouble came in the post-war recession, which hit the economy of the new Czechoslovakia particularly hard. In 1922 Bat'a met with his employees and won their agreement to a pay cut which would enable the firm to lower its prices and win more orders, particularly in export markets. In exchange, Bat'a made up part of the pay cut by providing services such as subsidised food stores and housing. The tactic worked, and by 1923 the company was prospering again and Bat'a was able to restore wages to their former levels.

During the mid-1920s, as the company continued to grow, Bat'a introduced many of the organisational reforms that would go to make up the Bat'a system. The company also continued to expand internationally. When exports to the USA were hurt by the introduction of import tariffs following the crash of 1929, Bat'a switched his attention to other markets. By 1930 he had ventures in China and India as well as in several European countries, and at the same time began opening his own retail outlets. Bat'a factories were now producing 100,000 pairs of shoes a day, and by 1932 there were over 650 retail outlets selling Bat'a shoes in thirty-seven countries.[2]

In July 1932, en route to a business meeting in Switzerland, Bat'a was killed when his plane crashed shortly after take-off from Zlín airport. He was only 56 at the time, and it is interesting to speculate on what he might have achieved had he survived. His half-brother, Jan Bat'a, took over as managing director. A very talented manager in his own right, Jan Bat'a led the company's dramatic worldwide expansion in the mid-1930s; by 1937 the company was making nearly 60 million pairs of shoes a year, and had 65,000 employees in sixty-three countries.[3]

In 1939, Czechoslovakia was annexed to Nazi Germany. Jan Bat'a tried, unsuccessfully, to prevent the company from being taken over by the German army, and then went into exile in the United States. As he had negotiated with the Nazis to try to save the company, he was then blacklisted by the Allied powers and in 1941 went into further exile in Brazil, where he once again went into business. Another member of the family, Tomik Bat'a, went to Canada in 1939 and re-established the company in Ontario, and it was this offshoot which grew into the modern Bata Corporation. Worse was in store for the company in Zlín; bombed and badly damaged by the US Air Force in 1941, it was taken over by the Soviet army in 1945 and nationalised by the communist Czech government in 1946. The Bat'a system of management was progressively dismantled by first the Nazis and then the communists, and Bat'a's legacy was all but forgotten. Since the collapse of the Czech communist regime and the beginning of liberalisation in 1989, however, interest in Bat'a has revived both in the Czech Republic and abroad. In May 2001, the first ever academic conference on the Bat'a system was held in Zlín.

To understand what was so special about Bat'a, and to understand how he was able to build such a hugely successful business in so short a time, it is necessary to understand the Bat'a system of management. This system was built, first of all, on an ability to analyse, understand and learn. Bat'a himself set the pace in this regard. Recognising that the USA was fast becoming the world leader in both technology and management methods, he visited the country three times: once in 1904, again in 1911 to study machine production methods and learn about mass production, and again in 1919 to look at the methods used by American shoe-makers. Also in 1919, he went to Detroit, and was given a tour of the state-of-the art production plant at Highland Park where the Model Ts were assembled, and also had a meeting with Henry **Ford**. Bat'a greatly admired Ford, and the latter's management philosophy as expressed in books such as *Today and Tomorrow* (1926) has echoes in Bat'a's thinking and practice.

At the most basic level, Bat'a relied on using the best and latest technology to achieve volume production of high quality products. Milan Zeleny, one of the world's leading authorities on Bat'a, notes that he 'never hesitated to replace a good machine with a better one, even if the latter was not yet worn out'.[4] Like many great entrepreneurs, he constantly tried to improve on existing technology; if the machines to fit his purpose were not available, he would build his own. By 1926 all the Zlín operations were using electric-powered production line machinery, devices which Bat'a referred to as 'electric robots'. He also sought maximum technical efficiency, insisting that all machines had to have standardised, interchangeable parts to speed up repairs. In a radical innovation, he did away with the standard belt transmission system as used in most assembly lines (in belt transmission, all machines on a line were powered from the same source), and instead located each machine on an independent platform with its own electric motor. This allowed the plant to be reconfigured more quickly to make new products, and reduced costly set-up and configuration times. Zeleny comments that Bat'a never bothered to patent most of these devices, confident that his competitors could not catch up with him in any case.[5] Many of the technologies he developed in the 1920s did not come into standard use elsewhere in the world until three or four decades later.

As well as technical efficiency, Bat'a also sought maximum organisational efficiency. His principal method for achieving this was radical decentralisation, with individual business units given near-total autonomy, asked to set their own targets and made responsible for meeting them. Every shop and every department became an independent accounting unit. Relationships between them were handled by a series of contracts, functioning in effect as an internal market, with shops 'selling' 'products' to each other during the various phases of production. Prices for these transfers were set centrally on a six-monthly basis in order to regulate the production flow, but it was up to the business units themselves to negotiate times of delivery, quantity and quality.

This heavily decentralised system was held together by several devices. First, there was the company's central analysis department, which played a number of critical roles. It monitored external market conditions, and made sure that all work units were regularly briefed on these. It also monitored the internal contracts and handled inter-unit accounting, providing weekly digests and other statistics for top management. The analysis department reported directly to the chief executive.

Second, every senior employee at the Zlín plant carried a pager and his own signal in Morse code. When head office wished to contact an employee or someone in his or her department, that employee's signal was transmitted over the pager system, and the latter would then telephone head office as soon as possible. This allowed comparatively rapid direct communication between all departments and head office.

Finally, Bat'a himself believed in managing through direct contact with his workforce, and in leading by example. Famously, in 1931 he had a new office building built in Zlín and established his own office in a lift. When someone needed to see the chief executive, they did not need to come to his office; he brought his office to them.

Bat'a believed in efficient management, but it was an article of faith for him that the success of the company required the result of the efforts of all its employees, not just a few. In 1924, introducing the company's first-profit sharing scheme, he told his workers:

> We are granting you a share of the profits not because we feel the need to give money to people out of the goodness of our hearts. No, in taking this step we have other goals. By doing this, we want to achieve a further decrease of production costs. We want to reach the situation in which shoes are cheaper and workers earn even more. We think that our products are still expensive and workers' salaries too low.[6]

Profit-sharing schemes had a long history in Europe before Bat'a. In the nineteenth century Ernst Abbé, head of the optical instrument maker Carl Zeiss in Jena, Germany, had introduced a very successful and widely emulated profit-sharing scheme, and in the 1920s many German and central European firms were bringing in such schemes. Some business owners and managers believed that profit sharing could help to combat the rising power of the trade unions and the political left; others were genuine philanthropists who wanted to help their workers. Bat'a was neither. As in the speech above, he makes it clear he is not *giving* his workers anything; rather, he is holding out an opportunity for them to *take* profits if they choose to do so by working hard and advancing the company's goals. This does not mean he was ungenerous: on the contrary, he also offered subsidised housing and health-care facilities among many other benefits. But he was pragmatic enough to realise what many other originators of profit-sharing schemes failed to notice: that charity, or even its appearance, will not motivate workers, whereas the belief that they are earning more through their own efforts usually will.

The components of the Bat'a system, then, were an emphasis on technology and on achieving a requisite organisation that would simultaneously create efficiency and innovation and motivate the workers. Allied to this was a strong sense of moral and social responsibility. He stood for election as mayor of Zlín in 1923, and worked hard to modernise the town and provide it with new facilities. Although there is more than a whiff of paternalism about this, it seems clear that Bat'a did feel a strong sense of obligation to the community where he had grown up. He also believed in the need for Czechoslovakia and indeed all of Europe to be strong, especially economically, to ward off the threats posed by extremist politics of both the right and the left. He frequently warned against the dangers of both communism and fascism, with the result that he was pilloried by both parties: the political right hated him for upsetting the status quo, while the left believed that his progressive labour policies were distracting workers from the real goal of a socialist revolution.

Any consideration of the Bat'a case raises an important question. If this experiment was so successful, why did managers in other companies not rush to copy it, and why are they not doing so now? What barriers prevent managers and organisations from adopting new systems which are proven to be successful? Why instead do they cling onto old and often outmoded organisations and systems? In such cases, it is common to defend the status quo by arguing that Bat'a and others like him are one-offs: that they were only able to succeed because of particular circumstances in their time and place, or that their success was due mainly to personal leadership qualities and would not outlive the leader.

The second of these is easy to refute in this case. Although charismatic leadership was certainly one reason for his success, the Bat'a system survived Bat'a himself and was employed with great success by the new managing director, Jan Bat'a. Whether it would have carried on for longer had the Nazi occupation and the Second World War not intervened is of course unknowable. But there are a number of other examples of radical experiments in management systems that have had a considerable lifespan. For example, in New York State in 1880 the quasi-religious group the Oneida community dissolved its social organisation following disputes between the elders and the group's founder, John Humphrey Noyes, but decided to retain ownership of the community's very successful business operations by creating a corporation and giving shares to each member of the former community. Pierrepont Noyes, the son of the founder, took over as general manager of Oneida in 1894 and reformed its management but left the ownership structure intact; he also introduced a number of welfare and other services for employees, and Oneida went on to become a profitable and prosperous company for decades. In Britain, the employee ownership scheme established by department store owner John Lewis was derided by many when it was launched in 1928, but continues to operate and now has some tens of thousands of employee-owners.

The most dramatic example, perhaps, is MCC (Mondragón Cooperatives Corporation), which has its origins in a production cooperative established in the village of Mondragón in the Basque region of Spain in 1956. The founder was the village priest, Father José Maria Arizmendiarrieta, and his initial motive was to establish a business which could provide work and skills to local people. The initial cooperative spun off several other ventures, which in turn multiplied until it was the major employer in the region. In 2001, the Mondragón Cooperatives Corporation included around 120 cooperatives with operations in twenty-three countries and a combined annual turnover approaching $6 billion, and was the eighth largest business entity in Spain. Throughout the group's history, only one of the cooperatives has ever gone bankrupt.[7]

So, radical forms of management can achieve lasting success. But was Bat'a, like Noyes, Lewis and Arizmendiarrieta, able to succeed only because he was the right person in the right place at the right time? That may indeed be part of the answer (but it can also be argued that one of the qualities of *any* successful manager is the ability to recognise opportunities when they come and then capitalise on them). It is worth noting, however, that Bat'a often succeeded in inauspicious circumstances: during both the recession of the early 1920s and the depression of the 1930s, he continued to grow and expand his business. The resilience of the system suggests that it was more than just a by-product of its environment.

Research on Bat'a is continuing, and more Czech scholarship in this field is now being translated and made widely available. From what we know already, we can deduce two important implications for management from Bat'a's career: first, innovation does not apply to technology only, but should be applied to systems and organisations as well; and second, the courage to innovate can produce some startling results. Bat'a is a key figure because he shows what can happen, or be made to happen, when managers free themselves from constraints and begin thinking outside the box.

See also: **Cadbury, Drucker, Ford**

Major works

Most of Bat'a's writings have not been published in any language other than Czech, and many of his papers remain unpublished. *Knowledge in Action* (1992), a translated collection of Bata's papers and speeches, is very valuable.

Knowledge in Action: The Bata System of Management, Amsterdam: IOS Press, 1992.

Further reading

Milan Zeleny, who teaches in the USA and the Czech Republic, is the leading authority on Bat'a writing in English. Cekota's biography is valuable, if somewhat hagiographic.

Cekota, A., *Entrepreneur Extraordinary: The Biography of Tomas Bata*, Rome: Edizioni Internazionali Soziali, 1968.
Zeleny, M., 'Bat'a System of Management: Managerial Excellence Found', *Human Systems Management* 7(3) (1998): 213–19.
—— 'Bat'a, Tomás', in M. Witzel (ed.), *Biographical Dictionary of Management*, Bristol: Thoemmes Press, 2001, vol. 1, pp. 56–63.

Notes

1 Biographical details for this chapter are taken from Bat'a's own book, *Knowledge in Action: The Bata System of Management*, reprinted in translation in 1992 by IOS Press, and also from two secondary sources: A. Cekota, *Entrepreneur Extraordinary: The Biography of Tomas Bata*, Rome: Edizioni Internazionali Soziali, 1968, and M. Zeleny, 'Bat'a, Tomás', in M. Witzel (ed.), *Biographical Dictionary of Management*, Bristol: Thoemmes Press, 2001, vol. 1, pp. 56–63.
2 Zeleny, 'Bat'a, Tomás', p. 57.
3 *Ibid.*, p. 58
4 *Ibid.*, p. 61
5 *Ibid.*, p. 61
6 T. Bat'a, *Knowledge in Action: The Bata System of Management*, Amsterdam: IOS Press, 1992, p. 181.
7 MCC, 'The Mondragón Experience', online at http://www.mondragon. mcc.es/ingles/experiencia.htm, 18 February 2002.

MAX BOISOT (1943–)

Max Boisot's name is not widely known outside academic circles in management, and his inclusion as a key figure here may come as something of a surprise. Yet his theories of information and organisation are highly original and innovative, and have had considerable impact on our current thinking about knowledge management. His view of the role of information within organisations is unique in that it takes account of differing organisational cultures. Cross-cultural management is another of his interests, and he played an important role in the 1980s in bringing Western-style management education to China.

Boisot was born in 1943. He originally trained as an architect, and enjoyed a successful career as an architect and planner before moving into management studies. He studied architecture first at the University of Cambridge and then at the Massachusetts Institute of Technology, where he also took a diploma in town planning; he was later to take a PhD from Imperial College in London. After a spell in management with the construction firm Trafalgar House in London, Boisot co-founded the architectural and planning partnership Boisot Waters Cohen in 1972. From 1975 to 1978 he was a consultant on building projects in France and the Middle East.

In 1979 Boisot moved into management studies, spending two years with the Euro-Asia Centre at Insead, and then five years as an associate professor at the École Superiéure de Commerce de Paris. Here he developed his interests in managing international businesses and managing across cultures. He was one of the prime movers behind the China–EC Management Programme, the first MBA programme to be run in the People's Republic of China, and in 1984–9 he served as dean and director of the programme in Beijing. The programme has today evolved into the China–Europe International Business School (CEIBS) in Shanghai, where Boisot remains a visiting professor. In 1994 Boisot also set up the Euro–Arab Management School in Granada, Spain, for the European Commission. He is currently professor of strategic management at ESADE at Barcelona.

This brief summary of his career shows a number of different influences and ideas, and all of these are reflected in his work on organisations. Good architecture takes account of both physical structures and the needs and activities of the human beings that inhabit them, and this link between behaviour and structures is readily apparent. So too is the influence that different cultures can have on both structures *and* behaviour, to the extent that Boisot is sometimes described as an anthropologist of management. Finally, the international dimension of his work and career allows Boisot to draw freely on explanatory concepts from many different cultures. Unlike much of modern management thinking which is strongly grounded in Western, especially American, culture, Boisot is an internationalist in the fullest sense of the word and his work refers easily and naturally to the problems of management within and across different cultures.

Many earlier discussions of organisational culture had tended to discuss culture as a feature or attribute of organisations. There was often an implicit assumption that all business organisations are basically the same, and that different cultures then create adaptive responses which are in turn responsible for diversity between organisations. Boisot, however, argues that culture is not just a superficial set of features and attributes, but is rather at the core of every organisation and influences how organisations function at the most basic of levels. Borrowing from the techniques of anthropology and his own experiences as an architect, and also from his experiences in international business, Boisot has developed what he calls his theory of 'culture space' or 'C-space', an organisational dimension within which communication and the circulation of knowledge take place.

To fully understand Boisot's approach to management, it is first necessary to see how he views knowledge, one of the critical components of any organisation and therefore necessary to its management. Boisot adopts the standard hierarchy of data–information–knowledge, which is common in Western philosophy and has its roots in Plato, although he appears to accept that Eastern schools of thought see the subject somewhat differently. Beginning at the bottom, *data*, says Boisot, is 'a discrimination between physical states'.[1] Data exist independently of the thought processes of the person who perceives them, usually through sensory processes (sight, touch, hearing, etc.). Data may, or may not, convey *information* to the person who perceives them, but whether they will do so depends on that person's prior stock of *knowledge*. Boisot gives the example of a set of traffic lights turning from green to red. These will produce sensory data, which convey information to the person seeing them (the information being, 'stop the car'), but only if that person has prior knowledge (he or she knows that it is dangerous and illegal to drive through a red light). The same data would convey no information at all to a Kung bushman from the Kalahari desert. On the other hand, the latter would be capable of looking at marks in the sand (apprehend data) and conclude that there were lions in the area (information) because he knows what a lion track looks like (knowledge).

This sounds simple, but in fact, the implications are profound. First, it is necessary to bear in mind the distinction between the three levels of the hierarchy. Far too many people confuse data with information, and information with knowledge. (One major work on knowledge management appeared a couple of years ago with the following line in its index: 'Knowledge: *see* information'!) Second, the need for prior knowledge in order to understand and interpret data is of critical importance. Without prior knowledge, assimilating information becomes an act of faith: we have to take what we hear and see on trust. This point was made some years ago by Michael Polanyi in his discussion of how people learn. Taking the example of a medical student learning how to interpret an X-ray, Polanyi points out that on seeing an X-ray for the first time, the student has no idea what he or she is looking at, and can only take for granted that what the instructor is showing them is a real picture of a part of the body. With experience and personal knowledge, however, the student learns to interpret the picture for himself or herself.[2] (Much the same process occurs for students of management as well, of course.)

It is for this reason that organisations value knowledge, for without stocks of prior knowledge to draw on, new data cannot be correctly interpreted. Knowledge, as noted, circulates in an organisational dimension which Boisot calls 'C-space', but how it circulates and to what extent depends on the type of knowledge. Boisot goes on to classify knowledge along two dimensions: codification and diffusion. On the first dimension, *codified* knowledge is knowledge that can be easily set out and transmitted, while *uncodified* knowledge is more implicit and difficult to transmit. On the second dimension, *diffused* knowledge is that which is easily and readily shared, while *undiffused* knowledge is not readily shared. From this, Boisot sets out a fourfold typology of knowledge:

1   Proprietary knowledge: codified but undiffused (easily transmitted but not widely shared)
2   Personal knowledge: uncodified and undiffused (not easy to transmit or share)
3   Public knowledge: codified and diffused (easy to transmit and widely shared)
4   Common sense: uncodified and diffused (not easy to transmit, yet widely shared).

Proprietary knowledge is often connected to specific things or artefacts which belong to a person or organisation and thus have an identifiable owner. It may well be written down or at least set out clearly, but the owners of the knowledge will often feel they have a vested interest in not sharing it, in order to protect their own position, power, competitive advantage, etc. Personal knowledge, on the other hand, is very often locked up in our own minds, and is rarely codified in any form. This makes it hard to share with other people even if we want to; good communications skills (and, of course, a motive for sharing in the first place) are necessary.

Public knowledge is the easiest form of knowledge to acquire, as it is highly codified and widely available in books, newspapers, over the Internet or, if the original owners are feeling proactive and ready to share, through newsletters, meetings, briefings and other devices for communicating knowledge. Common sense is perhaps the most difficult area of knowledge to grapple with: it consists of a series of shared sets of knowledge and/or beliefs about certain subjects which remain highly uncodified. We all know it is foolish to stick our hand in a fire, yet fires do not contain large signs beside them saying 'Do not touch' (although if health and safety officials were to have their way, this probably would happen).

Having defined knowledge, Boisot now returns to culture. The organisation's culture defines its cultural space, and the shape of C-space in turn makes some forms of knowledge dominant. Boisot says that the different kinds of knowledge are analogous to different forms of organisational culture, each of which privileges one kind of knowledge over the others. He calls his four forms *markets*, *bureaucracies*, *fiefs* and *clans*:

- *Markets* are cultures where public knowledge predominates. Knowledge has some of the attributes of a commodity, is well defined and is easily and frequently shared.
- *Bureaucracies* are cultures where proprietary knowledge predominates. Knowledge is codified, but the custodians of knowledge often adapt a protective attitude towards it, seeing their role as guardians of knowledge rather than as providers of it. Knowledge in these organisations is equated directly with power.
- *Fiefs* are cultures where personal knowledge predominates. Again, the guardians of knowledge tend to keep it close to themselves and do not share easily; but in addition, knowledge tends not to be codified. Organisations led by strong charismatic leaders who do not delegate and tend to give orders rather than explaining can be classed as fiefs.
- *Clans* are cultures where common-sense knowledge predominates. Knowledge tends not to be recorded or transmitted formally, yet through informal channels everyone has access to the same knowledge and can draw on it.

Of these four types, bureaucracies and fiefs are of course the most common in business, as in most fields of human organisation.

Bureaucracies are dominated by the upper tiers of management, fiefs by a few strong leaders, but in both cases knowledge and power are concentrated at the top. The obvious route for breaking away from this has been the market model. Tomás **Bat'a** was the first in the modern period to go down this road, with his radically decentralised organisation tied together by an internal market that encouraged the sharing of information and knowledge. Others have tried it since, but the idea has never really caught on. To develop a market model of organisation requires those at the top of the organisation to surrender their custodianship of knowledge, and this means giving up power.

An alternative model which has been tried is the clan. Attempts to deliberately create clans require an evolution from the fief model. There is still a strong leader, but the latter behaves as a guide and *paterfamilias* rather than an autocrat. The most radical experiment with clan organisations in the West is probably Semco in Brazil, whose chairman and owner, Ricardo Semler, effectively abolished much of the company's organisational hierarchy over a period of several years.[3] Different cultures around the world can be seen to favour different organisational cultures as well. Fiefs and bureaucracies are most common in the Anglo-Saxon world; East Asia is conducive to clan models, such as the 'Confucian family business', though bureaucracy has a long tradition here as well. Fiefs and clans are common in the Arab world, and also in Latin America. This idea of organisational culture based on knowledge makes an interesting contrast with other models, which tend to take social values and psychological attributes as their basis for comparison: most notably in the work of Geert **Hofstede** and also Charles Hampden-Turner and Fons Trompenaars.

Boisot's contribution, then, has been twofold. First, he has given us a new way to look at culture as an organisational variable by showing how it shapes one of the organisation's most important assets, its knowledge. Second, on the reverse side of the coin, he has provided a classification of different types of knowledge, and shown that just as knowledge itself is not unitary in nature, so there is no one single route to knowledge management. Knowledge, culture and organisation all play off each other and shape each other, and the result is a series of combinations each of which is as unique and complex as human nature itself.

See also: **Argyris, de Geus, Drucker, Hofstede, Simon**

Major works

Information and Organizations: The Manager as Anthropologist, London: Fontana, 1987.
(ed.) *East–West Business Collaboration: The Challenge of Governance in Post-Socialist Enterprises*, London: Routledge, 1994.
Information Space: A Framework for Learning in Organizations, Institutions and Culture, London: Routledge, 1995.
Knowledge Assets: Securing Competitive Advantage in the Information Economy, Oxford: Oxford University Press, 1998.

Further reading

To put Boisot's work in perspective, compare it with some of the other major works which deal with organisational knowledge, and also with the role of culture.

Albert, S. and Bradley, K., *Managing Knowledge: Experts, Agencies and Organizations*, Cambridge: Cambridge University Press, 1997.
Cortada, J.W. (ed.), *The Rise of the Knowledge Worker*, Oxford: Butterworth-Heinemann, 1998.
Cutcher-Gershenfeld, J., *Knowledge Driven Work*, Oxford: Oxford University Press, 1998.
De Geus, A., *The Living Company: Habits for Survival in a Turbulent Environment*, 1997.
Drucker, P., *The New Realities*, Oxford: Heinemann, 1989.
Hampden-Turner, C. and Trompenaars, F., *The Seven Cultures of Capitalism*, Garden City, NY: Doubleday, 1993.
Hofstede, G., *Cultures and Organisations: Software of the Mind*, London: McGraw-Hill.
Nonaka, I. and Takeuchi, H., *The Knowledge-Creating Company*, Oxford: Oxford University Press, 1995.
Semler, R., *Maverick! The Success Story behind the World's Most Unusual Workplace*, London: Arrow, 1993.
Senge, P.M., *The Fifth Discipline: The Art and Practice of the Learning Organisation*, New York: Doubleday, 1990.
Venzin, M., *Crafting the Future: Strategic Conversations in the Knowledge Economy*, St Gallen: University of St Gall, Institute of Management.

Notes

1   M. Boisot, *Knowledge Assets*, Oxford: Oxford University Press, 1998, p. 12.
2   M. Polanyi, *Personal Knowledge*, Chicago: University of Chicago Press, 1962.
3   R. Semler, *Maverick!*, London: Arrow, 1993.

JAMES BURNHAM (1905–87)

James Burnham was a right-wing philosopher who devoted most of his career to warning of the dangers of totalitarian control. In his most famous work, *The Managerial Revolution* (1941) he argued that two trends, the increasing professionalisation of management and the separation of ownership and control, were creating a situation in which a professional managerial 'class' was threatening to dominate society. Fears of a 'dictatorship of the managers' proved groundless, but Burnham's work has important implications not only for the role of management in society but also for the balance of power with responsibility in the management of very large organisations. The collapse of the giant energy corporation Enron in late 2001 has brought into sharp relief many of the issues on which Burnham wrote.

Burnham was born in Chicago on 22 November 1905. His father was a vice-president of the Burlington Railroad, and Burnham grew up in a well-to-do family. He attended Princeton University, where he took a BA in philosophy, and then studied at Balliol College, Oxford (which by coincidence was also the venue for a major series of conferences on the study and practice of management, the bi-annual Rowntree Conferences). In 1930 he was appointed to the philosophy department at New York University as a lecturer, where he remained for twenty-three years.

Like many other middle-class young men and women in the 1930s, Burnham was attracted to left-wing politics. In 1935 he joined the Fourth International Party, founded by Leon Trotsky, and quickly became a central figure in American Trotskyite politics, contributing articles to journals such as *Partisan Review* and *New International*. He corresponded with Trotsky, then in exile in Mexico, on a number of issues, and was generally a supporter of the Soviet Union.

The scales dropped from Burnham's eyes, as they did from so many others, in 1939 when the Soviet Union allied itself with Nazi Germany on the eve of the Second World War. Disillusioned, Burnham publicly questioned whether the Soviet Union was a socialist state at all. This provoked a quarrel with Trotsky, who, for all his hatred of Josef Stalin, was still a supporter of the Soviet ideal. In March 1940 Burnham resigned from the Fourth International Party, but continued his attacks on Trotsky up until the latter's murder by Stalin's agents a few months later.

Burnham had rejected communism as a political ideology, but he remained strongly influenced by Marxist ideas, particularly the concept of the dialectic as a historical force. From rejecting communism he moved to a position of rejecting all authoritarianism, a category in which Burnham included not only Stalinism and fascism but even mild forms of state intervention such as Roosevelt's New Deal in the USA, the programme of state intervention designed to provide welfare and stimulate economic recovery during the Great Depression of the 1930s.

From this position, Burnham moved almost inevitably towards libertarianism. Leaving academia, he took a post as senior editor of the right-wing American journal *The National Review*, and worked closely with its founder and owner, William F. Buckley Jr. Throughout the Cold War he continued to be an implacable opponent of the Soviet Union, and was vehemently opposed to any form of compromise with communism. In one notable late work, *Suicide of the West* (1964), he attacked the European colonial powers for withdrawing from their colonies and opening up the newly independent states to Soviet influence. With the election of Ronald Reagan in 1980, the kind of intransigent opposition to the Soviet Union that Burnham favoured came to dominate American political life; his ideas were now widely recognised, and in 1983 Burnham received the Presidential Medal of Freedom. He had suffered a stroke in 1987 which compelled his retirement, and he died at home in Connecticut in July 1987.

In *The Managerial Revolution* (1941) and *The Machiavellians* (1943), Burnham uses the Marxist dialectic to formulate his own vision of social conflict. In every society, he says, there are two elites: those who have power, and those who are attempting to seize it from the former group. Both these groups are in fact minorities, and neither represents the working class nor has their best interests at heart. *The Machiavellians* is an attempt to ground this view of society in the work of earlier writers and thinkers, notably **Machiavelli** himself, whom Burnham praises for being prepared to reveal the truth about how power is acquired and used, and also later figures such as Vilifredo Pareto, Roberto Michels and Georges Sorel.

In the 1940s, Burnham believed that the struggle was between the owners of capital – the classical 'capitalists' – and the controllers of capital – the managers. He considers the notion of the separation of ownership from control and with it, the professionalisation of management. The idea of the separation of ownership and control goes back to at least 1917 and the writings of the German politician and businessman Walter Rathenau, and was discussed in the USA by William Zebina Ripley, the fiery Harvard professor who bitterly criticised the American financial system in books such as *Main Street and Wall Street* (1927). One of Ripley's PhD students was Adolph Berle, who with Gardiner Means wrote the classic *The Modern Corporation and Private Property* (1932), the first full exposition of the idea. According to Berle and Means, the increasing size and complexity of corporations was leading to a de-personalisation of ownership: rather than a handful of owners closely tied to the business and involved in its management, corporations now had many thousands of shareholders who were remote from the business. Operational control of these corporations had now passed into the hands of their professional managers, who in turn were not usually shareholders and had no stake in the control of the company.

Debate has continued as to whether the separation of ownership and control has been for the best. Some, such as Alfred **Chandler**, argue that it has: in *The Visible Hand* (1997), Chandler ascribes much of America's twentieth-century business success to the rise of professional management and the removal of business owners from positions of control. Chandler believes that professional managers have been able to manage in a disinterested fashion, putting the goals of the corporation and the shareholders above their own goals; they tend to be better trained and more disciplined in their approach than 'amateur' owner-managers. That view has largely prevailed in the business world to this day; early in 2002, for example, the *Financial Times* wrote disapprovingly of the dismissal of the 'professional' Jac Nasser from his post as CEO of Ford and the resumption of control by Bill Ford, a member of the founding family and a major shareholder. Others, most notably William Ripley, have disapproved of the separation of ownership and control and argued that owners were surrendering their rights to managers without proper say in or scrutiny of how their assets were being managed.

Burnham, however, believed that the separation of ownership from control in business enterprises was just one stage in the process of the transfer of power from the old elite, the capitalists, to a new one, the managerial middle class. He argued that the logical conclusion to the process described by Berle and Means was that the managers, once they had taken control, would then proceed to take ownership as well. As he says: 'Ownership *means* control; if there is no control, then there is no ownership ... If ownership and control are in reality separated, then ownership has changed hands, to the "control", and the separated ownership is a meaningless fiction.'[1] He cites the example of the Merovingian kings of France in the seventh and eighth centuries who handed over control to their officials, the mayors of the palace; in the end the kings became no more than figureheads, and the mayors easily displaced them and became kings in turn.

There is another element to this trend: Burnham believes that managers are motivated to take control not for the good of the companies they manage but to secure their own positions. As long as they lack control, they can be hired and fired by the capitalist owners like any other employee. They need control in order to consolidate their own positions of power and make themselves secure. Moving on to take ownership is just a further step in that consolidation of power. This assumption of control by the managerial elite is what Burnham calls the 'managerial revolution'. In the 1940s he saw this revolution in terms of a global struggle for power. The world was in the process of transition, from a bourgeois capitalist society into a managerial society. He saw the first manifestations of this transition in the form of fascism and communism, where in both cases he believed that technocratic elites had hijacked what had begun as populist movements, and as a first step had seized control of the apparatus of state power. What then followed were centralised planning, expropriations and nationalisation, gathering both control and ownership into the hands of the elite. It was on this issue that he broke with the communists, who believed that a democracy controlled by the workers was still possible; to Burnham the workers were irrelevant, pawns in the global struggle between capitalism and managerialism.

There are of course flaws in this argument. First, whether the technocrats of Soviet Russia or Nazi Germany can be fairly compared with the professional managers of the free economies of the West is very much a moot point. They share a professionalism and discipline of approach but little more, and their guiding ideologies could scarcely be more different.

Second, although Burnham believed that managers would in the end develop a class identity similar to that of capitalists and workers, there has in fact been little sign of this happening. Managers have been very slow to develop a sense of managerial identity. Different cultures have also approached this issue differently. In post–Second World War Japan, managers have perhaps come closest to developing a class identity, but that identity has been strongly conditioned by and even contained within their loyalty to their companies; more than in any other country, Japanese managers have tended to regard themselves as servants, rather than masters, of their corporations. In Britain, there was dogged resistance to the very idea of professionalisation, and Sir Charles Renold, chairman of the British Institute of Management in the 1940s, went so far as to resign his post in protest over a move by the Institute to recognise management as a profession. And in the USA, managers have still tended to identify themselves with entrepreneurs. John Galt, the free-wheeling hero of Ayn Rand's *The Fountainhead* (1971), is a classic American managerial type: independent, arguing against state control and corporatism and for the free market and competition. In general, managers have remained tribal in outlook, loyal to their companies and the people in their own environment rather than to other managers in other places.

Yet, there are increasing signs that Burnham may have been onto something. Management did not turn into a dictatorial class, but as time passes, the line between ownership and control is once more becoming blurred. In the 1980s and 1990s executive share ownership plans (ESOPs) and similar devices allowed managers to acquire increasing numbers of shares in the companies they managed as part of their remuneration packages. It is not uncommon for senior managers to be millionaires or multi-millionaires, on paper at least, thanks to ownership of shares in their companies. They are becoming owners, and even if they are still minority owners, their access to positions of power in and out of the boardroom means that corporate governance increasingly reflects their interests as owners.

This trend has been one of the most important lessons to be learned from the Enron disaster. Enron, once one of the world's largest companies, collapsed in late 2001 amid allegations of financial irregularities and lack of transparency. At the time of writing the ultimate causes of Enron's collapse are still far from clear, but what is known is that the chief executive and several senior directors had very large portfolios of Enron shares, and that at least some of the company's moves in the months before the collapse were aimed at protecting those investments, or at least at enabling the directors to sell shares and cash in before the collapse. This is not responsible management, and it makes a mockery of the Chandler thesis that the separation of ownership and control leads to better governance. Incidents such as the Enron collapse have fortunately been comparatively few, but as managers become capitalists in their own right, there is the strong danger that they will recur.[2]

If taken at face value, *The Managerial Revolution* (1941) predicts a kind of Orwellian dystopia that we now know did not happen. Read more deeply, it has powerful implications for business ethics, corporate governance and the distribution of power in society. Burnham, like Ripley before him but from a different perspective, warns of the dangers of owners and shareholders becoming complacent and failing to scrutinise the activities of the managers who look after their assets. He warns too that managers, seeing the profits being made by the owners of capital, will inevitably want to have their share, and the fact that they have access to the mechanisms of power will enable them to take that share. What prevents this from escalating into a full-scale struggle for power and an exercise of naked greed? Government regulation has a role to play, but mostly we are constrained by our innate senses of ethics, of justice and morality, of basic right and wrong, which form a framework that guides our actions. When a corporation such as Enron steps outside that framework, the result is havoc. What Burnham does is to strip away the niceties and conventions and show us the worst that could happen, a cautionary tale which helps us to understand why acting ethically is actually in everyone's best interests.

See also: **Chandler, Drucker, Fukuzawa, Handy, Machiavelli**

Major works

Burnham was a prolific writer. *The Managerial Revolution* is his major work on the subject of management, but the other works listed below make useful background reading.

The Managerial Revolution: Or, What is Happening in the World Now, New York: Putnam, 1941.
The Machiavellians: Defenders of Freedom, New York: Putnam, 1943.
The Struggle for the World, London: Jonathan Cape, 1947.
Suicide of the West: An Essay on the Meaning and Destiny of Liberalism, London: Jonathan Cape, 1964.

Further reading

Francis is the standard biography, written in light of the Reaganite renewal of interest in Burnham; George Orwell's critique of him is fascinating reading, brilliantly written as one would expect.

Berle, A.A. and Means, G.C., *The Modern Corporation and Private Property*, New York: Macmillan, 1932.
Francis, S.T., *Power and History: The Political Thought of James Burnham*, New York: University Press of America, 1984.
Orwell, G., *James Burnham and the Managerial Revolution*, London: Socialist Book Centre, 1946.
Rand, A., *The Fountainhead*, New York: New American Library, 1971.
Ripley, W.Z., *Main Street and Wall Street*, New York: Brentano, 1927.
Witzel, M., 'Burnham, James', in M. Witzel (ed.), *Biographical Dictionary of Management*, Bristol: Thoemmes Press, vol. 1, pp. 109–13.

Notes

1 J. Burnham, *The Management Revolution*, New York: Putnam, 1941, pp. 87–8.
2 And recur they have; since the first draft of this book was written, at least three other companies – Global Crossing, Tyco and WorldCom – have been found to have been using similar unethical practices.

EDWARD CADBURY (1873–1948)

Edward Cadbury was the son of George Cadbury (1839–1922), the chocolate maker and social reformer. He joined the family firm on leaving school, and by 1900 was a senior manager responsible for planning and overseas sales. The period 1900–20 saw Cadbury Brothers grow from being a successful British firm with a turnover of £1 million into a position as the world's leading chocolate maker with a turnover of £8 million. Cadbury worked closely with his father and fully shared his views on personnel management, social responsibility and ethical business. But whereas the father was a paternalistic manager of the old school whose ambitions did not extend beyond the United Kingdom, the son was a professional manager in the modern sense, whose successes laid the groundwork for the modern multi-national, Cadbury Schweppes. Edward Cadbury's career shows how the virtues of socially responsible business can be combined with modern management disciplines to achieve both a harmonious company and worldwide commercial success.

Like their chocolate-making rivals, the York-based Rowntree family, the Cadburys were devout Quakers. George Cadbury was a lifelong abstainer from alcohol, tobacco, coffee and tea, and taught in the company-run Sunday school every week for more than twenty years. He and his brother Richard had inherited a struggling chocolate business from their father, John Cadbury, while still in their twenties. Turning the business around, they built it up into one of the country's leading chocolate makers, rivalling the established leaders, Rowntree and the family firm of Fry, also owned by Quakers. By the mid-1870s the firm had outgrown its premises in central Birmingham. Seeking room to expand, George Cadbury built a new factory on a greenfield sight in the village of Bournville, just outside Birmingham. Along with the factory he built large-scale housing and public amenities for workers, borrowing ideas from earlier schemes such as Robert **Owen**'s New Lanark and Titus Salt's Saltaire, built just outside Bradford.

Bournville became one of the most famous of the late Victorian 'social experiments' that combined industrial management with social reform: William **Lever**'s Port Sunlight and the huge complex of housing and social amenities built by Alfred Krupp for his steelworkers in Essen, Germany, are other notable examples. George Cadbury believed that he had a responsibility to the people who worked for him that went beyond the simple relationship between capital and labour: he was responsible also for their physical and spiritual health and well-being. Workers at Bournville were provided with housing, education for themselves and their children (including the Sunday school mentioned above), health care, exercise facilities, and shops selling subsidised food and clothing.

To observers in the twenty-first century this may seem paternalistic, and perhaps it was; but it is important to remember the environment in which Cadbury operated. Victorian England was suffering all the familiar problems of rapid industrialisation, including poor-quality housing, poor health (it was an epidemic of typhus in the slums of Bradford that finally propelled Titus Salt to move his workers out to the purpose-built village of Saltaire), little or no education and rising urban crime. Men like the Cadburys could not solve all of society's ills, but they could and did try to look after their own workers.

But Bournville was not just an exercise in pure philanthropy. In today's language, we would say that the Cadburys believed they were investing in their workforce. A better-fed, healthier, happier, better-educated worker would be more productive and a greater asset to the firm. What was good for the community was good for the company, and vice versa. George Cadbury was happiest when he could introduce measures that helped employees and the company in equal measure. For example, he built swimming baths near the factory and encouraged employees to use these: the result was both improved employee health and fitness, and greater cleanliness in the factory.[1] The company's personnel management policies showed a similar approach of enlightened self-interest. In the 1880s the Cadburys cut working hours, not solely to benefit the employees but also because research was showing that workers on an eight-hour shift were more productive than those working ten hours.

However, it was in their experiments in industrial democracy that the Cadburys showed themselves at their most pioneering. In this area, George Cadbury and his son Edward worked closely together, and the results are described in detail by Edward Cadbury in his book *Experiments in Industrial Organization* (1912). The Cadbury system had three main elements: (1) the provision of employee welfare, as discussed above, with the aim of improving employees' physical and moral health; (2) a mixed wages policy which included piece work and productivity bonuses; and (3) a system for employee participation and involvement through a suggestion scheme and works committees.

The 1880s was a time of widespread discussion about the best means of remunerating employees in order to encourage productivity in both Britain and the USA. Basically, there were three schools of thought:

1 Pay high wages across the board in order to attract the best quality of worker. This was the system initially adopted by Henry **Ford** at Highland Park, to great effect.

2 Pay on a piece-rate basis, with workers earning more for greater effort, the system advocated by F.W. **Taylor** and many of the pioneers of scientific management.

3 Pay bonuses for overall productivity, encouraging workers to meet certain targets, seen as cheaper and easier to implement than piece rates.

All three systems were perceived to have problems. High wages across the board meant higher costs, and there was no guarantee that high levels of productivity could be maintained. Piece rates seemed attractive, but in practice employers tended to cut the rate once production targets had been reached, meaning employees ended up working harder for the same money. Productivity bonuses suffered from the same problem; in addition, American workers were resistant to these as it meant the hard-working employee earned the same bonus as one who did little or no work.

The Cadbury company solved the problem by adopting a mixed system with elements of all three. They paid a good daily wage, enough to support a worker and his family. Piece rates were then paid on top of this for workers who managed to exceed their personal quotas. On top of this again, productivity bonuses were paid when the company as a whole hit its financial and quality targets. Though complex to implement, the system ensured workers could profit both by their own efforts *and* the general prosperity of the company.

The employee participation system was well ahead of its time, and Edward Cadbury played a leading role in this. As he describes in *Experiments in Industrial Organization* (1912), all employees were encouraged to make direct suggestions for improvements: for new products, for new production methods, for new administrative procedures, or 'any suggestion on any other subject, so long as it relates to the works at Bournville in some way'.[2] Prizes were given for the best suggestions, regardless of whether or not they were implemented. Nevertheless, a great many were. Edward Cadbury tracked the number of suggestions carried forward, and found that over time 20 per cent on average were accepted, and 5–10 per cent were actually put into practice.

As well as the suggestion scheme, employees also had a voice through the two works committees (there were separate committees for male and female workers). These committees were not just for show: they had a powerful voice in the running of the company, functioning at times almost as surrogate boards of directors. Each committee included a mix of people nominated by the directors, foremen and heads of sections, and workers nominated from the factory floor. Each was chaired by a director: Cadbury himself was chairman of the Women's Works Committee for many years (the only man serving on it), and had a lifelong interest in the problems and challenges faced by women in the workplace. These committees served as conduits for employees' views on virtually every aspect of the business. They had power of scrutiny over plans for new machinery, buildings and other facilities, health and safety, employee complaints, cases of employee distress and many other issues. Notably, the women's committee had virtually the same powers as the men's committee.

On one level, then, Cadbury can be seen as a classic example of Victorian industrial paternalism, albeit carried to greater lengths than in most other companies of the day. On another level, however, the Cadbury system resulted in a very strong, highly flexible organisation which, thanks to the strong levels of employee commitment and participation, could draw on a large bank of experience and intelligence to solve problems and undertake what amounted to continuous improvement. The employee participation system in particular meant that Cadbury was constantly upgrading its processes and products. Herbert **Casson** regarded Cadbury in the 1920s as one of the best-run companies in Britain, if not the world, and summed up the key to its success very succinctly: 'At Cadbury, everybody thinks.'[3]

That strength enabled Cadbury Brothers to successfully challenge Rowntree for market leadership, and to grow rapidly into a worldwide company. The rivalry with Rowntree could only have one end. Joseph Rowntree was a talented manager, but ultimately a conservative one. He believed that the company's key success factor was product quality, and never stinted on measures to improve the quality and purity of his chocolate. But he detested advertising, considering it dishonest and believing that if a product was of good enough quality it would sell itself; the product's features were advertising enough. Only reluctantly did he begin advertising in the 1890s when Cadbury Brothers began eating into his market share. The Cadburys, on the other hand, recognised the power of advertising in reinforcing a brand. Joseph Rowntree's son, Benjamin Seebohm Rowntree, tried to recover lost ground in the 1920s by becoming more efficient and introducing scientific management techniques from the USA, but by the end of the decade was prepared to throw in the towel and offered a merger with

Cadbury. The normally astute Edward Cadbury then made one of his few mistakes: he rejected the offer, assuming Rowntree would fail and he could then buy the company at a low price. Affronted, Rowntree withdrew his offer and then proceeded to revolutionise his own marketing approach; by the mid-1930s he had recovered and was competing strongly with Cadbury again.

Edward Cadbury's other notable achievement was the internationalisation of the firm. While still in his twenties, he took over the post of export manager and oversaw the great export drive in the decade before the First World War that saw Cadbury profits grow fivefold in ten years. After the war, high tariffs began to hamper exports so Cadbury changed strategies and set up local subsidiaries, first in Canada and Australia, later in continental Europe and Asia. Today, Cadbury Schweppes is one of the largest global corporations in the food and beverage sector. A later member of the family, Adrian Cadbury, served as chairman from 1975–89 and then went on to chair the Cadbury Committee on the Financial Aspects of Corporate Performance in 1991–2; its recommendations, encapsulated in Cadbury's book *The Company Chairman* (1995) are a major landmark in British thinking on corporate governance.

See also: **Bat'a, Casson, Lever, Taylor, Urwick**

Major works

Cadbury's writings were confined to his earlier career. *Experiments in Industrial Organization* is his most significant work, describing the industrial democracy reforms carried out by his father and himself. The two early works are an attack on the evils of 'sweating' labour, arguing that shorter hours actually lead to greater productivity, and a discussion of women in the workplace, a subject that was to interest Cadbury throughout much of his career.

(With G. Shann) *Women's Work and Wages*, London: T. Fisher Unwin, 1906.
(With G. Shann) *Sweating*, London: Headley Brothers, 1908.
Experiments in Industrial Organization, London: Longmans, Green & Co., 1912.

Further reading

Gardiner is a slightly hagiographic biography of George Cadbury; there is no book-length biography of his son. Wagner is a recommended study of Quaker management philosophy, not only at Cadbury but also at Rowntree and Fry.

Cadbury, A., *The Company Chairman*, 2nd edn, Hemel Hempstead: Director Books, 1995.
Fitzgerald, R., *Rowntree and the Marketing Revolution, 1862–1969*, Cambridge: Cambridge University Press, 1995.

Gardiner, A.G., *Life of George Cadbury*, London: Cassell, 1923.
Wagner, G., *The Chocolate Conscience*, London: Chatto and Windus, 1987.
Williams, I.A., *The Firm of Cadbury, 1831–1931*, London: Constable, 1931.

Notes

1   The provision of exercise facilities for employees is no longer common, but was at one time a regular feature of employee benefits. This innovation spread around the world: in the 1940s Abul Hassan Ebtehaj, governor of Bank Melli in Iran, introduced a gymnasium and weight-training room for all employees, making use of the latter compulsory for the Bank's notoriously flabby security guards!

2   E. Cadbury, *Experiments in Industrial Organization*, London: Longmans, Green & Co., 1912, p. 212.

3   H.N. Casson, *Creative Thinkers: The Efficient Few Who Cause Progress and Prosperity*, London: Efficiency Magazine, 1928, p. 165.

HERBERT N. CASSON (1869–1951)

Herbert Casson was a highly prolific writer on management, with a career as a management guru spanning some four decades. A skilled writer who was also a successful entrepreneur, he used his own experiences and acute observations of the world around him to develop a philosophy of management based on the concept of 'efficiency'. He published more than seventy books, which by the time of his death had sold more than half a million copies around the world. Something of a maverick, he was never really accepted by the business academic community in either Britain or America. His books were popular and populist, highly entertaining and full of penetrating insight.

Casson was born in Odessa, Ontario on 23 September 1869, the son of a Methodist missionary. During his youth the family moved around the remote bush towns of northern Ontario, as his father was routinely posted to a new parish every three years. The years 1877–80 saw the Casson family living in the frontier province of Manitoba, whose population was mostly nomadic Plains Indians and Métis (mixed race peoples), and years later Casson recalled watching armed Métis horsemen riding into the trading post where his father's church was located. He says that he had little formal education as a boy, but those years growing up in the wilderness taught him self-reliance and an ability to turn his hand to whatever was required. By the time he was in his teens, too, he had acquired an almost insatiable appetite for knowledge of every sort, a trait that would stay with him for the rest of his life.

In 1890 Casson went to Victoria College in Toronto on a theology scholarship, and graduated with a joint degree in theology and philosophy in 1892, having doubled his course-load in order to do both degrees at once. He was then offered a position with the Methodist church as minister in the small town of Owen Sound. He served here for less than a year; in his autobiography Casson is vague about the details, saying only that men flocked to hear his sermons while women left in droves. In 1893 he was put on trial for heresy by the Methodist church council, and on being convicted resigned from the church and emigrated to the USA.

In Boston, Casson found work with a publishing company and for a time was an editorial assistant on the *Encyclopedia of Social Reform*, edited by the Christian socialist William Bliss. His own visits to the poverty-ridden slums on the south side of Boston shocked him, and he converted from Methodism to socialism almost overnight. His own brand of socialism was more radical than that of Bliss, though he stopped short of communism. Already a highly effective speaker and writer, within a few months Casson had become one of the leading 'Red' agitators in America, drawing audiences of thousands to his lectures and rallies. Among the friends he made during this period, friends he was to mention with affection even forty years later, were the British socialist Keir Hardie and the American trade union leader Samuel Gompers. He visited Britain with Hardie, and conceived the idea of one day returning there to live.

In 1898 the outbreak of conflict with Spain over Cuba brought war fever to America. Casson was opposed to the war, and tried to organise a pacifist movement. To his shock, his socialist followers deserted him en masse, all clamouring for war with Spain. Many years later, Casson's tone in his autobiography still betrays his bitterness: 'Everything that I had built up in six years was destroyed in a week.'[1]

To get away from it all and consider his next move, Casson joined the Ruskin Colony, a socialist commune founded in Tennessee the previous year. He went to Ruskin expecting to find consolation for his disappointments among like-minded souls. He found instead faction fighting, bad food and filth. He stuck it out for six months, before deciding that if this was the best that socialism could do he wanted no part of it. As he wrote later:

> this strange adventure cured me of all sympathy with Socialism or Communism. It swept my mind clear of all the

plausible theories of social democracy. It opened my eyes to the fact that there is no tyrant like the mob – that the most efficient thing in every nation is the leadership of the 'Efficient Few' ... As soon as I left Ruskin Colony, I became a defender of civilization.[2]

Rejecting socialism, Casson now decided to see what capitalism might have to offer. He had heard something of the reputation of John Patterson, the owner and chief executive of National Cash Register Company, and he travelled north to Dayton, Ohio to see the company and meet its leader. Patterson was one of the great entrepreneurs of late nineteenth-century America. Close to bankruptcy after his mining equipment business had failed, Patterson saw one of the early cash registers, patented a few years earlier by James Ritty. Convinced of the machine's potential, Patterson bought Ritty's struggling company and made it into a huge success, doing business across America and around the world. An eccentric hypochondriac who lived on diets of hot water and baked potatoes (and sometimes forced his unfortunate directors to do the same), Patterson was a ruthless competitor who would use any tactics available to drive off competition: some years later, he and his sales director Thomas Watson (the future founder of IBM) were indicted on anti-trust charges. But he was also a brilliant marketer, who built up a highly trained and professional sales force, and a superb manager of people. His plant at Dayton was a model of cleanliness and efficiency; he paid his employees well and offered them a wide range of subsidised benefits.[3]

Casson visited Patterson and was once again an overnight convert, this time to capitalism. Moving to New York, he began to make a new career for himself, this time as a journalist. By 1900 he was a regular columnist for Joseph Pulitzer's *New York World*, and became editor of the paper's Forum page, where he began to specialise in interviews with the wealthy and powerful. Beginning with politicians and academics, Casson then went on to interview leading scientists including Marconi, Tesla, Einstein and Alexander Graham Bell, and then leading businessmen. Among his major coups was the first published interview with the Wright Brothers shortly after they had made the first powered flight at Kitty Hawk, North Carolina in 1903.

In 1905 Casson moved to *Munsey's Magazine*, whose owner and editor, Frank Munsey, asked him to write a series of interviews and profiles on the steel barons. These were later collected and published as *The Romance of Steel: The Story of a Thousand Millionaires* (1907), one of Casson's finest books. His vivid pen-portraits of the great figures of the steel industry, based on personal acquaintance, offer genuine insight into these men and how their minds worked. Andrew Carnegie he describes as 'one of the most sagacious men I have ever known'; Henry Clay Frick was 'a man of steel – keen, hard and competent'; Charles M. Schwab was 'always uncomfortable in the midst of his grandeur'.[4] He went on to interview and work with others of the giant figures of American industry, becoming friendly with the Rockefellers and advising them for a time on how to handle the negative publicity surrounding the company following the publication of Ida Tarbell's *The History of Standard Oil Company* in 1904 and the succeeding anti-trust suit against Standard.[5]

In 1908 Casson met the engineer and efficiency expert Harrington **Emerson**, and was invited by the latter to join his consultancy company. This was to be a life-changing experience for Casson, who discovered in Emerson's philosophy of efficiency 'that he knew clearly what I had discovered for myself vaguely'.[6] The two men worked together for only a year, but that was long enough for Casson to take on board Emerson's principles and make them the basis of his own theories about management. He then became interested in applying the principles of efficiency to advertising and marketing; finding Emerson had no interest in this field, Casson struck out on his own, researching and writing one of his most famous books, *Ads and Sales* (1911), which he claimed as the first attempt to apply scientific principles to the marketing and selling of goods.[7]

In 1911 Casson was able to put his principles into practice when he teamed up with an old friend, H.K. McCann, formerly advertising manager for Standard Oil, and they founded the advertising partnership which later became known as McCann-Erickson. The business was a huge success, and Casson sold out in 1914 as a wealthy man. Fulfilling a long-standing dream, he emigrated to Britain and settled down, intending to retire.

The First World War broke out shortly after Casson arrived, and British industry went onto a war footing. The quest for greater industrial efficiency became an urgent national need. Filled with a desire to do something patriotic for his adopted country, Casson discovered that scientific management theories, in particular Emerson's principles of efficiency, were barely known in Britain. He made it his task to cure this defect. Beginning with a series of lectures to the managers of British firms, he then picked up his pen and began writing again, not only books but also a journal, *Efficiency*, which he edited and partly wrote. His publishing company, also called Efficiency, published his own works and those of others interested in scientific management. His populist and approachable style made him hugely popular as a consultant, but at the same time made it difficult for him to be accepted by the British establishment; although he did once give a paper at the Rowntree Conferences in Oxford, he did not serve on any of the committees or institutions to support the management movement which sprang up in Britain during and after the war. Why he pursued a solo course is hard to determine: the British establishment's contempt for an outsider may have been part of it, but in fairness it should be added that Casson was a prickly individual, highly intelligent but also highly arrogant; to say that he did not suffer fools gladly is to put it mildly.

Although his book sales and lectures made him even more wealthy, Casson pursued his career with the avidness of one who has found a vocation. He never slackened the pace of his work, writing two or three books a year, editing his journal and endlessly touring and lecturing. In 1950, at the age of 71, he embarked on a ten-month lecture tour of Australia, New Zealand and Fiji. He died at home in London on 4 September 1951 shortly after his return.

Summing up Casson's broad-ranging ideas is not an easy task. The theme of efficiency – personal and organisational – is a constant that runs through nearly all of his writings. He usually begins his books by discussing the current failings of management and how these can be cured through the application of efficiency. One of the most common flaws in management, he found, was that managers did things, not because they had reasoned and found that this was the best way, but because that was how things had always been done. Tradition, rather than reason, dominated the culture of most organisations. In characteristic style, he remarks on what he often found:

> Managers had never studied management. Employers had never studied employership. Sales managers had never studied the art of influencing public opinion. There were even financiers who had never studied finance. On all hands I found guess-work and muddling ... A mass of incorrect operations was standardized into a routine. Stokers did not know how to stoke. Factory workers did not know how to operate their machines. Foremen did not know how to handle their men. Managing directors did not know ... the principles of organisation. Very few had LEARNED how to do what they were doing.[8]

The result, he says, is confusion, error and myth:

> There are nearly as many myths and delusions in business as there were in ancient philosophies and religions. I have seen many an industrial process that was as absurd as a ceremonial in a temple in Thibet.[9]

In order for managers to be effective, says Casson, they must first be willing to learn. Learning can – and should – come from a variety of sources, and that includes being willing to swallow one's pride and call in outside consultants. Managers should cultivate an attitude of mind that constantly questions accepted certainties and looks for new and better ways of doing things. Scientific principle, for Casson, meant not so much the research and application of scientific standards (though this was important), but also the quest for new knowledge, for exploration and discovery that characterised the great figures in science such as Einstein and Marconi.

Like Peter **Drucker** two decades later, Casson believed that management is purposive action. It is the task of the manager to get things done, to lead the business forward. He begins by defining action as 'the creation of causes that are likely to produce a certain desired effect'; the manager's task is to 'first study the nature of the desired effect, then create the causes that are most likely to produce it'.[10] He classes actions into two types: *routine*, or doing what was done before, and *creative*, or doing something new. He accepts the need for routine action in day-to-day management, but argues that creative action is essential if the company is to move forward. In a passage that has echoes of Tom **Peters** and even Chris **Argyris**, Casson calls for managers to develop an 'action habit of mind' in which creative thinking is foremost and the search for improvements is a constant.[11]

This linkage between action and management is the second constant theme through Casson's work. The worst sin that a manager can commit is to become complacent and do nothing: as he says with his usual bluntness, 'It would be far safer, sensible and more profitable to dismiss a do-nothing director and put a bag of sand in his chair.'[12] On leadership, for example, he asserts that managers must lead by example as much as by command, and that real authority in the workplace derives from respect rather than titles or positions. He also takes a dynamic view of how businesses function, and advocates planning and process engineering: 'Work travels. Every job has a Cook's Tour through the factory; and it should not start until its journey has been planned and everything made ready for it.'[13] He adopts Emerson's concept, derived from military science, of the line and staff principle in organisation: the line represents the functional aspects of the business that make and sell products, while the staff is the creative core that generates new knowledge and looks to make improvements in every field. The two are not separate, but rather have a constant interchange of ideas and information.

Casson was strongly authoritarian in outlook, and often advocated the development of an 'Efficient Few' who would provide prosperity and leadership for the many, but he was also very much interested in human nature and its impact on business and management. Like Emerson, he preferred an organic model of organisation to the mechanistic model used by **Taylor** and others in the scientific management movement. Like Emerson and another early writer on organisation, Charles Knoeppel, Casson often used the human body as a metaphor for organisation, noting how all its parts have their separate functions yet always work in harmony, the whole system regulating and correcting itself without active direction. He also became interested in psychology, and attempted to apply motivational theory and analysis of human needs to understanding behaviour in both the marketplace and the workplace. In marketing, for example, he argues that whether a good will satisfy a need is far more important as a selling point than price: price does not matter nearly so much as the nature of the proposition.

> I once saw a millionaire Pittsburgher buy a painting of a cow for £11,000. He could have bought the cow herself for £15. But the painting had become famous. It was the only one of its kind. Everybody wanted it. And the Pittsburgher wanted it more than he wanted £11,000.[14]

Casson was one of the major forces in introducing the American techniques of scientific management to Britain after the First World War. He himself argued that there was nothing distinctly 'American' about these methods, any more than there was anything distinctly 'American' about electricity or the principles of astronomy. It is difficult to assess his impact on management, but it seems certain that his influence did not long survive him; he is rarely cited in management literature past about 1950. As noted, the popular and populist tone of his writing meant that he sometimes had difficulty in being taken seriously. But Casson had a powerful vision of what management should be, and this included a number of surprisingly modern concepts such as dynamic organisation and the need for continuous learning. More recently there has been a revival of interest in his work, and he is now becoming recognised as one of the twentieth century's great management thinkers and writers.

See also: **Drucker, Emerson, Mooney, Morgan, Taylor, Urwick**

Major works

As noted, Casson wrote over seventy books. Some are re-hashes of earlier work; others are comparatively simple manuals or self-help books. *Ads and Sales* became a classic work on advertising and marketing. *Lectures on Efficiency* is regarded as one of his better books, being a collection of six lectures delivered to the managers of the Manchester engineering firm Mather & Platt. *Creative Thinkers* is an important work on knowledge and learning.

The Romance of Steel: The Story of a Thousand Millionaires, New York: A.S. Barnes, 1907.
Cyrus Hall McCormack: His Life and Work, Chicago: A.C. McClurg and Co., 1909.
Ads and Sales, New York: 1911.
The Axioms of Business, London: Efficiency Exchange, 1915.
Lectures on Efficiency, Manchester: Mather & Platt, 1917.
Human Nature, London: Efficiency Magazine, 1918.
Men at the Top: Twelve Tips on Leadership, London: Efficiency Magazine, 1927.
Creative Thinkers: The Efficient Few Who Cause Progress and Prosperity, London: Efficiency Magazine, 1928.
The Story of My Life, London: Efficiency Magazine, 1931.
How to Get Things Done, London: Efficiency Magazine, 1935.
What Makes Value?, London: Efficiency Magazine, 1937.

Further reading

Ernest Casson's biography is a continuation of the autobiography, filling in the years of his father's life after 1931. Melluish is the only English-language book-length assessment of Casson's work.

Casson, E.F., *The Life and Thoughts of Herbert N. Casson*, London: Efficiency Magazine, 1952.
Melluish, W. (ed.), *Efficiency For All*, Kingswood: The World's Work Ltd., 1948.

Notes

1 H.N. Casson, *The Story of My Life*, London: Efficiency Magazine, 1931, p. 57.
2 *Ibid.*, pp. 60–1.
3 Originally Patterson had begun offering meals in the factory canteen for free, and was astonished when employees refused to eat there. Realising that they objected to being treated as charity cases, he began offering meals for ten

cents, below cost but enough to make the workers feel they were paying for something; thereafter the canteen was full.

4   *The Story of My Life*, pp. 107–8.
5   Tarbell was one of the group of journalists known as the 'Muck-Rakers' who campaigned against abuses and corruption in business and politics. Her work on Standard Oil resulted in the company being prosecuted for violation of anti-trust laws and ultimately broken up. Tarbell herself went on to become a noted writer on business issues, including the role of women in the workplace.
6   *The Story of My Life*, p. 152.
7   Not altogether true: earlier attempts had been made by Walter Scott and Arch Shaw in the USA, and a call for advertising to be conducted along scientific lines had been made by the Briton Donald Nicoll in 1878 in his book *Publicity*. It is fairer to say that *Ads and Sales* was the first formal application of scientific management to sales.
8   *The Story of My Life*, pp. 222–3.
9   *Ibid.*, p. 227.
10   H.N. Casson, *How to Get Things Done*, London: Efficiency Magazine, 1935, p. 13.
11   H.N. Casson, *Creative Thinkers: The Efficient Few Who Cause Prosperity and Progress*, London: Efficiency Magazine, 1928, p. 149.
12   W. Melluish (ed.), *Efficiency For All*, Kingswood: The World's Work Ltd, 1948, p. 134.
13   *How to Get Things Done*, p. 25.
14   H.N. Casson, *Axioms of Business*, London: Efficiency Exchange, 1915, p. 65.

ALFRED D. CHANDLER (1918–)

Alfred Dupont Chandler is a historian of business and management at Harvard Business School. His work has been profoundly important in two fields: business and management history, where he remains the world's most authoritative figure, and business strategy, a discipline he is sometimes credited with having invented. Some of his later work, comparing the historical development of business in the USA with that in Britain and Europe, is regarded as controversial. His enduring contribution has been to show how the study of the past, of what managers *did*, can be used to gain new insights into the nature and practice of management today.

Chandler was born in Guyencourt, Delaware on 15 September 1918. His family had been prominent in business in America for several generations. His great-grandfather was the business journalist Henry Varnum Poor, one of the founders of Standard and Poors; there was also, as his second name suggests, a family connection with the du Ponts, originally a family of French emigrés who had founded a successful gunpowder business. This had been taken over by Pierre **du**

Pont, who had turned the family firm into one of the world's largest makers of gunpowder and explosives; following the First World War, du Pont had gone on to acquire a controlling interest in General Motors and had put together the management team and the organisation that would ultimately lead to GM taking over from Ford as the world's leading car maker. Business, therefore, was, if not exactly in Chandler's blood, then certainly very prominent in his environment.

Chandler attended Harvard University, graduating with a degree in history. A classmate and fellow member of the Harvard Sailing Club was the future US president John F. Kennedy. Like Kennedy, Chandler joined the US Navy during the Second World War, reaching the rank of lieutenant-commander. Demobilised in 1945, he returned to the study of history, completing his PhD at Harvard with a thesis on Henry Varnum Poor (published in book form in 1956). He taught history from 1950–63 at the Massachusetts Institute of Technology, and from 1963–71 at Johns Hopkins University in Baltimore. In 1971 he was appointed to the post of professor of business history at Harvard Business School (he is now a professor emeritus). Harvard is almost unique among major business schools in that it has a strong focus on business and management history, dating back to the influence of its founding dean, the economic historian Edwin **Gay**, and continuing through prominent historians such as N.S.B. Gras and Henrietta Larson. Under Chandler, however, business history has cemented a place in the core of the Harvard Business School curriculum, and he has been influential (often indirectly) in the development of business history teaching elsewhere.

It is through his writing, however, that Chandler has expressed his ideas most clearly and in the most influential manner. As well as the study of Henry Poor, Chandler has produced three major works: *Strategy and Structure* (1962), *The Visible Hand* (1977) and *Scale and Scope* (1990). All three have been best-sellers and all three have won awards: *The Visible Hand* became the first business book to win a Pulitzer Prize. Although there are common themes in all three books, they look at management in different ways. *Strategy and Structure* is in essence a look at corporate responses to the challenges of growth and diversification, and shows how managers responded to the strategic imperatives they faced by developing new forms of organisation. *The Visible Hand* argues that these new forms were accompanied by, and in part enabled by, the development of management as a profession. Finally, *Scale and Scope* attempts to explain the comparative success of large US businesses relative to their German and British counterparts by suggesting that the failure of the latter two countries to develop professional management until relatively recently has been responsible for their lagging behind the USA. (Any student coming to Chandler for the first time might consider reading the three books in order, as the later works are in part conditioned by the conclusions of the earlier.)

Strategy and Structure (1962) is built around four detailed case studies in business history: Du Pont, General Motors, Standard Oil (New Jersey) and Sears Roebuck. All four were highly successful firms, dominating their respective sectors from the 1920s onward. Chandler argues that this success was in part based on the early adoption of a new form of business organisation, the multi-divisional form or M-form, which allowed these corporations to grow and diversify. This diversification proceeded through the establishment of a number of semi-independent operating divisions, focused either geographically or on a particular group of products. All the divisions were then subject to supervision from corporate headquarters, but were required only to conform to the overall strategic plan; operating responsibility was devolved to the divisions themselves. Going further, Chandler argues that virtually all the successful companies in the US between 1920 and 1960 adopted this organisational form, and that it played a central role in the rapid growth of American businesses throughout this period.

This is not to say that the M-form was a rigid model; it could be adapted in any number of ways, and the four corporations Chandler has studied in detail each adapted the form to their own needs. This brings Chandler to his most important conclusion, namely that 'structure follows strategy'. He sees the choice of an organisational structure as a decision which must always be contingent on the strategy being followed: 'The thesis ... is then that structure follows strategy and that the most complex type of structure is the result of the concatenation of several basic strategies.'[1] In each of the four cases he describes, the companies in question were first faced with the need to make a fundamental change in strategy, resulting from changes in technology and in their core markets. The strategic response in each case was diversification; the M-form was then adopted as a means of carrying out this strategy.

In ascribing to the M-form the greater part of responsibility for American business success, Chandler may be guilty of oversimplification; powerful though it undoubtedly was, the M-form was by no means the only corporate response to strategic change. There are other elements in the mix as well. In each case Chandler discusses, the reorganisation that led to the adoption of the M-form had a champion: Pierre du Pont at Du Pont and later General Motors,

Alfred Sloan at General Motors, Robert Wood at Sears Roebuck and Walter Teagle at Standard Oil. It was the relationships between these men and their executives and employees that often determined the nature and success of the reorganisation; and one often overlooked aspect of *Strategy and Structure* is how it highlights the close links between leadership and corporate reorganisation and rejuvenation.

To succeed, the M-form required the existence of a strong and professional management hierarchy; the new decentralised organisations required strong management both at headquarters and in the divisions. In his next major work, *The Visible Hand: The Managerial Revolution in American Business* (1977), Chandler considers how the rise of large-scale business in the USA was accompanied by the growth of a professional managerial class and the separation of ownership from control. Curiously, he makes little mention of the earlier work of Adolph Berle and Gardiner Means on this subject, *The Modern Corporation and Private Property* (1932); and, despite the sub-title of his own work, Chandler mentions James **Burnham**'s *The Managerial Revolution* (1941) only in a footnote. A reason for this may be his own stance; whereas Berle, Means and Burnham were sceptical or downright opposed to the separation of ownership and control, Chandler strongly endorses it.

He starts from a picture of US business before the Civil War: small in scale, localised, usually family-owned and managed. Larger businesses began to emerge 'when administrative coordination permitted greater productivity, lower costs and higher profits'.[2] The key factor here was that some activities which had been carried out *between* firms (distribution, marketing, production of components, etc.) could be internalised and carried out *within* firms, provided the firms had the managerial resources to do so. More management makes possible more internalisation, with more control and greater economies of scale. Hence the title of the book, *The Visible Hand*: a direct reference to Adam Smith's 'invisible hand' of market forces that guides and regulates the economy. Chandler substitutes, in part at least, market forces for human agency; the visible hand is that of professional management, which guides and controls the destiny of the corporation.

The introduction of professional management thus both accompanies growth and is a pre-requisite for it. As the business grows, the salaried managers within its upper ranks become more highly skilled and their work becomes more technical and complex. As this process of growth in size and complexity continues, the owners of the business find that they can no longer directly control the business, and increasingly delegate that control to the managers, leading to the aforementioned separation of ownership and control. This in turn leads to a changing strategic emphasis; professional managers, says Chandler, are more likely to emphasise long-term growth and stability rather than short-term profits. Finally, the size, economic power and strategic direction of these large business units changes and alters the economy itself, especially the industry sectors in which these firms operate. The final picture is a transition to what Chandler calls 'managerial capitalism', in which the chief decisions that determine the present and future trajectory of the business enterprise are made by its professional managers.

The first industries to adopt professional management on a large scale, he says, were the railways and the telegraph companies, where the problems of management across large spatial distances were particularly acute:

> Administrative coordination of the movement of trains and the flow of traffic was essential for the safety of passengers and the efficient movement of a wide variety of freight across the nation's rails. Such coordination was also necessary to transmit thousands of messages across its telegraph wires. In other forms of transportation and communication, where the volume of traffic was varied or moved at slower speeds, coordination was less necessary.[3]

When other industries began to grow, companies within them often borrowed the techniques already developed in the railway and telegraph industries; and indeed, it can be observed that many of the most prominent business managers of the late nineteenth century had at least some background in either industry. So, the railways and the telegraph had a dual function: they developed techniques for coordinated management of large organisations over large geographical space, and they provided marketing and distribution opportunities which made physical growth possible. Chandler cites the example of the meat-packing industry, where the railway enabled firms such as Armour and Swift to develop large, vertically integrated organisations based on the large-scale rearing of livestock in the West and Midwest and selling meat in the urban centres of the East. Other industries, such as steel, coal and oil, were also enabled to grow in this fashion. And, as firms and sectors grew, they developed management hierarchies and underwent their strategic transformations each in turn, thus creating the managerial revolution.

Chandler argues, then, in favour of managerial hierarchy. It is essential, he says, for continued growth, and once firmly established can become an organisation's greatest source of power. In the 1920s and 1930s, the USA led the world in the development of professional management hierarchies, and it was this development in turn which enabled the growth of the M-form and the rise of the US economy to world dominance. For Chandler, there is no doubt that managerial capitalism is superior to other forms.

To assert this, he turned in his third major work, *Scale and Scope* (1990), to a comparison of US business organisations with those of two of its major competitors, the UK and Germany. Germany, Chandler found, was dominated by what he calls 'cooperative managerial capitalism'. German firms tended to adopt a model of business much like that of the USA, characterised by hierarchies of professional managers, but for a variety of social and cultural reasons they preferred to conduct networks of interfirm alliances rather than engage in full-scale competition. This professionalism, in his view, did much to explain Germany's economic resurgence after the Second World War. The British economy, on the other hand, comes in for severe criticism. The UK clung for far too long (in Chandler's view) to a model which he describes as 'personal capitalism', whereby the owners of businesses continued to exercise control and failed to hand over to professional managers. This lack of evolution and failure to separate ownership and control stifled the growth and competitiveness of British industry and was a major factor in its postwar decline.

Scale and Scope has been heavily criticised, especially outside the USA. Of Chandler's major works, it is probably the least successful, in that it does not fully demonstrate its thesis: that the transition to 'competitive managerial capitalism' enabled the USA to achieve economic power over and above that of its main rivals. Arguments can be advanced against this thesis on many levels. It is not at all clear that US economic dominance is due *solely* to any particular managerial form or structure. Chandler may also have been guilty of selecting his data to fit his thesis; neither the Far East nor Southern Europe, especially Italy, where there have been and continue to be many examples of successful firms based on personal/family models of capitalism, figure in his analysis. His analysis of the British case also has flaws; professional management had advanced rather more rapidly in Britain than he allows, and there is a tendency to discount successful British firms that were managed personally by their owners, such as Imperial Chemical Industries, British Petroleum or Cadbury, all world-beating companies in the 1930s and again in the 1950s. That there was strong resistance to the professionalisation of management in Britain is not in doubt, but there were many other economic and institutional factors behind Britain's comparative decline.

A more serious criticism, voiced in particular by David Teece, is that while the M-form and professional managerial hierarchy may have been responsible for building American dominance, they look increasingly unlikely to sustain it. Even before the publication of *Scale and Scope*, other American management gurus such as Tom **Peters** and Rosabeth Moss Kanter were attacking the idea of hierarchy, equating it with bureaucracy and inflexibility. Economies of scale and cost reduction were proving no match for flexible strategies that allowed first-mover advantage and rapid development and improvement of new products. Teece notes that many internalised activities are now moving back out into the market as companies shed or contract out peripheral activities in order to concentrate on their core capabilities; higher transaction costs are a price worth paying in order to gain greater flexibility and speed of response.

These criticisms aside, Chandler's work has much of enduring value and has changed the way we perceive and do management. He notes how changes in one sector, such as transportation, can have knock-on effects for many other sectors; a revolution in one business in one field can then lead to much more widespread change, as we are seeing today with advances in information technology. His work on the relationship between strategy and structure remains pivotal to modern strategic thinking. Finally, Chandler has created an awareness that management is a historical concept, one that has developed over time and will continue to do so. His style of historical analysis, if not necessarily his conclusions, provides a sound platform for the consideration of future trends, and brings the role of historical understanding to the forefront of management thinking.

See also: **Burnham, du Pont, Gay, Medici, Mintzberg, Mooney, Ohmae, Porter**

Major works

Chandler's major works are comparatively few. All are easy reading and make their points clearly and well. *Strategy and Structure* contains a wealth of historical detail in its four case studies, along with some fine analysis. The two later works tend to be broader in focus with fewer detailed case studies.

Henry Varnum Poor: Business Editor, Analyst and Reformer, Cambridge, MA: Harvard University Press, 1956.

Strategy and Structure: Chapters in the History of American Industrial Enterprise,
Cambridge, MA: MIT Press, 1962.
The Visible Hand: The Managerial Revolution in American Business, Cambridge, MA:
Harvard University Press, 1977.
Scale and Scope: The Dynamics of Industrial Capitalism, Cambridge, MA: Harvard
University Press, 1990.

Further reading

Berle, A.A. and Means, G.C., *The Modern Corporation and Private Property,* New
York: Macmillan, 1932.
McGraw, T.K., *The Eternal Alfred Chandler: Essays Towards a Historical Theory of Big
Business,* Boston, MA: Harvard Business School Press, 1998.
Teece, D.J., 'The Dynamics of Industrial Capitalism: Perspectives on Alfred
Chandler's *Scale and Scope'*, *Journal of Economic Literature* 31 (1993): 199–225.

Notes

1   A.D. Chandler, *Strategy and Structure,* Cambridge, MA: MIT Press, 1962,
    p. 14.
2   A.D. Chandler, *The Visible Hand,* Cambridge, MA: Harvard University Press,
    1977, p. 6.
3   *Ibid.,* p. 485.

ARIE DE GEUS (1930–)

Arie de Geus is a former executive with Royal Dutch/Shell who,
together with Peter M. Senge, is responsible for the development of
the concept of the 'learning organisation'. In the early 1990s it was
Senge, through his best-selling book *The Fifth Discipline* (1990), who
did most to disseminate and popularise the concept. More recently,
however, de Geus has produced an important body of writing in his
own right, notably *The Living Company* (1997), in which he takes an
organic and holistic view of organisations and closely links their ability
to learn with the extent to which they are integrated into their
environment. Though his work has been greeted with none of the
fanfare that surrounded *The Fifth Discipline,* de Geus offers an
important organisational model for the future, one which stresses
the links between organisation and knowledge, between strategy and
environment.

De Geus was born in Rotterdam on 11 August 1930. After
studying economics at Erasmus University he joined the Royal
Dutch/Shell group in 1951, remaining with the corporation until his
retirement in 1989. His career included postings overseas to Turkey

and Brazil; the last ten years were spent in the UK, and from 1981 he was coordinator for Royal Dutch/Shell group planning. He has also served as chairman of the Netherlands–British Chamber of Commerce, and since his retirement from Shell has been a visiting fellow of London Business School and has worked with Peter Senge at the Massachusetts Institute of Technology.

The careers of Senge and de Geus have intersected at several points. Born in 1947, Senge studied engineering at Stanford University and then system dynamics at the Massachusetts Institute of Technology, where he received a doctorate in 1978. Senge was strongly influenced by Jay Wright **Forrester**, the great pioneer of system dynamics at MIT, and in the 1980s he began a research programme applying Forrester's concepts to mental systems, notably to human learning. This brought him into contact with de Geus, then still at Shell, whose own research team was studying learning methods and coming to focus on the idea of continuous learning. The now famous concept that the ability to learn continuously may be a company's only sustainable source of competitive advantage has been attributed to both de Geus and Senge; it certainly appears in de Geus's seminal *Harvard Business Review* article of 1988, 'Planning as Learning', and in his own introduction to *The Fifth Discipline*, the multinational bestseller that first popularised the idea of the 'learning organisation' in the early 1990s, Senge attributes the idea to de Geus. It seems likely, however, that it came out of their shared work at MIT and Shell in the mid- and late 1980s.

Both de Geus and Senge have also been credited with inventing the concept of the 'learning organisation', but that term has an older provenance; it appears, for example, in **Peters** and Waterman's *In Search of Excellence* (1982). In his work at Shell and after, however, de Geus has developed the idea of the learning organisation to its highest state. For de Geus, a learning organisation is not just an organisation that acquires knowledge; it also knows how to use and manage that knowledge effectively to create competitive advantage, and does so on an ongoing basis. Using concepts that relate to Chris **Argyris**'s action research, Peter Senge's ideas on mental systems and even Max **Boisot**'s ideas on the relationship between communication and culture, de Geus conceives of the learning organisation as being organic rather than mechanistic in nature. Picking up a metaphor first used by Harrington **Emerson** and Herbert **Casson** in the early twentieth century, de Geus compares the learning organisation to a living organism. Internally, it consists of a number of self-regulating systems, through which learning happens, not as a result of command and control, but as a natural part of business activity. His argument is that learning organisations in fact learn as entities, and that the sum total of their acquired knowledge is greater than the pooled knowledge of the individuals who make up the organisation.

What then distinguishes a 'learning organisation' from its opposite? In fact, there are probably no 'non-learning organisations' *per se*, just as a complete 'learning organisation' is probably an impossibility. There are no blacks and whites here, but rather shades of grey; companies should be measured, and measure themselves, on a sliding scale of learning effectiveness. Definitions of what a learning organisation is are deliberately fuzzy. De Geus and Senge have offered the following requirements for the creation of a learning organisation:

1 'personal mastery', or the acquisition of personal skills and knowledge which enable learning on the part of individuals;
2 the development of a shared vision or 'mental model' of the organisation, its goals and its best interests, a vision that all members of the organisation can buy into;
3 the ability to think together and learn together in teams, together with an ability to see and understand the interdependence between a company and its environment.

The most important kind of knowledge is not 'snapshots' of individual situations, but knowledge that helps in the understanding of cycles and causes, allowing us to not only understand what is going on around us at the present, but also to understand what may happen in the future.

Learning organisations learn, in part at least, from their environment. Here again there is a clear parallel with living organisms, which acquire nurture and sustenance (food, water, oxygen, etc.) from their environment; learning companies use their environment to acquire knowledge. In *The Living Company* (1997), de Geus builds on his original model of the learning organisation by stressing the links between companies and society. He argues that companies should seek to develop strong bonds with their stakeholders – customers, suppliers, shareholders, etc. – and develop a 'harmony of values' with them. These strong relationships enable a greater depth of learning, learning that can be vitally relevant to the needs and interests of the company.

In this vision, the 'learning organisation' becomes the 'living company' in which learning is a built-in system that enables companies to grow organically and become self-aware. Companies do not, and cannot, exist in isolation. Their relationship with their stakeholders is not merely one of social responsibility or business ethics. Domagoj Racic, in his profile of de Geus for the *Biographical Dictionary of Management* (2001), suggests that de Geus's greatest contribution may be this merging of ethical, organisational and knowledge issues into a single concept. Forrester, and after him Senge, drew out the importance of systems and thinking; Boisot has shown the links between knowledge, communication and culture; and Charles **Handy** has shown how corporations respond to human ethical issues. With the idea of the living company, de Geus offers a model that encapsulates all these concepts. As Racic says, it is too soon to tell how influential this model will be on business thinking and practice. What is certain is that it is the most original and innovative model of business to emerge in the latter half of the twentieth century, and the only one so far posited that offers a vision of sustainable success in the uncertain environment of the twenty-first century.

See also: **Argyris, Boisot, Drucker, Follett, Forrester, Handy, Nonaka**

Major works

De Geus's writings include two important journal articles and one major book.

'Planning as Learning', *Harvard Business Review,* March–April 1988: 70–4.
'The Living Company', *Harvard Business Review,* March–April 1997: 51–9.
The Living Company: Habits for Survival in a Turbulent Environment, London: Nicholas Brealey, 1997.

Further reading

Nonaka, I. and Takeuchi, H., *The Knowledge-Creating Company,* New York: Oxford University Press, 1995.
Racic, D., 'De Geus, Arie', in M. Witzel (ed.), *Biographical Dictionary of Management*, Bristol: Thoemmes Press, 2001, vol. 1, pp. 217–18.
Senge, P.M., *The Fifth Discipline: The Art and Practice of the Learning Organization*, New York: Doubleday, 1990.

W. EDWARDS DEMING (1900–93)

William Edwards Deming was one of the leading figures in the quality movement of the 1950s to 1970s. His early work involved the development of statistical quality control (SQC) on production lines. His work was largely ignored in the USA, but in the early 1950s, during the period of post-war reconstruction, Deming and another quality control expert, Joseph Juran, were invited to Japan to demonstrate their methods. SQC became a key part of the Japanese drive for quality, most notably in the Toyota Production System. In the late 1970s, as American firms found themselves under increasingly fierce competition from Japanese firms producing low-cost, high-quality goods, Deming and Juran were rediscovered and quality issues became integrated into Western management thinking and practice. Today, Deming-influenced practices can be seen in firms of every size all around the world, his name forever associated with the concept of total quality management (TQM).

Born in Sioux City, Iowa on 14 October 1900, Deming grew up on his family's farm in Wyoming. After leaving school he studied engineering at the University of Wyoming and mathematics at the University of Colorado before going on to take a PhD in mathematical physics at Yale University. While at Yale, he spent his summers working at the Western Electric Company's telephone assembly plant at Hawthorne, near Chicago. During Deming's time at Hawthorne the company was being intensively studied in one of the most famous pieces of business research ever conducted, the so-called Hawthorne investigations led by Elton Mayo and Fritz Roethlisberger of Harvard University. This study focused on the effects of environmental conditions on productivity (see the **Argyris** entry elsewhere in this book). Deming, according to Andrea Gabor's biography, claimed to have been unaware of the research (if so, he must have been the only person in the factory who was), but his time at Hawthorne did teach him much about factory management and the mistakes being made in terms of both machine and human efficiency.

The job also changed his career in another way. Western Electric was a subsidiary of American Telephone & Telegraph (AT&T), and while at Hawthorne Deming came across the pioneering work in statistical quality control being undertaken by Walter Shewhart, then employed in doing research for AT&T. SQC itself had its origins in research on agricultural productivity undertaken in Britain; Shewhart's contribution was to develop statistical sampling methods that could identify defects or variations in quality during the production process.

This was an important step forward. The system of machine production developed by Richard Arkwright and those who came after him in the Industrial Revolution offered the promise of 'building in' quality through correct specifications and design of the machinery and production processes. In practice, this seldom happened; some problems were caused by incorrect specifications, while defective machinery and mistakes by the workforce created others. One of the driving forces behind the development of scientific management was the need to reduce production costs, and both Frederick **Taylor** and Harrington **Emerson** urged the importance of correct specifications and investment in training and maintenance to make sure the specifications were achieved. But the only way to determine the quality of goods remained the final inspection of the finished product coming off the assembly line. Shewhart's view was that the causes of defects needed to be detected as soon as possible, and then those causes should be eliminated.

Inspired by what he had learned, Deming made Shewhart's acquaintance and learned more about SQC directly from him. While working for the Census Bureau in Washington, DC, Deming was also able to take a year's study leave in London, where he worked with Sir Ronald Fleming, the British statistician who had originally developed the SQC concept. He became an authority on the techniques of SQC in his own right, and during the Second World War was employed in teaching those techniques to engineers and factory managers. After the war, however, interest in the subject died away. Deming, now teaching at New York University, could only watch as a great chance to improve quality and production methods disappeared. Although he was writing from a position of hindsight, he notes in his 1986 book *Out of the Crisis* that even in the late 1940s he could see that American industry was in danger of losing its competitive edge.

With US business losing interest, Deming began taking on consulting assignments for foreign governments interested in using SQC. In 1947 he accepted an assignment in Japan, spending some months there and travelling widely around the country helping to set up the systems for a national population census. There he found that, unlike in the USA, leading industrialists were aware of SQC and of his own and Shewhart's work; moreover, they were already beginning to apply it. The Japan Union of Scientists and Engineers (JUSE), formed in 1946 to assist in the reconstruction of Japan after the war, was already studying the techniques, and the talented young mathematician Ishikawa Kaoru was beginning to hold seminars on the subject for industrialists. Deming had conversations with a number of prominent people in JUSE during his stay, and in 1950 was invited back to Japan to give a series of lectures on SQC. He returned to teach further courses there in 1951 and 1952, and was thereafter a frequent visitor to the country. In 1951 the Deming Prize for research in quality management was created in his honour, and in 1960 he received the Order of the Sacred Treasure from the Emperor Hirohito.

Deming might have remained forever in obscurity in his own country, had he not done his work in Japan so well. Once associated with cheap consumer goods of inferior quality, by the 1960s Japanese industry was producing a wide range of low-cost, high-quality goods that began to flood into world markets. American firms in particular had failed to appreciate the importance of quality, thinking themselves invulnerable to foreign competition; by the 1970s, US makers of automobiles and electrical/electronics goods in particular were under serious threat. Leading the charge in Japan was Toyota under the leadership of **Toyoda** Kiichiro, who had working for him two talented production engineers, Ohno Taiichi and Shingo Shigeo. Together they created the famous Toyota Production System, with elements such as *poka-yoke* (zero defects), *kaizen* (continuous improvement) and total quality management. Thanks to the efforts of Ishikawa and his colleagues at JUSE, similar techniques were developed in other firms.

In 1980, as the Japanese onslaught on US domestic markets reached its height, NBC television in the USA screened a documentary film entitled *If Japan Can, Why Can't We?* Viewers were shocked to learn that the techniques of quality control which had made Japanese industry so strong had been invented in the USA – so the film said – and taken to Japan by Deming and his colleague, Joseph Juran. It was immediately assumed that quality control, having been invented in America, could easily be learned by American companies. However, the result, as Deming himself noted, was an instant obsession with statistical control, completely overlooking the philosophy of quality control that the Japanese had adopted and developed so effectively. A famous story of the time concerned an American computer firm buying microchips from Japan which set a standard of one defect in 10,000 components, and sternly warned its Japanese supplier that in a forthcoming order for 100,000 chips, only ten defects would be tolerated. When the order arrived, in addition to the 100,000 chips there came a small box containing a further ten chips. When queried about these, the Japanese supplier solemnly informed its American customer that 'these are the ten defects you asked for'.

During the 1980s Deming was for a time the best-known management guru in the world. His mature philosophy of total quality management was developed at that time. To Deming, quality was more than just a set of techniques for quality control and standardisation. Quality had to become a mindset, embraced by the entire company. *Out of the Crisis* (1986), his most famous book, describes how a quality system can be introduced, while his last work, *The New Economics for Industry, Government, Education* (1993), published in the year of his death, urges the importance of quality thinking for national competitiveness and prosperity. He died at home in Washington, DC on 20 December 1993.

As the above might suggest, consideration of Deming's career and influence falls into two parts. There is, first, work on statistical quality control, where he was an undoubted pioneer and leader, developing on the ideas of Shewhart and Fleming. At the heart of SQC is the measurement of variations or deviations from the required standard; these variations are measured through sampling at various stages of the production process. Once variations are found, causes are then looked for. Deming classed the causes of variation into two types: 'common' and 'special' (Shewhart, and also Juran, termed these as 'random' and 'assignable'). Special causes are the result of specific incidents, and are usually attributable to the actions of individual workers. Common causes are built into the production process and thus beyond the control of individual workers: they are therefore the responsibility of management. Deming argued that 94 per cent of all variations were due to these common causes, and one of management's most important tasks was the identification and prevention of these at source by removing the cause. It is worth emphasising that Deming believed that the primary responsibility for quality lay with management; he was adamantly opposed to the 'blame the worker' culture which held that poor quality was due solely to low skills and/or poor performance by workers. From Shewhart, too, Deming adopted the 'plan, do, check, act' cycle in which actions and events are constantly monitored and defects or problems noticed quickly and eradicated. This became famous in Japan as the 'Deming cycle'.

How much did Deming influence Japan, and how much did Japan influence Deming? Early claims by some of Deming's supporters – though not by Deming himself – that he had taught quality control to the Japanese are exaggerated. As noted, SQC was already known in Japan and several organisations, including JUSE, were actively involved in its development and implementation. That Deming assisted greatly in this cannot be doubted, as his expertise and experience in the field were very valuable; even today, many Japanese business people are genuinely appreciative of Deming's work in their country. But he was not the sole mover behind the Japanese quality drive.

As for influence the other way, there seems little doubt that Japanese ideas on total quality management, in particular, influenced Deming's later thinking. He was a frequent visitor to Japan and on friendly terms with many senior industrialists and engineers, and it would have been odd indeed if an interchange of ideas had not gone on. Deming's ultimate philosophy of quality management is encapsulated in his Fourteen Points, first published in book form in 1986, but a system which had been undergoing development for many years. The Fourteen Points, paraphrased slightly, are:

1 Create constancy of purpose.
2 Adopt a new philosophy for leadership and purpose.
3 Cease dependence on inspection to achieve quality; build quality into the product in the first place.
4 End the practice of awarding business on the basis of price; consider the total cost of good and bad quality.
5 Undertake continuous improvement of both production and service.
6 Institute training on the job.
7 Institute leadership.
8 Drive out fear, enabling everyone to work effectively for the company.
9 Break down barriers between departments.
10 Eliminate slogans, exhortations and targets.
11 Eliminate work standards, quotas, management by objectives and management by numbers; replace these with leadership.
12 Remove the barriers that rob workers of the right to workmanship, both on the shop floor and in management.
13 Institute a rigorous programme of education and self-improvement.
14 Put everyone in the company to work to accomplish the transformation.

The influence of the Japanese approach to total quality can be quickly seen. Continuous improvement, building in quality at the beginning of the process, total company transformation and constancy of purpose are all core elements of the Toyota Production System and of the Japanese philosophy of TQM more generally.

It is points 8 through 12 that are perhaps most intriguing. Deming, the man many people associate with statistical control, is arguing here for an end to statistical targets, to exhortations to higher productivity, to barriers between workers and management. In their place, he says, give workers pride in their work and managers pride in their companies; lead them and encourage them, but give them space to do what they do best. Instead of targets and goals, we have an open-ended system which challenges everyone in the company to do their utmost not to achieve some desired end, but simply for the sake of doing the task well. He condemns leaders who use statistical targets as clubs to hold over workers, threatening them if they do not perform. Targets, he says, are not a substitute for leadership; if workers do not see the reason for producing better quality, it is up to the leaders to show them why this is important, not to drive them forward without purpose.

It is interesting to compare Deming on this point with the other two leading quality gurus, Joseph Juran (1904–) and Philip Crosby (1926–). Juran in some ways was Deming's superior in the techniques of SQC, and some authorities credit him with an even greater influence in Japan than Deming. Working independently of Deming, Juran argues likewise that to achieve quality, management needs to move away from statistical targets and towards a culture of continuous improvement, backed up by training and motivation. Crosby, an engineer with Martin and then ITT for many years, developed his own fourteen points which likewise include training, motivation and the commitment by top management to improving quality; the major difference from Deming and Juran is that Crosby continues to advocate goal-setting. Crosby also urges managers to consider the costs of bad quality in terms of repairs, replacement of defective products and lost customers.

For decades a prophet without honour in his own country, Deming did ultimately receive the recognition he deserved. Unlike Crosby and Juran, Deming never really considered his views on quality to constitute a 'system'. SQC was a set of techniques for achieving quality; but their use alone did not ensure quality. There was no golden road to quality. His fourteen points are not a prescription for quality itself, but rather for thinking *about* quality and for developing a mindset – personal and corporate – that would make sustainable quality possible. That perhaps has been his enduring legacy: quality management is not just another item in the management toolkit but an all-embracing philosophy that has implications for leadership, motivation and knowledge management.

See also: **Babbage, Emerson, Matsushita, Peters, Taylor, Toyoda**

Major works

Deming's early work mostly took the form of lectures and articles. His mature philosophy and approach to quality can be found in two books:

Out of the Crisis, Cambridge, MA: MIT Center for Advanced Engineering Study, 1986.

The New Economics for Industry, Government, Education, Cambridge, MA: MIT Center for Advanced Engineering Study, 1993.

Further reading

Brocka, B. and Brocka, M.S., *Quality Management: Implementing the Best Ideas of the Masters*, Homewood, IL: Business One Irwin, 1992.
Butman, J., *Juran: A Lifetime of Influence*, New York: John Wiley, 1997.
Crosby, P.B., *Quality is Free: The Art of Making Quality Certain*, New York: McGraw-Hill, 1979.
Gabor, A., *The Man Who Discovered Quality*, New York: Times Books, 1990.
Juran, J., *Juran on Leadership for Quality: An Executive Handbook*, New York: The Free Press, 1989.
Kilian, C.S., *The World of W. Edwards Deming*, 2nd edn, Knoxville, TN: SPC Press, 1992.

PETER DRUCKER (1909–)

Peter Drucker is arguably the most popular and widely read management writer of all time. A guru who fully deserves his status, he regularly tops opinion polls among business men as the most influential management thinker and writer of the twentieth century. He has written more than twenty major books and innumerable articles, published over a span of more than sixty years. His interests and ideas range across the full spectrum of management, from ethics to technology, from economics to knowledge management. Probably more than any other individual, he has defined the nature of management and the tasks and purpose of the manager in modern business and society. Among the many honours he has received throughout his career is one unique among management gurus: a Korean businessman, whose admiration of Drucker's works reached the point of total adulation, changed his own name to 'Peter Drucker' in honour of his hero.[1]

Drucker was born in Vienna on 19 November 1909. His father, Adolph Drucker, was a lawyer and leading member of the liberal intelligentsia of pre-war Austria-Hungary, whose friends included the economist Joseph Schumpeter. Drucker was educated at the Vienna Gymnasium, and while in his teens flirted briefly with socialism. At seventeen he moved to Germany, working for a time in Hamburg before moving to Frankfurt where he attended university, graduating with a doctorate in international law in 1931. By this time he was also working as a financial journalist for a Frankfurt daily newspaper and was learning about economics and business. Implacably opposed to the

Nazis, Drucker returned to Austria following Hitler's rise to power in 1933, but stayed there only a short time. Moving to London, he worked for several years as a merchant banker, and also came to know John Maynard Keynes. In 1937 he moved to New York where he found work as a journalist and financial advisor. In 1941 he took up an academic post at Bennington College in Vermont, moving to New York University in 1952. Now living in Los Angeles, he no longer teaches but continues to be an active and prolific writer.

From the mid-1930s, and especially from the 1940s, the most important aspect of Drucker's career has been his writing, and the stages in his intellectual development can be charted through his books. Drucker has always been eclectic, and there are many crossovers of interest within his works; nonetheless, it is possible to categorise his books into three rough stages. These are:

1   The 'economics' books of the early period, including *The End of Economic Man* (1939), *The Future of Industrial Man* (1942) and *Concept of the Corporation* (1946).
2   The 'management' books from the 1950s through to the 1970s, including notably *The Practice of Management* (1954), *The Effective Executive* (1966) and *Management: Tasks, Responsibilities, Practices* (1974).
3   The 'philosophical' books from the mid-1970s to the present, beginning with *The Unseen Revolution* (1976) and including *Innovation and Entrepreneurship* (1985), *The New Realities* (1989), and *Managing in a Time of Great Change* (1995).

In the first stage, Drucker was concerned with the nature of economic society and the new world that was emerging out of the old order in the first half of the twentieth century. *The End of Economic Man* (1939) discusses the rise of totalitarianism and some possible responses to it by the free world. *The Future of Industrial Man* (1942) takes the latter theme forward, arguing that an industrial society and a free society are not incompatible. His influences in this period are strongly liberal: Schumpeter, the existentialist philosopher Søren Kierkegaard and the German Jewish industrialist Walter Rathenau, assassinated by the Nazis in 1922. In America, he read and was impressed by *The Modern Corporation and Private Property* (1932) by Adolph Berle and Gardiner Means: like James **Burnham**, though from a different political angle, Drucker was opposed to the divorce of ownership from control in corporations. That, said Drucker, led to power without responsibility. Peter Starbuck sums up his argument as follows: 'Management's first responsibility was to produce economic results as profits; the second responsibility was to work in a manner that was for the good of society while never attempting to take over the work of society.'[2] Wealth and freedom, for Drucker, were necessary co-equals; one was of no use without the other, and he concluded that the free market offered the best opportunity to achieve both.

His next step was to begin to study more deeply the mechanisms of the market, and in particular Western capitalism's most important institution, the corporation. *Concept of the Corporation* (1946) is a study of General Motors, at the time the world's largest corporation with over half a million employees worldwide. Founded by the talented but feckless entrepreneur William C. Durant in 1908, the company had been taken over by Pierre **du Pont** in 1920. Du Pont used his organisational skills to achieve a transformation similar to that he had already worked at his own company, the gunpowder maker Du Pont. Diversifying the firm through the multi-divisional form later described by Alfred **Chandler** in *Strategy and Structure* (1962), Du Pont also brought in a highly professional and talented management team, including Alfred P. Sloan and James D. **Mooney**, to run the company. By 1940 GM was admired not only for its profitability but also for its highly successful organisation and structure. Taking GM as the ideal of the modern corporation, Drucker began to examine exactly what it was that the corporations and their managers did. *Concept of the Corporation* remains one of the best case studies of organisation ever written; it does more than just describe the workings of the organisation, peeling back the layers to reveal a deeper understanding of what made GM and its people tick.

One of the critical conclusions of *Concept of the Corporation* was that the success of management is judged by results – always presupposing, of course, that those results are obtained in an ethical manner. There now began the second 'stage' of Drucker's writings in which he looked at management as an activity, profession and discipline. *The Practice of Management* (1954) is his first attempt to sum up what management is; many still regard it as his best book. The work of top management consists of setting policies, measuring performance and evaluating results. Following Henri **Fayol**, he then lists the basic tasks of management as setting objectives, organising, motivating, measuring and communicating. Absolutely essential is the relationship between managers and workers: the latter are to be regarded, not as tools for getting a job done, but as a resource for achieving greater objectives. The better the relationship between the two parties, the more valuable this resource becomes. In another passage which has echoes of the later work of Chandler, Drucker urges managers not to put too much emphasis on organisation and structure. Two questions need to be answered: what kind of business are we, and what kind of business should we be? Only when these have been answered can a decision be made as to the appropriate structure.

In *The Practice of Management* and later in *Managing for Results* (1964), Drucker introduced two terms that have since been criticised: management by objectives (MBO) and management by results. Both have been regarded as leading to a management style that is fixated on targets and standard setting; the quality guru W. Edwards **Deming**, for example, was strongly opposed to management by objectives, which he regarded as standing in the way of the only legitimate goal of management, continuous improvement. But this is a misreading of Drucker's intention. With management by results, in particular, Drucker is attempting to turn managers away from a rigid adherence to task and routine and towards a mindset that focuses on new and creative ways to achieve results profitably. Influenced here by Schumpeter's work on entrepreneurship and innovation, Drucker began to increasingly stress the central importance of innovation to management.

His philosophy of management reaches its mature form in *Management: Tasks, Responsibilities, Practices* in 1974. Here again he begins with the notion that managers should move away from the idea of managing processes and instead seek to manage for results. He emphasises the central importance of the manager to the business enterprise; the manager's function is that of a catalyst, pulling together the otherwise static resources of production and making them active. Quite literally, it is the manager who breathes life into the enterprise and makes it function. It was possible that in the future workers would become redundant, having been replaced by automation; but machines could never replace the spark of life provided by management. In the future, said Drucker, it was possible that *all* employment would be managerial in nature, and we would then have progressed from a society of labour to a society of management (contrast this with Burnham's vision outlined in *The Managerial Revolution* (1941)).

The first tasks of the manager, then, are to harness resources and create production. The second set of tasks concern guidance and control. In Drucker's view, this role is almost entirely proactive: 'Economic forces set limits to what a manager can do. They create opportunities for management's action. But they do not by themselves dictate what a business is or what it does.'[3] In a famous statement, he assigns to managers the primary role not only for creating the enterprise but also for creating its markets:

> There is only one valid definition of business purpose: *to create a customer.* Markets are not created by God, nature or economic forces, but by the people who manage a business. The want a business satisfies may have been felt by customers ... but it remained a potential want until business people converted it into effective action. Only then are there customers and a market.[4]

Theodore Levitt, himself a marketing guru of some note, later credited Drucker with being the first to have this insight and to bring marketing to the popular notice of American business leaders. This is to overstate the case somewhat. Early twentieth-century writers on advertising and marketing such as John Lee Mahin and Herbert **Casson** had made much the same point, the latter commenting in his book *Ads and Sales* (1911) that: 'It is not true that new goods are manufactured to supply the demand. There is no demand. Both the demand and the goods have to be manufactured. The public has always held fast to its old-fashioned discomforts, until the salesman persuaded it to let go.'[5] But although the lesson had been articulated frequently and well, it had been lost or forgotten by American businesses in the interval. It is fair to say that Drucker helped to bring marketing ideas back to the forefront of business thinking, paving the way for the later work of Levitt and, especially, Philip **Kotler**.

On managers, therefore, fall the twin tasks of pulling together the labour and resources to create production, and of creating markets in which the resulting products can be sold. Through both of these tasks managers must strive to add value, creating something that is greater than the sum of the resources put in. Here Drucker departs from scientific management, which stresses the most *efficient* use of resources; instead, he emphasises a creative environment in which managers use resources in the most *effective* way in order to achieve the goals of the enterprise. This combination of catalyst and proactive control comes very close to a direct identification of the enterprise with its managers. Drucker does not go so far as to say that the managers *are* the enterprise, but he repeatedly stresses their paramount role; earlier, he had commented that: 'The enterprise can decide, act and behave only as its managers do – by itself the enterprise has no effective existence.'[6]

Turning to the responsibilities of management, Drucker argues that these are threefold: (1) to achieve economic performance; (2) to make work productive so that performance can be achieved more easily; and (3) to manage the social impacts that the enterprise will inevitably have on its environment. He speaks of 'responsibilities' rather than leadership, urging that managers should cause things to be done without necessarily having to directly lead the effort themselves. In his view, managers should be the pivot around which the organisation revolves, rather than directors controlling from the top down or officers leading from the front. Particularly important is the third set of responsibilities, those to society. The social dimension of work must never be forgotten, and this grows even more important as the enterprise grows larger and more powerful; at one point Drucker even comments that increased social responsibility is part of the price that must be paid for commercial success.[7] As one reviewer comments:

> Drucker never loses sight of the public good that rests within the organisation in general and the corporation in particular. Corporations must be managed, not only according to a set of pragmatic rules, but within a philosophical framework that conforms to the role of the organisation in industrial society.[8]

Here again Drucker is saying nothing new: the argument that corporations are, in part at least, social instruments goes back to Berle and Means, to William Zebina Ripley, the Harvard professor of economics who taught Adolph Berle and wrote a penetrating series of essays on corporate America entitled *Main Street and Wall Street* (1927), and even further back to the lawyer and historian John Davis, whose study *Corporations* (1902) reached many of the same conclusions as Drucker about the relationship between business and society. Again, however, what is important about Drucker is his ability to get this message across to his audience and make them hear and understand it.

It is this ability which characterises the third phase of his writings, when he begins to turn away from the core discipline of management to its impact on society and its future. In *Innovation and Entrepreneurship* (1985), for example, he returns to the Schumpeterian themes that he had discussed in the 1950s and sets out anew the importance of both, not only in the successful management of business enterprises but in creating wealth and maintaining a strong and free society. In *The New Realities* (1989), he talks about the links between technology, politics, government, economics and the environment, and how these are impacting on management as a function and a profession. In a chapter entitled 'Management as a Social Function and Liberal Art', he writes on how the impact of knowledge is changing the fundamental assumptions that underlie much management thinking. In the early twentieth century, the task of managers was to coordinate and direct the efforts of large, low-skilled labour forces. By the end of the century, workforces were smaller, better educated and more knowledgeable, and this required a different approach to their management. Since the 1980s, Drucker has also been leading the way in calling for the development of knowledge management as a discipline.

An eclectic man, Drucker has also written a historical novel and curated an exhibit of Japanese art. He likes to think of himself as an intellectual rather than an academic. Certainly his thinking is not always original: he is a brilliant synthesiser of ideas rather than a creator of new paradigms. His greatest talent is as a communicator: he is able to package ideas within an easy-to-read, common-sense style that speaks directly to business men and women without talking down to them. As an aphorist he rivals even Herbert Casson (for example: 'Most sales training is totally unjustified. At best it makes an incompetent salesman out of a moron.'). He has the ability to reach an audience given to few other writers on management.

His work has been criticised, particularly as noted above with reference to management by objectives. Drucker has appreciated that management by objectives, if mishandled, can become an organisational strait-jacket, and has redoubled his efforts in calling for more flexibility and customer focus. A more serious complaint may be that he has created, even if unwittingly, the idea of a 'transferable manager', whereby the skills of management are more important than the nature of the business and a trained manager can manage equally well in any kind of business. Drucker himself has never accepted this, and again has repeatedly argued that managers must know the business they are in; but the perception that management skills are entirely generic and easily transferred has remained strong. Against this, however, there remains the fact that Drucker's thirty-five books and over one hundred essays and articles make him the most widely read and referred to management guru of our time.

See also: **Casson, Fayol, Handy, Peters, Simon, Urwick**

Major works

Drucker has produced a phenomenal volume of writing, to which he continues to add even though he is in his early nineties. *Management: Tasks, Responsibilities,*

Practices sums up his most important thinking on the nature and purpose of management; *Innovation and Entrepreneurship* and *The New Realities* are highly topical even though more than fifteen years old. *Adventures of a Bystander* is his autobiography.

The End of Economic Man, London: William Heinemann, 1939.
The Future of Industrial Man, New York: The John Day Company, 1942.
Concept of the Corporation, New York: The John Day Company, 1946.
The Practice of Management, London: Heron Books, 1954.
Managing for Results, New York: Harper & Row, 1964.
The Effective Executive, New York: Harper & Row, 1966.
Technology, Management and Society, New York: Harper & Row, 1970.
Management: Tasks, Responsibilities, Practices, New York: Harper & Row, 1974.
The Unseen Revolution, New York: Harper & Row, 1976.
Adventures of a Bystander, New York: Harper & Row, 1979.
Innovation and Entrepreneurship, New York: Harper & Row, 1985.
The New Realities, New York: Harper & Row, 1989.
Managing in a Time of Great Change, Oxford: Butterworth-Heinemann, 1995.

Further reading

There have been a number of studies of Drucker, nearly all affectionate. Tarrant is one of the best reviews of his work, including a chapter entitled 'The Sayings of Chairman Peter' which includes many of Drucker's best aphorisms.

Beatty, J., *The World According to Drucker*, London: Orion Business Books, 1998.
Bonaparte, T.H. and Flaherty, J.E. (eds), *Peter Drucker: Contributions to Business Enterprise*, New York: New York University Press, 1970.
Starbuck, H.P., 'Drucker, Peter Ferdinand', in M. Witzel (ed.), *Biographical Dictionary of Management*, Bristol: Thoemmes Press, 2001, vol. 1, pp. 242–52.
Tarrant, J.J., *Drucker: The Man Who Invented Corporate Society*, London: Barrie & Jenkins, 1976.

Notes

1   I am indebted to Peter Starbuck, Britain's leading scholar on Drucker, for this startling piece of information.
2   H.P. Starbuck, 'Drucker, Peter Ferdinand', in M. Witzel (ed.), *Biographical Dictionary of Management*, Bristol: Thoemmes Press, 2001, vol. 1, p. 245.
3   P. Drucker, *Management: Tasks, Responsibilities, Practices*, New York: Harper & Row, 1974, p. 88.
4   *Ibid.*, p. 89.
5   H.N. Casson, *Ads and Sales*, New York: 1911.
6   P. Drucker, *The Practice of Management*, New York: Harper & Row, 1954, p. 7.
7   *Management: Tasks, Responsibilities, Practices*, p. 289.
8   J.J. Tarrant, *Drucker: The Man Who Invented Corporate Society*, London: Barrie & Jenkins, 1976, p. 84.

PIERRE DU PONT (1870–1954)

Between 1902 and 1929, Pierre du Pont took over and restructured two failing companies, the gunpowder maker E.I. Du Pont de Nemours and the car maker General Motors. In each case, he put into place a management system and organisation that turned the firms into competitive giants that dominated their respective industries. Often overshadowed at General Motors by his friend and successor Alfred P. Sloan, du Pont played an important role in establishing the organisation and systems that were to be so successful under Sloan's leadership.

Du Pont was born in Wilmington, Delaware on 15 January 1870. His great-grandfather, Eleuthére du Pont de Nemours, was a French chemist of some note, who had studied under Antoine Lavoisier and was a friend of the engineer Robert Fulton. It was Fulton who persuaded du Pont to leave France, then ruled by Napoleon, and emigrate to the USA, where he founded a gunpowder works near Wilmington in 1802. The firm was moderately prosperous under du Pont's sons Alfred and Henry and Alfred's son Lammot (Pierre's father) who served as president from 1872 to 1884. Following Lammot du Pont's death in the latter year, however, the management of the firm, which remained in family hands, became increasingly moribund.

Pierre du Pont studied chemistry at the Massachusetts Institute of Technology and then joined a cousin, Coleman du Pont, as a manager at the Johnson and Lorain Steel Company, which had works in Pennsylvania and Ohio. Unlike the rest of his family, Coleman du Pont was a progressive manager who sought to improve efficiency; in 1896, he sought out the rising engineer Frederick W. **Taylor** and employed him to install a new cost and control system at the company's steelworks, based on Taylor's system of scientific management. After several years the cousins sold their company to the J.P. **Morgan**-backed United States Steel, and Pierre du Pont then spent several years running the street car system in Dallas, Texas.

In 1902 he returned to Delaware and backed Coleman du Pont and another cousin, Alfred, in buying out the company from the older generation of owner-managers, who had been on the verge of selling the company to one of its competitors. He took on the post of treasurer with specific responsibility for reorganising the company's finances, but he also helped create the executive management committee, to which the board of directors agreed to devolve responsibility for the day-to-day running of the company, and as a member of that committee he played a major role in all the organisations that followed.

The subsequent reorganisation of Du Pont happened at an astonishing speed. Alfred **Chandler**, who studied Du Pont in detail in later years, remarked that the transformation at Du Pont happened in months whereas in other organisations it took years. Within two years of taking over, the three young du Ponts had installed a professional management team including former associates from Johnson and Lorain: some of these men, such as Arthur Moxham and John J. Raskob, went on to become famous names in American management in their own right. In particular, Pierre du Pont expanded the staff of the treasury office from twelve to over 100, including talented control accountants such as Russell Dunham and Donaldson Brown. At the same time, Du Pont had bought out most of its rivals (this led to the acquisition of other able managers such as J. Amory Haskell, who came to Du Pont with the acquired companies) and by 1904 controlled 70 per cent of the gunpowder and explosives market in the USA.

Rapid expansion required an organisation to support it. The du Ponts created a divisional structure, based around three operating divisions plus a sales division, a purchasing division and a headquarters division. The three operating divisions rationalised all the company's interests in black powder, smokeless powder and dynamite, respectively, combining all the plants and production facilities for each under a single management. The sales division likewise merged all the company's sales offices and brought them under central control, at the same time establishing a more professional sales organisation with full-time sales staff and regular training courses to help the staff learn more about the products they were selling (particularly essential in the case of explosives). The company's product line required a broad range of raw material inputs, sometimes of small or irregular quantities; the purchasing division was established to speed up and standardise raw material supplies. It accomplished this in the main through vertical integration up the supply chain, setting up its own transport and raw materials production facilities, notably its own nitrate mines in Chile.

Perhaps most radical of all was the establishment, as an adjunct to the headquarters, of a development department under the management of Arthur Moxham. This department had three operating units, which Chandler rather confusingly also refers to as 'divisions'. The experimental division, based near Wilmington, supervised research laboratories, investigating in particular problems of process control. The raw materials division worked closely with purchasing, monitoring raw materials quality and investigating new sources. Finally, the competitive division worked with the sales department to provide information on competitors and customers. Moxham reported to and was a member of the executive committee, which also included the three du Ponts and the head of each operating division. This committee was the primary instrument through which the activities of the divisions were coordinated.[1] Among the development department's rising stars was Walter Carpenter, who would later become president of Du Pont and a director of General Motors.

In his own financial office, Pierre du Pont concentrated initially on improving the quality of financial information. Both he and Russell Dunham had worked with F.W. Taylor and absorbed many of his ideas on cost analysis and control, and together they developed a sophisticated and highly accurate system of cost accounting. Turning their attention to accounting for profits, they rejected the standard definition of earnings as a percentage of sales (or alternatively, of costs) and instead chose to focus on the rate of return on capital invested. By 1910 there was a further advance as Donaldson Brown worked out a method of calculating turnover (the value of sales divided by total investment) and then relating this to earnings as a percentage of sales. These methods, pioneered at du Pont, remain standard accounting tools in business today. As Alfred Chandler says:

> In carrying out this work, Pierre du Pont and his division heads pioneered in the ways of modern industrial accounting. They were among the first industrialists to end the long separation between cost, capital, and financial accounting. They did so, in part at least, by replacing renewal accounting with modern industrial asset accounting. By 1910 they had developed accounting methods and controls that were to become standard procedure for twentieth-century industrial enterprises.[2]

Elsewhere, looking back over the transformation of Du Pont by 1910, he comments: 'the Du Pont company employed nearly all the basic offices and methods used today in the general management of modern industrial enterprise'.[3]

In 1909, Pierre du Pont took over as president of the company and guided its rapid expansion during the First World War. Production of smokeless powder rose from 8 million tons in 1913 to 455 million tons in 1917. Thanks to its efficient organisation and accounting systems, the company coped almost effortlessly with the rapid expansion. Only at the top was there trouble. A dispute developed between Coleman du Pont and the rest of the family over some share dealings by the latter, and Pierre sided with Coleman. He resigned the presidency in 1919. By this time, however, he had a new interest: he had taken a substantial stake in the troubled car maker General Motors, and since 1915 had been a member of its board. In 1920, the affairs of GM reached a crisis.

General Motors had been founded in 1908 by William C. Durant, a Flint, Michigan-based carriage and wagon maker who in 1904 entered the car industry, buying the fledgling Buick company and setting out to challenge Henry **Ford** for leadership of the car market. General Motors became his vehicle for acquiring other small companies, including Cadillac, Oldsmobile and Chevrolet. Although GM made a profit of $10 million in 1909 and the Chevrolet in particular became a success, coming second only to the Model T Ford in terms of units sold, Durant made a series of bad investments and acquisitions. He lost control of the company in 1910–15, returning as president in 1916 with the financial backing of Pierre du Pont. Durant continued to expand and diversify, but his headstrong temperament and risky approach to management led to clashes with du Pont, who was much more methodical and systematic. By 1920, Buick and Chevrolet were making money but the rest of the group was sliding into the red. Durant was ousted again, and du Pont took over as president.

Du Pont's first task was to overhaul the management structure of General Motors and bring in the requisite talent at the top. He used his Du Pont corporate connections well in this regard, bringing Walter Carpenter onto the board of directors; he also brought in a Briton, Harry McGowan, chairman of Nobel Explosives in the UK and a friend and long-time business associate. John Raskob, Donaldson Brown and Amery Haskell came across from Du Pont to strengthen the management team. He also headhunted talent from inside and outside the group, promoting promising managers. Alfred P. Sloan, president of United Motors, GM's wholly-owned parts supplier, was a former associate of Durant, but he had also instituted systems of accounting and control at his subsidiary based on those at Du Pont. Pierre du Pont and Sloan had formed a strong relationship and knew they could work together; Sloan was brought onto the board and made du Pont's *de facto* deputy. Plucked from near obscurity was James D. **Mooney**, then head of a small GM subsidiary called Remy Electrics, who by 1922 had been promoted to run all of GM's operations outside the USA.

Another important hiring was that of William Knudsen. Henry Ford's talented head of production left Ford Motors in 1921 after a quarrel with his employer; du Pont immediately hired him and put him in charge of production of the Chevrolet, where he worked closely with Sloan. The development and marketing of the Chevrolet as a higher quality alternative to the Model T was a central feature of GM's competitive strategy over the next decade; in 1922 the Model T was outselling the Chevrolet by five to one, but by 1929 Chevrolet had overhauled its rival and forced the Model T off the market.

Stage two of the restructuring was to implement on a group-wide basis the kinds of accounting and control systems du Pont had developed and which Sloan had implemented. Stage three was an overhaul of the structure of the company. Pierre du Pont and Sloan felt that General Motors was too large for the kind of functional divisions that had worked so well at Du Pont. Instead, they opted for a 'business unit' approach with the core operating divisions defined by the markets they served. They developed what Sloan later called the price pyramid, with one division at the top, Cadillac, selling small numbers of highly priced cars, and another at the bottom, Chevrolet, selling a large volume of inexpensive cars; the other three divisions were positioned in between at various levels on the pyramid. Parts and accessories continued to function as autonomous divisions. Virtually all responsibility for day-to-day operations and line management was handed over to the divisions, and the enlarged and strengthened headquarters took over responsibility for planning, forecasting, assessments of quality and progress towards goals, measuring managerial effectiveness and a variety of other staff functions. Peter **Drucker** would later describe GM as the ultimate example of the line and staff model of organisation.

At the top of the organisation was a four-man executive committee consisting of du Pont himself, Sloan, Raskob and Haskell, who handled all major operating decisions that did not require board approval. By 1924 this committee had been expanded to ten, but it remained small and flexible enough to allow the corporation to respond quickly to events and sort out problems as they arose. Sloan would later add further interdepartmental and interdivisional committees to ensure better and more frequent communications between the line and staff and between the different operating units.

Du Pont stepped down as president of General Motors in 1924, feeling that the business would be better handled by Sloan, whose career and background were in the automobile business, and who had a better feel for the market. He remained chairman of the board until

1929 and a director for many years thereafter, but increasingly his attention was taken up by outside causes; he was active politically (although a Republican, for a time he supported Franklin D. Roosevelt) and he was a vigorous campaigner in favour of repeal of the prohibition laws. He died at home in Wilmington on 5 April 1954. Sloan, meanwhile, went on to make General Motors into the world's largest corporation, for the time being eclipsing his rival Ford; a brilliant marketer and leader of people, Sloan never forgot that it was du Pont's method of organisation and principles of accounting and control that gave him a platform from which to build his later success.

It is interesting to compare du Pont's approach to management with that of two other great corporate architects of the twentieth century, Harold Geneen of ITT in the 1960s and 1970s, and more recently Jack **Welch** at General Electric in the 1980s and 1990s. Of the two it is Geneen who resembles du Pont most closely, with his emphasis on financial information and control being essential to the management of large conglomerates; but whereas du Pont sought to minimise risk, Geneen relished it. In the end he went too far, and anti-trust suits were launched which broke up the company. Welch too has been a risk-taker, and has also relied on a far more personal style of management, identifying himself much more clearly with the company than du Pont ever did. It remains of course to be seen whether the GE edifice built up by Welch will survive his reign; but the two companies built up by du Pont proved to be durable and lasting.

Alfred Chandler has commented that 'only two basic organizational structures have been used for the management of large industrial enterprises. One is the centralized, functional departmentalized type ... the other is the multidivisional, decentralized structure'.[4] Pierre du Pont was closely involved in the design, development and implementation of both these forms in their early years. Chandler and Salsbury assess his impact in the following terms:

> During that generation, the coming of the modern corpora-
> tion was one of the most important developments in the
> American economy. And of that generation, few men were
> more involved than Pierre du Pont in the shaping of this
> powerful economic institution.[5]

See also: **Chandler, Emerson, Ford, Mooney, Welch**

Major works

Du Pont left behind no written descriptions of his work. The main authorities for his work are Chandler, who undertook comprehensive research on both GM and Du Pont from company records, and Sloan's autobiography. Drucker mentions du Pont but tends to award most of the credit for GM's success to Sloan.

Further reading

Chandler, A.D., *Strategy and Structure: Chapters in the History of American Industrial Enterprise*, Cambridge, MA: MIT Press, 1962.
Chandler, A.D., *The Visible Hand: The Managerial Revolution in American Business*, Cambridge, MA: Harvard University Press, 1977.
Chandler, A.D. and Salsbury, S., *Pierre S. du Pont and the Making of the Modern Corporation*, New York: Harper & Row, 1971.
Drucker, P., *Concept of the Corporation*, New York: The John Day Company, 1946.
Sloan, A.P., *My Years with General Motors*, New York: Doubleday, 1964.

Notes

1   This divisional structure at du Pont strongly resembled the 'line and staff' model of organisation advocated by Harrington Emerson, in which the 'line' or operating departments are complemented by a 'staff' or advisory department at head office. Whether the du Ponts were directly influenced by Emerson is not known, but later at General Motors the line and staff model was explicitly developed, and is referred to both by Drucker in his study of the corporation and James Mooney, one of its senior executives.
2   A.D. Chandler, *The Visible Hand*, Cambridge, MA: Harvard University Press, 1977, p. 445.
3   *Ibid.*, p. 449.
4   *Ibid.*, p. 463.
5   A.D. Chandler and S. Salsbury, *Pierre S. du Pont and the Making of the Modern Corporation*, New York: Harper & Row, 1971, p. 592.

HARRINGTON EMERSON (1853–1931)

Harrington Emerson was an engineer and management consultant in late nineteenth- and early twentieth-century America. He is usually spoken of as one of the leaders of the scientific management movement, and is included alongside the likes of Frederick W. **Taylor**, Henry L. Gantt and Frank and Lillian **Gilbreth**. However, Emerson's ideas on management differed considerably from those of Taylor in particular. Emerson's primary emphasis was on 'efficiency', a word he introduced into the modern management lexicon; his approach to the subject amounted to a complete management philosophy, including ideas on requisite organisation, employee motivation and training and quality standards. Whereas Taylor's version of scientific management concentrated on technical efficiency, bringing each individual production process as near to perfection as possible, Emerson's view of efficiency embraced the entire organisation from top to bottom.

Emerson was born in Trenton, New Jersey on 2 August 1853. His father was a professor of political economy who taught at several European universities; Emerson himself was educated at schools in Paris, Munich, Siena and Athens before studying engineering at the Royal Polytechnic in Munich. While in his late teens he witnessed the events of the Franco-Prussian war, which made a deep impression on him; he later said that he had been equally impressed by the French character and resolve in the face of adversity and the military efficiency of the Prussians. In particular, he became interested in the victorious Prussian commander, Field-Marshal Helmuth von Moltke, and subsequently made a thorough study of Moltke's principles of organisation. An eclectic, Emerson sought knowledge wherever he could find it; he was later to say that the three most important influences on his management methods had come from studying and working with a European music teacher, a breeder of racehorses and a railway surveyor.[1]

Returning to the USA, he taught modern languages at the University of Nebraska from 1876 to 1882 before embarking on a career as an entrepreneur, investing in property and setting up a number of engineering ventures. He surveyed routes for submarine cables to Alaska and Asia for the US government, and later undertook a survey of coalfields in the western states. There are also references to his prospecting for gold in the Yukon in the 1890s, and he may have been involved in the Klondike gold rush of 1898. Also during the 1890s, he began a series of private consultancies with railway firms with a view to 'systematising' the management of railway maintenance and repair shops in particular. Railway locomotives were the single most expensive items of equipment that railways owned, and they were also the most complex and required the greatest maintenance. Improving locomotive reliability and shortening maintenance times could save a company hundreds of thousands of dollars a year.

By 1900 Emerson was so successful as a consultant that he abandoned most of his other ventures and set up his own consulting firm, the Emerson company, and took on associates. By now he was also branching out into consulting for manufacturing companies. His initial focus was on cost reduction and waste elimination, but gradually he began to look beyond this narrower remit towards the idea of more holistic reorganisation and restructuring in order to achieve greater efficiency. What he was now doing was effectively process engineering, examining the whole range of activities associated with planning, scheduling and production, aiming to treat the firm as a harmonious whole, not a series of independent functions.

The job that made his name was the reorganisation of the machine shops of the Santa Fe Railway from 1904 to 1907. Employing thirty-one assistants, Emerson went through the entire motive power department of the railway from top to bottom, measuring and collecting data. The result was a programme of improvements, known as 'betterment works', which had two goals: to restore labour peace, and to improve workplace efficiency. Emerson saw these two goals as being linked; indeed, the first goal was contingent on the second. Reforms to the system of supervision and labour management could not proceed until the workers' own tasks and tools had been standardised. Emerson's team focused on the routing and scheduling of work, ensuring that jobs were carried out according to standard procedures: 'All the work in the machine shop was arranged so that it could be controlled from dispatch-boards located in a central office; likewise on a bulletin-board was indicated the progress of repair of each locomotive.'[2]

Once tasks and duties were standardised, everyone in the shop knew what was expected of them and according to what schedule, and a major source of workplace friction was removed. The second half of Emerson's task was the introduction of a bonus system which rewarded those workers who performed efficiently and well. Although Emerson insisted that the standardised times which formed the basis of work schedules were ones which any worker could achieve, nonetheless, 'the schedule is a moral contract or agreement with the men as to a particular machine operation, rate of wages and time'. Gaining the informed consent of the workers to the new system was vital, and 'extreme emphasis was laid on the individual character of the relations of men and management'.[3]

By 1906, the Santa Fe Railway had achieved cost savings of around $1.25 million. The work attracted much interest and publicity, and suddenly Emerson became one of the most sought-after consultants in the USA. By 1915 he had introduced his efficiency methods into more than 200 firms, including many railways and mining firms but also a number of manufacturers. He continued to develop his system, producing his famous 'twelve principles of efficiency'. He also attracted talented partners, including Herbert **Casson** who went on to become one of efficiency's foremost proselytisers, and Charles

Knoeppel, a former associate of F.W. Taylor who later became one of the pioneers of the discipline now known as organisation behaviour. In 1921 Emerson served as a member of Herbert Hoover's Commission on the Elimination of Wastes in Industry. He retired in the late 1920s and died in New York on 23 May 1931.

As noted above, Emerson was responsible for introducing the word 'efficiency' into the language of business. He saw 'efficiency' as being based on natural principles; nature, he believed, was ultimately efficient, and there were plenty of examples in the natural world to prove this. Indeed, one of the most efficient organisms in the world was the human body, incredibly complex yet largely self-regulating and highly efficient in its usage of inputs such as air, water, food, etc. Achieving efficiency, then, was not about *imposing* an efficiency system; rather it was about structuring an organisation so that efficiency would be achieved naturally. Accordingly, the best way to achieve efficiency is to eliminate inefficiency.

Inefficiencies, says Emerson, come in two forms: there are inefficiencies in processes and materials, and there are inefficiencies in people, societies and nations. The first type is in many ways the least harmful. When inefficient materials are used, they simply give way; when inefficient processes are in place, when the limits of their efficiency are reached, they simply stop working. The second is much more serious in that 'to the inefficiency of an individual or a nation there is no predeterminable limitation'.[4] Human inefficiency is constant, especially when it is embedded in a society or culture. Yet, despite the importance of human inefficiency, Emerson notes that the attention of science is largely focused elsewhere: 'In the passion for modern scientific accuracy it has proved more interesting, and more has been done to solve the lesser problem of efficiency in process or material, almost wholly ignoring the larger problem of individual or national efficiency.'[5] Here, at least, we see a clear break between Emerson and the Taylor school of scientific management, for whom process inefficiencies were all important.

In order to achieve human efficiency, says Emerson, two conditions are necessary: the right *standards*, and the right *organisation*. Of these, it is clear that the organisation must come first. In *Efficiency as a Basis for Operations and Wages* (1909), Emerson devotes three full chapters to the 'line and staff' method of organisation. The line and staff model is in practice made up of a blend of two organisational sub-models, the line organisation and the staff organisation. The line organisation is hierarchical and functional; each member knows his or her place and carries out allotted tasks on a procedural basis. The staff organisation is organic and interdependent, with members relying on each other to carry out their work. A crucial distinction between the two is the role of knowledge. In the line organisation, 'one man knows much more than any other' and that person guides the organisation; so, if the leader loses direction, the organisation is lost as well. In the staff organisation, knowledge is held in common: 'The strength of the staff organisation lies in its ability to multiply many-fold the effectiveness of other staff members, all co-operating to make possible such a wonderful thing as a man, a humming-bird, a midge, or a yellow-fever microbe.'[6]

The best organisations are those that combine the line and staff principles, creating a mix of organism and construct. At a simple level, Emerson uses the example of a baseball team. The batting side uses the line principle: each man comes to the plate in turn in a pre-arranged order and bats without any dependence on his team-mates. The fielding side use the staff principle: pitcher, catcher and fielders work together as a unit, all depending on each other to some degree. The two sides alternate these functions as the game progresses from innings to innings, each depending on the other for ultimate success. The origin of the concept, however, comes not from sport but from military science: Emerson regarded Field-Marshal von Moltke as the greatest exponent of the line and staff principle, and frequently referred to Moltke in his own work. During the Franco-Prussian war, the well-drilled Prussian line performed on the battlefield exactly as it should have, guided by the seemingly omnipresent and omniscient staff. The French, relying almost exclusively on the line principle, could not respond effectively and were defeated.

Emerson links the need for standards to the adoption of the staff principle. Line organisation, he says dismissively, 'needs few standards, usually crude and often fictitious. Seniority or precedence is one of its standards, and closely interwoven is the fundamental standard of immediate and unquestioning obedience almost as automatic as the obedience of sheep to the leader.' Staff, on the other hand, have 'an unlimited multiplicity of scientific standards, higher than all personality ... The staff expert receives from his chief principles which are higher than the chief, since they are part of the eternal laws of the universe.'[7] It is here that Emerson has most in common with the other proponents of scientific management: he believes that adherence to standards of measurement and process that are based on science will eliminate inefficiencies, and thus lead perforce to efficiency. He also believes in a process of continuous improvement, with standards constantly being revised in the light of new knowledge: 'Staff standards are based on specific human authority only until new facts substitute better authority.'[8] Likewise, Emerson is clear that standards do not exist for their own sake:

> Staff standards are not theoretical abstractions but scientific approximations, and are evolved for the use of the line, the sole justification of standards being that they will make line work more efficient. Staff standards, being for the benefit of the line and often entrusted to line officials, must be put in the form of permanent instructions so that all may understand what is being aimed at, and deviations by the line be noted and reprimanded.[9]

In order to set and achieve standards, it is first necessary to conduct a detailed audit of five different areas of the business: (1) methods of materials handling; (2) condition of machines and tools; (3) labour audits, noting discrepancies between what workers are supposed to be doing and what they are actually doing; (4) relationships between current costs and standard costs; and (5) the speed of movement of work through the shop. Each of these five lines of investigation is then developed as a field of measurement and control. The experts of the staff then devise and institute five corresponding standardised systems for: (1) materials handling so as to eliminate wastage; (2) maintenance to keep machines in good repair; (3) wages to ensure workers are motivated and rewarded; (4) costings to ensure that profit and loss can be measured accurately; and (5) task and process times to ensure that work moves through the plant or shop at a natural rate, unhindered by delays.

The final refinement of the Emerson philosophy was the famous 'twelve principles of efficiency'. These are, in summary form:

1 Clearly defined ideals: the organisation must know what its goals are, what it stands for, and its relationship with society.
2 Common sense: the organisation must be practical in its methods and outlook.
3 Competent counsel: the organisation should seek wise advice, turning to external experts if it lacks the necessary staff expertise.
4 Discipline: not so much top–down discipline as internal discipline and self-discipline, with workers conforming willingly and readily to the systems in place.
5 The fair deal: workers should be treated fairly at all times, to encourage their participation in the efficiency movement.

6 Reliable, immediate and adequate records: measurement over time is important in determining if efficiency has been achieved.

7 Despatching: workflow must be scheduled in such a way that processes move smoothly.

8 Standards and schedules: the establishment of these is, as discussed above, fundamental to the achievement of efficiency.

9 Standardised conditions: workplace conditions should be standardised according to natural scientific precepts, and should evolve as new knowledge becomes available.

10 Standardised operations: likewise, operations should follow scientific principles, particularly in terms of planning and work methods.

11 Written instructions: all standards should be recorded in the form of written instructions to workers and foremen, which detail not only the standards themselves but the methods of compliance.

12 Efficiency reward: if workers achieve efficiency, then they should be duly rewarded.[10]

Emerson sees organisational efficiency as being achieved from the bottom up. The staff are there to serve the line, not the other way around; although the staff may have controlling positions, with powers of reprimand and discipline over the line, these functions are ultimately about moving the line to greater efficiency. The worker is there to assist his machine to run efficiently, not to exercise dominion over it; the foreman is there to help his workers achieve their targets, not to control them on behalf of the superintendent, and so on up the line to the chief executive who is ultimately the servant of the organisation, not its master.

Emerson also extends these principles beyond the organisation, seeing businesses in the context of broader society and arguing that more efficient businesses will make for more efficient societies. He was a strong critic of American society at the beginning of the twentieth century, which he saw as riddled with inefficiencies and ill-equipped to compete with either the established powers of Europe or the rising Japan. In part he blamed this situation on the European heritage; an admirer of European culture, he felt nonetheless that this culture had been adapted too uncritically in the USA, without proper regard for the actual pragmatic needs of the new American society. By adopting efficiency methods such as the line and staff principle (itself, of course, a product of Europe), he believed the USA could eliminate waste and become efficient and competitive:

> We have not put our trust in kings; let us not put it in natural resources, but grasp the truth that exhaustless wealth lies in the latent and as yet undeveloped capacities of individuals, of corporations, of states. Instead of oppression from the top, engendering antagonisms and strife, ambitious pressure should come from the bottom, guidance and assistance from the top.[11]

Although he is usually described as being part of the scientific management movement – Horace Drury was to claim that Emerson had 'done more than any other single man to popularise the subject of scientific management',[12] and Herbert Casson often called him the foremost exponent of scientific management – Emerson's relationship to the other figures of the scientific management movement is difficult to assess. He certainly knew of Taylor's work from an early stage, and Drury says he was among the audience when Taylor read his famous paper on shop management before the American Society of Mechanical Engineers in 1903. Drury says further that Emerson sometimes referred to Taylor as the source of his ideas. On the other hand, Emerson also believed that many of Taylor's ideas were over-ambitious and unlikely to succeed. The two men did not get on well, and were in fact temperamental opposites. And in his stress on human and organisational efficiency rather than process efficiency, Emerson took a markedly different approach to the subject than did Taylor.

Another difference lay in the fact that, while Taylor was happy to use and develop standardised production systems, Emerson's approach was instead to emphasise operational flexibility. Drury notes that 'Emerson's methods are flexible, rather than stereotyped; his time studies and standards are approximate rather than exhaustively exact; and he relies much on the self-direction of his subordinates.'[13] He always believed that it is much more important to get the organisation right than it is to set exact measurements. Efficiency, in the final analysis, is about eliminating waste, not creating systems.

Although linked with scientific management, Emerson's work is closer to a philosophy than a science. In the final analysis, for all his devotion to New World-style organisation and principle, Emerson was at least as much a product of Europe as of America, and science and art would always be co-equal in his thinking; management was not only about results, but about higher things as well. He rejected the idea that business is about 'supernal men working through principles to realize supernal ideals', but he believed that what is good for business is also good for society. As he concludes in The Twelve Principles of Efficiency

(1913): 'It is impossible that righteousness married to wisdom should rule without immensely benefiting humanity.'[14]

See also: **Casson, Drucker, Fayol, Follett, Gilbreth, Mooney, Taylor, Urwick**

Major works

Emerson wrote a number of influential journal articles, principally for the New York-based *Engineering Magazine*. His ideas are developed to their fullest extent in two major works.

Efficiency as a Basis for Operations and Wages, New York: John R. Dunlap, 1909.
The Twelve Principles of Efficiency, New York: Engineering Magazine Co., 1913.

Further reading

There is as yet no published book-length biography of Emerson and his ideas, an omission that needs to be rectified. Two good portraits can be found in Casson's autobiography and Drury's survey of scientific management, both based on personal knowledge of the subject. Robert Hoxie's study of scientific management and labour has a good analysis of Emerson's views on personnel management. It is also useful to compare Emerson's works with those of some of the other leaders of the scientific management movement, Taylor, Gantt and the Gilbreths.

Casson, H.N., *The Story of My Life*, London: Efficiency Magazine, 1931.
Drury, H.B., *Scientific Management: A History and Criticism*, New York: Columbia University Press, 1915.
Gantt, H.L., *Work, Wages and Profits*, New York: Engineering Magazine Co., 1910.
Gilbreth, F. and Gilbreth, L., *Primer of Scientific Management*, New York: Van Nostrand Co., 1912.
Hoxie, R.N., *Scientific Management and Labor*, New York: D. Appleton & Co., 1915.
Taylor, F.W., *The Principles of Scientific Management*, New York: Harper & Row, 1911; repr. Norwalk, CT: The Easton Press, 1993.

Notes

1   H.B. Drury, *Scientific Management: A History and Criticism*, New York: Columbia University Press, 1915, p. 113.
2   *Ibid.*, p. 127.
3   *Ibid.*
4   H. Emerson, *Efficiency as a Basis for Operations and Wages*, New York: John R. Dunlap, 1909, p. 23.
5   *Ibid.*
6   *Ibid.*, pp. 55–6.
7   *Ibid.*, pp. 96–7.
8   *Ibid.*, p. 98.

9 *Ibid.*
10 H. Emerson, *The Twelve Principles of Efficiency*, New York: The Engineering Magazine Co., 1913.
11 *Efficiency as a Basis for Operations and Wages*, p. 242.
12 *Scientific Management*, p. 116.
13 *Ibid.*
14 *The Twelve Principles of Efficiency*, p. 423.

HENRI FAYOL (1841–1925)

Henri Fayol was a French mining engineer who developed, independent of the American scientific management movement, a general theory of business administration. His most notable work, *Administration industrielle et générale* (General and Industrial Management) (1925), is an attempt to classify and set out the duties and functions of management. Unlike F.W. **Taylor** and his followers in scientific management, Fayol concentrated on the duties of senior managers rather than on managing individual processes. His ideas are at once more abstract and more flexible than those of Taylor, and while he has his modern critics, his approach to management continues to have appeal.

Fayol was born on 29 July 1841 in Galata, the suburb of Constantinople where most Westerners who worked in the Ottoman Empire lived. His father was an engineer who had originally gone out to Turkey to establish a foundry for casting cannon barrels; later he was appointed as superintendent of works for a French-financed project to build a bridge over the Golden Horn between Constantinople and Galata. The family returned to France around 1847, and Fayol was educated at schools in Valence and Lyon and then the mining school at St Etienne. He was recruited straight from the school at age nineteen to join the mining company Boigues Rambourg, being selected by the general manager of the firm's mine at Commentry, Stephane Mony. When Mony made senior partner of Boigues Rambourg and returned to Paris, Fayol took over as general manager of the Commentry mine.

Mony was a dynamic leader who was ahead of his time as far as the French mining industry was concerned. He converted the company from a partnership into a joint stock company, renamed Commentry-Fourchambault Company, and pushed for further expansion. However, following Mony's death in 1884, control passed into the hands of one of the owners, Anatole le Brun Sessevale. Faced with an ongoing depression in the iron and steel industry, Sessevale could not manage effectively, and instead embarked on a six-year-long internecine feud with his fellow directors. By 1888 the firm was on the edge of bankruptcy; the one business unit that was functioning well was the Commentry mine. When Sessevale was finally forced out of office, the board of directors at once appointed Fayol to succeed him as president. His appointment seems to have been provisional in the first instance, as he was not appointed to the board of directors but instead was employed by them; an unusual situation which suggests that the board regarded him as more of a general manager than a president.

In retrospect, it is easy to understand the board's possible unease at promoting a 47-year-old with no senior management experience or training to the head of a large company. Yet Fayol proved to have an innate understanding of his task. He was, as he later said himself, a far better manager than he had been an engineer. His first task was to put the company back onto a sound financial footing. Pursuing economies of scale, Fayol took over and merged a number of smaller mining and smelting companies, culminating in 1892 with the acquisition of the iron and steel mills of the Decazeville Company: the firm was then renamed the Compagnie Commentry, Fourchambault et Decazeville. By 1900 the company was one of the largest producers of iron and steel in France and regarded as a vital national industry, especially given the expansion and rearmament of the French army in the decade before the First World War. A grateful board of directors finally voted Fayol onto the board of the company he had led for the last twelve years.

Over the next two decades Fayol continued to lead the now prosperous company. He also became increasingly interested in the problems of management, in particular whether there were general principles of management that could be applied across the board. His own experience and his observations of others suggested that such principles could indeed be drawn and further, that the tasks and activities of management could be classified into various standard types. Sasaki notes that Fayol was also strongly influenced by the positivist philosophy of Auguste Comte and Claude Bernard, a philosophy 'in which inference is directly and accurately applied to a variety of facts gathered through observation and experiment'.[1]

He first expounded his views in a paper to a congress of the Société de l'Industrie Minérale in 1908. This brought him immediate attention within France. Over the next seven years he continued to refine his views, finally publishing them as an essay in a French mining journal in 1915 as 'Administration industrielle et générale' (the book form did not appear until 1925, the year of his death). The essay made Fayol France's leading national expert on administration and management, and a school of thought known as 'Fayolism' began to grow, opposed to and sometimes directly challenging the 'Taylorist' American ideas of scientific management, imported into France in the years after 1905 by the chemist Henri Le Chatelier and the naval architect Charles de Fréminville. Fayol retired as president of Commentry-Fourchambault-Decazeville and turned to full-time consulting, working with the government of Belgium after the First World War and later helping the French government reorganise the Ministry of Posts, Telegraphs and Telephones.

Fayol's later years were marred by a squabble between his own followers and the Taylorists. In 1919 he helped to found the Centre d'Études Administratives (Centre for Administrative Management) to promulgate his theories on administration. In the following year, however, Le Chatelier and Fréminville founded a rival body, the Conférence de l'Organisation Française (French Conference on Scientific Management). A bitter rivalry soon developed between the two schools. Finally, at the Second International Management Conference in Brussels in 1925, matters came to a head. Fayol, after some negotiation with Fréminville, announced publicly that there was no conflict between his ideas and those of Taylor, and the two organisations agreed to merge, with Fréminville as president. Fayol himself died at home in Paris on 19 November 1925.

In *Administration industrielle et générale* (1925), Fayol begins his exposition by stating that all business enterprises, in whatever field, are characterised by six types of activity: production, commerce (or selling/marketing), finance, security, accounting and management. As businesses become larger, so the importance of management grows, as it is necessary to control and coordinate the elements of the other five. From this basis, Fayol proceeds to his statement of the tasks of management. Originally composed of five elements, this later grew to seven, summarised by the acronym POSDCORB: planning, organising, staffing, directing, co-ordinating, reporting and budgeting. Again, every manager, no matter what business they are involved in, will be involved in these tasks to some degree.

The POSDCORB concept has been developed and expanded on, not always in beneficial ways, and it was partly in reaction to this that Peter **Drucker** in the 1950s and 1960s tried to simplify the tasks of the manager to a few basic precepts such as innovation and marketing. But the basic POSDCORB concept works; it is hard to envision a management position, even today, which does *not* involve most if not all of the seven elements. There are differences between the requirements of different management positions, of course, but these are differences of degree rather than kind. A simple test of the validity of the concept is to consider any management position, take away one or more of the elements above from the manager's responsibility, and then consider the ways in which this removal increases risk and uncertainty for the manager involved.

If POSDCORB has endured, Fayol's equally famous 'fourteen principles' of management have not. These, paraphrased to an extent for brevity, are:

1 division of labour, so as to achieve the maximum efficiency from labour;
2 the establishment of authority;
3 the enforcement of discipline;
4 unified command, so that no employee reports to more than one supervisor;
5 unity of direction, with all control emanating from one source;
6 subordination of individual interests to the interest of the organisation;
7 fair remuneration for all (though Fayol was not in favour of profit sharing);
8 centralisation of control and authority;
9 a scalar hierarchy, in which each employee is aware of his or her place and duties;
10 a sense of order and purpose;
11 equity and fairness in dealings between staff and managers;
12 stability of jobs and positions, with a view to ensuring low turnover of staff and managers;
13 development of individual initiative on the part of managers;
14 *esprit de corps* and the maintenance of staff and management morale.[2]

These fourteen principles, especially those such as the division of labour, centralisation of authority and scalar hierarchy, are very much products of their time; seventy years later, they were declining in popularity, seen as products of the past. Stability of jobs and positions, too, is increasingly becoming a memory. Yet some of the fourteen points – unity of direction, a sense of order and purpose, equity and fairness – remain highly relevant. The problem for today is how to adapt Fayolism so as to hang onto the relevant aspects and excise those portions which are no longer relevant.

Fayol's use of the term *l'administration* later caused considerable confusion in English-language writings on management. The British writer Oliver Sheldon, for example, took a keen interest in Fayol and incorporated some of the latter's ideas into his own very popular *The Philosophy of Management* (1924). Sheldon tried to draw a distinction between 'administration', a set of organisation-wide functions carried out by the directors and senior executives, and 'management', more micro-level activities carried out lower down the organisation: administration was about setting policy, management was about completing tasks. The distinction between the two was seen as being the difference between the ideas of Fayol and those of F.W. Taylor.

In fact, the more correct translation of *l'administration* in the sense that Fayol uses it is 'management'. Fayol was right when he said that there was no fundamental incompatibility between his ideas and those of Taylor. Many of the differences that arose between his supporters and those of Le Chatelier and Fréminville were personal and nationalistic, with supporters of the home-grown doctrine of Fayolism rejecting the alien intrusion of American Taylorism. Another, more lasting division later grew up between students and practitioners of public and private sector management. Luther Gulick, the head of the Institute of Public Administration at Columbia University and the man who did perhaps more than any other to shape modern approaches to civil service administration worldwide, admired Fayol and preferred the term 'administration' to 'management'. Today the division is almost complete: 'administration' refers to government, while 'management' refers to the private sector. On both sides, there is a damaging failure to realise that many of the tasks and practices are the same.

In later years, indeed, Fayol would be criticised by many for being too close to Taylor and for encouraging the establishment of strong managerial bureaucracy and rigid division of labour. Like Taylor, he too believed in universal precepts of management. But, setting the misunderstanding over *l'administration* aside, there were still substantial differences between their approaches. Taylor's view of the organisation was ultimately a mechanistic one, in which perfection of the whole was achieved through perfection of the sum of its parts. Fayol was in many ways closer to **Emerson**, or even the **Gilbreth**s, in encouraging a holistic outlook of organisation and seeing principles of management as a framework rather than a critical path to success. Again, linguistic difficulties often intervene in our understanding of Fayol. Considering the tasks of management, for example, Fayol uses the term *prévoyance*, which in the original has connotations of foresight and anticipation of needs; but in the English translations this appears as 'planning', with strong connotations of direction and command.

As Sasaki notes, Fayol's views on management's purpose and tasks were later displaced in the mainstream of thinking by the American Chester Barnard in *The Functions of the Executive* (1938), which drew on the POSDCORB concept to some degree but placed much more emphasis on concepts such as open systems and bounded rationality, strongly emphasising the fuzzy nature of organisational life and personal decision making. This was later to be developed still further by Peter Drucker in books such as *The Practice of Management* (1954). Set against that kind of approach, Fayol does indeed look overly mechanistic. Yet Fayol himself was aware of the importance of change and flux, commenting that 'there is nothing absolute in management': 'Seldom do we apply the same principle twice in identical circumstances; allowance must be made for changing circumstances.'[3] It should never be forgotten that Fayol was no academic theorist, but a practitioner with a long record of successful management in tough circumstances. His experience showed him that the only management that could succeed was management conducted according to first principles.

See also: **Drucker, Emerson, Ford, Gilbreth, Taylor, Urwick**

Major works

Administration industrielle et générale was Fayol's major work. It was originally published as an essay in a French mining journal, and only appeared in book form in France in 1925. The translations of Storrs and Gray, listed separately, are the best known and most widely available; Gray takes the liberty of 'rephrasing' some of the original language, and Storrs is preferred. *L'incapacité industrielle de l'État* is a polemic against state management of industrial enterprises.

L'incapacité industrielle de l'État, Paris: Dunod, 1921.
Administration industrielle et générale, Paris: Dunod, 1925.
C. Storrs, trans., *General and Industrial Management*, London: Pitman, 1949.
I. Gray, trans., *General and Industrial Management*, New York: David S. Lake, 1984.

Further reading

Brodie and Lepawski have detailed, if dated, analyses. Urwick represents an attempt to reintegrate 'Fayolism' into the main current of management thinking; Wren is a good modern analysis; and Sasaki is very good on background.

Barnard, C.I., *The Functions of the Executive*, Cambridge, MA: Harvard University Press, 1938.
Brodie, M., *Fayol on Administration*, London: Lyon, Grant & Green, 1967.

Lepawski, A., *Administration: The Art and Science of Organisation and Management*, New York: Alfred A. Knopf, 1949.

Sasaki, T., 'Fayol, Henri', in M. Witzel (ed.), *Biographical Dictionary of Management*, Bristol: Thoemmes Press, 2001, pp. 293–5.

Urwick, L., 'The Function of Administration', in L. Gulick and L. Urwick (eds), *Papers on the Science of Administration*, New York: Institute of Public Administration, 1937.

Wren, D.A. (ed.), 'Henri Fayol and the Emergence of General Management Theory', *Journal of Management History* 1(3) (1995): 5–12.

Notes

1   Sasaki, Tsuneo, 'Fayol, Henri', in M. Witzel (ed.), *Biographical Dictionary of Management*, Bristol: Thoemmes Press, 2001, p. 294.

2   This summary comes from Sasaki (2001). For a more detailed explanation see the Storrs translation of *General and Industrial Administration* and also Brodie's *Fayol on Administration*.

3   *General and Industrial Management*, Storrs translation, London: Pitman, 1949, p. 19.

MARY PARKER FOLLETT (1868–1933)

Mary Parker Follett was a social scientist who challenged the precepts of scientific management and helped lay the foundations of the human relations school of management. In particular, she suggested that the only viable form of control was coordination: organisations based on command and control were inefficient and would not survive. She challenged also the role of specialist 'experts', and argued that the best learning is that which we acquire for ourselves, rather than relying on others to do our thinking for us. A critical, independent thinker, Follett had a powerful impact on management theory in the 1920s and 1930s, and her ideas continue to resonate today.

Follett was born in Quincy, Massachusetts into an old New England family on 3 September 1868. She studied at Radcliffe College, taking a mixed degree in philosophy, law, history and political science, and spending part of her time studying at Newnham College, Cambridge and the Sorbonne in Paris; she graduated *magna cum laude*. Settling in Boston with her long-time companion Isobel Briggs, Follett became involved in the establishment of centres for educational services in working-class districts of the city; later, these services would also provide vocational education and help people find jobs. Her major interest had been in politics (while still at Radcliffe she had written an important and highly regarded book, *The Speaker of the House of Representatives* (1896)), but her work in Boston gave her greater interest in economic and social issues. Her next book was the thoughtful *The New State-Group Organization* (1918). Now rarely read, this book is an analysis of the relationship between the individual and society and the role that relationship plays in the maintenance of democracy. In this book, Follett anticipated many of the conclusions of postmodern scholars of politics and society such as Anthony Giddens.

From here, Follett went on to a consideration of how individuals function in society. Her next book, *Creative Experience* (1924) introduced ideas from sociology and psychology and on the role of personal knowledge into her thinking. The book appeared at a time when management theorists and practitioners were becoming increasingly interested in the interaction between individuals and organisations (which could be considered as miniature constructs of society as a whole) and the new discipline of organisation behaviour was just starting to emerge. *Creative Experience* was picked up and read by Henry Metcalf, director of the Bureau of Personnel Administration in New York who, with his colleague Ordway Tead, was one of the leading writers and teachers on organisation and personnel management. Metcalf saw the potential of Follett's work for management, and invited her to give a course of lectures at the Bureau. These in turn were widely noticed, in Britain as well as the USA. Benjamin Seebohm Rowntree, chairman of the chocolate maker Rowntree & Co. in York and a businessman keenly interested in the problems of management, invited Follett to give a lecture at one of the bi-annual Rowntree Lecture Conferences which he organised at Balliol College, Oxford. Here she came into contact with the leading intelligentsia of British management, including Oliver Sheldon and Lyndall **Urwick**. Urwick became a strong supporter and disseminator of her ideas and encouraged her to write more directly on management. Follett also returned to the UK to give more lectures, notably at the London School of Economics.

Follett felt welcome in the UK and found that her ideas were given a warm reception there, even more so than in the USA. She decided to make her life in Britain. In 1928, after the death of Isobel Briggs, Follett moved to London, where she lived in Chelsea with another friend, Dame Katherine Furze. In 1933 she returned briefly to Boston to settle some financial affairs before moving to the UK for good, but she fell ill and died there on 18 December 1933 at the age of 65.

Creative Experience is a book that arrived, so far as management theory was concerned, at exactly the right time. By the mid-1920s, the scientific management movement dominated management thinking in both the USA and many parts of Europe. However, scientific management was not regarded with universal enthusiasm. It had a tendency to lead to bureaucracy and technocracy, and, especially, it emphasised the role of the technical expert, appearing to downgrade (and in many cases actually doing so) the roles of not only the worker on the shop floor but also of line managers, who often felt that the technical and efficiency experts were taking control of the business out of their hands. Follett opens her book by questioning the role of these experts and indeed the whole concept of what she calls 'vicarious experience'; that is, relying on the experience and skills of others rather than acquiring knowledge for ourselves. She questions whether experts can be regarded as custodians of truth, in the same way that it is questionable whether the law is really the guardian of truth. She does not dismiss experts out of hand, and acknowledges that their own experience and knowledge means that they *do* have access to truth, or at least some of it. What is dangerous, she feels, is the way in which others rely unquestioningly on experts to do their thinking for them.

What is the alternative? Follett's view is that people should gather their own information, make their own decisions, define their own roles and shape their own lives. At the same time, however, she rejects empiricism: experience should not be used to create rigid theories and concepts, but rather to inform the mind and 'liberate the spirit', in a process which she calls 'evocation'. In this way, experience can become truly creative, a powerful force that creates advancement and progress.

This has strong echoes of modern work on knowledge management, where it is now generally accepted that, in order to understand and make use of new information that comes to us, we need a grounding in prior knowledge which enables us to interpret the new information and determine what is valid and relevant. Moreover, it suggests that experience and knowledge are in themselves motivating forces. Follett's view of society, and of organisations, is that people at all levels should be motivated to work and participate, and at the same time to acquire experience. The importance of psychological theory is evident throughout *Creative Experience*, and Follett makes reference to concepts such as Gestalt. Ultimately, however, this is not a book about psychology any more than it is about any other branch of knowledge. Follett believed in the unity of knowledge, and she draws on political, social, economic and legal theory as well as psychology and biology to construct a holistic picture of how we think, feel and experience, not only as individuals but also as individuals-in-groups.

This was a major contribution to the nascent discipline of organisation behaviour, and it was justly recognised as such at the time. The interest in her work within the field of management and administration studies may have taken Follett somewhat by surprise, as she had never written on this subject before. But as Lyndall Urwick and Edward Brech comment in their short study of her work and influence, Follett did not so much change direction to study business and management, but rather she incorporated these fields into her already broad area of interest. Her subsequent lectures at the Bureau of Public Administration, the Rowntree Conferences and the London School of Economics show how she applied a wide range of theories from many disciplines to the problems of management. She spoke constantly of the need for personal growth and development as a key to management success. The gathering of experience and knowledge, she argued, broadened the person and made the manager more effective and better able to maintain and coordinate relationships both within the organisation and outside it. Among other contributions at this point, Follett laid the groundwork for a relational or network theory of management by suggesting that such relationships were all-important to both business and social effectiveness.

It is her work on coordination and control, however, that has had the most lasting impact. In one of her most important lectures, 'The Process of Control', delivered in 1930 and later reproduced by Urwick and Luther Gulick in *Papers on the Science of Administration* in 1937, Follett again introduces the role of knowledge management. The purpose of control, she says, is not to control people but to control *facts*; in other words, the real control that matters is the control of information. Second, effective control of this sort cannot stem from one source; to be effective, control has to be 'the correlation of many controls rather than a superimposed control'.

> The ramifications of modern industry are too wide-spread, its organization too complex, its problems too intricate for it to be possible for industry to be managed by commands from the top alone. This being so, we find that when central control is spoken of, that does not mean a point of radiation, but the gathering of many controls existing throughout the enterprise.[1]

What we think of as 'control', then, is in reality 'coordination'. In a famous and often cited passage, she goes on to offer four fundamental principles of coordination:

1 coordination as the reciprocal relating of all the factors in a situation;
2 coordination by direct contact of the responsible people concerned;
3 coordination in the early stages;
4 coordination as a continuing process.[2]

The first of these harks back to Follett's philosophy in *Creative Experience*. When two or more people work together, she says, they combine their thinking through a process she calls 'adjustment'. In a game of doubles tennis, for example, each player has to adjust their thinking to take account of the movements and actions of their partner. In a large business organisation, the heads of each department constantly 'adjust' their thinking to reflect the actions and activities of their colleagues and their departments. This adjustment is reflected in the way in which each head controls his or her own department. At the same time, of course, they are *also* adjusting their thinking to a whole host of other factors going on in the environment around them. All these different sets of thinking interpenetrate each other, and the activities of any one department reflect this combined thinking set which governs its coordination. Thus no department exists in isolation, nor is the organisation merely a set of departments set side by side: rather, it is a unified whole bound together by this set of dynamic, constantly changing relationships. This in turn affects everything that the organisation and its members do.

Follett advocates that coordination should be handled directly by the responsible managers who are in direct contact with the workers, not from unseen figures on high. By coordination at the early stages, she means that coordination should be built into a system from its inception. However, coordination does not stop with the design of the system: it is also a continuous process, one which must happen as a natural part of management. She advocates continuous coordination on the grounds that it leads both to easier problem solving and to the generation of knowledge which can improve working methods in the future. In a pre-figuring of later work on strategy and planning, she also argues that continuous coordination creates what later become known as 'feedback loops', whereby plans and policies can be easily adjusted in the light of fresh information.

Follett rejects the mechanistic view of organisation advocated by many in the scientific management movement, and opts instead for a social and biological model. This is most clear when she discusses the nature of control. Famously, she argues that 'organisation *is* control', organisations in effect have no other purpose *but* control. But again, she emphasises that the real nature of control is the coordination of the parts:

> Biologists tell us that the organizing activity of the organism is the directing activity, that the organism gets its power of self-direction through being an organism, that is, through the functional relating of the parts.
>
> On the physiological level, control means co-ordination. I can't get up in the morning, I can't walk downstairs without that co-ordination of muscles which is control. The athlete has more of that co-ordination than I have and therefore has more control ...
>
> This is just what we have found in business.[3]

There is no such thing as forcible control in business. Control by attempting to force one element to perform an action alone, says Follett, is not control at all. In the reality of business life, even the most autocratic board of directors does not have sole control; as soon as lower layers of management are added, responsibility is delegated and control is shared, and from that moment on coordination becomes a necessity.

The most important control of all, Follett concludes, is self-control. In a passage which is a direct appeal to greater democracy in industrial organisations, she argues that a form of collective control which coordinates the actions of all members of the organisation by allowing them to participate in the control process is the right way forward for industry:

> If you accept my definition of control as a self-generating process, as the interweaving experience of all those who are performing a functional part of the activity under consideration, does not that constitute an imperative? Are we not every one of us bound to take some part consciously in this process? Today we are slaves to chaos in which we are living. To get our affairs in hand, to feel a grip on them, to become free, we must learn, and practice, I am sure, the methods of collective control. To this task we can all devote ourselves. At the same time that we are selling goods or making goods, or whatever we are doing, we can be working in harmony with this fundamental law of lie. We can be assured that by this method, control is in our power.[4]

Pauline Graham, the foremost modern scholar on Follett, believes that many of the latter's ideas are just as relevant today as they were at their inception (Graham has, indeed, produced a book of management precepts for modern use derived from Follett). It is hard to argue with this view. Follett's human-centred and holistic approach to organisation, emphasising relationships, communication and coordination, is very much in line with modern thinking. If her ideas on management have a weakness, it is that (again like modern thinking) they do not perhaps give enough consideration to the potential need, at least, for outright control and regulation for ensuring security and probity. A Follett-style organisation works so long as its members are motivated to work together for the good of the organisation and society. The task of the controller/coordinator must also be to motivate with this view in mind. As Gareth **Morgan** has pointed out, no metaphor of organisation, no matter how powerful, ever presents more than a partial picture of the whole.

This quibble aside, Follett has given us a set of persuasive and powerful ideas on how to manage organisations by coordinating knowledge and relationships. She anticipated much modern thinking in this field many decades in advance, and remains one of modern management's most original and enduring thinkers.

See also: **Argyris, Emerson, Fayol, Gareth Morgan, Simon**

Major works

Creative Experience is regarded as Follett's masterwork. 'The Process of Control' is regarded as being one of her best essays on management. The collected essays by her admirers Henry Metcalf and Lyndall Urwick are essential reading for students of Follett's views on management and organisation.

The Speaker of the House of Representatives, New York: Longmans Green, 1896.
The New State-Group Organization: The Solution for Popular Government, New York: Longmans Green, 1918.
Creative Experience, New York: Longmans Green, 1924.
'The Process of Control', in L. Gulick and L. Urwick (eds), *Papers on the Science of Administration*, New York: Institute of Public Administration, 1937, pp. 159–69.
Metcalf, H.C. and Urwick, L.F. (eds), *Dynamic Administration: The Collected Papers of Mary Parker Follett*, Bath: Management Publications Trust, 1941.

Further reading

Graham is Follett's biographer and has produced excellent studies of her work, superseding the earlier study by Urwick. The short assessment of her career by Urwick and Brech is worth reading.

Graham, P., *Dynamic Managing: The Follett Way*, London: British Institute of Management, 1987.

—— (ed.), *Mary Parker Follett: Prophet of Management*, Boston, MA: Harvard Business School Press, 1995.

Urwick, L.F. (ed.), *Freedom and Coordination*, London: Management Publications Trust, 1949.

Urwick, L.F. and Brech, E.F.L., *The Making of Scientific Management*, vol. 1, *Management in British Industry*, London: Management Publications Trust, 1949; repr. Bristol: Thoemmes Press, 2002.

Notes

1 M.P. Follett, 'The Process of Control', in L. Gulick and L. Urwick (eds), *Papers on the Science of Administration*, New York: Institute of Public Administration, 1937, p. 164.
2 *Ibid.*, p. 161.
3 *Ibid.*, pp. 166–7.
4 *Ibid.*, p. 169.

HENRY FORD (1863–1947)

Henry Ford is probably the single most famous business leader of all time. Over the course of the past hundred years he has been admired and reviled in almost equal proportions. To some, he was the paragon of American entrepreneurial genius, who revolutionised American culture and lifestyles by bringing cheap motoring to the masses, beginning America's long love affair with the automobile. To others, he was the instigator of a dehumanising, deskilling system of mass production which has oppressed the lives of millions around the world. His admirers included Vladimir Ilich Lenin, who instructed *Pravda* to serialise his books; his detractors included Aldous Huxley, whose characters in the novel *Brave New World* pray to 'Our Ford' rather than 'Our Lord'.

Part of the problem stems from the fact that Ford's own life and career changed dramatically over time. Even the most sympathetic observer has difficulty in reconciling the enlightened employer and talented engineer who designed the Model T and built the Highland Park production plant with the paranoid and bitter old man who neglected his company, hired mafia thugs to beat up employees and, if witnesses are to be believed, drove his only son into an early grave. There were two sides to Henry Ford, and any appreciation of him needs to look at both.

Ford was born near Dearborn, Michigan on 30 July 1863. After a rudimentary education, at sixteen he apprenticed as a machinist in

Detroit, supplementing his meagre wages by working part-time as a watch repairman. He was particularly interested in gears and their functions, and at one time contemplated making a career as a watchmaker. Returning to Dearborn in 1882, Ford set up a small machine shop undertaking general repair work, mostly on farm machinery. In 1888, now aged twenty-five, he married a local girl, Clara Bryant, and then returned with his wife to Detroit, where he found a job with the Edison Illuminating Company. Here his natural talent as an engineer allowed him to prosper and he was quickly promoted, rising to become chief engineer for the Chicago area in 1893 (his only son, Edsel Ford, was born that year). His ability had also brought him to the notice of Thomas Edison, who later became a close friend.

From the beginning, Ford had been fascinated with automobiles and the potential they offered, and certainly by the 1890s he was experimenting with designing and building motor cars. His experience with watches and gears helped him solve the problem of how to convert the motive power provided by a steam or internal combustion engine into drive through the wheels. His simple design for a transmission led to his development of a working automobile in 1896. The car, which he called a quadricycle, ran on bicycle wheels and weighed only 500 pounds. Ford promptly sold it to raise capital for further experiments, continuing to make and sell similar prototypes for several years.

In 1899 Ford resigned from Edison and, with capital from a local timber merchant, set up the Detroit Automobile Company. This failed quickly, largely thanks to Ford's own inexperience with production problems. In 1900 he tried again with the Henry Ford Company. As with the previous firm, this was plagued with problems and made few cars, but did develop a successful design for a racing car. Ford became suddenly enthusiastic about racing cars, so much so that he neglected his business and was finally ejected from the firm by his partners (ironically, the Henry Ford Company was bought by Cadillac and ended up becoming part of General Motors). Ford went on to set up a partnership with the former racing car driver Tom Cooper, and together they built a racing car, the 999, which set the world land speed record in 1902.

But although racing cars were exciting, the chances of getting rich were small. Ford's original vision had been of building cheap, affordable cars that could be marketed to the masses. By 1903, he not only had the engineering experience but also the contacts, the backers and above all the management team to make that vision a reality. Backing this time came from Alexander Malcolmson, a Detroit coal dealer; other partners were John and Horace Dodge, who supplied the original engines for Ford cars. Canadian-born James Couzens, a former employee of Malcolmson, was appointed treasurer and handled much of the initial marketing and administration work. With this team, Ford Motor Company was founded in Detroit in June 1903.

The early years were plagued with problems. Ford first had to fight off a patent infringement suit from the Association of Licensed Automobile Manufacturers, which claimed to have sole rights to make and sell gasoline-powered automobiles. He then had to make plain his own vision of the company's future as a producer of cheap, low-cost cars, fighting his corner against Malcolmson, who wanted to make high-priced, luxury vehicles. Ford pointed out that every other car maker was then competing in this market, so it made sense to go down-market where the competition was almost non-existent. He won his case eventually, forcing Malcolmson out in 1906, and finally getting down to the serious business of making cars. The first important design was the Model N, a cheap runabout which went on sale later that year with a showroom price of $600. Sales were good, sufficient to convince Ford that his original approach was the correct one. He now began development of the two innovations that were to make his name: the Model T Ford, and the production plant at Highland Park.

The Model T, nicknamed 'Tin Lizzie' by the millions who owned and drove it, is the car that brought mass motoring to America and so changed the shape of American culture for all time. Designed by Childe Harold Willis and engineered by Ford himself, the Model T went on sale in 1908 for $825. With a 22-horsepower engine and advanced chassis and steering design, the car was technologically advanced when first launched, yet its design was so simple that interchangeable parts could easily be mass produced and then assembled. Between 1908 and 1927, 17 million Model Ts were sold, more than all other models of car put together at the time. Ford worked constantly to bring unit costs down, so successfully that by the mid-1920s the price of a new Model T had fallen to $275. This was a recipe with which other motor car companies could not compete; even their most successful rivals, such as William Durant at Chevrolet/ General Motors and John North Willys at Willys Overland, sold only a small fraction of the number of cars that Ford did. From being a luxury, the car was transformed almost overnight into a mass consumer good. Middle-class and even prosperous working-class households could afford a car. This ability to see the potential of the car market played a central role in Ford's success.

The dominance of the Model T was made possible in large part by the impressive organisation that existed to build it. Designed by architect Albert Kahn and purpose-built for the production of the Model T, the plant at Highland Park, Michigan covered sixty-two acres. It featured the largest assembly line yet seen in the world, and had been carefully engineered to increase car production to speeds beyond anything yet attempted; instead of 12–14 hours to assemble a finished car, the previous norm, Model Ts could now be assembled from stocks of finished parts in an hour and a half. The opening of Highland Park in 1910 sent a shock through the business world. Visitors from other companies and even other countries flocked to see it; among those who learned from Ford's production methods was the Czech shoemaker Tomas **Bat'a**, who would later establish his own revolutionary approach to management in Europe. Ford won plaudits not only for his mechanical engineering but also for his attention to detail and carefully engineered production system, which was based in large part on the methods of scientific management advocated by Frederick W. **Taylor**, but also owed much to earlier mass production systems such as that developed by the inventor of the combine harvester, Cyrus Hall McCormick at International Harvester. Ford's achievement was to combine a whole series of earlier ideas and systems into a single, smoothly running production process.

In terms of worker relations, also, Ford was seen by many as a visionary. In 1914 he cut the working day to eight hours, believing this to be the optimum working day for worker efficiency, and also initiated the famous $5 daily wage, nearly double the going rate in the industry. On one occasion when Highland Park advertised for workers the plant received nearly 1,000 applications for every vacancy, meaning that Ford's production chiefs, William Knudsen and Charles Sorenson, could take their pick of the most skilled and best qualified workers. Despite the later connotations of deskilling and dehumanising labour associated with mass production, Highland Park was at the time nearly as famous in the world of labour as it was in the world of management. When Sorenson visited the Soviet Union and toured a truck factory near Moscow in the late 1920s, he was astonished to be greeted with shouts of 'Hi, Charlie!' by the men on the production line. It transpired that several had worked at Highland Park before the First World War and had spread the plant's reputation among their colleagues.

A further factor in Ford's success was his management team. By 1910 he had working for him three of the best senior managers in America at the time. James Couzens, as well as managing the company's finances, put together its distribution system and set up a nationwide network of franchised dealerships which was one of Ford's great early strengths, allowing mass production to be complemented by mass marketing. The Danish-born engineer William Knudsen came to Ford from a subsidiary company which Ford purchased in 1911, and by 1916 was in charge of all production not only at Highland Park but at nearly two dozen subsidiary plants making parts and sub-assemblies across the USA. His deputy, Charles Sorenson, was a draughtsman who had worked with Ford and Cooper in their racing car days and had risen through the ranks to become production manager for the Model T.

But by 1920, Ford was beginning to lose his grip. The first signs of cracks came with the break-up of the great management team. One after another, the top managers and directors quarrelled with Ford and departed. James Couzens was the first to go, leaving Ford and business altogether and embarking on a career in politics (he later became a US senator). More serious was the defection of Knudsen in 1920, to Ford's rival General Motors. At GM, Knudsen took over responsibility for production of the Chevrolet, then being outsold by the Model T at a ratio of 7:1; seven years later, the resurgent Chevrolet had driven the Model T from the market. General Motors, reformed and restructured by Pierre **du Pont** and Alfred P. Sloan, was now a stronger, more flexible, better managed company than Ford; with James **Mooney** in charge of international business, it was also becoming dominant overseas. And Ford was also losing sight of the most important element in his mix, the customers. The famous comment, 'A customer can have a car of any colour he wants, so long as it is black', which dates from this period, may be apocryphal but is nonetheless indicative of a mindset in which production was now the only thing that mattered.

There were increasing signs too of mental illness, and his son Edsel, who had succeeded Couzens as company secretary and treasurer at the age of twenty-two, was one of the chief sufferers. Charles Sorenson, who remained loyal to Ford almost until the end, nonetheless concurred that by the early 1920s Ford was paranoid and showing signs of delusions, and that his son was the victim of an increasingly violent series of rages. Although Edsel Ford had taken over the presidency of the firm, he became increasingly unwell with stomach ulcers and then cancer, finally dying in 1943; Sorenson, who normally tolerated no criticism of his chief, believed that Ford himself was largely responsible for his son's death.

It was Sorenson and Edsel Ford who finally persuaded Ford that the Model T's day was done, and production stopped for six months in 1927 while the plants retooled for its successor, the Model A. This was successful, but not so much as to prevent General Motors from taking over as the country's leading car producer in terms of units sold. A new production plant at River Rouge, Michigan was set up to make the Model A; larger and less efficient than Highland Park, it suffered from a series of problems that delayed production and impacted on profitability. Workplace morale also declined. Ford, though vehemently opposed to unions, had always treated his men fairly and well, but now he began cutting wages and increasing hours. When the workers threatened to unionise, Ford hired Harry Bennett, a former prizefighter and mafia enforcer from Chicago, who set up the infamous Ford Service Department, a gang of toughs who broke up union meetings and terrorised pro-union workers. In 1940 Ford refused to participate in the government's aircraft manufacturing programme largely because of a paranoid delusion that President Franklin D. Roosevelt was out to destroy him (the fact that William Knudsen was in charge of the programme probably did not help allay Ford's suspicions). Edsel Ford and Sorenson finally persuaded him to take part, and the Willow Run production plant was established near Ypsilanti, Michigan to make heavy bombers; even so, Ford would never go near the plant, convinced that if he did he would be assassinated by government spies. Harry Bennett was now virtually in control of both the company and Ford himself, and Sorenson recalls the sight of Clara Ford in tears at the thought of what 'that monster' was doing to her husband.

The death of Edsel Ford in 1943 brought about the final crisis. Now partially paralysed by a stroke, Ford announced he was resuming the presidency of the firm. This led to a revolt by his own wife and his daughter-in-law, Edsel's widow, who threatened to sell their shares in the firm to General Motors unless Ford retired altogether. He finally gave way, and Clara Ford was able to intervene with the government to secure the release from service in the US Navy of Henry Ford II, Edsel's son. After the war the younger Henry Ford began the long task of rebuilding the company, hiring in new management talents such as Robert Macnamara and Lee Iacocca.

What, then, are we to make of Henry Ford? His career is open to many different interpretations, all of which have an element of truth. In business history, however, it has become fashionable to compare Ford unfavourably with his rivals at General Motors, notably Alfred Sloan. General Motors was progressive and innovative, Ford was conservative and unreceptive to change; General Motors was focused on the market, Ford was focused on production; General Motors was divisionalised and efficient, Ford was centralised and inefficient; and most of all, General Motors was managed by professionals with a separation of ownership and control, while Ford was managed by its family owners.

All of these notions can be challenged. General Motors initially had little separation of ownership and control, especially under Durant and du Pont, while Ford, in the early stages at least, had a number of brilliant managers on his senior staff. The problem, as Nevins and Hill point out in the second volume of their magisterial account of the Ford company, is that most comparisons are valid depending on when they are made. The Ford of 1934 is by no means the same as the Ford of 1914. That Ford himself went on too long is undeniable; equally, it is hard to deny his successes in the early years, or his impact on management both in the car industry and more generally.

Nevins and Hill describe Ford's basic managerial insight as being based on five related facts:

> that the American people needed cars in millions; that a single durable inexpensive model could meet that demand; that when new technological elements were woven together to create mass production, they could furnish millions of cheap vehicles; that price reduction meant market expansion; and that high wages meant high buying power. This was as obvious, when demonstrated, as Columbus's art of standing an egg on its end. Until then it was so far from clear that Ford had to battle his principal partner and the current manufacturing trend to prove it. A special kind of genius lies in seeing what everybody admits to be obvious – after the exceptional mind thinks of it; and Ford had that genius. It changed the world.[1]

Ford was probably at his happiest when designing. Dearborn Engineering, the corporate research and development group, centred around Ford himself and, in the years before 1920 at least, was a hive of activity and ideas. These ideas concerned process as well as product. Highland Park was every bit as revolutionary as the car it created; River Rouge, though more control-oriented, still had its share of technological and engineering wizardry. To the end of his days, Ford possessed an almost intuitive understanding of production engineering and process flows. Virtually every mass production system developed in the world since owes at least something to Ford and his ideas.

Insight into Ford's views can be found in his books. Although these must be used with care, as their primary purpose was often self-aggrandisement, there are frequent passages where he muses to his co-author Samuel Crowther on his purpose and goals. The following, from *Moving Forward* (1931) is interesting on a number of levels:

> Through all the years that I have been in business I have never yet found our business bad as a result of any outside force. It has always been due to some defect in our own company, and whenever we located and repaired that defect our business became good again – regardless of what anyone else might be doing. And it will always be found that this country has nationally bad business when business men are drifting, and that business is good when men take hold of their own affairs, put leadership into them, and push forward in spite of obstacles. Only disaster can result when the fundamental principles of business are disregarded and what looks like the easiest way is taken. These fundamentals, as I see them, are:
>
> (1) To make an ever-increasingly large quantity of goods of the best possible quality, to make them in the best and most economical fashion, and to force them out onto the market.
> (2) To strive always for higher quality and lower prices as well as lower costs.
> (3) To raise wages gradually but continuously – and never to cut them.
> (4) To get the goods to the consumer in the most economical manner so that the benefits of low-cost production may reach him.
>
> These fundamentals are all summed up in the single word 'service' ... The service starts with discovering what people need and then supplying that need according to the principles that have just been given.[2]

As a statement of philosophy, this shows both the strengths and weaknesses of Henry Ford's approach to management. On the one hand there is the attention to quality, to the product and, importantly, to the needs of the market. On the other hand, there is the ignoring of competition and the centring of responsibility on the manager himself. Part Frederick Winslow Taylor, part Friedrich Wilhelm Nietzsche, here is a portrait of the executive as superman, capable of solving all problems through authority and control. It is a philosophy which, like the man himself, is full of contrary aspects and is not capable of being sustained for long.

See also: **Arkwright, Bat'a, du Pont, Taylor, Toyoda, Welch**

Major works

Ford wrote a number of journal articles and several books in which he set out his own philosophy of management, usually working with a co-writer, Samuel Crowther. As noted above, these need to be handled with care, but there is still much to be learned from them.

My Life and Work, New York: Doubleday, 1922.
Today and Tomorrow, New York: Doubleday, 1926.
My Philosophy of Industry, London: Harrap, 1929.
Moving Forward, New York: Doubleday, 1931.

Further reading

Nevins and Hill's three volumes are still the best account of the company and its founder, if at times too uncritical. Sward is an interesting look at the Ford myth. Beasley's biography of William Knudsen is a useful counterweight, and Sorenson's autobiography is full of insights although it too should not be accepted uncritically.

Beasley, N., *Knudsen: A Biography*, New York: McGraw-Hill, 1947.
Nevins, A.N. and Hill, F.E., *Ford: The Times, the Man, the Company*, New York: Charles Scribner's Sons, 1954.
—— *Ford: Expansion and Challenge, 1915–1933*, New York: Charles Scribner's Sons, 1957.
—— *Ford: Decline and Rebirth*, New York: Charles Scribner's Sons, 1962.
Sorenson, C. and Williamson, S.T., *Forty Years with Ford*, London: Jonathan Cape, 1957.
Sward, K., *The Legend of Henry Ford*, New York: Rinehart, 1948.

Notes

1   A.N. Nevins and F.E. Hill, *Ford: Expansion and Challenge, 1915–1933*, New York: Charles Scribner's Sons, 1957, p. 614.
2   H. Ford and S. Crowther, *Moving Forward*, New York: Doubleday, 1931, pp. 2–3.

JAY WRIGHT FORRESTER (1918–)

Jay Wright Forrester is a scientist and professor of management at the Massachusetts Institute of Technology. His name will forever be associated with the concept of system dynamics, a technique for modelling systems as they develop over time, and one which encourages thinking about management – and a broad range of other issues – as something that happens in a constantly changing environment, rather than in static situations. His ideas and techniques have been widely diffused. Much of his influence on management has been indirect: system dynamics does not raise the instant cheer of recognition that accompanies terms such as, for example, management by objectives or core capabilities. Yet the influence of system dynamics can be seen in areas as various as forecasting, resource planning, organisation behaviour and the concept of the learning organisation. As twenty-first century managers learn to accept and manage through continuous change and ambiguity, system dynamics becomes an increasingly important concept.

Born in Arnold, Nebraska on 14 July 1918, Forrester grew up on a cattle ranch. After taking a degree in electrical engineering at the University of Nebraska, he joined the research faculty of the Massachusetts Institute of Technology in 1939, where he worked on servomechanisms for weapons and radar during the Second World War. After the war he was appointed to head MIT's digital computer laboratory in 1946, where he developed and built the Whirlwind, an early high-speed digital computer; he also did pioneering work on flight simulators. In 1952 he became head of the digital computer division at the Lincoln Laboratory at MIT, where he worked on magnetic core memory (MCM) for computers. In 1956 he patented an improved version of MCM, which had originally been developed by Wang An at Harvard in 1951.

Wang, an expatriate from war-torn China, and Forrester, the rancher's son from Nebraska, had a similar vision of the future of the computer: each believed that computers had wide potential for application, especially in industry. But whereas Wang chose to pursue his vision by going into business himself, setting up Wang Laboratories in 1951 and going on to lead the way in the commercial development of computers for almost three decades, Forrester remained in academia and pursued his research in other directions. In 1956 he joined the Sloan School of Management at MIT as professor of management, and began research on social systems. His unique approach, rooted in his own background in servomechanics, electronics and cybernetics, gave him new insights into the problems of organisation and management. He remained with the Sloan School until his retirement in 1989.

The catalyst for the development of Forrester's ideas on system dynamics is usually considered to be his work with General Electric in the 1950s, when he noted that managerial interventions in some areas, such as inventory and human resources management, were actually worsening the problems they were intended to solve. Studying the situation, he identified what he termed 'feedback loops'. In essence, when problems arose, managers took what they believed to be the appropriate corrective actions, and these actions had consequences within the system. A single 'feedback loop' thus comprised the original situation, the management action taken, and the resulting impact on the system.

However, many of these corrective actions had consequences which went beyond the initial situation, and these could cause further distortions elsewhere in the system. Let us take a hypothetical example. The maintenance department of a factory has a high wages bill (situation). Management believe the best way to reduce this bill is to cut staff (action). As a result, the maintenance department now has fewer staff (result). However, if manpower is reduced by too much, or if key staff with specific technical skills are let go, there is a knock-on effect for factory maintenance which causes problems elsewhere in the company. Other managers now have to take other actions, generating other feedback loops. What started off as a single problem can spread into a multiplicity of other problems and responses. Forrester termed this 'oscillation', referring to how a pendulum will swing further and faster as more pressure is applied to it.

In effect, inappropriate management action was generating internal, or endogenous, 'noise' that was cluttering the system and making it more difficult to manage effectively. Forrester's achievement was to define the feedback loops and to measure the noise or oscillation that they produced, then re-design the management system so as to reduce them. The result was what he first called 'industrial dynamics' in the 1961 book of that title, but which later became known as 'system dynamics'.

System dynamics has three principal components. The first is the understanding of the nature and working of feedback loops. Understanding feedback loops requires the collection of information about the original problem, followed by controlling action, followed then by new information collection to monitor the results and determine success or failure, and also to measure the consequences for other parts of the system. Second, Forrester introduced the use of computer modelling to understand the process over time, and to calculate the downstream effects of a particular action or intended action. This was a critical new technique at the time, as it allowed managers to literally 'see' the consequences of possible actions before taking them. Simulation also allows a number of alternative decisions and actions to be compared and evaluated to determine the best possible outcome.

The third feature was the one that Forrester himself believed to be most important: mental models. He argued that the most important feature of any social system – including business organisations – is the set of unwritten assumptions we all share as to the causes of particular events and phenomena. This goes beyond *how* we make decisions and *what* decisions we make into the altogether more fuzzy domain of *why* we make the decisions we do. For any simulation or model to be accurate, therefore, the modellers or designers of the simulation need to understand the mental models of the managers in question. How they think and react and share information have powerful impacts on the systems they manage.

This was revolutionary and complex stuff, and even today system dynamics remains a hard concept for many managers to grasp. In part this is because it is both hard and soft: it relies on quantifiable data and information to create technologically based models and simulations, yet at the same time it places great emphasis on fuzzy factors, on uncertainty and on human behaviour. There is a temptation, of course, to use system dynamics to 'harden' managerial behaviour by producing mechanistic solutions to problems in social systems; critical comparisons have been made with the 'one best way' approach of scientific management. Another trend is to create industry-wide models that predict how the banking industry or the oil industry as a whole will behave, which tend to assume that all managers will need to react in more or less the same way to the challenges that are arising. This is damaging, as it closes doors to imagination and creative management.

Nor did Forrester ever intend that system dynamics should be used in this way. In the 1960s, futurologists such as those of the RAND Corporation were indeed seeking predictive models which would allow them to estimate the future with some accuracy. But Forrester argued that the prevalence of mental models makes such predictivity impossible. Every organisation was a social system with its own mental models, and in certain circumstances would behave differently from others. There were, obviously, decisions which had favourable or unfavourable consequences, but there were no black and white, right or wrong options. Every system and every management team needed to work out its own way forward.

These ideas have consequences for a wide range of business activities. System dynamics is of course widely used in forecasting and modelling future activity of markets and economies, where it has become an invaluable tool. There are also important applications in resource planning and supply chain management, and the influence of system dynamics can be seen in the concept of just-in-time management, where companies run a series of continuous feedback loops with their suppliers. Decision sciences use system dynamics to model the consequences of particular decisions and to seek optimum solutions to problems. Chris Argyris adapted the concept of feedback loops into his studies of organisation behaviour. Most recently, the concept of shared mental models has been at the heart of the 'learning organisation' concept devised originally by Arie **de Geus** and Peter Senge in the late 1980s and early 1990s (Senge had studied and worked closely with Forrester and was heavily influenced by him). Indeed, it can be argued that the learning organisation is itself a kind of mental model, and that the concept cannot be successfully implemented until the members of the organisation are prepared to adapt their individual thinking to encompass it.

In later years, Forrester applied his system dynamics to understanding the problems of urban decay and regeneration, the results being described in his book *Urban Dynamics* (1969). He also began an important association with the Club of Rome, a private thinktank established in the 1960s to consider world economic growth and its associated problems, such as environmental damage, uneven economic development and the gap between rich and poor nations. Applying system dynamics to the world economy, Forrester and his colleagues argued that growth at then current rates was unsustainable and would have to slow down at some point, or else the problems of inequality and environmental damage would overwhelm it. This argument was set out in his book *World Dynamics* (1971), and also – and more forcefully – in the work of another of his students and fellow member of the Club of Rome, Donella Meadows, who developed in more detail the thesis of sustainable development. Meadows and Forrester were heavily criticised by many economists, who believed that high growth was ultimately sustainable. Today the debate rages on and has become part of the central *problematique* of globalisation for both its defenders and its opponents.

System dynamics is a concept that is at once both very simple and very complex. Its effective use requires considerable training and experience, and only a minority of managers today fully understand it. Yet it has had ramifications in our thinking, not only about global economy and competition, but also about how we manage in organisations, why we take the decisions we do, and how we learn and employ knowledge. Building on the earlier works on organisational psychology and cybernetics by the likes of Herbert **Simon** and Norbert Wiener, Forrester has created a robust system which allows managers to estimate the impacts of their own decisions and behaviour and to construct rational approaches to complex problems.

See also: **Argyris, Babbage, de Geus, Follett, Gates, Maslow, Simon, Taylor**

Major works

Industrial Dynamics is the first setting out of system dynamics theory, and is Forrester's most influential book. *World Dynamics* reflects on his work with the Club of Rome. The collected papers contain a number of important later articles. See also Legasto *et al.* in the following section.

Industrial Dynamics, Portland, OR: Productivity Press, 1961
Urban Dynamics, Portland, OR: Productivity Press, 1969
World Dynamics, 2nd edn, Cambridge, MA: Wright-Allen Press, 1973 (first published in 1971).
Collected Papers of Jay W. Forrester, Cambridge, MA: Wright-Allen Press, 1975.

Further reading

There is now a considerable literature on system dynamics in everything from forecasting to organisation and knowledge management, and only a small sample can be given here. Legasto *et al.* is a good general work, while the other two books listed are primarily concerned with modelling applications in practice.

Legasto, A.A., Forrester, J.W. and Lyneis, J.M. (eds), *System Dynamics*, Amsterdam: North Holland, 1980.
Meadows, D.H, Meadows, D.L. and Randers, J., *The Limits to Growth*, New York: Universe Books, 1972.
Morecroft, J. and Sternman, J. (eds), *Modelling for Learning Organisations*, Portland, OR: Productivity Press, 1994.
Richardson, G.P. (ed.), *Modelling for Management*, Aldershot: Dartmouth, 1996.

FUKUZAWA YUKICHI (1835–1901)

Fukuzawa Yukichi was an economist and educator who played a central role in the modernisation of Japan following the Meiji Restoration of 1868. He founded Keio University and published a number of very popular books and journal articles, using both channels to introduce Western ideas into Japan. He believed that adopting such ideas was crucial if Japan was to survive as a strong independent state, but at the same time he argued that the Japanese needed to preserve the essentials of their own proud and ancient culture. Much of his work was aimed at business and industrial leaders, and it was from the foundations laid down by Fukuzawa and others like him that Japan rose to become one of the economic leaders of the world.

Fukuzawa was born in Osaka on 10 January 1835, the second son of a minor *samurai* (member of the warrior class). His father died when he was still very young, and Fukuzawa grew up in conditions of considerable poverty in the small town of Nakatsu in northern Kyushu, the family's ancestral home. In 1854 his elder brother, who held a minor administrative post in Nagasaki, suggested Fukuzawa should come there to study, and in particular to learn Dutch. The suggestion was an important one, and came at a critical time.

For several centuries, Japan had existed in virtual isolation from the rest of the world. The emperors of Japan held their offices only nominally, with real power being vested in the *shoguns*, the military leaders who also controlled the civil administration. The *shoguns* sought to consolidate their own power through a rigorous control of state and economy, fearing that foreign influences could mean the end of their own power. Only a very limited foreign trade was allowed, primarily with Dutch merchants and their agents, and through one port only: Nagasaki.

In 1853, an American naval squadron under Commodore Matthew Perry, through a mixture of force and bluff, succeeding in opening other Japanese ports to American trade. Other Western nations quickly followed suit. Japan in the 1850s was relatively prosperous and there was little real economic hardship, but the country was technologically three centuries behind the Western powers. Perry's 'black ships', so-called because of their iron hulls, inspired fear in the inhabitants of the coastal cities. Thinking Japanese realised that there were just two choices ahead: to submit to foreign domination and colonisation, processes which were already underway in nearby China, or to forcibly advance the Japanese economy and technology to the point where it could compete with the West on equal terms.

Fukuzawa's move to Nagasaki, therefore, was prompted by a desire to learn as much as possible about Western culture, economy and technology. However, he found the opportunities for learning in Nagasaki were limited, and in 1855 he moved to Osaka where he joined the private school of a local Dutch-speaking physician, Ogata

Kouan. Here Fukuzawa was able to study not only the Dutch language but also Western science through Dutch textbooks. He was the academy's star pupil, and in 1858 moved to Tokyo to set up a Dutch school at the behest of his family's feudal overlord.

In the same year, the Treaty of Friendship and Commerce between Japan and the USA opened the port of Yokohama, near Tokyo, to American and British merchants. Fukuzawa visited Yokohama and came away convinced that the English-speaking nations were those that Japan should seek to emulate. He began studying English, and in 1860 volunteered to join the Kimura embassy to the USA, thus becoming one of the first Japanese to visit that country. The visit greatly improved his knowledge of Western science and economics and also helped him to master the English language. Returning to Japan, he worked briefly as an English-language translator in the office of the *shogun*, and then in 1862 was appointed as a member of the first Japanese mission to Europe. In 1867 he was sent to the USA again as a member of a purchasing mission for the Japanese navy.

At home, in intervals between overseas journeys, Fukuzawa published his observations in the three-volume work *Seiyo Jijo* (Conditions in the West) between 1866 and 1870, and this work became standard reading for any Japanese interested in Western economics. In particular, Volume 1 gave a comprehensive description of how Western businesses were managed, operated and owned. His school had meanwhile expanded and was teaching the English language and English economics, the latter gleaned from both British and American sources. In early 1868 he renamed the school Keio Gijuku (Keio College); today this institution is known as Keio Gijuku University and is one of the leading universities in Japan.

In the meantime, those around the emperor realised that, while the *shoguns* remained in power, there would be little chance of modernising Japan. Accordingly, they plotted to overthrow the shogunate and restore direct imperial rule. In 1867 the 15-year-old emperor Mutsuhito took the title *meiji tenno* (enlightened emperor; he is usually known in the West as the Meiji emperor) and began the process of removing the *shoguns* and their supporters in the large feudal clans from power. In 1868 there was a military showdown between the forces of the emperor and those of the *shogun*, culminating in the Battle of Ueno, which by coincidence took place close to Keio College (according to tradition, Fukuzawa refused to interrupt his lecture on Francis Wayland's *Elements of Political Economy* even once the battle had started). The imperial forces won the day and the restoration of imperial power was proclaimed, with a strong mandate for modernisation and industrialisation in Japan.

Fukuzawa, as one of Japan's leading experts on the West, was at once offered a senior position in the new government. He declined, however, feeling he could do more as an educator. His next book, a series of essays entitled *Gakumon no Susume* (Recommendation for Learning) (1872–6) was a practical encouragement of learning and education, but also an assertion of these things as a natural right. Basing his views in part on Jean-Jacques Rousseau's concepts of human freedom, Fukuzawa argued that all human beings had a right to be free and prosperous, and that education was the best route to achieve these things. His arguments for both personal and national education struck a powerful chord with the new mood in Japan, and increased Fukuzawa's authority and standing.

Enlightenment, again on both a personal and a national basis, became one of the core concepts of Fukuzawa's thinking over the next decade. His philosophy blended Japanese concepts of personal enlightenment through education, derived from Confucianism and Buddhism, with Western concepts such as utilitarianism, the seeking after the greatest good for the greatest number. He also emphasised the *laissez-faire* economic doctrines developed by the French physiocrats and later by Adam Smith.[1] He particularly admired the American Francis Wayland, and translated the latter's *Elements of Political Economy* (1841) into Japanese. In the late 1870s he produced two masterful syntheses of Japanese and Western civilisation aimed at showing the way forward for development in Japan: *Bunmeiron no Gairyaku* (An Outline of the Theory of Civilisation) (1875) and *Minkan Keizi Roku* (Political Economy for Citizens) (1877), both showing how the Japanese could learn from the West and adapt the best Western ideas to the needs of Japan.

To promote his views and those of others, Fukuzawa embarked on a number of ventures, including a publishing company and a journal, *Jiji Shimpo* (Timely News). The latter, founded in 1882, became the leading progressive journal in Japan, and Fukuzawa himself was a regular contributor on a broad range of topics, ranging from business management to the need for female emancipation.

Even before the Meiji Restoration, Fukuzawa had been aware of the need for more and better education for business people. In the 1860s he acquired a copy of one of the leading textbooks of the period, *Bryant and Stratton's Common School Book-keeping*, and immediately digested its contents and importance. Book-keeping courses were added to the syllabus at Keio College (Fukuzawa's wife was one of the first pupils) and in 1873 Fukuzawa translated the book into Japanese. It went on to have a wide dissemination and helped to bring up-to-date accounting methods into Japanese businesses as they prepared for growth and expansion. Iwasaki Yataro, founder of the recently established shipping firm Mitsubishi Shokai, shared many of Fukuzawa's views and recruited several Keio graduates to his management team. As well as teaching accounting at Keio, Fukuzawa helped set up several other colleges for training in accounting methods: one of these, Tokyo Commercial College, founded in 1875, went on to become Hitotsubashi University, another of Japan's leading universities today.

Although a fierce critic of Japan's feudal order, Fukuzawa did not believe that the Japanese should abandon their own ancient culture. The latter had many virtues and many strengths, such as dedication, integrity and desire for the good of others, all of which were embedded in *samurai* culture. In one of his later books, *Jitsugyo Ron* (Essays on Industry and Business) (1893), he argued that what was needed instead was an adoption of the techniques and practices of Western business: not only up-to-date accounting methods but also improved production methods and competitive practices. Fukuzawa rightly foresaw that Japanese business would have to go beyond Japan's borders and compete with Western rivals on the world stage. Writing in the 1890s, Fukuzawa believed that Japanese industry was not yet ready for that level of competition, but he urged politicians and industrialists alike to look forward to that day and prepare for it. Once again, he urged the importance of education, training and skills in making Japanese industry competitive.

In his later years Fukuzawa became politically more conservative, particularly in terms of Japanese foreign policy. He believed that Japan had a leadership role to play in Asia; China, Japan's ancient rival, was now rotten and about to fall into the hands of the Western powers or to be dismembered altogether. He therefore supported Japanese aggression on the Asian mainland, particularly the taking over of Korea and the Sino-Japanese War in 1894–5, which Japan won easily thanks to its updated army and modern weapons. The Sino-Japanese War convinced many in Japan that the country could now compete militarily and economically with the West. In 1904, three years after Fukuzawa's death, Japan went to war against one of the greatest Western powers, Russia, and again was the victor. Japan had now arrived as a world power. Unfortunately, these victories also sowed the seeds of Japanese militarism which, especially after the death of the Meiji Emperor in 1912, became the ruling creed in Japanese political circles. The ultimate result was the Japanese invasion of China in the 1930s and defeat in the Second World War in the 1940s.

Fukuzawa died in Tokyo on 3 February 1901. By the time of his death his efforts had worked a mighty transformation in Japanese society. Most importantly of all, he had set the scene for Japan's industrial transformation. As noted above, he personally trained several leading managers of the new shipping company Mitsubishi, which rose with astonishing rapidity to rival the leading British and American shipping firms in Asian waters. He also trained many of the managers who took over the ancient and largely moribund Mitsui company, based around the Tokyo department store Echigo-ya, and turned it into the largest company in Japan. Chief among these was Fukuzawa's own nephew, Nakamigawa Hikojiro, who studied at Keio and was the first editor of *Jiji Shimpo*, before going on to become managing director of Mitsui and its leader and guiding hand through the years of high growth. Otaguro Jugoro, who graduated from Fukuzawa's Tokyo Technical College, also played a leading role in the transformation of Mitsui. Hibi Osuke and Kobayashi Ichizo were Keio graduates who worked for Mitsui before going on to careers as retail entrepreneurs, Kobayashi as founder of the Hankyo Department Store in Osaka and Hibi as founder of the Mitsukoshi chain. Matsunaga Yasuzaemon, who studied at Keio but did not graduate, dominated the Japanese electric power industry for decades.

One of the most impressive of Fukuzawa's alumni was Muto Sanji, who graduated from Keio and briefly taught there before going on to spend several years working and studying in the USA. In 1893 he joined Mitsui, where he worked closely with Nakamigawa. In the following year he was sent to Kanebo, a small cotton-spinning company which was a Mitsui affiliate, and tasked with expanding the company and building up an export base. He began by working on the shop floor and studying the machine processes, noting where defects occurred and the problems, both human and machine, that led to loss of product quality. Between 1896 and 1900 Kanebo bought up half a dozen rival firms, expanding very rapidly, and Muto was made chief manager. In moves that echo not only the work of his contemporary, Frederick W. **Taylor**, in America but also the later work of W. Edwards **Deming** in Japan, Muto studied individual processes in order to find ways of improving them, introduced quality inspection during the manufacturing process and developed statistical methods for monitoring quality. He introduced the time-and-motion study method pioneered by the **Gilbreths**, and **Emerson**'s line and staff principle of organisation, and his paternalistic philosophy of employment, complete with full welfare provision for workers, is reminiscent of both the **Cadburys** in Britain and the later 'cradle to grave' social security policies of Japanese employers.

Fukuzawa encouraged the alliance of traditional Japanese values and culture with modern Western business techniques, and further encouraged business leaders to aim for national prosperity and strength, not just personal enrichment. There were others like him engaged in the same task, notably the banker Shibusawa Eiichi who founded Daichi Bank and was an important incubator for new businesses: he was said to have helped personally to found over 500 new companies during the course of his career. But, of his generation, it is Fukuzawa's intellect and philosophical approach to economics and business that continually stand out. Modern Japanese business owes much of its character and culture to his work.

See also: **Deming, Ibuka, Matsushita, Toyoda**

Major works

Regrettably, not all of Fukuzawa's major works have been translated.

Seiyo Jijo (Conditions in the West), Tokyo, 3 vols, 1866–70.
Gakumon no Susume (Recommendation for Learning), Tokyo, 1872–6; trans. D.A. Dilworth and U. Hirano, *An Encouragement of Learning*, Tokyo: Sophia University, 1969.
Bunmeiron no Gairyaku (An Outline of the Theory of Civilisation), Tokyo, 1875; trans. D.A. Dilworth and G. Cameron Hurst, *An Outline of a Theory of Civilisation*, Tokyo: Sophia University, 1970.
Minkan Keizi Roku (Political Economy for Citizens), Tokyo, 1877.
Jitsugyo Ron (Essays on Industry and Business), Tokyo, 1893.

Further reading

Blacker remains the best English-language study of Fukuzawa and his influence, and much of this chapter has been based on him. The short biographies by Nishikawa and Sasaki are full of value. Wayland is of interest for his influence over Fukuzawa. Kuwahara's article on Muto Sanji is the only English-language study of this remarkable man.

Blacker, C., *The Japanese Enlightenment*, Cambridge: Cambridge University Press, 1964.
Kuwahara, T., 'Muto Sanji', in M. Witzel (ed.), *Biographical Dictionary of Management*, Bristol: Thoemmes Press, 2001, vol. 2, pp. 732–7.
Nishikawa, S., 'Fukuzawa, Yukichi', in M. Warner (ed.), *Handbook of Management Thinking*, London: International Thomson Business Press, 1998, pp. 233–7.
Sasaki, T., 'Fukuzawa Yukichi', in M. Witzel (ed.), *Biographical Dictionary of Management*, Bristol: Thoemmes Press, 2001, vol. 1, pp. 336–8.

Wayland, F., *Elements of Political Economy*, 4th edn, Boston, MA: Gould and Lincoln, 1841 (suggested as the edition Fukuzawa most likely used; the book went through nine editions in all).

Note

1   The term *laissez-faire* does not actually appear in Smith's *The Wealth of Nations* (1776), but the concept is widely discussed there.

BILL GATES (1955–)

Bill Gates is no ordinary multi-billionaire. He has been at the centre of developments in computer software since the 1970s, and has done more than almost any other single individual to shape the information revolution in modern business and society; only Tim Berners-Lee, the creator of the World Wide Web, can claim to be his equal in influence. Gates has also shown himself to be one of the most talented entrepreneurs of his generation, building up a company of global influence based on an almost instinctive understanding of the principles of marketing and an ability to manage a flexible, sometimes volatile but always creative organisation. In an industry where companies rise and fall almost overnight, Gates's company Microsoft has proved to be one of the few enduring success stories.

William Henry Gates III was born in Seattle, Washington on 28 October 1955. He was educated at Lakeside School in Seattle, where he shone at science and particularly maths, and reportedly was tested as having an IQ of between 160 and 170. He became interested in computers while at school, and befriended another young computer enthusiast, fellow pupil Paul Allen. While still in their teens, Gates and Allen set up their first computer company, Traf-O-Data. Computers in the early 1970s were still relatively primitive affairs, large and slow, and used primarily to conduct numerical analysis. Gates and Allen, however, were among those who believed that computers were the technology of the future.

Bitten by the bug, Gates went off to Harvard University and also took a summer job working for the electronics company Honeywell in 1974 (Allen had also taken a job at Honeywell). He entered the mainstream of the computer world just as it was on the basis of a major revolution. This was the introduction of the integrated circuit, or microchip. The process of making microprocessors on silicon chips had been developed by Robert Noyce and Gordon Moore at Fairchild Semiconductors in the late 1950s, and in 1968 they and a third member of the Fairchild team, Andrew **Grove**, had set up a new company, Intel. The Intel 8080 microprocessor, introduced in 1974, showed Gates the direction in which the computer industry was heading. Ten times more powerful than any previous microprocessor, the 8080 could make smaller, cheaper computers run more quickly.

Gates and Allen had been experimenting since their school days with writing programmes in the computer language BASIC (Beginners All-purpose Symbolic Instruction Code), which had been developed in 1964 to allow multiple users to work on the same computer. Gates thought that BASIC programmes could be written for the 8080 microchip, but although he offered his services to a number of companies, none was interested. Other developments were going on around him, however, and in 1975 the computer company Altair launched the first true microcomputer based around the 8080 chip. In order to prove their own theories, Gates and Allen acquired an Altair 8080 and in the space of a few weeks showed it was possible to write software programmes for it.

Rather than try to persuade other companies to develop their innovation, they decided to go down the long and difficult route of commercialisation themselves. From the beginning, however, Gates and Allen were fully aware of the potential of what they had done. As Gates later wrote in his book *The Road Ahead* (1995), the introduction of programmable microprocessors opened the door to software as an industry in its own right. Software no longer had to be tied to a particular piece of hardware, and the same piece of hardware could load and use multiple programmes, and be augmented with new programmes as the need arose. Hitherto, all the emphasis had been on hardware, with American companies such as IBM and DEC vying for control with the rising Japanese firms. Rather than challenge them, Gates thought he could develop this new industry in parallel with the hardware makers, selling products both to them and directly to computer users.

Gates left university and Allen quit his job with Honeywell, and the two men pooled their resources and set up a company, Micro-Soft, in Albuquerque, New Mexico. Soon after, however, they relocated the firm, now called Microsoft, back to their native Seattle. They deliberately chose not to get involved in the Silicon Valley ratrace, but to remain detached and able to work at their own speed without influence from other companies in what was already a highly volatile and excitable industry. Seattle also gave them access to several excellent universities which, thanks to the presence of the aircraft manufacturer Boeing, had strong engineering and electronics departments.

Microsoft struggled initially, but by the end of 1976 was making headway as the Altair 8080 became popular with hobbyists and computer enthusiasts. Soon they had branched out and were writing programmes for other manufacturers, sometimes in other languages. Gates's most important move, however, was to set up relationships with computer makers, initially with Steve Jobs's Apple Computers and later with Tandy and, by 1980, IBM. The computer companies made the hardware; Microsoft provided the operating system software under licence, and it was bundled with the hardware and sold as a finished product. Microsoft then wrote further software applications which could be sold directly to the consumer. The IBM deal in particular was a turning point; IBM's decision to enter the personal computer market on a large scale turned that market upside down. In its quest for dominance over its smaller rivals, IBM determined to develop an entirely new operating system, and contracted the development of this to Microsoft. The result was MS-DOS, an instant success thanks to its ease of use and flexibility. Within three years, every major computer maker except Apple had abandoned its own operating system and adopted MS-DOS as standard.

Apple, however, remained a serious rival. Though MS-DOS was very flexible, Apple, with its graphic interface controlled through use of a mouse rather than a keyboard, was more user-friendly. Microsoft accordingly began developing similar graphic interface operating systems, beginning with Windows 1.0 in 1984. The real breakthrough came with Windows 3.0 in 1990, which was installed on over 70 million computers in that year alone. By 1990, Microsoft's earnings had topped $1 billion for the first time. The launch of Windows 95 five years later caused a near sensation, as millions of computer users disposed of their old machines and acquired new, more powerful computers capable of running the new software. As Gates and Allen had forecast, software was no longer an adjunct to hardware; rather, the reverse was now true.

Focusing to a large extent on software and applications, Gates had to a large extent overlooked the development of the Internet; certainly, in a lapse for one normally so prescient about technology developments, he had not anticipated the speed with which it would develop and become omnipresent. In 1981 the British telecommunications engineer Tim Berners-Lee, then working at the European Particle Physics Laboratory in Geneva, developed a software programme for storing information which eventually evolved into the development of hypertext mark-up language (HTML). By 1989 he had developed his ideas into a global hypertext communications project, using three basic elements: HTML itself, uniform resource locators (URLs) and hypertext transfer protocols (HTTP). These were, and are, the basic building blocks of the World Wide Web, which was launched in 1991. From there, Internet usage grew at an astonishing rate, from a few tens of thousands of mostly institutional users in 1991 to hundreds of millions of households a decade later.

The key software application for accessing the web was the web browser, and first-mover advantage in this market was essential. Gates failed to take it, surrendering the advantage to Netscape, whose Netscape Navigator became virtually the industry standard by 1995. Only in that year did Microsoft launch its own browser, Internet Explorer 1.0. Netscape, however, continued to dominate the market and was following the Microsoft pattern of selling directly to computer makers who bundled the programme with the operating system and other software applications sold as a package to the end customer. In a highly controversial move, Microsoft then embedded the Internet Explorer programme into the Windows operating system, meaning that anyone who had Windows installed on their computer automatically had Internet Explorer as well. This removed the need to purchase Netscape separately. It also brought accusations that Microsoft was attempting to create – or protect – a monopoly, and a major anti-trust suit by the US Federal Government which at time of writing has still not been resolved.

The world's richest man, Gates heads a company which is admired by some as the most successful entrepreneurial venture of the twentieth century, and reviled by others as a threat to competition and democracy. Gates himself has been widely discussed and fiercely criticised. His technological accomplishments, notably MS-DOS and Windows, the two most widely used software programmes of all time, are well-known. What is less frequently discussed is his impact on management.

The first and most obvious impact, of course, is that on how business is done through the use of the computer. In the 1830s, Charles **Babbage** believed that computers had the potential to revolutionise commerce by speeding up operations and making them more accurate and reliable. With the development and ready availability of small, fast, inexpensive computers, that vision has become a reality. Computers have in one form or another entered nearly every aspect of the workplace, from computerised ordering of stock and computer numerical control of production machines, to computerised machines dispensing money and other services and computerised monitoring of sales through EPOS (electronic point of sale) data, to name just a very few. Of all these impacts, the development of personal computers allowing individual managers to not only access the Internet but also set up local communications networks such as intranets has perhaps been most important. Nearly every modern theory of organisation from the learning organisation to the virtual organisation is predicated on the widespread availability of the microcomputer and the software Gates invented and sold.

But why did Gates succeed when so many others fail? The electronics industry has perhaps the highest failure rate of any industry in the world; the average Silicon Valley software or electronics firm usually lasts less than a year. But Microsoft has endured for nearly thirty years, and has grown steadily throughout that time. What has made Bill Gates different?

For a start, it is important to realise that Gates is not just another computer whizzkid, talented in that field though he undoubtedly is. He is also a natural entrepreneur, with a marketing instinct that in the past has allowed him to forecast developments before they happen, and an understanding of where market power lies. Two points stand out: his early belief that the microcomputer was the way of the future, when the industry's main players, IBM and DEC, were prepared to dismiss it, and his understanding that the key to lasting competitive success was to offer partnerships with the hardware makers that would bundle hardware and software together as a single consumer product. In the former he resembles Steve Jobs, the visionary founder of Apple and one of the instigators of the personal computer boom, but also Wang An, the Chinese-American electronics engineer who founded Wang Laboratories in the 1950s. In both cases, a strong personal vision and commitment to that vision was the key to success, as it has been with Gates.

Second, Gates realised early on that one of the keys to success in the computer industry is scale. Hewlett Packard, founded in 1938, and IBM, founded in 1924, have survived and prospered despite vicissitudes, to a large extent because they have been large enough to take the punishment during times of difficulty. Intel, the chip maker, has had the same experience. Size matters in this industry not so much for economies of scale, though these do help, but because in a rapidly changing and highly volatile industry it is often hard to predict the nature and extent of the next downturn. Big firms can absorb losses and innovate their way out of trouble; smaller firms, with fewer resources, go to the wall. This too was the philosophy of Larry Ellison of Oracle, who engaged in a relentless programme of expansion from the late 1970s into the 1990s in the belief that only big companies could survive a major crisis in the industry; the same principle can be glimpsed in the strategy of Son Masayoshi, the Japanese software and e-commerce entrepreneur, who likewise expanded rapidly during the 1990s.

Third, and linked to the above, there is the need for innovation. Gates is more aware than anyone else that the software industry never stands still, largely because he himself helped create the present dynamic atmosphere. In the 1990s, Gates argued that the primary business of Microsoft was not software, but intellectual property, and much of his strategy was based on a constant infusion of new talent and new ideas:

> We've always had the most aggressive approach of any software company in finding people with top IQs and bringing them in. We also pushed to the absolute limit the people we brought in from overseas. Finally, we designed a development methodology that could make use of different individuals' talents.[1]

Knowledge, then, lies at the heart of the Microsoft system; acquiring and developing knowledge and turning it into products is what the company does. Gates's approach emphasises decentralisation and personal responsibility, but there is also plenty of pressure: Microsoft development teams are constantly pressed for results and challenged to go beyond the limits set for them. Employees are paid for results, and profitability is seen as everyone's business. According to one developer:

> One of the reasons our products are so successful is that everybody takes responsibility for them. You own this thing, you make it great; you're responsible for it. Your input is taken seriously. It doesn't matter what level you are at, or where you are, you compete like hell for the business.[2]

Intermediating between teams and coordinating their efforts is Gates himself. By 1995, he said he was spending about half of his time on marketing and the other half on working with the project teams and recruiting new personnel. Gates made himself available to every employee via e-mail, and promised a swift response to any query directed to him. The result, as Philip Rosenzweig concludes, was 'a flat, flexible, highly internally competitive firm where results are produced in a kind of pressure-cooker atmosphere'.[3]

In an industry with few borders, location matters. Based near Seattle, Microsoft is to some extent isolated from the hectic world of Silicon Valley, and there is some protection from other firms trying to poach talented employees, many of whom like the lifestyle of the Pacific Northwest and want to remain there.

There are downsides to the Microsoft approach. The internal pressure is very severe; project teams are even sometimes set up in competition with one another, and this kind of atmosphere does not suit every employee. There is also a sense of intellectual arrogance, and fools are not tolerated: Gates himself once commented that to let in 'mediocrity' would be the ruin of the organisation.[4] Microsoft employees have a reputation for saying what they think, and bouts of 'flaming' on the internal e-mail system are not uncommon. The internal competition has led to accusations of some fairly unethical dealings, of project teams spying on each other and senior managers monitoring their juniors' e-mail.

More seriously, Gates's aggressive competitive approach has long had its critics, who accuse him of trying to create a monopoly and drive other software makers out of business. The Explorer affair brought this to a head, and the resulting court action has yet to be concluded. The onset of the Internet and Gates's initial failure to respond led many to conclude that Microsoft's day as the dominant player within the industry might soon be over; long accustomed to being in the position of the faster, more flexible, smaller rival fighting off larger, slower competitors, Microsoft now started to look as old and slow as the companies it had demolished. Such criticisms now look premature. Microsoft did react, and react powerfully. First-mover advantage has never been a necessity in Microsoft's strategic thinking, where the emphasis tends to be on the best product rather than the first product and on strategic alliances to ensure eventual dominance rather than capturing market share through direct consumer sales.

Gates's phenomenal success as an entrepreneur has been based only partly on his technical skills and ability. His understanding of the market and of strategic leverage has been complemented by his ability to put together a fast, flexible, thinking organisation that emphasises knowledge and creativity and demands productivity. Not everyone likes working there, but it is impossible to deny that the combination gets results. At Microsoft, Gates has created a model of organisation, creativity and strategy that may turn out to be one of the best recipes for success in the emerging world of global business.

See also: **Babbage, Ford, Ibuka, Welch**

Major works

The Road Ahead, despite its name, also functions as Gates's autobiography to that point, telling the story of the rise of Microsoft and giving some very useful insights into Gates's management thinking and style. *Business @ the Speed of Thought* is speculative but interesting.

(With N. Myhrvold and P. Rinearson) *The Road Ahead*, New York: Viking Penguin, 1995.
(With C. Hemingway) *Business @ the Speed of Thought: Using a Digital Nervous System*, New York: Warner Books, 1999.

Further reading

Gates and Microsoft have generated a huge output of comment in newspapers and journals, much of it polemical and devoted to either attacking Gates or defending him (and mostly the former). Objective assessments of his works are hard to find. The passages on Microsoft to be found in Kalthoff *et al.* are frustratingly scanty extracts from a case study of Microsoft conducted by Philip Rosenzweig, then of Harvard Business School, in the early 1990s. All of the other works below need to be treated with caution.

Kalthoff, O., Nonaka, I. and Nueno, P., *The Light and the Shadow*, Oxford: Capstone, 1997.
Lowe, J.C., *Bill Gates Speaks: Insights from the World's Greatest Entrepreneur*, New York: John Wiley, 1998.
Manes, S. and Andrews, P., *Gates: How Microsoft's Mogul Reinvented an Industry and Made Himself the Richest Man in America*, New York: Touchstone, 1994.
Wallace, J., *Overdrive: Bill Gates and the Race to Control Cyberspace*, New York: John Wiley, 1998.
Wallace, J. and Erickson, J., *Hard Drive: Bill Gates and the Making of the Microsoft Empire*, New York: Harperbusiness, 1993.

Notes

1 Quoted in O. Kalthoff, I. Nonaka and P. Nueno, *The Light and the Shadow*, Oxford: Capstone, 1997, pp. 44–5.
2 *Ibid.*, p. 46.
3 *Ibid.*, p. 160.
4 Quoted in *ibid.*, p. 46.

EDWIN GAY (1867–1946)

Edwin Gay was an economic historian who became the first dean of Harvard Business School and made it into the world's premier institution for graduate management education, a position it arguably still holds today. Admired around the world, Harvard has influenced several generations of management teachers and students, in Europe and Asia as well as the Americas. Gay did more than just set up the administration and organisation of the school; he also laid down many elements of its philosophy and pedagogy, including the case study method of teaching, practical assignments with companies and an approach to classroom instruction which emphasised dialogue between teachers and students, not simply lectures. All these methods are still in use in business schools today. It is scarcely an exaggeration to say that Gay shaped the nature of modern management education.

Gay was born in Detroit on 27 October 1867, the son of a wealthy business man. He was educated at schools in Michigan and later in Europe. Returning home briefly, he took a bachelor's degree in history and philosophy from the University of Michigan and married a classmate, Louise Randolph, in 1892. The couple then returned to Europe where Gay undertook graduate studies in medieval history at the University of Berlin, later moving on to studies in Leipzig, Zurich and Florence. Although it was Edwin Gay who finally received a PhD from Berlin in 1892, the Gays were a scholarly team and worked together on many projects. Both later recalled their twelve years in Europe as an idyllic time, the happiest of their lives.

In 1902 they returned to the USA and Gay was offered a post as instructor in economics at Harvard University. His intellectual ability, but even more his abilities as an administrator, marked him down for early promotion; by 1906 he was professor of economics and chairman of the department. When Harvard's president, Charles Eliot, began developing his plans for a graduate school of business administration, Gay was one of his principal advisors. Despite some opposition from the university establishment, the Harvard Graduate School of Business Administration was opened in 1908.

Eliot's first choice for dean of the new school was William Lyon Mackenzie King, formerly an instructor in economics at Harvard and now deputy minister of labour in the Canadian government. King turned down the post (he went on to become Canada's longest serving prime minister), and in February 1908 the post was offered to Gay. He accepted with reluctance, realising that this would mean curtailing his work in his main field of interest, economic history. Persuaded to take on the post, however, he then worked indefatigably to make Harvard Business School a success, winning praise from the school's supporters and opponents alike.

By 1917, the School was prospering and Gay felt able to step down. After serving as an advisor to the US Shipping Board during the First World War, Gay, for reasons that are not entirely clear, chose to leave academia altogether and accepted an offer to become editor of the

New York *Evening Post*. This was not a success, and the newspaper went bankrupt in 1924. Gay then returned to Harvard and became once more a professor of economic history, remaining there until his retirement in 1936. The Gays then moved to California, where Edwin Gay served on the research staff of the Huntingdon Library for another ten years. He contracted pneumonia in January 1946, and died in hospital at Pasadena on 8 February of that year.

When Gay assumed the post of dean of Harvard Business School, management education in the USA was in its infancy. Beginning in the 1840s there had appeared what were known as 'management colleges', one of the best known of which was Duff's Management College in Pittsburgh, where H.J. **Heinz** was once a pupil. These colleges taught book-keeping and accounting, and some also taught rudimentary management techniques, such as some of the basic principles of marketing. Courses were short and focused on the basics; in essence, these colleges were the modern descendants of the *scuole d'abaco* of medieval Italy, with curricula that were only a little more sophisticated. Experiments in more formal management training had begun in Britain early in the nineteenth century, and the establishment by the East India Company of a training college at Hayleybury, Buckinghamshire in 1805 marks the beginning of a trend towards greater sophistication. In the USA, universities were taking an interest in management education by the 1890s; the University of Pennsylvania's Wharton School had been founded with a view to providing more detailed training in financial management, while Dartmouth College's Tuck School had a strong bias towards the problems of labour and personnel management.

Important though the contributions of these two schools were, there was a still a vast need for management education. The new, large corporations that were coming to dominate American business required many layers of management, and moreover, required managers with technical skills in many fields, not just in shop management but also in marketing and sales, distribution, personnel management, and so on. When setting up a school to meet this need, Gay had no real models to work from apart from the very recent experiences of Wharton and Tuck. He had not only to design the administrative structure of the school, but also to create its teaching materials and pedagogical methods virtually out of nothing.

Gay saw this, not as an insurmountable challenge, but as a great opportunity. President Charles Eliot, his friend and mentor, later said that Gay 'transferred himself body and soul to the new School, put all his time and strength into it'.[1] Heaton, Gay's biographer, summed up the latter's attitude to his new task:

> To fashion, build, and manage a school which would train men for business as a profession; to bring his wide range of knowledge to bear on planning and guiding that training; to inculcate an awareness of the social obligations and consequences of business enterprise; and to do this for a country that was travelling fast toward economic maturity and pre-eminence – here indeed was a call to active service that could not be declined.[2]

Gay's guiding philosophy for the new school rested on two key ideas. The first was that the task of the manager was to make things that could be sold for a profit while at the same time behaving in an ethical manner. The second was that the School's own task should then be 'to experiment and to learn what the *content* and *form* should be for the training of mature students primarily for "making" or "selling" '.[3] He went on to state that the most important qualities of a successful manager were courage, judgement and sympathy. He believed that it was the School's role to inculcate and strengthen these qualities in managers.

By his own admission, Gay had no business or management experience. However, he knew where to find such people and how to recruit them to his cause. This was not entirely an easy task. Some of the business people he approached were opposed to the idea of the School, believing that management was an inborn capability and could not be taught. Others were supporters but lacked the time to commit. Still others did come to the School but proved to be incompetent teachers. Patiently, Gay built up his cadre of experienced teachers, some full-time members of staff, others business people who taught on an occasional basis. Early important recruits to the full-time faculty were W.J. Cunningham and Paul T. Cherington. The latter became the School's first professor of marketing and established its marketing department, which quickly grew to rival the one at Northwestern University in Chicago, and Cherington himself went on to become one of the twentieth century's most important writers on marketing. Gay several times approached Frederick W. **Taylor**, the founding father of scientific management, but was repeatedly rebuffed; he then turned his attention to Taylor's associate Carl Barth, and by dint of persistence eventually persuaded Barth to give a course of lectures. Barth was won over, and in turn persuaded Taylor, who taught occasionally at the school until his death in 1915. Other important supporters included the publisher Arch Shaw, the banker T.W. Lamont and the economist Wesley Clair Mitchell.

But although Gay put together the academic team, the approach to teaching was all his own. It was Gay who determined that the degree awarded by the new School would be called Master of Business Administration (MBA), a title which has now been adopted around the world and remains one of the most important academic business qualifications. Looking for ways of developing teaching material, Gay studied the case study method pioneered by Harvard Law School, and felt that teaching cases could be used equally well in the classroom for business students. There was no pre-existing body of case material, so Gay sought out Arch Shaw, a publisher and writer who had been a partner of W.K. Kellogg in the original Battle Creek Toasted Corn Flake Company, and asked for his help. Shaw began building up a bank of written case studies, and also provided 'living cases' which gave students the chance to talk to managers and study problems in action, not just in the abstraction of the classroom. Shaw and Cherington also set up the School's Bureau of Business Research, one of whose principal functions was to provide material for cases.

In addition, Gay's classroom teaching methods were novel. He felt that traditional 'chalk and talk' lectures were inappropriate for management students, as they were not sufficiently challenged; students needed to be drawn into dialogue with the lecturer in order to challenge their own thinking and show that they were learning. Older lecturers were often uncomfortable with this, so Gay recruited new, young scholars such as Melvin Copeland, who later succeeded Cherington as head of the marketing department. These younger scholars were given broad latitude to develop their own methods, but were put under considerable pressure to succeed. Copeland, for example, was recruited in 1909 and asked to design and teach a marketing course, a thing he had never done before, at thirty-six hours' notice. He later recalled meeting Gay some weeks after the course began. When the dean asked how the course was going, Copeland replied, 'I have found enough to talk about so far.' 'That is not the question', replied Gay. 'Have you found enough to keep the students talking?' Copeland, taking the broad hint, abandoned his lecturing style for one of classroom discussion, and followed this through the rest of his career. Much later, he realised that Gay had selected him as a 'guinea pig' for the introduction of classroom discussion and the case study method in marketing.[4]

The effort of establishing the School exhausted Gay, and fatigue was one of the factors that lay behind his resignation in 1917, and perhaps behind some of his subsequent misjudgements. Certainly he later came to regret taking on the task, which forced him to give up his historical research; although he later returned to the study of history, he never again felt the passion for it that he had in his youth. He came to regard his own career as a failure, and told friends that his taking on the deanship of Harvard Business School was his greatest regret. Yet Harvard Business School, and the world of management education in general, can hardly share that regret. Harvard went on to become the world's leading business school, training tens of thousands of managers for US and foreign firms as well as leading academics in many fields. Its model has been emulated in nearly every country where post-graduate management education exists; its teaching methods, such as the case study and classroom dialogue, are standard tools, and Harvard remains the largest single generator of case study material on management. Heaton sums up Gay's methods and approach:

> The early history of the School had something of the flavour of a cause, a crusade or a movement beyond the frontier of educational settlement, with Gay as leader, inspirer and challenger. He never told his colleagues what to do, for he would not have known what instructions to give. Instead he sent them off to explore, with a double piece of advice: to remember that there were no experts in this new field and that the printing of a statement did not make it authentic. His own faith, resourcefulness and expenditure of energy impelled them to give the best that was in them, so that each man made his full contribution to the policies and programs that were a team product rather than the achievement of any one person.[5]

See also: **Babbage, Chandler, Fukuzawa, Porter, Taylor**

Major works

Unsurprisingly, Gay produced no major works on management or management education; during his tenure at Harvard Business School he was too busy, while in later years he was disinclined to return to the subject. Most of his own output was on medieval and early modern history.

Further reading

Copeland's history of Harvard Business School offers an in-depth assessment of Gay's approach to teaching management. Heaton is a full biography, sympathetic to the subject but very detailed.

Copeland, M.C., *And Mark the Era: The Story of Harvard Business School*, Boston, MA: Little, Brown, 1958.

Heaton, H.K., *A Scholar in Action: Edwin F. Gay*, Cambridge, MA: Harvard University Press, 1952.

Notes

1   Quoted in H.K. Heaton, *A Scholar in Action: Edwin F. Gay*, Cambridge, MA: Harvard University Press, 1952, p. 74.
2   *Ibid.*, p. 69
3   *Ibid.*, p. 76.
4   M.C. Copeland, *And Mark the Era: The Story of Harvard Business School*, Boston, MA: Little, Brown, 1958, pp. 59–60.
5   Heaton, *A Scholar in Action*, p. 81.

FRANK BUNKER GILBRETH (1868–1924)
LILLIAN GILBRETH (1878–1972)

Frank and Lillian Gilbreth were a husband and wife team of management consultants who played a central role in the development of scientific management. Frank Gilbreth initially pioneered the concept of 'motion study', which combined with F.W. **Taylor**'s method of 'time study' became the technique of 'time and motion study', the basis of most production and efficiency studies for many decades thereafter. Lillian Gilbreth was a pioneer in the application of psychology to the problems of management. They worked closely together as professional consultants, and nearly all their books were co-authored. After Frank Gilbreth's early death, Lillian Gilbreth carried on running the consultancy business and continued to develop her ideas on the importance of the human factor in business and management. She was an inspirational role model to women in business around the world, some of whom, such as her British friend Anne Shaw, rose to high positions in industry.

Frank Bunker Gilbreth was born in Freeport, Maine on 7 July 1868. After finishing school, although he had passed his entrance examinations for the Massachusetts Institute of Technology, he decided instead to study mechanics in a more practical way and took a job with a construction company. Although his first job was as an apprentice bricklayer, Gilbreth seems to have been on a 'fast track plan' for promotion into management: he was made chief super-intendent of the company at the relatively young age of 27. By this time he had developed a number of methods, both technical and procedural, for improving efficiency at work, including the rudiments of what later became known as motion study. In 1895 he decided to set up his own construction company, based in Boston. By 1900 he was running a very successful business with branches throughout the USA, and had also established a branch office in London.

Lillian Moller was born in Oakland, California on 24 May 1878, the daughter of a business man and leading citizen of the town. Intellectually gifted, she attended the University of California at Berkeley against the wishes of her parents, who did not feel it appropriate that girls should attend college. She studied English literature, taking a BA in 1900 and an MA in 1903 with a thesis on Ben Jonson. She planned to carry on for a doctorate, but took a year out to travel in Europe. She then met Frank Gilbreth in 1903, and they were married in 1904. She later went on to take a PhD in psychology from Brown University in Rhode Island.

From the outset of their marriage the Gilbreths worked as a partnership, first to run the business and later to develop jointly their efficiency methods and turn them into an important system of management. Their early works were officially authored by Frank Gilbreth alone, but his wife played a major role in their composition. From 1912 onward their works were formally co-authored. Lillian Gilbreth also wrote one book of her own during this period, *The Psychology of Management* (1914), based on her PhD thesis.

Increasingly, the Gilbreth business turned away from construction and towards consulting. Frank Gilbreth had read Frederick W. Taylor's 1903 work *Shop Management* and had become very enthused by it. He contacted Taylor, and the latter and the Gilbreths worked together for a number of years. Taylor was, as far as is known, punctilious in giving the Gilbreths credit for their contributions to scientific management, but some of his followers were less scrupulous and tried to claim credit for Taylor for such major ideas as motion study. This, plus personal differences, ultimately led to a split between the Gilbreths and Taylor. Their mutual friend Henry Gantt tried to mediate between them, until he too fell out with Taylor around 1913. Gantt and the Gilbreths remained close friends. Lillian Gilbreth, however, never fully forgave Taylor: her verdict on the latter to Lyndall **Urwick** – 'You see, Colonel Urwick, Taylor was not a very nice man' – has passed into the folklore of management history.

With the deaths of Taylor in 1915 and Gantt in 1919, Frank Gilbreth became the senior figure in the scientific management movement. By 1920, he was known worldwide for his views on management, and was regularly sought after as a lecturer in both the USA and Europe. In 1924, he was invited to Europe to present a keynote paper at the First International Management Congress. A few days before sailing, however, on 14 June 1924, he died suddenly of a heart attack in Montclair, New Jersey. Lillian Gilbreth, who had planned to stay at home and look after the business and their large family (twelve children: six boys and six girls) instead took her husband's place at the conference and delivered the paper.

Returning home after the conference, she found that most of the firm's consulting clients had cancelled their contracts, assuming the firm would be wound up after her husband's death. Gilbreth had to set about rebuilding the business, which took up much of her time and energy through the 1920s. She continued to pioneer new methods of workplace efficiency, but also turned to efficiency in the home, a subject which she and her husband had already given some attention. The Gilbreths had been very interested in what is now called ergonomics, that is, the scientific layout of a workplace that will minimise fatigue while improving work performance. Gilbreth spent much of the 1920s designing ergonomic kitchens that would reduce labour for housewives. These designs proved very successful and garnered much publicity.

Gilbreth also became an important authority on the role of women at work. In 1929 she was invited by President Herbert Hoover to join the government's Emergency Committee on Unemployment, set up at the onset of the Great Depression. In the 1930s she became a visiting lecturer on workplace organisation and methods at Purdue University, and following the Second World War she became an authority on the new discipline of 'home economics', departments for the study of which were being established at many universities, as well as continuing to hold a number of consulting posts for government: she served, in turn, the administration of presidents Hoover, Roosevelt, Truman, Eisenhower, Kennedy and Johnson. In the 1960s she was known as 'America's First Lady of Engineering' and, despite being in her eighties, continued to write and lecture. One of her last tasks was to ensure that her husband's papers and work were preserved for posterity. She died in Phoenix, Arizona on 2 July 1972.

The Gilbreths' contribution to management takes several forms. There is, first and most famously, their work on motion study and fatigue, which became part of the core of scientific management but which also contributed to the foundation of ergonomics. Second, and of equal importance, is Lillian Gilbreth's contribution to the psychology of management. Third, Lillian Gilbreth was an active teacher both before and after her husband's death, and trained some of the most important figures in the business world. Finally, in her later years Lillian became an important role model for women in management.

Frank Gilbreth initially became interested in motion study while working in construction. Observing the movements of bricklayers, he realised that the number of individual movements the layer made when transferring each brick from the pallet to the wall being built could be reduced. This would have the double impact of speeding up the work and reducing the amount of energy the worker would have to expend, cutting down on fatigue. The Gilbreths' subsequent work on motion study was similar to Taylor's time studies in that each task was broken down into its component parts and the individual elements studied: not to determine the time each took, but to determine the movements and efforts required in each case. Motion was classified into various types, such as turning, selecting, lifting, loading, and so on: these generic classifications were known as 'therbligs' (an anagram of 'Gilbreths'). By using therbligs as the building blocks of each task, the Gilbreths were able to re-engineer tasks in a systematic manner so as to save labour and improve productivity. Gilbreth developed a number of technical devices to aid in motion study, such as freeze-frame photography and the cyclegraph, a device which consisted of small electric light bulbs strapped to a worker's limbs which, when filmed, showed acceleration and deceleration of movement graphically on a screen.

This approach was similar to that of Taylor, then, in that it involved the scientific study of minutely divided labour. It was similar too in the resistance that it met. Workers felt – and rightly in some cases – that employers were using the Gilbreth method to sweat more labour out of them without increasing pay. The combined Taylor–Gilbreth system, by now known as time and motion study, had become a common efficiency tool by the 1920s, and its use was an equally common bone of contention between big corporations and big unions. But whereas Taylor ultimately gave up on trying to persuade workers that his system could benefit them, the Gilbreths never ceased to argue for the benefits of their work. By 1914–15 they were becoming increasingly interested in the problems of fatigue and in trying to re-engineer both tasks and workplaces to cut down on injuries, accidents and industrial illnesses.

Two important advances during this period have had lasting impacts. The first was the discovery that the design of workspace was often as important as the human effort required in producing fatigue. Using the principles of therbligs again, the Gilbreths began designing new forms of workstation for assembly line workers, using therblig analysis to detect areas where the workstation could be reconfigured to reduce unnecessary motions. These studies form the basis of the modern discipline of ergonomics, in which incorrect workplace configuration is widely accepted as being a major cause of employee fatigue and illness, and effort is accordingly devoted to correct design. Moving out of the industrial arena, Gilbreth also applied his techniques to areas such as hospital operating theatres, where he was able to significantly reduce the times required for operations by redesigning the theatres and repositioning staff. Later, Lillian Gilbreth used the ergonomics principles in designing kitchens and other domestic workspaces, leading to the development of yet another new discipline, home economics.

The second important advance was in the employment of disabled workers. The aftermath of the First World War saw the return to the USA of many young men who had been injured in the fighting and could no longer work in conventional ways. The Gilbreths turned their techniques of job analysis to the problem, and found that many tasks and workplaces could be altered to suit the requirements of disabled workers; often, indeed, the amendments required were only minor ones. This was an important step forward in the acceptance of disabled workers into the workplace.

Lillian Gilbreth was also one of the first people to discuss the idea of a 'psychology of management', which she defined as 'the effect of the mind that is directing work upon that work which is directed'. Although the concepts of psychology had been applied to business before, notably in the work of Walter Scott at Northwestern University on the psychology of advertising and industrial psychology, Gilbreth was one of the first to make a direct link between mental states and subsequent action by managers as well as workers. Her conclusion was radical for the time, and showed how the Gilbreths' thinking was beginning to diverge from that of Taylor:

> It has been demonstrated that the emphasis in successful management lies on the *man*, not on the *work*; that efficiency is best secured by placing the emphasis on the man, and modifying the equipment, materials and methods to make the most of the man. It has, further, been recognized that the man's mind is a controlling factor in his efficiency, and has, by teaching, enabled the man to make the most of his powers.[1]

The effect of Gilbreth's work and of other psychologically based studies that followed it was to begin to turn the focus of organisation thinking away from structure and control and towards the individual as the primary element that composed the organisation. In seeking a behavioural explanation for workplace performance and motivation, Gilbreth directly anticipated Abraham **Maslow** and Herbert **Simon**'s work four decades later.

As well as consulting services, the Gilbreths also trained a number of other engineers in the techniques of scientific management and helped diffuse the discipline very widely. The two founders of scientific management in Japan, Araki Toichiro and Ueno Yoichi, were both influenced by the Gilbreths. Araki was taught by Lillian Gilbreth during his four years of study in the USA, and Ueno had a long correspondence with both Gilbreths: his book the *Human Psychology of Industrial Efficiency* (1919) was inspired by both motion study techniques and the application of psychology to management. A later member of the Gilbreth consultancy team was the Briton Anne Shaw, who worked for the company for a time before returning home to take a job with the Metropolitan-Vickers Electrical Company. Here she set up an internal centre for efficiency studies that was copied by a number of other British firms, and in the late 1930s and 1940s she was involved in British management education, setting up a number of training programmes. The Motion Study Society of Britain was originally named the Anne Shaw Society in her honour, and she received the CBE for services to industry.

Shaw was a lifelong friend of Lillian Gilbreth and regarded her as a role model, as did many thousands of other working women. Widowed while still in her forties with a large family to support, Gilbreth overcame stereotyping and prejudice to become one of the most respected figures in American industry. By showing that it was possible for women to succeed in business, she encouraged many others to try.

The story of the Gilbreths is one of the most remarkable in the history of management. Partly because of their personal circumstances, they continue to attract much interest and their views have passionate supporters, who are keen to distance the ideas of the Gilbreths from those of Taylor. The major difference between them is that Taylor's idea of efficiency focused on time while those of the Gilbreths focused on motion. It has been argued therefore that Taylor was concerned with getting work done quickly while the Gilbreths were concerned with getting it done well. This is a crude over-generalisation. Both were concerned with efficiency, and speed and quality of work were components which figured in both systems. In fact, time study and motion study were highly complementary, as both Taylor and Gilbreth immediately recognised. The rhetoric of their later followers has done much to obscure the fact that scientific management could not have been developed without the major input of both.

From a modern perspective, there is much to admire in the Gilbreths' work aside from their contributions to scientific management in its narrow sense. The attention to the workplace environment, both physical and mental, led to major contributions to ergonomics and industrial psychology. The Gilbreths did indeed work on efficiency techniques, and it is for this that they are most famous, but they also took a much broader and more holistic view of the workplace and the relationship between workers, managers and environment. It is in this latter context that their work remains most relevant today.

See also: **Emerson, Fayol, Follett, Taylor, Urwick**

Major works

All works unless indicated were formally co-authored. *Primer of Scientific Management* was a widely read textbook. *Motion Study* was the first full explication of the principles of the topic, developed in later books. *The Psychology of Management* is a major early work in its field.

(F.B. Gilbreth) *Motion Study*, New York: Van Nostrand Co., 1911.
Primer of Scientific Management, New York: Van Nostrand Co., 1912.
(L.E. Gilbreth) *The Psychology of Management*, New York: Sturgis & Walton, 1914.
Fatigue Study, New York: Sturgis & Walton, 1916.
Motion Study for the Handicapped, New York: Macmillan, 1920.
(L.E. Gilbreth) *The Quest of the One Best Way: A Sketch of the Life of Frank Bunker Gilbreth*, Chicago, IL: Society of Industrial Engineers, 1924.
(L.E. Gilbreth) *The Home-Maker and Her Job*, New York: D. Appleton, 1927.

Further reading

Secondary writings on the Gilbreths are relatively rare. *Cheaper by the Dozen* and *Belles on Their Toes* are two light-hearted accounts of life in the Gilbreth household, where motion study was also (necessarily, given the size of the family) a major feature. Yost is the best biography of the couple, by a friend of the family. Spriegel and Meyers is a useful collection of articles. Graham and Ferguson's complementary articles are useful analyses.

Ferguson, D., 'Gilbreth, Frank Bunker', in M. Witzel (ed.), *Biographical Dictionary of Management*, Bristol: Thoemmes Press, 2001, vol. 1, pp. 371–5.
Gilbreth, F.B. Jr and Carey, E.G., *Cheaper by the Dozen*, New York: Thomas Y. Crowell, 1949.
—— *Belles on Their Toes*, New York: Thomas Y. Crowell, 1949.
Graham, L. and Ferguson, D., 'Gilbreth, Lillian Evelyn Moller', in M. Witzel (ed.), *Biographical Dictionary of Management*, Bristol: Thoemmes Press, 2001, vol. 1, pp. 375–9.

Spriegel, W.R. and Meyers, C.E. (eds), *The Writings of the Gilbreths*, Homewood, IL: Irwin, 1952.

Yost, E., *Frank and Lillian Gilbreth: Partners for Life*, New Brunswick, NJ: Rutgers University Press, 1949.

Note

1   L. Gilbreth, *The Psychology of Management*, New York: Sturgis & Walton, 1914, p. 3.

ANDREW GROVE (1936–)

Andrew Grove is chief executive officer of Intel, the world's largest maker of semiconductors. Like his younger contemporary Bill **Gates**, Grove has succeeded in building an organisation that has survived and prospered during a time of great turmoil in the information technology industry, when thousands of other companies have gone to the wall. He is also a thoughtful and persuasive writer on management, who draws on a wealth of personal experience of both success and failure to develop his ideas on leadership and organisation. In an era when many management books take an optimistic, 'gung-ho' approach, providing recipes for success which anyone can follow, Grove takes a darker view. Management in an age of turmoil and change is hard, and is getting harder. The title of his best book sums up his philosophy: *Only the Paranoid Survive* (1996).

Grove was born Andras Grof in Budapest, Hungary on 2 September 1936. His childhood was spent in Hungary during the Second World War and then under the post-war communist regime. Like many other young Hungarians, he fled the country in 1956 after a short-lived uprising against the communist state was suppressed by Soviet military intervention. He arrived in the USA in 1957 and has remained there ever since, Anglicising his name and taking out US citizenship in 1962. Shortly after his arrival, he enrolled at City College, New York, working as a waiter to pay his way through an undergraduate degree. He then moved west to California and took a PhD in chemical engineering from the University of California.

Like many other successful business people, Grove now found himself in the right place at the right time. Since the Second World War, southern California had been a centre for research and development in high technology, and it was here that, in 1957, Robert Noyce had developed a process for making semiconductors on silicon chips. This was a major breakthrough, ultimately leading to the development of the microcomputer and the much more widespread diffusion of computer technology in business and society. In the early 1960s Noyce's company Fairchild Semiconductor, based in San Jose, California, was growing rapidly, and when Grove finished his doctorate he was immediately hired by Fairchild's research laboratory. Here he was promoted rapidly, becoming assistant head of research and development in 1967.

A brilliant scientist, Noyce was driven by a passion for innovation. He believed firmly that the best results in research occurred when companies were small and flexible; large firms stifle innovation and become moribund. When Fairchild grew too large for his comfort, he and his colleague and co-founder Gordon Moore simply left, moving from San Jose to Santa Clara and setting up a new company, Intel, to continue the development of semiconductors. Grove was invited to join them as head of operations, and he accepted. In 1976 he was appointed chief operating officer and was groomed to take over from Noyce who, true to form, resigned in 1979 to go and start another venture, Sematech. Grove was appointed president in Noyce's place in 1979, chief executive officer in 1987, and finally chairman of the board in 1996.

An energetic man, Grove also lectured at Berkeley between 1966 and 1972, and for many years wrote a column for a weekly newspaper, the San Jose *Mercury*. He has written several books, notably *High Output Management* (1983) and the more recent *Only the Paranoid Survive* (1996). Both books are notably different from the main stream of management writing today: *High Output Management* is aimed at the much despised class, the middle managers, whom Grove sees as the backbone of organisations, while *Only the Paranoid Survive* is one of the few reflective considerations of failure and its consequences to come out of recent years.

Grove's task on taking over Intel was, in effect, to prove his mentor Robert Noyce wrong: he had to show that a company could become large *and* remain flexible and innovative. In this, he has been outstandingly successful. Intel dominates the microchip industry, with a turnover of more than $30 billion worldwide, and it has achieved this position in the face of fierce competition both from inside the USA and from the Far East. Under Grove's leadership, it has reached this position not in spite of its size, but because of it. Economies of scale and management structure have given the company's research scientists both the freedom to create and the resources they need; the rest of the company then focuses on turning that creative output into practical products. One observer describes Grove's achievement in the following terms:

> From being an innovator, [Intel] became a company whose objective was to deliver – to make sure its good ideas were turned into practical products that customers could use, products that arrived on schedule and at prices that fell consistently year by year. This transformation was no mean feat. It forced Intel to become rigorously organized and focussed, and to find a balance that allowed it to keep firm control over its operations without jeopardizing the creativity of the scientists who were its greatest assets. The result of this transformation was that Intel rose to domination of its industry.[1]

Grove himself is a fervent believer in the power of technology. In 1996 he wrote that technology is a kind of unstoppable force, and that 'what can be done will be done'.[2] Like Robert Noyce, he believes that technological development and social progress are inextricably linked. More recently, he has argued for a greater shift to broadband technology, believing that this must play a key role not only in making American economy and society more prosperous but also in strengthening the US government and military's ability to respond to attacks such as those of 11 September 2001.[3] The importance of broadband, in Grove's view, is that it will greatly increase both the speed and dissemination of knowledge and information.

Information lies at the heart of Grove's management philosophy. In his own working life, he constantly collects and filters information, and he encourages all his employees to do the same. He believes too in the need for emotion and belief in work, and says that intuition is just as important as analysis. His view of the task of management is a flexible one: he argues that, as managers have limited time and energy, they should concentrate on doing those things that will have the maximum impact, moving to the point where their leverage will be greatest.

As noted above, *High Output Management* is aimed at middle managers, who Grove sees as 'the muscle and bone of every sizeable organization', but who are often ignored by theorists.[4] The book, which is written in a light and amusing tone, sets out to define what it is that managers do. In one metaphor, drawing on his personal experience, he compares the doing of management to a waiter serving breakfast. Both have the same basic tasks of production: 'to build and deliver products in response to the demands of the customer at a *scheduled* delivery time, at an *acceptable* quality level, and at the *lowest* possible cost'.[5] He argues that managerial activity should not be confused with output. Planning, negotiation, allocating resources and training are things that managers *do*; output is what they actually *produce*. At Intel, he says, the managerial output is not ideas, it is silicon wafers, just as the outputs of surgeons are healed patients, and so on. Management is a team activity, and so 'the single most important task of a manager is to elicit peak performance from his subordinates'.[6] Managers also need to know what motivates their employees; here Grove refers specifically to **Maslow**'s hierarchy of needs, and argues that managers need to be aware of how these needs motivate employees and subordinates.

There is a sense here that the basics of management are simple in theory, but that this is seldom the case in practice. The Prussian writer on military strategy, Karl von Clausewitz, had a dictum that 'Everything in strategy is simple, but that does not mean that everything in strategy is easy.' Clausewitz had developed the concept of 'friction', the concatenation of unforeseen events and forces that hampers plans and causes everything to work more slowly or less efficiently than forecasted. Grove does not refer specifically to 'friction', but this nagging sense of the unforeseen waiting to wreck plans is omnipresent in his later work. In *Only the Paranoid Survive*, written in the aftermath of a disastrous incident when half a billion dollars' worth of defective Pentium chips had to be recalled and replaced, Grove warns explicitly against managerial complacency:

> I believe in the value of paranoia. Business success contains the seeds of its own destruction. The more successful you are, the more people want a chunk of your business and then another chunk and then another until there is nothing left. I believe that the prime responsibility of a manager is to guard constantly against other people's attacks and to inculcate this guardian attitude in the people under his or her management.[7]

In an interview with *Forbes* magazine, Grove commented on the usefulness of fear as a creative force: 'It's fear that gets you out of comfortable equilibrium, that gets you to do the difficult tasks ... [it is] healthy, like physical pain is healthy. It warns your body that something is wrong.'[8]

Unlike many other theorists, who see change as a continuous process in the business environment, Grove sees major changes as taking the form of a series of flashpoints, which he labels 'strategic inflection points'. These are events, he says, in which the fundamentals by which a business has existed and operated suddenly change, sometimes without apparent warning. The appearance of one of these points can mean new opportunities, or it can mean the beginning of the end, depending on how the business responds. Formal planning cannot anticipate these kinds of changes, and therefore managers have to be able to respond to the unanticipated. The advent of the personal computer was an obvious example of a strategic inflection point, forcing companies such as IBM and DEC to adapt or go out of business; the break-up of Bell's monopoly of US telephone services was another. Intel's own decision to go into microprocessors was yet another, forcing existing makers of microprocessors to adapt to the sudden appearance of a giant in their midst.

One of the difficulties in dealing with strategic inflection points is recognising them when they arrive. How is management supposed to distinguish signals from noise, and understand what is truly important? The answer, says Grove, is for managers to engage in continuous and vigorous debate, sharing information and generating new ideas. Always challenge the data: ask what it is really telling you, listen to everyone around you. Everyone must be encouraged to speak; fear of punishment, in many organisations, is the great inhibitor of discussion, and this in turn leads to signals being missed. He recognises that many managers will not find this easy: 'With all the rhetoric about how management is about change, the fact is that we managers loathe change, especially when it involves us. Getting through a strategic inflection point involves confusion, uncertainty and disorder.'[9]

Passing through a strategic inflection point is tense and chaotic; there are no rules here, precisely because the ground rules themselves are changing. But, says Grove:

> at some point you, the leader, begin to sense a vague outline of the new direction. By this time, however, your company is dispirited, demoralized or just plain tired. Getting this far took a lot of energy from you; you must now reach into whatever reservoir of energy you have left to motivate yourself and, most importantly, the people who depend on you so you can become healthy again.[10]

He describes this kind of massive, transforming change as being like a sickness, and says that only those companies with sufficient strength and stamina will recover; in another metaphor, Grove describes passing a strategic inflection point as like crossing the Valley of Death. Once through the point, however, there is time to pause, make sense of the chaos around you, re-establish stability and then proceed towards new goals.

Grove has succeeded in a notoriously volatile industry because he has, by and large, lived and managed by his own rules. Intel has shown it can change course suddenly and respond to unforeseen change. At the time of writing, Grove is preoccupied with the problem of whether his adopted homeland can do the same. He sees the events of 11 September as a strategic inflection point for America, when old certainties have been swept away and nothing will be the same again. He speaks now of what he calls '10× forces', trends and changes that are ten times more powerful than anything we encounter in our normal lives, and that have the power to turn our lives upside down. As a country and as a people, Grove says, America needs to become robust enough to withstand these.

There is little doubt that Andrew Grove's outlook on life was in part shaped by his upbringing under totalitarian rule in Hungary. Equally, however, his attitude has been conditioned by spending all his working life in a volatile industry and watching thousands of other firms, some large and powerful, go to the wall. His philosophy of management is personal and psychological. Organisation and innovation are tools for success; but ultimately, management is about what goes on inside the manager's brain and how well he or she can think, communicate and anticipate.

See also: **Argyris, Babbage, Bat'a, Forrester, Gates, Handy, Maslow, Ohmae, Welch**

Major works

The two books listed here are both important and were both described in the chapter above. Grove has also written a number of technical works and journal articles.

High Output Management, New York: Random House, 1983.
Only the Paranoid Survive: How to Exploit the Crisis Points that Challenge Every Company and Career, New York: HarperCollins, 1996.

Further reading

Grove features in many collections of works on management gurus. The best and most insightful account is that of Jackson. Lewis's short article updates Grove's thinking to the post-11 September period.

Jackson, T., *Inside Intel: Andy Grove and the Rise of the World's Most Powerful Chip Company*, London: Penguin, 1998.
Lewis, D.C., 'Living Paranoid after 11 September: The Management Philosophy of Andy Grove', *Mastering Management Online* 11 (March 2002), online at www.ftmastering.com/index/march

Notes

1 T. Jackson, *Inside Intel*, London: Penguin, 1998, p. xiii.
2 A. Grove, *Only the Paranoid Survive*, New York: HarperCollins, 1996, p. 5.
3 D.C. Lewis, 'Living Paranoid after 11 September: The Management Philosophy of Andy Grove', *Mastering Management Online* 11 (March 2002), online at www.ftmastering.com/index/march
4 A. Grove, *High Output Management*, New York: Random House, 1983, p. ix.
5 *Ibid.*, p. 3.
6 *Ibid.*, p. 145.
7 *Only the Paranoid Survive*, p. 3.
8 Quoted in Lewis, 'Living Paranoid after 11 September'.
9 *Only the Paranoid Survive*, p. 123.
10 *Ibid.*, p. 139.

CHARLES HANDY (1932–)

Charles Handy has been variously described as Europe's leading management guru and the man who has brought philosophy back into the study of management. Originally a theorist on organisation behaviour, Handy has gone on to consider the nature of work and employment and the role of management in modern society, and to argue for a more holistic and ethical view of management as a discipline and practice. His work has resonances for economics, organisation theory and business ethics. In 2001, a poll of managers and academics conducted over the Internet to determine the most important management thinkers of all time ranked Handy as second only in importance behind Peter **Drucker**.[1]

Handy was born in County Kildare, Ireland on 25 July 1932, the son of an archdeacon. After taking a degree from Oriel College, Oxford (he also has an MBA from the Sloan School of Management at the Massachusetts Institute of Technology), he held managerial posts with Shell International and the Anglo-American Corporation. In 1967 he joined the faculty of the newly established London Business School as a lecturer on psychology in management, becoming a professor in 1972 and appointed to the board of governors in 1974. At LBS, Handy played an important role in raising the School's profile, and in the general revival of management education that took place in

Britain in the later 1970s. In 1977 he was appointed Warden of St George's House, Windsor, a private study and conference centre. He has also been closely involved with the Royal Society for the Encouragement of Arts, Manufacture and Commerce, serving as its chairman from 1987 to 1989. His two most famous works, *The Age of Unreason* (1989) and *The Empty Raincoat* (1994), gave him an international reputation and sold hundreds of thousands of copies. During the 1990s, while remaining a visiting professor at London Business School, Handy concentrated on writing and broadcasting, producing several more books and becoming a regular contributor to *Thought for the Day*, a religious-philosophical opinion programme broadcast by the BBC. He lives in Norfolk.

A prolific writer, Handy's work runs from *Understanding Organizations* (1976), a textbook on organisation behaviour that is conventional in style if far-reaching in content, through to *The New Alchemists* (1999), a series of portraits of visionary people who are changing the way we work and live. Although there are strong common themes running through all his work, in essence Handy's writings can be divided into three phases. First, there are the works on organisation behaviour, first outlined in *Understanding Organizations* and developed further in *Gods of Management* (1979). Next, Handy focused on the management of paradox, the central theme of both *The Age of Unreason* and *The Empty Raincoat*. The third stage moves beyond the study of paradox *per se* to a search for personal values and meaning in an increasingly paradoxical world; this is the central focus of works such as *Beyond Certainty* (1996) and *The Hungry Spirit* (1997). His later works show an intense concern for the plight of the individual and his or her social, psychological and spiritual welfare in an organisational environment of constant flux and change.

Understanding Organizations lays down solid principles which, as noted, permeate Handy's later and more personal writings. The most important of these is his conceptualisation of organisation culture. Cultures, says Handy, can be distinguished by certain features, notably the roles and functions of the individuals within them and the power that those individuals have. He describes four archetypes of organisation culture, which he calls 'power cultures', 'role cultures', 'task cultures' and 'person cultures'.

Power cultures (referred to in *Gods of Management* as 'club cultures'), are those where power is concentrated in the hands of a single dominant individual, such as the founding entrepreneur. All power flows from one central source in the organisation through a web-like network of influence and communication. Control is exercised on a personal level rather than through rules or procedures. Role cultures, by contrast, are hierarchical and bureaucratic. Organisations with a strong role culture tend to place a premium on functional specialisation: finance, marketing, production and other tasks are assigned to specific departments, often with some separation between the departments. Jobs and authority are strongly defined; reporting is vertical, with coordination taking place among a fairly narrow band of senior managers at the top of the organisation.

In task cultures, the primary orientation is on the job or project. Organisations which are based on this culture tend to be very flexible and adaptive; people are used to moving between groups and teams, which are formed and reformed as needed to undertake specific projects. Their major weakness is the lack of a leading or coordinating point. In power cultures, direction and control emanate from the centre, and in role cultures they come down from the top. In task cultures, there is no obvious focal point; with a lack of directed power may also come a lack of responsibility. Person cultures, on the other hand, exist only to assist and serve their members. Person cultures can also be thought of as clusters, with members drawn together almost at random on the basis of self-interest, with no other common bond. Organisations based on the person culture are rare: the examples Handy gives are barristers' chambers and hippie communes.

Handy does not assert the primacy of any one of these archetypes over the others. Just as the Greeks worshipped many gods, so there is room for many cultures in the organisational pantheon. Indeed, Handy's ideal organisation would have room for all four somewhere within it, reflecting the diverse nature of the groups and individuals involved. (His use of multiple metaphors here is suggestive of the work of Gareth **Morgan**, while his fourfold classification of archetypes is echoed in Geert **Hofstede**'s fourfold typology of organisation culture and Max **Boisot**'s archetypes of market, bureaucracy, fief and clan.) He does not believe that organisations are, or should be, homogeneous. All organisations, he says, have a tendency to subdivide themselves into groups. Groups have many names and functions, and organisations rely on them for a variety of purposes: to distribute, manage and control work, to solve problems and take decisions, to collect and process information and ideas, to coordinate activities within the organisation, to increase commitment and involvement, and to negotiate and resolve conflicts. Likewise, individuals also use groups for purposes of their own: as a means of satisfying social or affiliation needs, as a means of defining a concept of self, as a means of acquiring support for their own personal objectives, and as a means for sharing or taking part in a common purpose.

The effectiveness of groups depends in turn on a number of factors. Handy now considers these, dividing them into three classes: (1) 'givens', which include the size and composition of the group, the environment in which it works and the nature of its tasks; (2) 'intervening factors', which include the style of leadership, the processes by which the group carries out its work and the motivation of its members; and (3) 'outcomes', including the group's productivity and the resulting satisfaction of its members.

One of the most powerful and insightful aspects of *Understanding Organizations* is Handy's discussion of motivation. He acknowledges that it is only one of many variables which affect organisations (he lists over sixty in all), but says it is one of the most important. Handy describes what he calls 'motivation calculus'. Each of us as an individual has a set of needs. In order to fulfil these needs, we consider possible actions which could result in satisfaction, and then calculate the effort we would have to expend in order to carry out that action. However, this motivation calculus is not carried out in isolation. Each of us also has a psychological contract with the organisation to which we belong. These contracts, says Handy, can come in one of three types:

1   coercive, where we have no choice but to perform the duties required of us;
2   calculative, where our primary consideration is personal gain or reward;
3   cooperative, where we identify with the organisation's goals and make them our own, so that the maximum reward to the organisation is also the maximum reward to ourselves.

The nature of this contract serves as a variable affecting our motivation calculus and determining at least in part what actions we take. Thus, organisations are social organisms, and should not be viewed as mechanical constructs; they consist of overlapping networks of human relationships and are affected by personal feelings, emotions, needs and wants. They are also strikingly diverse. Handy believes in diversity as a positive force, but accepts that it can lead to conflict. His solution is decentralisation, or 'federalism', in which sub-groups work semi-independently, grouped in what he calls 'organisational villages'. These small sub-units can then work relatively free from central interference, and can develop the cultures that best suit their own group and individual needs.

In his next major work, *The Age of Unreason* (1989), Handy reinvents the organisational village as the 'shamrock organisation'. This is essentially a tripartite structure. The first leaf of the shamrock is composed of core workers, such as professionals and technicians, whose work is essential to the organisation. They are the prime repositories of organisational knowledge, and it is they who give the organisation its goals and direction. The workers in the core are well paid with large salaries and benefits, but in return they are expected to work long hours and give high levels of commitment.

The second leaf of the shamrock consists of the non-essential work which needs doing but which can be contracted out rather than being done within the company. Here, Handy is suggesting a move away from the 'internalisation' of functions which Alfred **Chandler** saw as typifying the large corporations of the early twentieth century. Whereas the early corporations internalised many business functions so as to cut transaction costs and achieve economies of scale, Handy sees the modern organisation as preferring to sacrifice cost savings in favour of flexibility and to focus on the core. This is also the case when we come to the third leaf, consisting of part-time and temporary workers who are hired as and when they are needed in order to meet peaks of labour demand. This third group, less well paid and less motivated, are obviously vulnerable, and organisations should resist the temptation to squeeze the maximum labour from them in exchange for the minimum reward; only good wages and rewards will ensure a good quality of output.

Handy then addresses at length the problem of managing these different cultures. His major concern is for managerial adaptability and flexibility, not just in terms of group effectiveness, but for the sake of managers themselves, who find the conflicts inherent in diverse groups are placing them under increasing levels of stress. Forced to manage conflicts between different cultures over time, often without clear objectives, managers are caught between the need to generate trust and the need to exercise control. Traditional forms of organisation may have been inflexible, but at least they provided short-term security. If these patterns of organisation persist, how will people develop their careers, provide for their families and their own old age? Who will train them and educate them? What other aspects of life and society can give them security? These conflicts are not always easily resolvable.

In his next major work, *The Empty Raincoat* (1994), Handy turned to one of the core psychological and social aspects of management: the management of paradox. The problem of paradox had already surfaced in his earlier work, but here Handy makes a determined effort to show how paradox can be understood and managed. He advises us that paradox cannot be avoided; it is here to stay. As in his writings on organisation, the first step to managing paradox is to classify it, and he opens the book by listing nine forms of paradox which confront us in our professional lives. These are, briefly:

1   The paradox of intelligence: intelligence is the greatest single source of wealth but it is also the most difficult to own and control.
2   The paradox of work: as our society becomes more efficient, there is less work to do and consequently more 'enforced idleness'.
3   The paradox of productivity: greater productivity has been achieved by fewer people working longer hours, with a consequent increase in unemployment and underemployment.
4   The paradox of time: greater efficiency has in theory led to more leisure time, yet the pressures on our time are greater than ever.
5   The paradox of riches: the increasing concentration of wealth in the hands of fewer people is actually leading to a slackening of demand.
6   The paradox of organisations: new business organisations have to be structured yet flexible, global yet local.
7   The paradox of age: every generation believes itself to be different from its predecessor, but assumes the next generation will be the same as itself.
8   The paradox of the individual: we seek to be individuals, yet we identify – and are identified by others – with the groups and organisations to which we belong.
9   The principle of fairness: justice demands that all should be treated equally, yet our system of distribution makes it inevitable that some will achieve and earn more than others.

Although *The Empty Raincoat* was hailed as a statement of the post-modern business dilemma, of the problems of management in an age of change and flux, Handy makes it clear that paradox is not new; indeed, it is a problem as old as society. But, as he says later in *The New Alchemists* (1999), some truths need resurrection rather than discovery. *The Empty Raincoat* is not a prescription for management, but rather an introduction to a new way of thinking, one in which variables are taken for granted and in which diversity, change, flux and paradox are assumed and understood. Paradox need not be seen as a barrier; it can even be an asset. To reach this point, however, we need to adopt a less mechanistic, scientific approach to management and pick up one that is more philosophical and humanistic, one in which a corporate scorecard includes assets such as the intelligence and knowledge of employees, levels of customer satisfaction, and contributions to social environmental well-being.

The ethics of business which Handy introduces here is one which focuses on personal welfare over profit. Managers are not technicians; they are moral beings, and without a sense of ethics, and indeed of faith, they become no more than automaton servants of their organisation, doomed to run down and die once the organisation itself runs out of energy to propel them. With the right inspiration, however, they can transcend the limits of organisation and reach out to touch the future. In doing so, they re-energise their organisations and propel them forward. People die, says Handy, but organisations can live forever.

Handy has bridged the gap between management thinking and philosophy, a gap which had widened immeasurably through the course of the twentieth century as mechanistic approaches to management dominated thinking and practice. He is the closest thing we have today to a philosopher of management, and yet his books go beyond management. *The New Alchemists*, his study of those people who are changing the world around us, includes inventors, doctors, designers and charity workers as well as business leaders. Charles Handy's work has given us new tools for understanding the dynamics of organisation and how human beings function in groups; but most important of all, he has reminded us that neither managers or management exist in isolation, but are subject to the same social forces and pressures as those around them.

See also: **Boisot, Cadbury, Chandler, Drucker, Follett, Hofstede, Maslow, McLuhan, Gareth Morgan, Simon**

Major works

As noted, Handy is a prolific writer. All the works below are important to his thought, and remain in print.

Understanding Organizations, London: Penguin, 1976.
Gods of Management, London: Arrow, 1979.
The Age of Unreason, London: Business Books, 1989.
The Empty Raincoat, London: Hutchinson, 1994.
Beyond Certainty, London: Arrow, 1996.

The Hungry Spirit, London: Random House, 1997.
The New Alchemists, London: Hutchinson, 1999.

Further reading

There are few good independent studies of Handy. Carol Kennedy dips into his thought and ideas and compares them usefully to those of his contemporaries. Kurtzmann's interview is interesting if dated. My own previous writings on Handy form the basis for this chapter.

FT Dynamo, 'Thinkers 50 Survey', 15 January 2001, in association with Suntop Media, online at http://www.ftdynamo.com
Kennedy, C., *Managing With the Gurus*, London: Century, 1994.
Kurtzmann, J., 'An Interview with Charles Handy', *Strategy and Business*, 4th Quarter; 5 February 2001 [interview conducted in 1995], online at http://www.strategy-business.com/thoughtleaders/95405
Witzel, M., 'Handy, Charles', in M. Warner (ed.), *Handbook of Management Thinking*, London: International Thomson Business Press, 1998, pp. 273–8.
—— 'Handy, Charles Brian', in M. Witzel (ed.), *Biographical Dictionary of Management*, Bristol: Thoemmes Press, 2001, pp. 418–23.

Note

1   FT Dynamo (2001) 'Thinkers 50 Survey', 15 January 2001, in association with Suntop Media, online at http://www.ftdynamo.com

HENRY J. HEINZ (1844–1919)

Henry J. Heinz founded and built up one of the largest food products corporations in the world, and in doing so created one of the greatest brand names of all time. A gifted marketer, he used brilliantly showy appeals to attract public attention but then backed these up with high quality goods that were affordably priced. In doing so, Heinz took American marketing practice forward from the days of showmen such as P.T. Barnum and Sam Colt and the 'snake oil salesmen' of the nineteenth century, into a more modern mode of thinking where product features were tailored to customer needs and genuine relationships with both suppliers and customers were seen as essential to success. Above all, Heinz was one of the first marketers in America to appreciate the importance of quality.

Henry John Heinz was born in Pittsburgh on 11 October 1844, but grew up in nearby Sharpsburg, Pennsylvania. His father owned a brickworks, and Heinz for a time considered joining his father in the business on a permanent basis; he maintained a lifelong interest in brickmaking, and in later years used to astonish visitors by showing them piles of brick samples in his office and holding forth on the techniques by which they were made. He first became involved in the food industry at the age of eight, when he began selling surplus vegetables from the family garden; finding he was making a profit, he acquired more land and increased production, including setting up greenhouses. By the time he was sixteen he was employing other people to sell for him on contract and was supplying vegetables to several grocers in Pittsburgh. In 1859 he enrolled at Duff's Commercial College, a small training school in Pittsburgh, where he learned book-keeping and accounting and some basic management skills.

By the time he was in his early twenties Heinz was running a small but highly profitable business and beginning to specialise in the growing and production of horseradish. A friend, L.C. Noble, came into partnership with him, and the firm of Heinz and Noble was soon selling not only horseradish but also other products such as sauerkraut, pickles and vinegar, shipping as far afield as Chicago and St Louis. But they had expanded too soon, and the financial crisis of 1875 caught them without sufficient reserves; by the end of the year the company was bankrupt. Heinz later repaid his share of the debt in full.

Despite the bankruptcy, Heinz knew the market potential was there, and in 1876 he set up a new partnership with his brother and cousin. The new firm, F. and J. Heinz, invested in new food preparation equipment, in particular for the newly invented processes of preserving food in tinned metal containers. Through the 1880s Heinz launched a series of new canned and bottled food products, including such modern staples as canned vegetables, canned spaghetti and canned baked beans. In 1888 he bought out his partners and renamed the firm H.J. Heinz and Co. By 1890 this was one of the largest food-producing companies in the country; by 1900 it was one of the largest in the world, making over 200 products in nine factories and with branch offices around the globe.

Heinz himself became personally very wealthy. He built a large mansion, Greenlawn, near Pittsburgh, and became friendly with the likes of the steelmaker Henry Clay Frick and the engineer George Westinghouse; together, the group were dubbed the 'Pittsburgh millionaires'. Although his son Howard Heinz and others took over much of the daily management of the company after 1905, Heinz continued to be actively involved in its affairs until his death. He died at home on 14 May 1919.

The story of how the Heinz 57 Varieties brand was conceived is best told by Heinz himself, relayed by one of his close associates, E.D. McCafferty.

Its origin was in 1896. Mr Heinz, while in an elevated railroad train in New York, saw among the car-advertising cards one about shoes with the expression: '21 Styles'. It set him to thinking, and as he told it: 'I said to myself, "we do not have styles of products, but we do have varieties of products." Counting up how many we had, I counted well beyond 57, but "57" kept coming back into my mind. "Seven, seven" – there are so many illustrations of the psychological influence of that figure and of its alluring significance to people of all ages and races that "58 Varieties" or "59 Varieties" did not appeal at all to me as being equally strong. I got off the train immediately, went down to the lithographers, where I designed a street-car card and had it distributed throughout the United States. I myself did not realize how highly successful a slogan it was going to be.'[1]

Branding by the 1890s was already fairly sophisticated, even by modern standards. Some industries, notably soap, had established strong brands and supporting advertising and publicity campaigns. However, the common practice of the day was to brand individual products or product lines separately. In Heinz's case, given the broad range of products, this would have been so expensive as to be impracticable. His solution was to create a single corporate brand that could be applied across all products.

Heinz had already shown himself ready to innovate in marketing. He had devoted much time in the 1880s to setting up a large and well-trained sales force, and at his instigation the salesmen developed hitherto untried methods such as product demonstrations and free samples given away at public events. The latter were a particular inspiration, as they allowed the public to taste the product and assure themselves of its quality before buying. At the Chicago World's Fair in 1893, Heinz hit on another giveaway. Setting up a Heinz pavilion, he gave each visitor a free 'pickle pin' as a memento. Robert Alberts has called this 'one of the most famous giveaways in merchandising history', and notes that so many people crowded into the pavilion that the floors began to sag and had to be reinforced.[2]

In Pittsburgh in the late 1880s, Heinz built a new state-of-the-art factory in the grandiose, Pittsburgh-Romanesque style, and then opened it to visitors, providing guided tours. As many as 20,000 visitors a year came to visit the factory. His eye for promotional opportunities increased as time went on. In 1900 he sponsored the first advertising billboard lit by electric light bulbs, in New York City. The sign included 1,200 light bulbs, at a time when very few people had electric lighting at all, and was regarded as a technological marvel: the *New York Times* called it a 'work of advertising genius', and the billboard became an important tourist attraction in its own right until its demolition a few years later to make way for the construction of the Flatiron Building.

Perhaps the most ambitious of all Heinz's promotional efforts was the Heinz Ocean Pier in Atlantic City, New Jersey, sometimes called the 'Crystal Palace by the Sea' and sometimes, less reverently, 'The Sea Shore Home of the 57 Varieties'. Nine hundred feet in length, the pier featured a glass pavilion with a sun room and reading room, and of course a kitchen giving out free samples of Heinz products. At the height of its popularity before the First World War, the pier was attracting over 20,000 people annually. Its popularity declined in the 1930s, however, and the pier was finally abandoned after being badly damaged by a hurricane in the autumn of 1944.

The showmanship of Heinz's marketing and promotion efforts was intended to do no more than attract the public's attention and make it think about Heinz and his products. Once consumers were aware of his products, his purpose then was to make them into regular customers by providing high-quality goods cheaply. Earlier in the nineteenth century, Charles **Babbage** had pointed out that customers, when making a purchase, are taking a risk that the goods they buy may not be of satisfactory quality. If they cannot verify the quality themselves before purchase, they rely on the producer's trade mark or brand marque to signal probable quality. Heinz was probably not aware of Babbage, who was not widely read in America, but he understood the same principle and put it into practice. He insisted that all the goods his firm produced had to be of the best quality possible, and he made the company's name synonymous with quality in the public mind.

Quality, then, was one of Heinz's watchwords, and had been almost from the beginning of his career as a market gardener. In order to maintain quality finished products, he also needed to have the best quality raw materials. Purchasing was one area where Heinz never skimped or cut corners. In the 1880s he began developing purchasing arrangements with farmers, especially growers of cucumbers and cabbage used in making pickles and sauerkraut. Heinz would agree to purchase the farmer's entire output of a given crop at a previously agreed price, usually well above the average market rate; for their part, the farmers had to allow inspection of crops by Heinz technicians and to plant and harvest specific crops at specific times to ensure best quality of output. Heinz got the quality he needed; the farmers were well paid; and the agricultural community of the Midwest learned more about scientific farming methods (Heinz's farming technicians were hired from the country's leading agricultural colleges). Other crops were grown and harvested under direct supervision on the 16,000 acres of farmland the company owned, and Heinz also established his own plants for making bottles and tins and even owned his own railway cars, all to ensure that the supply process worked effectively and that food arrived at the canning and bottling plants fresh and in prime condition.

As well as seeking the best quality in his own products, Heinz and his managers were constant advocates of higher standards in the food industry. Heinz and his son both supported the Pure Food Crusade which began in the 1890s. Food adulteration and the risk to public health this caused were major public issues of the day, and several of the Muck-Rakers, the crusading journalists who campaigned for higher standards in public and business life from 1902 onwards, wrote articles on food adulterers and campaigned for tighter legislation. One of the results was the Pure Food and Drug Act of 1906, legislation which Heinz again supported. In both cases he was strongly at odds with the other major food producers, but Heinz was never afraid to court professional unpopularity in order to protect his standards.

Promotional activity was costly, as were the steps taken to protect quality. However, Heinz's first business training had been as a book-keeper, and he never forgot the painful lessons of his bankruptcy. Accordingly, he maintained strong financial controls. In the early stages of the business, Heinz served as book-keeper and accountant himself, and later continued to monitor closely the basic financial indicators. Yet Heinz was not a cost-cutting manager; he balanced financial requirements with the other needs of his business, and used accounting information to help determine where the most profitable opportunities lay. Heinz was one of those rare and imaginative managers who used accounting and financial data to explore opportunities for growth.

In employment, Heinz was strongly paternalistic in approach. He believed in hiring employees young, training them in his business methods and promoting on merit. He believed that all employees ought to feel part of the Heinz family. His was one of the first companies in the USA to introduce free life insurance for employees. In part this may have been a means of warding off industrial unrest, but Heinz's entire life and career were characterised by firmly held social principles. He was deeply religious, although his faith had different varieties, and he seems at times to have been a Lutheran, an Episcopalian, a Methodist Episcopalian and a Presbyterian (to the gentle amusement of his wife, an Ulster Protestant). He was for twenty-five years a Sunday school superintendent, and later served on the executive council of both the International Sunday School Association and the World Sunday School Association. He took his Christian values into both civic life and business life. He served as vice-president of the Pittsburgh Chamber of Commerce and on a number of other civic bodies. He was also a noted art collector and philanthropist; among his many civic roles in later life was the presidency of the Pittsburgh branch of the Egyptian Exploration Fund.

McCafferty, who knew him well, argued that Heinz was always guided by attention to business fundamentals: 'He was not a dreamer or a visionary, who went into business and by chance made a success. He was a businessman by origin, by preference, and by training.'[3] Yet attention to business fundamentals is not incompatible with being a visionary, and it seems most likely that Heinz was both at once; his particular genius lay in being able to translate his vision into reality. Robert Alberts has adduced what he calls the 'Eight Important Ideas' that guided Heinz's philosophy of business. These are:

1   Housewives are willing to pay someone else to take over a share of their more tedious kitchen work.
2   A pure article of superior quality will find a ready market through its own intrinsic merit – if it is properly packaged and promoted.
3   To improve the finished product that comes out of the bottle, can or crock, you must improve it in the ground, when and where it is grown.
4   Our market is the world.
5   Humanise the business system of today and you will have the remedy for the present discontent that characterises the commercial world and fosters a spirit of enmity between capital and labour.
6   Let the public assist you in advertising your products and promoting your name.
7   Good foods, properly processed, will keep without the addition of preservatives.
8   If people could work together in religion, then lasting peace might be found.[4]

Evidence of all these ideas can be seen in Heinz's approach to management, often co-mingled.

Although he has been best known for his marketing, Heinz succeeded because he was an all-rounder, equally accomplished in areas such as finance and production management, and topping it all off with a strong set of ethics and a personal philosophy that he was in business, at least in part, to do good for others. He remains something of an ideal type of business manager, conforming to nearly all the expectations set for management by theorists. In one area alone he falls down; he was a poor delegator and tended to centralise control. Yet that control was done with a light touch, and more closely resembles the 'coordination' discussed in the decade after his death by Mary Parker **Follett**, rather than strict command and control. It is for his marketing genius, however, that Heinz's name survives. He broke new ground in fields such as corporate branding, linking quality to marketing, and the use of publicity and promotion.

See also: **Babbage, Kotler, Lever**

Major works

Heinz wrote no major works. His ideas were, however, widely reported and quoted in other sources.

Further reading

Alberts's study of Heinz and his business is an outstanding work. McCafferty was Heinz's private secretary for a number of years and is good on detail but tends to idealise his subject.

Alberts, R.C., *The Good Provider: H.J. Heinz and His 57 Varieties*, London: Arthur Barker, 1973.
McCafferty, E.D., *Henry J. Heinz: A Biography*, New York: Bartlett Orr Press, 1923.

Notes

1   E.D. McCafferty, *Henry J. Heinz: A Biography*, New York: Bartlett Orr Press, 1923, p. 147.
2   R.C. Alberts, *The Good Provider*, London: Arthur Barker, 1973, p. 123.
3   McCafferty, *Henry J. Heinz: A Biography*, p. 137.
4   Alberts, *The Good Provider*.

GEERT HOFSTEDE (1928–)

Geert Hofstede is a Dutch academic who has led the way in the scientific study of cross-cultural management. His research into cultural differences within national subsidiaries of a single company, IBM, in the 1960s and 1970s opened the door to a greater understanding of worldwide variations in the psychology of work and of organisations, with major implications for organisation theory and human resources management, at the very least. Hofstede's model for cultural analysis has subsequently undergone revisions, and other explanations for cultural variation have since been developed. But Hofstede's lasting achievement has been to raise the importance of culture as a major issue when managing trans-nationally.

Gerard (Geert) Hofstede was born on 2 October 1928 in Haarlem, the Netherlands. He took an MSc in engineering from Delft University, then spent two years in the Dutch army before going into industry as an engineer. In 1965, in a change of career direction, he joined IBM's executive development department in Europe, and also began part-time studies towards a PhD in social psychology at the University of Groningen, completing this in 1967. From 1968 to 1971 he was manager of personnel research at IBM. He then moved into academia, and has held posts at a number of major European universities, culminating in a professorship of organisation anthropology and international management at the University of Maastricht. Retiring from that post in 1993, he continues to hold several fellowships. Among his major achievements are the founding of the Institute for Research on Intercultural Cooperation in 1980.

At IBM, one of Hofstede's roles included the conducting of inter-company surveys among the corporation's numerous subsidiaries and employees around the world. In 1968, he hit on the idea of conducting a survey which would attempt to measure differences in cultural values and traits between subsidiaries. In 1972, having left IBM but still in close contact with the company, he was able to conduct a second survey to confirm and validate the results of the first. The unique access to IBM (code-named HERMES in the original published study of 1980) allowed Hofstede to compare cultural values across the same company. This allowed him to overcome one problem which might have arisen in a similar study of this sort involving different companies, the impact of different managerial approaches methods on employee culture. At the time IBM (known not always affectionately as 'Big Blue' for the colour of its employees' uniforms) was famously monolithic in terms of its approach to company culture, and variances in managerial methods could be expected to be minimal.

In all, 116,000 employees took part in the survey, the largest survey of employee attitudes undertaken so far (the previous largest had been the long-term study at Western Electric's plant at Hawthorne, Illinois in the 1920s and 1930s which had studied some 10,000 people). Those surveyed came from over sixty nationalities and were employed in forty different subsidiaries. The analysis of the data necessarily took some time, and the results were not published until 1980 in Hofstede's first and still most famous book, *Culture's Consequences*.

Hofstede found that the differences in workplace cultural attitudes shown by the survey could be classified along four dimensions, and he developed a rating scale for each dimension. The original dimensions, described in *Culture's Consequences*, he described as *power distance, uncertainty avoidance, individualism/collectivism* and *masculinity/femininity*.

Power distance is Hofstede's term for the degree to which power within a society is distributed equally or unequally, and the extent to which that society accepts this distribution. Thus societies with a high power distance score not only show a tendency towards vertical hierarchies and strong definition of individual roles within those hierarchies, but also feature a strong acceptance of that situation by most members of society: most are happy to be part of a hierarchy, show little inclination to deviate from its rules, and may even be uncomfortable when asked to step outside the hierarchy and assume more personal responsibility. Low power distance scores, conversely, apply to societies where hierarchy is limited and loose and where individuals put more value on personal responsibility and show less deference to authority.

Uncertainty avoidance is the degree to which members of the society require structure and boundaries in the workplace. High uncertainty avoidance societies are those which are intolerant of risk, and also of ideas which may challenge accepted norms and standard ways of doing things. They may prefer the certainties of the present over the uncertainties of the future. In the workplace this can take the form of, for example, high degrees of specialisation and standardisation, or also high levels of employee security in the form of, for example, lifetime employment contracts. Low uncertainty avoidance societies are those where risk and paradox are more widely accepted.

Individualism/collectivism is the degree to which people act according to self-interest or the interests of the group. Societies which score on the individualist end of the scale tend to be societies which regard personal freedom and free will as important values, and which see personal independence as more important than the demands of society. Collectivist societies put it the other way around: the individual is expected to partly subordinate his or her personal needs to the needs of the group, team, organisation or community as a whole.

Masculinity/femininity should not be interpreted literally. This dimension is intended to measure the goal orientation of the society. Societies where earnings, promotion and status are seen as the most important work goals are classified as 'masculine', while those where quality of life and human relationships are prioritised are classified as 'feminine'.

The variations in these four dimensions are not either/or; Hofstede uses a ten-point scale to score each culture in each of the four dimensions. The results are not black and white, but rather shades of grey. Some cultures score high in some dimensions and low in others; some hover around the middle in all four, with only weak indicators in any dimension. Hofstede shows how each dimension is rooted not in the culture of the workplace but in much deeper, national, cultural attributes. Collectivist-minded workers are so because they grow up in societies, such as southern Europe or East Asia, where family and community relations are important; individualists, on the other hand, come from countries such as the USA or Australia where personal freedom is an important part of culture. Indeed, in later work comparing organisational cultures across both countries and companies, Hofstede argues that the former is by far the most important; organisational culture is in fact relatively weak at explaining cultural variations when compared to national culture.

One of the initial criticisms of Hofstede's work was that the data from Asian countries was comparatively weak and did not take account of all the variables that could be found there. The foremost of these commentators, Michael Bond from the University of Hong Kong, argued that in particular there was a difference in terms of time orientation between East and West. Workers and managers in Eastern cultures tended to be more long-termist in outlook, while those in the West were more short-termist. Subsequent collaborative work between Bond and Hofstede resulted in the adding of a fifth dimension, *time orientation*, to account for this variable. This update appeared in Hofstede's later book, *Cultures and Organizations: Software of the Mind* (1991), in which he also discusses in more detail the links between national and organisational culture.

This extra dimension is a valuable addition to the original model, but it does open up a can of worms and expose a weakness in the Hofstede approach. It is possible to think up an almost limitless number of additional 'dimensions' which could be added to the model concerning, say, attitudes to learning and knowledge, or market orientation, or whatever. This is of course a weakness with *any* basic typology; see the work of Max **Boisot** on communications and Michael **Porter** on strategy, for example. It is important to understand that the Hofstede scales are not meant to be an all-embracing description of the differences between every culture included. Rather, their purpose is to indicate that difference does exist – and can be shown to exist reliably and scientifically, not just as a series of impressions or personal biases. Some of his results are surprising. British culture, it has always been assumed, is strong on uncertainty avoidance. In fact, Hofstede's study shows a considerable tolerance of uncertainty, better than in many other European countries. Likewise, some Asian countries score higher on the individualism scale than might be expected.

Critics of Hofstede's work have attacked his methodology, his data and his conclusions. Yet virtually every criticism has in fact confirmed Hofstede's own central view: culture matters. Very few critics of Hofstede have argued that the idea of cultural difference is invalid; most believe he has not gone far enough in explaining it. In the years since the appearance of *Culture's Consequences* (1980) a number of other well-known studies of cross-cultural management have emerged, such as Hampden-Turner and Trompenaar's *The Seven Cultures of Capitalism* (1993) and Lessem and Neubauer's *European Management Systems* (1994). These works provide different perspectives on the issues of culture, but serve if anything to reinforce its importance.

That there are causal links between the national cultural background of workers, including their values, social mores and ideals, and their behaviour in the workplace may seem obvious now, but it was not always fully accepted before Hofstede; and indeed the idea is still resisted in some quarters. There persists a belief that, as proposed by scientific management, there is 'one best way' to manage, one unique set of principles which always apply in all situations. Hofstede suggests that, when managing people at least, different concepts and tools may be necessary at different times and places. Perhaps the most important implication of his work is that there are different ways to success in management, depending on the local culture in which managers operate. At the very least, sensitivity to local culture is important to avoid conflict and problems in the workplace.

Proponents of globalisation theory argue that, following Marshall **McLuhan**, in time differences between cultures will be ironed out, and that a single global culture will emerge as the result. That day still looks a long way off, and until it comes, Hofstede's ideas on the importance of cultural difference will continue to be important for any manager working outside the boundaries of their home culture.

See also: **Boisot, Follett, Fukuzawa, Matsushita, Gareth Morgan, Ohmae**

Major works

Cultures and Organizations updates and expands the original research published in *Culture's Consequences.*

Culture's Consequences: International Differences in Work-Related Values, Beverly Hills, CA: Sage, 1980.
Cultures and Organizations: Software of the Mind, London: McGraw-Hill, 1991.

Further reading

Hampden-Turner and Trompenaars, and Lessem and Neubauer, are examples of other comparative systems. Adler's work shows how Hofstede's influence has been diffused; she is a very important writer on organisation in her own right.

Adler, N.J., *International Dimensions of Organizational Behavior*, 3rd edn, London: International Thomson Publishing, 1997.
Hampden-Turner, C. and Trompenaars, F., *The Seven Cultures of Capitalism*, Garden City, NY: Doubleday, 1993.
Lessem, R. and Neubauer, F., *European Management Systems*, New York: McGraw-Hill, 1994.
Ohmae, K., *The Borderless World: Power and Strategy in the Interlinked Economy*, New York: Harper Business, 1990.

IBUKA MASARU (1908–97)

Ibuka founded the electronics company Sony, and built it up into one of the most prominent companies in the electronics industry. One of the great scientist-entrepreneurs, he combined technological knowledge with acute management ability, especially in marketing. He believed in constant innovation, in doing things that other companies were not willing to do, and in always leading the market in terms of new technologies. His approach to innovation and entrepreneurship was widely imitated in post-Second World War Japan, and he was a catalysing force in the drive towards Japanese technological and market leadership in consumer electronics worldwide.

Ibuka was born in Nikko, a town in the mountainous central region of Honshu to the north of Tokyo, on 11 April 1908, the son of a mining engineer. He became interested in radios while still a schoolboy, and in 1930 enrolled at Waseda University to study electrical engineering. He converted to Christianity around this time, and for the rest of his life remained a man of quiet but sincere belief. His career as an inventor began at university, where his most notable achievement was the development and patenting of luminous neon; this feat won him a prize for excellence at the Paris Exhibition of 1933, when he was still just 21 years old.

Graduating from Waseda in 1933, Ibuka worked with a film technology company, Photo Chemical Laboratory, and then joined the radio technology department at the newly established Japan Light and Sound Engineering in 1936. In 1940 he left to set up his own company, Japan Measuring Tools, which developed and manufactured high-technology electronics equipment such as oscillators and relays for the armed forces. Among his contacts was a young officer in the technical branch of the navy, Morita Akio, who became a close friend.

The Second World War ended in the Pacific in September 1945, leaving Japan in ruins and occupied by the victorious Allied forces. In October 1945, Ibuka and a small group of engineering friends, including Morita Akio, Iwama Kazuo and Tsukamoto Tetsuo, took over a third-floor room in the Tokyo Department Store, deserted but one of the few buildings still standing in downtown Tokyo, and set up a new business which they called Tokyo Communications Laboratory. There were just ten employees, and some, such as Morita, had to augment their salaries by teaching part-time. They began by making voltmeters, and gradually expanded into other radio components. Their aim now was to produce for the civilian market; the military market in Japan had disappeared with the defeat of 1945, but in any case it seems that, the horrors of wartime experience coupled with his religious principles, led Ibuka to concentrate on technology that could only be useful for purposes of peace and prosperity.

By the early 1950s the company, renamed Tokyo Telecommunications Engineering Company (Tokyo Tsushin Kogyo, or TTK) was branching out into fields such as tape recorders. In 1952, Ibuka visited the USA where he saw at first hand the new developments in transistor technology. Securing a licensing agreement from Western Electric, the main patent holder, Ibuka returned to Japan and convinced his colleagues to throw their resources behind the development of consumer products based on transistor technology. In 1955 TTK developed one of the world's first commercial transistor radios, and promptly began to mass produce low-price radios for the Japanese and world markets. Morita, making his own first trip to America in that year, came home convinced of the prospects for exporting. In 1958, in order to give itself a brand name recognisable in world markets, TTK changed its name to Sony, the word derived from the Latin word *sonus* (sound).

Through the later 1950s, 1960s and 1970s, the Sony brand became synonymous with high-quality radios, televisions, tape recorders and other consumer goods based on audio and visual technology. Sony introduced the first commercial video tape recorder, and later the first commercial video cassette recorder. As well as new product lines, the company was constantly searching for new technologies which would upgrade and improve existing ones. The company was also a leader in the development of compact products such as pocket radios and tape recorders and miniature televisions, all of which had immense consumer appeal worldwide. The acknowledged technological leader in consumer electronics for over three decades, Sony had a research and development budget more than double that of its rivals, such as Matsushita. Ibuka continually recruited talented graduates from Japan's top universities and technical schools in order to upgrade Sony's knowledge pool and R&D capabilities.

Ibuka believed that Sony's main competitive advantage lay in its ability to innovate continually and keep ahead of rivals. He was a strong believer in first-mover advantage with new products and new markets. He was willing to accept high development and marketing costs if this could give him the advantage he sought. There were of course failures. Etsuko Abe comments that Ibuka's concentration on transistors may have led him to ignore developments in integrated circuit technology and thus miss a competitive opportunity in this field. More famously, Sony launched the Betamax videocassette recorder, the first product of its type, with the aim of capturing the market and making the Betamax system the industry standard. However, on this occasion first-mover advantage did not work; a year later the Matsushita subsidiary JVC launched the rival VHS system which, while arguably inferior in terms of quality, was backed up by Matsushita's more powerful production and marketing systems.

The incident highlights the different approaches of Ibuka and **Matsushita** Konosuke. Both marketed consumer electronics goods, but Ibuka sought leadership through innovation and differentiation while Matsushita sought it through cost and price strategies. Both were phenomenally successful; for Ibuka, failures such as Betamax were very rare. His view, typical of scientist-entrepreneurs, was that the individual failures did not matter, so long as the overall balance of successes against failures remained in your favour.

Unusually for a large Japanese company, Sony tended to work on its own; it rarely formed alliances with other companies, and never compromised on its own brand name. Even when struggling in the early 1950s, TTK had refused lucrative offers to distribute imported electronics goods unless it could brand them with its own name. This may have meant that, in the early days at least, Sony missed out on some marketing opportunities through a lack of economies of scale, but at the same time it left Ibuka free of ties and able to innovate as he chose. His philosophy was one of 'not liking to do the same thing as others do',[1] meaning not only self-reliance and independence, but also a desire to explore new markets rather than compete with other firms in existing ones. He constantly challenged the existing limits of science and technology in his pursuit of the new. In his own words:

> While we should make less risky decisions based on scientific data, it is vitally important to keep up the sharp and bold spirit which enables us to challenge. If we become frightened and do nothing, Sony will become an old-fashioned firm. If you judge that it is good for Sony, you should daringly try it. Responsibility implies the boldness to fulfill it.[2]

Ibuka became chairman of Sony in 1971, and his friend and deputy Morita Akio took over as president and chief executive. In 1976 Ibuka retired, taking the post of honorary chairman, and Morita succeeded him as chairman. Morita was also a talented engineer who had played a major role in Sony's product development and marketing programmes, and under his leadership Sony continued to pioneer new products such as the Walkman personal cassette player and recorder. Morita retired in 1991. Following his own retirement, Ibuka Masaru received many awards, including the Order of Cultural Merit in 1992. He remains one of Japan's most admired entrepreneurs and innovators.

It has often been said, especially by outsiders, that Japanese firms prefer to imitate rather than innovate. Ibuka and Sony show how wrong that belief can be. Through a combination of personal belief and an ability to tap into a wider cultural desire for excellence – plus the sense of national pride that demanded a restoration of Japan's fortunes after the Second World War – Ibuka created one of the world's most innovative companies.

See also: **Babbage, Deming, Fukuzawa, Matsushita, Peters, Toyoda**

Major works

Regrettably, none of Ibuka's several books have been translated into English. The two works given below contain his fullest thinking on innovation and competitiveness; the second is a collection of transcripts of interviews with Ibuka, most done after his retirement.

Sozo Eno Tabi (Journey to Creation), Tokyo: Kosei Shuppansha, 1985.
Ibuka Masaru no Sekai (The World of Ibuka Masaru), Tokyo: Mainichi Shinbunsha, 1993.

Further reading

Morita's autobiography is a compelling account, full of detail about the Sony culture and Ibuka. Kono, Rafferty and Suzuki all have lengthy treatments of the development of Sony in comparison with other Japanese corporations. Abe and Sasaki are very useful introductions.

Abe, E., 'Ibuka, Masaru', in M. Warner (ed.), *Handbook of Management Thinking*, London: International Thomson Business Press, 1998, pp. 313–16.
Kono, T., *Strategy and Structure of Japanese Enterprises*, London: Macmillan, 1984.
Morita, A., Reingold, E.M. and Shinomura, M., *Made in Japan: Akio Morita and Sony*, London: Collins, 1987.
Rafferty, K., *Inside Japan's Power Houses: The Culture, Mystique and Future of Japan's Greatest Corporations*, London: Weidenfeld and Nicolson, 1995.
Sasaki, T., 'Ibuka Masaru', in M. Witzel (ed.), *Biographical Dictionary of Management*, Bristol: Thoemmes Press, 2001, vol. 1, pp. 467–9.
Suzuki, Y., *Japanese Management Structures, 1920–80*, Basingstoke: Macmillan, 1991.

Notes

1 From Sony's corporate history, quoted in E. Abe, 'Ibuka, Masaru', in M. Warner (ed.), *Handbook of Management Thinking*, London: International Thomson Business Press, 1998, p. 315.
2 *Ibid.*

PHILIP KOTLER (1931–)

Philip Kotler is the best-known writer on marketing in the world today. His contribution has been to change the way marketing is perceived, to move it from being a peripheral activity undertaken by an often isolated department to being a core activity which should feature in the thinking and actions of every department and every manager. Previous writing on marketing had tended to focus on what marketers *do*. Kotler changed the focus to the study of what marketing *is*, and in so doing demonstrated the central relevance of marketing to business in incontrovertible terms.

Kotler was born in Chicago on 27 May 1931. He took his BA at De Paul University and then studied for an MA in economics at the University of Chicago under the great exponent of the free market, Milton Friedman. He then attended the Massachusetts Institute of Technology, where he completed his PhD thesis in economics under the supervision of a Keynesian, Paul Samuelson, giving him the benefit of contrasting approaches to the subject. He embarked on a career in economics, teaching the subject at Roosevelt University from 1957 to 1961.

In the latter year, Kotler went to Harvard University on a post-doctoral fellowship. Here he met two leading academic figures in marketing: Robert Buzzell, who later became famous as one of the co-originators of the PIMS (profit impact of marketing strategies) model, and Jerome McCarthy, the man who popularised the concept of the 'four Ps' of the marketing mix (product, place, price and promotion).[1] Their ideas and work influenced Kotler's own outlook. It is probable that he was also exposed to the work of Theodore Levitt, who in 1960 had published the seminal *Harvard Business Review* article 'Marketing Myopia', one of the most influential writings on marketing of all time. Levitt had argued that, in reality, products are only means to ends; the ends themselves are the satisfaction of customer needs and wants. When customers focus on their products rather than their customers, they are doomed to fail. He cited the example of the US railway companies, who assumed that they were in the railway business and that therefore there was no competition between them and other transport media, such as roads and air. Wrong, said Levitt: all these companies were actually in the *transportation* business, as it was this service that the customer was buying, not the railways themselves. But the railway companies were blind to this, and so they failed to meet the challenge of competition and went out of business.

Back in Chicago in 1962 Kotler was offered a post at the Kellogg School of Business at Northwestern University. By now very much interested in the principles and concepts of marketing, he chose to switch to this discipline. He began as an assistant professor of marketing at Kellogg, was promoted to associate professor in 1965, professor in 1969 and distinguished professor in 1989. He continues to be a highly active teacher and writer in his field. His books have sold millions of copies around the world and have been translated into nearly thirty languages. He remains the recognised doyen of the academic marketing community.

Kotler brought to the study of marketing a wide range of concepts from other backgrounds, principally, but not exclusively, economics. This enabled him to take a fresh look at a subject that had been around for many decades. Northwestern itself was one of the first centres of marketing teaching in the USA. Walter Dill Scott, professor of psychology and later president of the university, had begun in the early years of the twentieth century to apply the concepts of psychology to advertising, and his *Theory of Advertising* (1903) and *The Psychology of Advertising* (1913) were landmark ventures in the application of scientific principles to an aspect of marketing. In the 1920s, Scott and Fred Clark had developed more detailed concepts of marketing based on a psychological understanding of customer needs and how to discern these and appeal to them. Although grounded in theory, the work of Scott and Clark was largely aimed at describing practical methods for finding and reaching customers, as was the work of another Chicago-based writer, Arch W. Shaw.

While Northwestern broke new ground in research into consumer psychology and motivation, a different kind of approach was being developed at the new Harvard Graduate School of Business Administration. Its first professor of marketing, Paul T. Cherington, helped set up the School's Bureau of Business Research in part to study marketing problems, and Cherington directed one of its first nationwide research studies, on the shoe industry. For Cherington, the primary problem faced by marketers was not so much finding customers as physically delivering goods to them. Given the state of the USA's transport infrastructure at the time, this was not unreasonable, but it did create an ethos in which pricing and distribution were emphasised over product and promotion. Cherington's successor, Melvin T. Copeland, redressed the balance somewhat and placed more emphasis on consumer theory. In general, however, as at Northwestern, the emphasis was on what marketers do. It was usually accepted that marketing, and sales and advertising, would be carried out by separate departments, albeit with line responsibility to a director at or near the top of the company.

By 1960, this view of marketing still largely held sway in US companies and even in academia. Marketing was a marginal activity carried out by specialists, and some companies would respond to economic downturns or loss of market share by dismissing the entire marketing department, believing their salaries to be an unnecessary expense.[2] It was applied largely to tangible products: the idea of marketing services was not yet taken seriously. Theodore Levitt's article on marketing myopia was a warning that this attitude could no longer be tolerated, but few outside academia paid much heed.

Kotler, looking back over this period of US business history, began by classifying approaches to marketing on five levels, each one of increasing sophistication. First there is the *production concept*, which 'holds that consumers will favor those products that are widely available and low in cost. Management in production-oriented organizations concentrates on achieving high production efficiency and wide distribution coverage.'[3] In economic terms, it is assumed that there will always be demand and that sales are dependent on the goods physically reaching the customer. Next comes the *product concept*, which 'holds that customers will favor those products that offer the most quality, performance, and features. Management in these product-oriented organizations focus their energy on making good products and improving them over time.'[4] The emphasis here has switched from price to the bundle of benefits the consumer receives when making the purchase, or in other words, from price to value. This, like the product concept, is an ancient approach to marketing and can be traced in economics literature as far back as the Middle Ages.[5]

Third, Kotler says, there is the *selling concept*. This 'holds that customers, if left alone, will ordinarily not buy enough of the organization's products. The organization must therefore undertake an aggressive selling and promotion effort.'[6] Here there is an active engagement with the market through various forms of selling, ranging from the 'soft sell', which emphasises educating the customer about the product and allowing the latter to make a free decision, to the aggressive 'hard sell', which emphasises completing the transaction. This approach was current at the beginning of the twentieth century when Scott and Cherington first began their work.

Fourth comes the *marketing concept*, which 'holds that the key to achieving organizational goals consists in determining the needs and wants of the target markets and delivering the desired satisfactions more efficiently and effectively than competitors'.[7] This approach, which had been outlined as long ago as the 1920s, had been developed in more detail by scholars and practitioners in the 1950s and 1960s, and was the prevailing academic orthodoxy in the late 1960s. This approach requires some active engagement by both parties, and assumes, as Melvin Copeland once argued, that the basic goal of both parties in an exchange is to complete a transaction; it falls to the marketer to find out what the needs of the customer are and attempt to deliver a product that meets as many of those needs as possible, making the transaction as satisfactory as possible.

Finally, Kotler offers his radical innovation, what he calls the *societal marketing concept*. This 'holds that the organization's task is to determine the needs, wants, and interests of target markets and to deliver the desired satisfactions more effectively and efficiently than competitors in a way that preserves or enhances the consumer's or society's well-being'.[8] The societal marketing concept has been controversial since the beginning, and has been part of Kotler's more general campaign to 'broaden' the concept of marketing; it was first introduced in a *Journal of Marketing* article co-written with Sidney Levy in 1969. Kotler and Levy argue that marketing is not just about commercial transactions; it is also about social values. Every product that is made and sold performs some sort of social function; every transaction has some social aspect; social values are part of all exchanges. Marketing is, whether it likes it or not, a social function. Thus, much of marketing is about communication – of needs, of wants, of offerings, of price and features – and all communication is value-laden.

Although this seemed radical, it was not without precedent; Drucker had argued from similar premises in the 1950s, and very early twentieth-century literature on the nature and function of the corporation showed ideas of a similar nature. But Kotler and Levy went further. They argued that it is possible to apply the value principles of marketing to non-commercial exchanges, such as services and products which are provided on a non-profit basis or even for free; more, it is possible to apply them to communications situations where no formal transaction takes place at all, such as elections of political candidates.

Kotler and Levy's articles caused something of a sensation, and distinguished marketing academics of the day rushed rebuttals into print. The most common criticism was that Kotler and Levy had 'broadened' marketing so far that it had disappeared; if the principles of marketing could be applied to all forms of exchange, commercial or otherwise, why call it 'marketing' at all? But Kotler, notably in his later work with Alan Andreasen, has pointed out that, while non-profit marketing and commercial marketing differ in many aspects, they are still based on the same fundamental principles.

Kotler thus creates a model of marketing as being founded on a few simple common elements, regardless of what is being marketed and to whom. These elements begin with analysis of the needs, wants and demands of the customer. *Needs*, he says, are the realisation of the lack of some basic requirement; *wants* are specific requests for products or services to fill needs; *demands* are wants backed up by the desire and ability to pay or otherwise make exchange.

Next in importance come the concepts of *value* and *satisfaction*. Customers, when faced with a variety of products, make their choice based on perceived value to themselves, not to the marketing company. Value thus depends on how well the product – or service, or other good – will satisfy a need, want or demand, regardless of what the selling party perceives value to be. Satisfaction, then, is the extent to which actual value realised by the purchase or acquisition of the product matches the pre-purchase assessment of value. If actual value is equal to or greater than perceived value, satisfaction will result, if not, then dissatisfaction will result.

Marketing, then, as defined by Kotler, is 'a social process by which individuals and groups obtain what they need and want through creating and exchanging products and value with others'.[9] Not until an understanding of that definition has been achieved should the company or manager proceed to the actual elements of *doing* marketing. Kotler is at pains to point out that while the marketing concept is actually a very simple one, doing marketing is quite complex and can be very costly. The activities associated with marketing include research and analysis, environmental scanning, forecasting of potential demand, identification of marketing segments and the needs of customers in those segments, development of new products which will better meet those needs, product life cycle planning, marketing strategy, pricing strategy, establishment and maintenance of distribution channels, communications and promotion, among others. Not for nothing are Kotler's books usually long and detailed. Again, however, he insists that these activities are common to all marketing activity, and are tasks which are carried out by every marketing department or organisation in some guise or other.

A market orientation – or better, a societal marketing orientation – is, he says, an essential pre-requisite for any marketing operation. Marketing should be part of the philosophy of all managers in that all should be focused on the needs and wants of the customer and be prepared to satisfy his or her demands. In structural terms, the marketing department must be at the heart of the organisation, not on its periphery.

To sum up, Kotler's contribution to marketing and to management generally has been threefold. First, he has promoted the importance of marketing, transforming it from a peripheral activity 'bolted onto' the more 'important' work of production to a core activity. Second, he has helped to shift the emphasis in marketing away from price and distribution issues to a greater focus on meeting customer needs and on the bundle of benefits the customer receives from a product or service. Third, he has broadened the concept of marketing from mere selling to a much more general process of communication and exchange, and has shown how marketing can be extended and applied to non-profit and non-commercial situations.

The result has been a full-scale transformation of thinking about marketing in US, and international, industry. Why has Kotler been so successful at reaching his audience in this way? There are probably several reasons. First, he was writing at the right time. In the 1970s, the long, post-Second World War honeymoon for US business came to an end; a combination of a domestic economy wobbling after the oil shocks and pressure from aggressive foreign exporters, notably Japan, meant the more thoughtful among US industrialists were receptive to new ideas. (Those who did not adopt new marketing concepts went, as Levitt in particular suggested they would, to the wall.) Second, Kotler in his writings has demonstrated the truth of his ideas, showing how companies who adopt the marketing outlook get results; his books are loaded with dozens of case studies of successful companies showing how it can be done. But third, and this may seem counter-intuitive, by taking a more philosophical approach and going into the heart of the marketing concept, Kotler convinced executives that marketing was not just another bag of tools but something that was central to their own objectives and purpose. This final point in particular has been his lasting legacy.

See also: **Babbage, Casson, Drucker, Heinz, Lever, Maslow, Porter, Toyoda, Urwick**

Major works

Kotler has written or co-written fifteen books and more than 70 articles. Any understanding of his approach should start with the following:

(With S.J. Levy) 'Broadening the Concept of Marketing', *Journal of Marketing* January (1969): 10–15.
(With A. Andreasen) *Strategic Marketing for Nonprofit Organizations*, Englewood Cliffs, NJ: Prentice-Hall, 1996.
Marketing Management, Englewood Cliffs, NJ: Prentice-Hall, 1997.

Further reading

The works below represent other important stages in the development of the marketing concept prior to Kotler.

Cherington, P.T., *The Elements of Marketing*, New York: Macmillan, 1920.

Clark, F.E., *Principles of Marketing*, New York: Macmillan, 1924.

Copeland, M.T., *Problems in Marketing*, Chicago, IL: A.W. Shaw, 1917.

Drucker, P., *The Practice of Management*, New York: Harper & Row, 1954.

Levitt, T., 'Marketing Myopia', *Harvard Business Review* July–August (1960): 45–56.

McCarthy, J., *Basic Marketing*, Homewood, IL: Irwin, 1960.

Scott, W.D., *The Psychology of Advertising*, Chicago, IL: Dodd, Mead, 1913.

Notes

1   Credit for first defining the four Ps is usually given to Neil Borden, but McCarthy explored the concept in more detail and made it into a central idea of marketing.

2   The author can testify from personal experience as a researcher that this response was still being used by British companies as late as 1990.

3   P. Kotler, *Marketing Management*, Englewood Cliffs, NJ: Prentice-Hall, 1997, p. 17.

4   *Ibid.*

5   Notably, to St Thomas Aquinas in his remarks on the 'just price' of goods.

6   *Marketing Management*, p. 19.

7   *Ibid.*, p. 22.

8   *Ibid.*, p. 29.

9   *Ibid.*, p. 4.

LAOZI (LAO TZU) (6th century BC)

Laozi, or Lao Tzu,[1] is one of the semi-legendary sages of ancient China and the founding father of the philosophical and religious movement known as Daoism (or Taoism). The essence of this movement's philosophy is found in the book *Daodejing* (*Tao Te Ching*), a title which translates roughly as 'Book of the Way and Virtue'. Along with Confucius, Laozi has been a major influence on Chinese thinking for two and a half millennia, and his thought has particularly important resonances in Eastern ideas about leadership and management. Laozi's ideas also passed into Western philosophy during the eighteenth-century Enlightenment, where the Daoist concept of *wu-wei* (non-action) was adapted by French economists as the concept of *laissez-faire*.

Little if any certain knowledge can be had of the life of Laozi, and it is even possible that he is an entirely mythical figure. Tradition says that he was a contemporary (in some accounts, the teacher) of Confucius. He is credited with writing the *Daodejing*, but as was common in ancient China, the original version was doubtless added to and amended many times; the text as we know it today probably reached its final form around 300 BC.

The *Daodejing* is divided into eighty-one short chapters, each consisting of a collection of sayings concerning the Way (*dao*) and the attainment of virtue (*de*). Running throughout the book are a number of themes: the need to avoid conflict and to achieve ends instead through peace and harmony; the need for effacement of the self and the pursuit of inner cultivation rather than striving for things of this world; the essential one-ness of the universe and all things in it; and the belief that true achievement comes not through action but rather through its opposite, *wu-wei*, or 'non-action'. These core principles have had a very powerful influence on Chinese thought and society, especially from the first millennium AD onwards when scholars increasingly sought to build a synthesis of Confucian, Daoist, Legalist and Buddhist ideas as a governing framework for society.

The *Daodejing* remains widely read in China, and the text is perceived as having important things to say about business culture and leadership. The book exhorts those in positions of power and authority to know much, but do little. *Daodejing* 8, for example, urges: 'In governing, know how to maintain order. In transacting business, know how to be efficient. In making a move, know how to choose the right moment.' *Daodejing* 17 says that the most effective form of leadership is that which motivates people rather than controlling them:

> The highest type of rule is one of whose existence the people are barely aware.
> Next comes one whom they love and praise.
> Next comes one whom they fear.
> Next comes one whom they despise and defy.
> When you are lacking faith,
> Others will be unfaithful to you.
> The Sage is self-effacing and scanty of words.
> When his task is accomplished and things have been completed,
> All the people say, 'We ourselves have achieved it!'

The highest form of rule, says the *Daodejing*, is that which is conducted according to the principles of virtue and the Way; the lowest is that which is conducted according to ritual and ceremony, for these are 'the beginning of all confusion and disorder' (*Daodejing* 38).

Another important aspect of the *Daodejing* is its emphasis on the importance of the intangible. This is highlighted in Chapter 11:

Thirty spokes converge upon a single hub;
It is on the hole in the center that the use of the cart hinges.
We make a vessel from a lump of clay;
It is the empty space within the vessel that makes it useful.
We make doors and windows for a room;
But it is the empty spaces that make the room livable.
Thus, while the tangible has its advantages,
It is the intangible that makes it useful.

The focus on the intangible leads to the concept of *wu-wei* or non-action, whereby the ruler does not do things; rather, he causes them to happen. In a society or organisation which is focused on the Way, right things happen naturally and of their own accord without need for the ruler's intervention; the task of the latter, then, is solely to guide the organisation along the Way and in accordance with the principles of virtue.

As noted, the *Daodejing* has had and continues to have an important influence in Chinese culture. However, the principles of Daoist thought also reached the West from an early period, and were a minor but important influence in the thinking of the eighteenth-century European enlightenment, as evident in the work of *philosophes* such as Montesquieu. The school of economists known as the physiocrats, including such pioneers of modern economic thinking as Quesnay, Cantillon, Argentan and Turgot, were also influenced by these ideas. They took *wu-wei* to mean that things happened best when they happened naturally, of their own volition, rather than being compelled or forced to happen. In economic terms, then, the state was required to create conditions in which economic good would result naturally, rather than to try to lead or direct economic activity. They termed this principle *laissez-faire*. Although Adam Smith does not use the term *laissez-faire* in *The Wealth of Nations* (1776), he was strongly influenced by the physiocrats, and he takes the concept of *wu-wei* a step further: he postulates that markets, if left unhindered by government intervention, will act naturally to do good and to distribute wealth where it is needed, the famous 'invisible hand'.

Important though it is, Daoism is only one system of Chinese thought that has had an impact on business. More famous and arguably more important is Confucianism. Confucius, a contemporary of Laozi, took a very different view of society. As Chen Huan-Chang shows in his *Economic Principles of Confucius and His School* (1911), the end goal of the Confucian system, like that of Daoism, was virtue, but virtue could only be reached through direct effort. In particular economic activity, in order to remain virtuous, must be managed and controlled. Doing this is the task of sages and kings, whom Confucius advises to remain above or outside the economic system and to act as external agents; hence his often repeated call for those in positions of power to avoid personal enrichment. Most notably, whereas Western economic theory often focuses on increasing supply in order to match demand, Confucius favours curbing demand so as to meet supply. He proposes not only economic controls (such as sumptuary laws to inhibit demand for luxuries) but also the curbing of human wants through moral and social education. Himself a government minister in a north Chinese kingdom of the pre-empire period, Confucius was once asked what should be done for the betterment of the people. His answer was twofold: educate them, and make them wealthy. Education bred an understanding of the uses of wealth; wealth made possible the benefits of education, and both led to self-development. Whereas Daoist thinking led to the idea of the free market, then, Confucian thinking led to the development of a managed economy.

Still further along this continuum is the Legalist school of thought attributed to Han Feizi, the minister and ideologue who influenced the first emperor of unified China, Qin Shi Huangdi (221–206 BC). Han Feizi rejected the Confucian notion that most men tend towards the good and can be relied upon to behave ethically through a social system which exerts pressure on people to conform. To him, the only way to achieve conformity was through the rule of law. His system of thought was based on three important principles. The first of these was *fa*, meaning roughly 'prescriptive standards', but also with connotations of law and punishment. People should comply with *fa* so that their behaviour conforms with the public good, or be punished as a result. The second was *shi*, meaning 'authority' or 'power'. The exercise of *shi* is necessary to ensure compliance with *fa*; but conversely, *shi* should also be governed by the dictates of *fa* to prevent abuses of power. The third was *shu*, the technique of controlling the bureaucracy by comparing 'word' with 'deed' (or more generally, potential performance with the actuality).

Elements of all three of these systems of thought can be found in modern China today, both in the system of government and the attitude towards economic control, and in managerial methods, systems of organisation and hierarchy, and workplace relations. The study of all three is therefore necessary to understanding Chinese business culture. But more than either of the others, Daoism has had a worldwide impact. The Daoist-inspired idea of the free market, radical for the eighteenth century in the West, has had a transforming effect not only on economies but also on companies and business methods. It has spread around the world and, in an apparent irony, is now finally making a return to its homeland.

See also: **Drucker, Fukuzawa, Handy, J.P. Morgan, Ohmae, Sunzi**

Major works

There have been many translations of the *Daodejing*. Quotations in this chapter are taken from Wu's translation, which is modern and accessible.

Tao Teh Ching, trans. J.C.H. Wu, London: Shambhala, 1990.

Further reading

Lafargue is a good introduction to the composition and nature of the *Daodejing*. Clarke gives more detail on the links between *wu-wei* and *laissez-faire*. Chen, recently republished, is indispensable on classical Chinese economic thought.

Chen, H., *Economic Principles of Confucius and His School*, New York: Columbia University Press, 1911, 2 vols; repr. Bristol: Thoemmes Press, 2002.
Clarke, J.J., *The Tao of the West: Western Transformations of Taoist Thought*, London: Routledge, 2000.
Lafargue, M., 'Daodejing', in E. Craig (ed.), *Routledge Encyclopedia of Philosophy*, London: Routledge, 1998, vol. 2, pp. 779–81.

Note

1   Lao Tzu is the presentation of his name in the older Wade-Giles romanisation of Chinese; the modern *pinyin* version, Laozi, is preferred here.

WILLIAM LEVER (1851–1925)

William Lever was one of the most successful of the late Victorian industrialists, who built up his company from a tiny regional base to become one of the first true multinationals. Described as a 'born marketing man', Lever built his success on the back of powerful marketing campaigns and the creation of some of the first internationally recognised brands in consumer goods. He was one of the most respected businessmen of his day, and his management methods were admired and widely imitated in Europe and America. Although he was very much a product of his own time, many of Lever's business methods seem surprisingly modern, and in terms of abilities and reputation, he compares favourably to such giant figures of modern business as Jack Welch.

Lever was born in Bolton, Lancashire on 19 September 1851, the son of a grocer. Despite his mother's wish that he should become a doctor, he joined his father in the family firm at age sixteen and was made a partner at twenty-one. By the time he was in his late twenties he had effectively taken over the business. Lever's father had built up a moderately prosperous business, but he was conservative in his instincts and did business by traditional methods. Lever, who by 1880 at least was aware of new techniques of advertising and promotion being developed in Britain and the USA, felt that there were opportunities for growth. He began studying his customers, mainly Lancashire housewives, observing their buying habits and spending power and especially looking at the products they needed and wanted most. He first built up a wholesale grocery business based out of Bolton and then began reaching out to customers across the northwest of England, directing his advertising and promotional efforts at both his own retail customers and the end consumers.

Studying the market, Lever, now in partnership with his brother James, was convinced that there were great opportunities to be found in soap. Rising working-class incomes and improved methods of production meant that soap, once a luxury, could now be offered for sale at a price most of the population could afford. A few firms had already ventured into this market, and one in particular, Pears, had shown that advertising could be very effective. Pears's gifted young general manager, Andrew Barrett, had in the 1870s launched advertising campaigns in the London area that had made Pears almost a household word in the capital: the strapline 'Good morning! Have you used Pears today?' entered popular culture for a time, and even featured in the libretto of a West End musical. In the northwest, however, the market was still wide open.

Even before beginning production, Lever's first step was to find a brand. As was common at the time, he sought advice from a trade mark agent. Officially, the main purpose of these agents was to register trademarks, but many also provided advice and suggestions for brand names and marks. After a long discussion with his agent, Lever came away with a list of possible names, but at first he was not satisfied with any of them. He spent two days in his office, trying to come up with a better name on his own. At the end of the second day he happened to look at the list again, and realised that the name he wanted had been there all along: Sunlight.

Lever's experience in the grocery trade had taught him that the two product features housewives prized most were reliability and cheapness. To be successful, the Sunlight brand had to deliver good quality at a reasonable price. Lever worked for several years to find reliable suppliers but was never satisfied with the quality of the products, and finally decided to expand vertically and set up his own factory. In 1885 he purchased the soap works Winser & Co. in Warrington, Cheshire, and recruited several top technicians to run the factory. Lever knew nothing about making soap, but he knew how to manage the people who did; under his direction, Sunlight became known as a product of good quality that provided good value for money. Demand grew rapidly, and the Warrington plant could no longer handle the necessary production. In 1889, the Lever Brothers factory at Port Sunlight on the Mersey opened, having been purpose-built on a greenfield site along with its surrounding village, shops and support services. Port Sunlight itself was later expanded several times, and by the early twentieth century more factories were opening on other sites. Over the period 1900–14 Lever Brothers expanded overseas, acquiring production facilities for raw materials in Africa and the Pacific, and also marketing its products in continental Europe, America and Australia. By the time the First World War began the company had operations on six continents.

Lever himself began to withdraw from active management about this time. He was briefly active in politics, and served as a Liberal MP from 1906–9. He was knighted in 1911, and made a baron in 1917. He set up other business ventures, notably purchasing the islands of Lewis and Harris in the Outer Hebrides and setting up a number of companies with a view to providing local employment; his interest in the Hebrides proved short-lived, but one of his companies, MacFisheries, went on to considerable prosperity. In 1922 Lever was made Viscount Leverhulme of the Western Isles. He spent the next three years working on projects for development in the Congo, a region which he felt had great potential for growth. He died in London on 7 May 1925, shortly after returning from his second visit to the Congo. His son, the second Viscount Leverhulme, succeeded him and had an impressive career in his own right, and was for many years chairman of the Federation of British Industries (ancestor to today's Confederation of British Industry).

Lever's most notable achievements as a business manager came in the field of marketing, and one observer has commented that 'by trade Lever was a grocer, and by profession a marketing man'.[1] Charles Wilson, whose study of Lever Brothers and its successor company, Unilever, contains some very detailed descriptions of Lever's management practices, notes that Lever's advertising programmes went through two phases. The first phase, to use modern terminology, was aimed at creating *product awareness*, providing information to customers and alerting them to the potential of the product itself. Later, when soap became an accepted product and many rival brands were fighting for market share, Sunlight's advertising switched its emphasis to *brand awareness*, with the goals of retaining customers and distinguishing the brand from its rivals. In terms of actual advertisements, Lever was by no means the most innovative; other advertisers, such as Pears, put together what were probably better campaigns. But Lever knew how to exploit advertising through scale. Between 1885 and 1905 he is estimated to have spent £2 million on advertising, a huge sum for the time and far more than any of his competitors. He also used other promotional tools in tandem with advertising, including product giveaways and, especially, contests with prizes. In these latter, in order to enter the contest, entrants had to send in a certain number of soap wrappers. These methods evoked derision at first from his rivals, but as they were shown to work, contempt turned into alarm, and then into imitation. Lever was also aggressive in terms of developing new products to follow Sunlight, and between 1885 and 1914 he launched a major new brand every two years.

Lever is also known as an exemplary Victorian entrepreneur in terms of his views on social welfare. Port Sunlight, like Bournville (built near Birmingham by George Cadbury), was conceived of as a model community which would provide workers with a better standard of living. Working in the rapidly growing cities of the northwest of England where poor housing and overcrowding were the norm, Lever was particularly convinced of the need for housing reform. He himself designed and laid out the town of Port Sunlight, and for the workers' housing set out precise requirements for living space, size of gardens and other features which he considered essential to healthy living. Lever was a paternalist, who rejected profit sharing on the grounds that the workers might spend their increased wages on things which were bad for them (such as drink), and instead set up a scheme which he described as 'prosperity sharing' in which the company's profits were ploughed back into inalienable benefits for the workforce such as housing, education and welfare. These benefits came with strict controls: Lever laid down regulations for the inhabitants of Port Sunlight governing details such as prohibiting the hanging of laundry in front gardens. His own office was a panopticon-like structure in the centre of the factory with walls made of glass, so that he could see every worker and note what was going on at all times.

Although 'prosperity sharing' was possible at Port Sunlight, it was not always possible at the other plants established by Lever Brothers as the firm grew; many were in urban areas and it was not possible to provide housing. In 1909 Lever abandoned his opposition to profit sharing and introduced a system of co-partnership in which employees received preference shares in the company. Lever himself had controlled virtually all the ordinary shares since 1895, when his brother had retired on grounds of ill health, and thus there was no danger of his losing actual control; but the employees gained the further benefit of dividends. The scheme seems to have been popular, and Lever Brothers could always rely on a loyal and efficient workforce.

Like many of his contemporaries, notably the American banker J.P. **Morgan**, Lever was opposed to competition on principle. He believed that competition ultimately meant ruin for many businesses, and this was to the long-term disadvantage of the consumer. In 1899 he began a policy of amalgamation with other soap makers in both the UK and the USA, and seemed on the way to acquiring a monopoly. Unfortunately for him, his attempt came at a time when public sentiment, spurred in part by the anti-trust movement in the USA, was against monopolies. In 1906 the newspaper proprietor Lord Northcliffe launched a campaign against Lever on the grounds that his monopoly was against the public interest (although the fact that concentration in the soap industry would mean fewer advertisers and less revenue for North-cliffe's newspapers may also have been a factor). Public pressure forced Lever to abandon his consolidation strategy, but Lever did have the satisfaction of suing Northcliffe and his papers for libel and winning over £140,000 in damages, a record sum for the time.

With the consolidation strategy abandoned, Lever now sought to protect his core business in other ways. As both wholesaler and retailer, he had been confronted by the problem of ensuring that the brand image he had created was backed up by product quality. His initial answer had been to take over the manufacturing process himself. However, soap quality depended to a great extent on the quality of the ingredients with which it was made. Concerned about securing adequate stocks of high-grade palm oil in particular, Lever then embarked on further vertical integration. His first plantations in the Solomon Islands in the South Pacific were established in 1905; by 1913 he had 300,000 acres under cultivation there. In 1902 he had begun to investigate supplies of palm oil in Nigeria, and followed this up in 1911 with the securing of a major concession in the Belgian Congo, the beginning of his interest in that region. By securing his own supply chain, Lever was able to keep prices low and to manage through the periodic fluctuations in the palm oil market, while his competitors who bought their supplies on the open market were less able to manage their risk effectively.

William Lever quite literally lived for business; it was his passion and his overriding interest. Even after he stepped back from the active management of Lever Brothers, handing over much responsibility to his son, he continued to set up business ventures in Scotland and Africa. He once summed up his own business and personal philosophy as follows:

> My happiness is my business. I can see finality for myself, an end, an absolute end; but none for my business. There one has room to breathe, to grow, to expand, and the possibilities are boundless. One can go to places like the Congo, and organize, organize, organize, well, very big things indeed. But I don't work at business only for the sake of money. I am not a lover of money as money and never have been. I work at business because business is life. It enables me to do things.[2]

Another observer sums up Lever as the 'representative member of the trading middle class which created so much of the wealth and set so much of the tone of Victorian England. All the roots of Lever's being sprang from it and all its precepts and ideals were his.'[3] But that is to suggest that Lever's relevance died with him, and this is far from true. He pioneered the mass marketing and mass advertising of fast-moving consumer goods, and his methods were used by many who came after him, not least his younger contemporary William Procter of the American firm Procter & Gamble. Lever understood all the core concepts of marketing: consumer needs and perceptions of value; designing products that would provide maximum value; the importance of product quality; the importance of effective communication and branding; and how to distribute and sell products at a location and price that were suitable for the customer. All his other work – the vertical integration, the consolidation strategy, the overseas expansion, even the enlightened self-interest evident at Port Sunlight – was aimed at supporting and reinforcing the core proposition he offered to his customers. Along with Henry **Heinz**, Lever was one of the first modern marketing men.

See also: **Bat'a, Cadbury, Ford, Heinz, Owen**

Major works

Lever left behind a number of speeches and letters, but no major works.

Further reading

Wilson is the acknowledged authority on the firm and its founder. Reader's essay is excellent and widely available.

Jolly, H.P., *Lord Leverhulme: A Biography*, London: Constable, 1976.
Reader, W.J., 'Lever, William Hesketh', in D.J. Jeremy (ed.), *Dictionary of Business Biography*, London: Butterworth, 1985, vol. 3, pp. 745–51.
Wilson, C., *The History of Unilever: A Study in Economic Growth and Social Change*, London: Cassell, 1954, 2 vols.

Notes

1   W.J. Reader, 'Lever, William Hesketh', in D.J. Jeremy (ed.), *Dictionary of Business Biography*, London: Butterworth, 1985, vol. 3, p. 748.
2   Quoted in C. Wilson, *The History of Unilever*, London: Cassell, 1954, vol. 1, p. 187.
3   Reader, 'Lever, William Hesketh', p. 746.

NICCOLÒ MACHIAVELLI (1469–1527)

Machiavelli was a Florentine statesman and diplomat whose major works, *The Prince* and *Discourses on the First Decade of Livy*, are widely considered to be the founding tracts of modern political science. Condemned for centuries for apparently condoning immoral and ethical behaviour, they have been re-examined in the twentieth century and recognised for what they are, seminal studies in the nature and exercise of power in organisations. Machiavelli's writing has important implications for business strategy and for ethics, but a deeper examination of his writing shows a highly advanced awareness of how organisations function and how individuals within them behave. Over the last thirty years Machiavelli has increasingly been studied from a management perspective, and he is now regarded as an important precursor to modern strategy and organisation theory.

Niccolò Machiavelli was born in Florence on 3 May 1469, the son of a lawyer and minor noble. He began his career in the Florentine civil service when the city was ruled by Lorenzo dei Medici, son of Cosimo dei **Medici**, and kept his post following the establishment of a republic under the fundamentalist Savonarola in 1494. He again survived the fall of Savonarola in 1498 and went on to achieve high rank under the subsequent moderate republican government, serving as secretary to the body known as the Ten of War and representing Florence on diplomatic missions abroad. After the return of the Medici to power in 1512 Machiavelli was removed from office, and in

1513 he was arrested, imprisoned and tortured. Released, he retired to his country estate at San Casciano, near Florence, and it was here that he produced his most famous writings: *The Prince, Discourses on the First Decade of Livy* and *The Art of War* (only the latter was published in his own lifetime). He recovered some public favour after 1521, but the second overthrow of the Medici in 1527 led to the end of his hopes. He died on 21 June 1527 after a short illness.

Machiavelli's most famous work is *The Prince*, a short treatise on political organisation and government. It is significant in that it is the first modern work on politics and statecraft to consider these subjects outside the framework of Christian ethics. Political leadership and decision making are evaluated not in terms of whether they are ethically 'right', but whether they are ultimately to the benefit of the state. The most sensational aspect of *The Prince* is Machiavelli's view that princes may – indeed, should – be cruel and dishonest if their ultimate aim is the good of the state. It is not only acceptable but necessary to lie, to use torture and to trample over other states and cities. Machiavelli accepts that these things are in and of themselves morally wrong, but he points out that the consequences of failure – the ruin of states and the sacking of cities – can be far worse. Princes should not hesitate to use immoral methods to achieve power, if power is necessary for security and survival.

The Prince was condemned in its own time and after for its apparent amorality and its preaching of the doctrine that the ends justify the means. Machiavelli was rehabilitated in the twentieth century when James **Burnham** pointed out that he was not passing judgement on princes, merely describing a kind of *realpolitik*. Burnham commended Machiavelli for telling the truth about how power is achieved and maintained, and went so far as to describe him as a defender of freedom and liberty. Antony Jay, in his popular work *Management and Machiavelli* (1967), also takes a value-neutral approach, seeing *The Prince* as a study in the dynamics of power within and between organisations. He points out that Machiavelli is not condoning unethical behaviour *per se*, but is instead removing administration from the ethical realm. Jay sees this as an equally valid approach to business: 'The only helpful way to examine organizations and their management is as something neither moral nor immoral, but simply a phenomenon; not to look for proof that industry is honourable or dishonourable, but only for patterns of success and failure ... and for the forces which produce them.'[1] This view remains controversial, and the question of whether management is or is not a value-neutral concept has not been satisfactorily answered by either side in the debate.

Jay's argument (well presented if not always convincing) is that large multinational corporations can be compared to Renaissance city-states in terms of how they acquire and wield power: 'The twentieth-century junior manager in Shell or ICI lives in a state of voteless dependence on the favour of the great just like the sixteenth-century Italian.'[2] This is the most common approach to the study of Machiavelli from a management point of view. For example, social psychologists such as Christie and Geis have used Machiavelli's principles to construct a typology of personal behaviour in organisations, and Adrian Furnham has commented more recently that individuals within organisations may similarly use Machiavellian principles to further their own interests at the expense of those around them.

The Prince can also be viewed as a study of the nature of leadership, and there are strong implications here for strategy. An often-discussed component of Machiavelli's thought is that of *virtú* (ability or capacity), which is the prime requisite of a successful leader; it is *virtú* that allows leaders to recognise and seize opportunities and to outthink and outfight their opponents. He recognises an important role for *fortuna* (serendipity or luck), in that unexpected events can upset even the most carefully laid plans. The nineteenth-century Prussian writer on strategy, Karl von Clausewitz, was very much influenced by Machiavelli, and the idea of *fortuna* can be seen in Clausewitz's concept of 'friction', the concatenation of unforeseen events and forces that interferes with the execution of plans. Machiavelli maintains that a sufficiency of *virtú* allows leaders to recognise when chance has given them an opportunity, and to take advantage of *fortuna* by reacting quicker than competitors or opponents. It is not clear whether *virtú* is an inherent capacity or whether it can be learned.

The emphasis on power and leadership in Machiavellian thought derives mostly from the study of *The Prince*, and is not entirely representative of his own views. The *Discourses on the First Decade of Livy*, a much more substantial work, offers many lessons for managers as well, ones which are probably even more relevant to the modern day. *Virtú*, Machiavelli says here, can be resident in organisations and peoples, not just in individuals. When this is the case, leadership by a strong dictator should be supplanted by popular systems which allow participation by all, such as democracy. And although leaders can use the kinds of strong methods described in *The Prince*, equally they should also take measures to secure the support of the populace and ensure participation. He contrasts two forms of rule, tyranny and the republic, and while recognising the weakness of each, believes that the latter offers more advantages in terms of flexible organisation and the ability to adapt to changing circumstances. That circumstances do change is a frequent theme (here Machiavelli introduces *fortuna* once more), and in a passage that strongly resembles later evolutionary theory of organisations, he argues that states must continue to grow and expand, or else they will weaken and die; maintaining the *status quo* is a strategy doomed to failure.

Machiavelli's arguments for participation make clear the nature and importance of organisational commitment, while his argument for political and governmental forms to be dynamic and adaptable according to circumstance and aims, also foreshadows the concept of organisational 'fit' developed in the second half of the twentieth century. Both his major works have important lessons for modern managers, and though the importance of the *Discourses* in particular is often understated, both have been major influences in how we think today about leadership, organisation, purpose and power.

See also: **Burnham, Chandler, Emerson, Medici, Mooney**

Major works

Two quite different books need to be read together to understand Machiavelli: *The Prince* is famous for its argument that the ends justify the means, while the *Discourses* are equally important in their argument for participation, commitment and popular support.

Il principe (The Prince), trans. G. Bull, Harmondsworth: Penguin, 1961.
Discorsi sopra la prima deca di Tito Livio (Discourses on the First Decade of Livy), ed. B. Crick, trans. L.J. Walker as *The Discourses*, Harmondsworth: Penguin, 1970.

Further reading

Jay is the best known study of Machiavellian principles in management. Price is a good summary, but concentrates too much on *The Prince* and not enough on the *Discourses*. Gilbert shows Machiavelli's importance to modern strategy and leadership.

Burnham, J. *The Machiavellians: Defenders of Freedom*, London: Putnam, 1943.
Christie, R. and Geis, F., *Studies in Machiavellianism*, New York: Academic Press, 1970.
Furnham, A., 'Beware the Big Mach', *Financial Times Mastering Management Review* 13, 1999, pp. 10–11.
Gilbert, F., 'Machiavelli: The Renaissance of the Art of War', in P. Paret (ed.), *Makers of Modern Strategy*, Princeton, NJ: Princeton University Press, 1986, pp. 11–31.
Jay, A., *Management and Machiavelli*, London: Hodder & Stoughton, 1967.
Price, R., 'Machiavelli, Niccolò', in M. Warner (ed.), *International Encyclopedia of Business and Management*, London: Routledge, 1996, vol. 3, pp. 2607–13.

Notes

1   A. Jay, *Management and Machiavelli*, London: Hodder & Stoughton, 1967, p. 35.
2   *Ibid.*, p. 26.

MARSHALL McLUHAN (1911–80)

Marshall McLuhan was one of the great thinkers of the twentieth century on communication and culture. He coined two concepts which have entered both academic thinking and popular imagination: 'the global village', referring to the increasing trend towards world-wide cultural convergence, and 'the medium is the message', referring to the impact of technology on communications. He was himself a superb and innovative communicator, easily bridging the gap between academia and popular culture, and his work at the Centre for Culture and Technology in Toronto both made his academic reputation and turned him into a pop icon in the 1960s. His works on the relationship between culture and communication have had considerable influence on advertising and marketing, and his work has also had an influence on the ongoing debate over globalisation.

Herbert Marshall McLuhan was born in Edmonton, Alberta on 21 July 1911. He attended the University of Manitoba, where he took BA and MA degrees, and then went to Britain to take his PhD at the University of Cambridge. From 1936 onward he taught at a series of US universities including the University of Wisconsin, the University of St Louis and Assumption University. In 1946 he moved to the University of Toronto, where he was made a professor in 1952. His work in Toronto in the 1960s made his academic reputation and turned him into a pop icon; his books, including *The Mechanical Bride* (1951), *The Gutenberg Galaxy* (1962), *War and Peace in the Global Village* (1968) and *Culture is Our Business* (1970), sold widely around the world. A superb communicator himself, McLuhan also contributed a number of journal and newspaper articles and had a high media profile. In 1977 he appeared in a cameo role as himself in the Woody Allen film *Annie Hall*.

Among his other posts, McLuhan chaired the Ford Foundation Seminar on Culture and Communication from 1953 to 1955, and founded the Centre for Culture and Technology at the University of Toronto in 1963. In 1973 he was appointed by the Vatican as a consultant to the Pontifical Commission for Social Communication. He was widely consulted by world leaders including US president

Jimmy Carter and Canadian prime minister Pierre Trudeau. Active to the end, he was working on several books and a conference lecture at the time of his death.

McLuhan's work was characterised by three principal themes. The first is the concept of art as cognition, referring to the symbolic meanings to be found in visual messages ranging from art to advertising. The second is that technology is an extension of man; the content of any message is inevitably affected by the technology used to communicate it. Third, McLuhan believed that human development had passed through two ages, the primitive and the industrial or 'typographical', and had now entered a third age, the technological.

In *The Mechanical Bride*, McLuhan explores the relationship between art and popular culture by deconstructing a series of print advertisements, showing the symbolic elements present in each. His conclusion is that advertisements are a kind of folklore. Returning to this theme in *Culture is Our Business*, he describes advertisements as 'the cave art of the twentieth century'.[1] His views on advertising were not always laudatory:

> Ours is the first age in which many thousands of the best-trained individual minds have made it a full-time business to get inside the collective public mind. To get inside in order to manipulate, exploit, control is the object now. And to generate heat not light is the intention. To keep everybody in the helpless state engendered by prolonged mental rutting is the effect of many ads and much entertainment alike.[2]

Understanding Media (1964) marked McLuhan's first major exploration of the second theme, the impact of technology on media. The text of this book begins:

> In a culture like ours, long accustomed to splitting and dividing all things as a means of control, it is sometimes a bit of a shock to be reminded that, in operational and practical fact, the medium is the message. This is merely to say that the personal and social consequences of any medium – that is, any extension of ourselves – result from the new scale that is introduced into our affairs by each extension of ourselves, or by any new technology.[3]

McLuhan goes on to describe the negative and positive effects of this principle. Automation, for example, eliminates jobs; it also, he claims, creates new roles for people in relation to their work, replacing associations destroyed by the immediately preceding mechanical revolution. The same point is made with relation to media; mankind graduated from an oral to a written culture through the introduction of the printing press, but television and radio were now returning people to an oral culture.

This concept of a circular process, or of humanity returning to an earlier way of life through technology, is the third major theme in McLuhan's work. 'If Gutenberg technology retrieved the ancient world and dumped it in the lap of the Renaissance,' he wrote, 'electric technology has retrieved the primal, archaic worlds, past and present, private and corporate, and dumped them on the western doorstep for processing.'[4]

The best summary of the fundamentals of McLuhan's thought can probably be found in *Laws of Media* published in 1988, some years after his death. The original intention was to produce a second edition of *Understanding Media*, but the analysis goes far deeper than the original book. Here, McLuhan defines four fundamental principles which have ramifications for communicators in every field, including – especially – advertising. They are:

1   Every technology extends some organ or faculty of the user.
2   When one area of experience is heightened or intensified, another is diminished or numbed.
3   Every form, pushed to the limit of its potential, changes its characteristics.
4   The content of any medium is an older medium (i.e. new media subsume all older forms of media).

At the nexus of the interrelationship between culture, communication and technology is the theme of globalisation, especially cultural globalisation but probably extending to the economic and political spheres as well. McLuhan argued that advances in communications technology were increasing the reach of media to the extent that global communications and global culture were now a possibility, and in the 1960s he coined the phrase 'the global village' to describe this phenomenon. He believed that human development has passed through two ages: the primitive, which has existed before the introduction of mass communication; and the industrial or 'typographical', which has succeeded the invention of the mechanical printing press by Gutenberg in the fifteenth century. By the end of the Second World War, this age too was passing and a third age, the technological, was beginning, ushered in by the appearance of broadcast media such as radio and television but also by continuing advances in print media such as photography.

The speed and reach of these new media were making the broadcasting of global messages possible. Merging the two concepts of the global village and 'the medium is the message', we see a technologically defined world in which the ability to communicate is as important as the message being communicated. This principle has, if anything, become more important as time has gone on.

McLuhan's main impact in managerial terms has been in the fields of marketing and advertising. Barry Day's study of McLuhan's relevance to advertising remains important, commenting that 'McLuhan is saying something that every good advertising man senses for himself, though rarely crystallizes or formalizes to anything like this extent.'[5] That the medium used can have a greater impact than the message is clearly a concept of vital importance for advertisers. Day spells out five points from McLuhan's work which advertisers need to take into account:

1   advertising must be alive to its environment;
2   advertisers must try to predict the environment;
3   each medium should be used for what it can do best;
4   the audience should participate as far as possible;
5   the picture should always tell the 'real' story.

McLuhan's views on the importance of language and symbol are less well known but equally important. The importance of technological media in the 1990s, as satellite television girdles the globe, is easy to see, but McLuhan defined media as any 'extension of self' and thus by definition included more mundane forms of communication. Language, he felt, was the most powerful metaphor of all. The late Pierre Trudeau, formerly prime minister of Canada and an admirer of McLuhan, noted in a letter to him that: 'the *effects* of language as media are quite different from the input or intended meanings. All inputs have side effects which are usually considered irrelevant by the speaker or sender.'[6]

McLuhan's work is open to criticism. Like most modernists, he greatly overestimated the immediate impact of the printing press, and greatly underestimated the penetration of the written word before Gutenberg; as a result, he placed more emphasis on the technology and less on the education required to use it. Education, not technology, has always been the key barrier to the assimilation of written words. His strong focus on media meant that at times McLuhan also ignored the impact of other forms of technology; the revolution in travel may have done as much to create a 'global village' as the revolution in communication. Interestingly, McLuhan also failed to foresee how the computer revolution would develop, giving people the ability to manipulate and control the media before and as it reached them. From the medium is the message, we are now moving towards a paradigm where the viewer is the medium. Nevertheless, McLuhan remains one of the seminal thinkers of his age, one whose views continue to resonate both in business management and in society more broadly.

See also: **Boisot, Gates, Hofstede, Kotler, Ohmae, Simon**

Major works

McLuhan was a prolific writer whose books are often imaginative in terms of layout as well as content. Recommended from a management perspective are the following:

The Mechanical Bride: Folklore of Industrial Man, New York: Vanguard, 1951.
The Gutenberg Galaxy, New York: McGraw-Hill, 1962.
Understanding Media: The Extensions of Man, London: Routledge and Kegan Paul, 1964.
(With Q. Fiore) *War and Peace in the Global Village*, New York: McGraw-Hill, 1968.
Culture is Our Business, New York: McGraw-Hill, 1970.
(With E. McLuhan) *Laws of Media: The New Science*, Toronto: University of Toronto Press, 1988.

Further reading

There have been some excellent studies of McLuhan. Day, as noted, explores his relevance to advertising, while Neill and Curtis offer good critiques. Sanderson and McDonald is a collection of articles, and Molinaro *et al.* is McLuhan's collected correspondence, which also offers insights. Lewis Mumford presents a different, less optimistic look at the global village (Mumford was a fierce critic of McLuhan).

Curtis, J.M., *Culture as Polyphony: An Essay on the Nature of Paradigms*, Columbia, MO: University of Missouri Press, 1978.
Day, B., *The Message of Marshall McLuhan*, London: Lintas, 1967.
Molinaro, M., McLuhan, C. and Boyd, W. (eds), *Letters of Marshall McLuhan*, Toronto: Oxford University Press, 1987.
Mumford, L., *The City in History*, New York: Harcourt, Brace & World, 1961.

Neill, S.D., *Clarifying McLuhan: An Assessment of Process and Product*, Westport, CT: Greenwood Press, 1993.

Sanderson, G. and Macdonald, F. (eds), *Marshall McLuhan: The Man and His Message*, Golden, CA: Fulcrum, 1989.

Notes

1   M. McLuhan, *Culture is Our Business*, New York: McGraw-Hill, 1970, p. 7.
2   M. McLuhan, *The Mechanical Bride*, New York: Vanguard, 1951, p. v.
3   M. McLuhan, *Understanding Media*, London: Routledge and Kegan Paul, 1964, p. 7.
4   *Culture is Our Business*, p. 7.
5   B. Day, *The Message of Marshall McLuhan*, London: Lintas, 1967, p. 1.
6   M. Molinaro, C. McLuhan and W. Boyd (eds), *Letters of Marshall McLuhan*, Toronto: Oxford University Press, 1987, p. 542.

ABRAHAM MASLOW (1908–70)

Abraham Maslow was a psychologist who founded what later became known as the humanistic school of psychology. His principal subject of study was human motivation. He is most famous today for developing his 'hierarchy of needs', which explains people's motivation and behaviour as the results of different sets of needs which drive them. Although Maslow's ideas were not immediately accepted by his fellow psychologists, they were picked up and adapted by a number of prominent organisation theorists, notably Rensis Likert, Frederick Herzberg and Douglas McGregor, who used the hierarchy of needs to explain many aspects of organisation behaviour. The hierarchy of needs concept also has important implications for marketing in explaining consumer behaviour. It remains a highly important concept in both fields.

Maslow was born in New York City on 1 April 1908, the son of Russian immigrants. He studied psychology at the University of Wisconsin, completing his BA in 1930 and his PhD in 1934. He taught psychology at Brooklyn College from 1937 to 1951, and then moved to Brandeis University where he set up and chaired the psychology department. In 1961 he retired from Brandeis and moved to California, where he worked with several research centres. He died at Menlo Park, California on 8 June 1970.

Maslow's intellectual influences were many, and included not only the psychology of Freud and Wilhelm Reich, but also the Gestalt theories of Kurt Goldstein and the pragmatic philosophy of William James and John Dewey. His work on human motivation began in the 1940s; its first full exposition came in his book *Motivation and Personality* (1954). Rejecting both the psychoanalytical and behavioural schools of psychology, Maslow sought an explanation for human motivation in the inner core that he felt all humans possessed. This inner core is not inherited or genetic: indeed, Maslow strongly rejects biological determinism. Rather, it is composed of a complex assortment of feelings, emotions, desires, needs and wants. Everyone has this core, but its composition can differ from person to person, and it manifests itself in each individual in different ways at different times. Our needs are not static, says Maslow; as we satisfy one need, others on the hierarchy then become more manifest and must be satisfied in turn. This work was considered highly unorthodox at the time of its publication, so much so that for a time Maslow was virtually ostracised in the American psychological community; it was not until much later that he was recognised as a true pioneer in psychology and his work given the attention it deserved.

The hierarchy of needs suggests that all human beings are motivated to undertake actions – including purchasing goods and services, and going to work – by their inner needs. These needs can be classified into various types. Not every type of need is of equal importance at any given time: Maslow says that some needs will always override others. Once these dominant needs are satisfied, however, other needs then demand attention and our behaviour changes as we seek to satisfy these. For example, when we are hungry, that need tends to override all others and our behaviour is dominated by the need for food. Once we have eaten, however, the need for food is satisfied and then other needs come into play. This progression from one set of needs to another results in a 'hierarchy' of needs. Where we are on this hierarchy at any given moment determines much of our motivation and actions, both as consumers and in the workplace.

Maslow grouped our needs into five categories in ascending order:

1   physiological needs;
2   safety needs;
3   belongingness and love needs;
4   esteem needs;
5   self-actualisation needs.

Those needs at the bottom of the hierarchy are the most prepotent; that is, they override other needs further up the hierarchy. They are also, in most ordinary life, the needs most easily met. Those at or near the top are the most complex and difficult to satisfy; indeed, many people never get as far as the fifth stage of the hierarchy.

Physiological needs are requirements for the basic things that allow us to live, such as air, water and food. We may lack many things in life, but if we lack food, we will probably choose to eat before doing anything else. Moreover, as Maslow notes, we will choose to make the search for food the most important thing in our lives, and, depending on how hungry we are, this desire for food will tend to override other ideas which we might otherwise think of as important, such as freedom, love, ethical behaviour towards our fellows and so on. In economic terms, a hungry man will buy food before he buys a car; a hungry woman will take a job for lower wages than one who has enough to eat.

However, once the need for food and other basic necessities for life to continue are filled, our outlook changes. As soon as physiological needs are met, says Maslow, then 'at once other (and higher) needs emerge, and these, rather than physiological hungers, dominate the organism'.[1] The next set of needs constitute what Maslow terms *safety needs*. These can be described generally as the need for physical security for ourselves and those we are close to, which manifests itself in a desire for security, stability, law and order, and freedom from physical threat. In civilised societies where the threat of physical violence is comparatively rare, we can still see safety needs manifested in areas such as desire for job stability and security, the need for protection against illness and old age through insurance and pensions, and so on. Safety needs also manifest themselves more generally in a common preference for familiar over unfamiliar things and an avoidance of situations where we are uncertain or do not know how to react.

Once physiological and safety needs are satisfied, there then emerges a third set of needs, for *belongingness and love*, sometimes also referred to in Maslow's later writings as 'social needs'. Fourth comes the need for self-esteem. This is actually a complex set of needs, and Maslow breaks it down into two parts:

> first, the desire for strength, for achievement, for adequacy, for mastery and competence, for confidence in the face of the world, and for independence and freedom. Second, we have what we may call the desire for reputation and prestige ... status, fame and glory, dominance, recognition, attention, importance, dignity, or appreciation ... Satisfaction of the

self-esteem need leads to feelings of self-confidence, worth, strength, capability, and adequacy, of being useful and necessary in the world. But thwarting of these needs produces feelings of inferiority, of weakness, and of helplessness.[2]

Ultimately, says Maslow, failure to satisfy these needs when they are dominant can lead to neurosis and personality breakdown.

Last of all, highest in the order, there is the need for *self-actualisation*. Maslow borrows this term from the Gestalt theories of Kurt Goldstein, but similar terms also exist in Daoist and Buddhist psychology. In essence, even if our physical and social needs are met, even if we are well fed, safe and secure, love and are loved, and have respect and sense of worth, there exists something more; a need to do what we feel we are called to do. The drive for self-actualisation does not exist in everyone, and exists more powerfully in some people than in others. In those for whom self-actualisation is a strong force, however, there will be a driving force to achieve something on which the person places a high personal value. Great entrepreneurs are driven by this need, as are many political and religious leaders and great humanitarians.

The hierarchy of needs appears to be a simple concept, but Maslow warns against treating it as such: there are a number of complicating factors. The hierarchy of needs describes our *basic* needs, but there are also others which stand outside the hierarchy: Maslow lists for example the desire to know and understand, and also aesthetic needs (for beauty, attractive surroundings and so on). He also points out that the hierarchy of basic needs is not fixed; for some people, for example, self-esteem needs are more important than social needs and will be actualised earlier. In most cases, however, these variances in the hierarchy are indications of pathological personalities. Needs can also be influenced by culture; that is to say, the relative importance and nature of various needs may depend on the culture into which the individual has been born or is currently living. Finally, Maslow says that a need does not have to be 100 per cent satisfied for the next need in the hierarchy to become dominant: thus a starving man does not have to completely satiate his hunger before he begins to consider his needs for safety, nor do our needs for belongingness need to be completely filled before we seek esteem. This leads to situations where multiple needs may be present in varying degrees, and this is especially true as we move more towards the higher end of the hierarchy.

This description of the hierarchy of needs, though necessarily simplified, shows how it can be a very powerful tool for understanding human motivation in business and economic contexts. The social psychologist Frederick Herzberg, for example, used Maslow's concepts when studying motivation at work to develop a dual scale of motivational factors: inner or actualisation factors, in which the worker is motivated by internal needs, and atmosphere or 'hygiene' factors in which the worker is motivated by external stimuli. Herzberg thus succeeded in filling an important gap in organisation theory, which had previously focused in large part on environmental stimuli, and had failed to account for inner human needs. More famously, Douglas McGregor's development of Theory X and Theory Y is based on Maslow's concept, with Theory X representing the bottom of the hierarchy or physiological needs and Theory Y the top end or social/ psychological needs.

Marketers too have become interested in the hierarchy of needs. In practical marketing terms it has become customary to talk of the 'bundle of benefits' attached to a product or service; it is perceived that consumers often make purchases to satisfy several needs simulta- neously, and when faced with a choice among products or brands will usually buy the one capable of satisfying the greatest number of needs at once. Thus a car buyer who considers safety as his or her primary need will buy the car that has the most safety features (or alternatively, the cheapest car so as to minimise financial risk); the buyer who emphasises belongingness needs will buy the car that will earn him or her the greatest admiration and respect of friends, family and colleagues; and the buyer who emphasises self-esteem needs will buy the car that makes him or her feel good about themself. Motivation theory has been applied in this way in both consumer research and in the design of advertising and promotions.

The hierarchy of needs is not by any means a complete explanation for motivation in either the workplace or the marketplace, but as a starting point for understanding how people behave *en masse*, it has proved its worth. The challenge, of course, is to find out what motivates people at a given time, which depends in turn on where they are on the hierarchy of needs and which set of needs is dominating or overriding the others. Often companies will choose simple responses: for example, relocating plants to developing countries where workers are likely to be motivated by lower level needs and will work for less money (and with fewer complaints about infringements of workers' rights and health and safety rules, perhaps). But there are other, more complex ways of using the hierarchy as a tool for assessing the needs and motivations of individuals. Research into this complex concept is still ongoing, and will have much more to tell us in the future.

See also: **Argyris, Kotler, Morgan, Simon**

Major works

Motivation and Personality is the work that first sets out the full hierarchy of needs. *Towards a Psychology of Being* is more 'pure' psychology, but still of interest to management. *The Farther Reaches of Human Nature* is a collection of articles put together shortly before Maslow's death and published posthumously.

Motivation and Personality, New York: Harper & Bros, 1954.
Towards a Psychology of Being, Princeton, NJ: Van Nostrand, 1962.
The Farther Reaches of Human Nature, New York: Viking, 1971.

Further reading

Rose includes an excellent study of Maslow's influence. McGregor and Herzberg are foundations texts for modern organisation theory.

Goldstein, K., *The Organism*, New York: American Book Company, 1939.
Herzberg, F., *Work and the Nature of Man*, Cleveland, OH: World Publishing Co., 1966.
McGregor, D., *The Human Side of Enterprise*, New York: McGraw-Hill, 1960.
Rose, M., *Industrial Behaviour: Theoretical Development since Taylor*, London: Penguin, 1978.

Notes

1   A. Maslow, *Motivation and Personality*, New York: Harper & Bros, 1954, p. 38.
2   *Ibid.*, p. 45.

MATSUSHITA KONOSUKE (1894–1989)

Matsushita Konosuke is known in Japan as the 'god of management'. From an impoverished background, he founded a small electronics business and built this into a global corporation, becoming Japan's richest man. His philosophy of management, based around the concept of 'peace through prosperity' included such concepts as low-priced, mass-produced consumer goods to enhance the quality of everyday living, mutual support and respect between the corporation and its employees, and close relations with distributors and customers.

His ideas were widely admired and imitated in Japan, and in the 1980s became popular in the USA and Europe as well.

Matsushita was born in the Wakayama Prefecture on 27 November 1894. His father had been a prosperous landowner, but managed to bankrupt the family through a disastrous speculation in the rice market when Matsushita was five years old. At age nine, as the family was no longer able to support him, he went on his own to Osaka and took a job with a maker of *hibachis* (charcoal braziers). Later he worked for a bicycle maker, which gave him his first experience of working with machinery. As he himself later noted, working for these small shops also gave him an understanding of business and of how markets worked; throughout his later career, Matsushita always showed great understanding of the problems facing small suppliers and retailers.

The introduction of electric street lighting and trams in Osaka fascinated him, and at age fifteen he took a job with the Osaka Electric Light Company as an assistant electrician. By twenty-three he was an inspector, his practical knowledge of electrical engineering supplemented by a series of night school courses. With his wife and his brother-in-law as partners, Matsushita decided to set up his own business, initially named Matsushita Electric Company, working out of his own apartment. Initially he made electric sockets and plugs, and did good business. Real success came, however, with the development of a battery-powered bicycle lamp, which he made and sold under the brand name National. This was an instant success, and Matsushita prospered through the 1920s. Further diversification into other electrical goods, including irons and radios, followed. The initial impact of the Great Depression initially hit the company hard, as demand for consumer goods dried up, but Matsushita persuaded his workforce to take a pay cut – as an alternative to forced lay-offs – and redoubled his marketing efforts. The company's fortunes soon recovered, and it converted into a joint stock company in 1935.

During the Second World War Matsushita, like other electrical goods and electronics makers, was perforce involved in wartime production. As a result, following the defeat of Japan and the occupation of the country by Allied forces, Matsushita was proscribed by the Allied occupation administration headed by General Douglas MacArthur. Matsushita himself was removed from his post at the head of the company, and plans were drawn up for its dissolution. The company union, then involved in negotiating with management for a wage increase, broke off its campaign to present a petition – with over 15,000 names – to the authorities on behalf of Matsushita workers, urging that the founder be reinstated. Startled by the novelty of workers petitioning to keep a chief executive rather than have one sacked, the authorities gave in and allowed Matsushita to stay. However his activities were under legal restriction until 1951, when the outbreak of the Korean War meant that the USA had urgent need of Japanese allies and Japanese electronics goods; only then were the last restrictions on Matsushita lifted.

Matsushita responded by immediately increasing production and looking for new markets, especially in the USA. Forbidden to make alliances with other Japanese firms, he made them overseas instead, setting up a licensing and marketing agreement with the Dutch electronics maker Philips in 1952. Already involved in radios, Matsushita expanded into the whole range of consumer electrical goods including washing machines, refrigerators, vacuum cleaners, electric stoves and irons, water heaters and, soon after, televisions. Initially, low labour costs in Japan allowed Matsushita competitive advantage in world markets; when wages began to rise, he was one of the first Japanese entrepreneurs to appreciate the competitive advantages of locating production in Southeast Asia. As financial restrictions eased, the corporation began to diversify still further, buying up or taking major stakes in many other Japanese firms in other industrial sectors.

One of Matsushita's last strategic decisions was the outwitting of his rival **Ibuka** Masaru at Sony over the introduction of the videocassette recorder. Sony, as was its wont, was ahead of the market in terms of new product development, and launched the Betamax system ahead of any of its rivals. The Matsushita subsidiary JVC was then working on a rival system, VHS. Matsushita persuaded JVC's management to delay launching VHS, taking time to work out defects in the product and get it as close to Betamax standards as possible, and then launch it as a mass-produced and mass-market consumer good. The strategy worked: arguably an inferior product, VHS was supported by Matsushita's superior production, marketing and distribution facilities, and ended up dominating the market and becoming the industry standard.

Matsushita Konosuke retired from the corporation in 1973, though he remained on the board as a 'special advisor' and continued to have influence. Much of his later work was devoted to a charitable foundation, the Peace and Happiness Through Prosperity Institute, which he had founded in 1946. In the 1960s he set up a second foundation, the purpose of which was to educate and train Japan's future business and political leaders. He also became involved with overseas academic institutions, endowing a chair in management at the

Sloan School of Management, of the Massachusetts Institute of Technology. He died in Osaka on 27 March 1989.

As a manager, Matsushita was highly observant and borrowed freely whenever he found good managerial ideas in other companies. An early admirer of Henry **Ford**, he read Ford's books and followed many of his ideas on mass production. With the Model T, Ford believed that mass production could provide goods at much lower cost and therefore lower retail price, bringing what had once been luxury items into the reach of millions. Matsushita followed a similar approach, and was an early Japanese convert to the idea of mass production. He adopted the multi-divisional form or M-form used at Du Pont and General Motors, among others, to facilitate rapid expansion in the 1930s. He was a great admirer of the Toyota system of production developed by **Toyoda** Kiichiro and his managers, in particular just-in-time methods, where again he was an early adopter.

Yet he also had his own strong philosophy of management, and following his retirement, Matsushita wrote a number of books disseminating this philosophy. This was composed of two major elements: the notion of peace and happiness through prosperity, and the idea of close and harmonious relationships between all major stakeholders, including workers, customers and suppliers.

As described above, Matsushita had grown up in poverty, and his early life had been full of hardship. He was not alone in this. The Westernisation and industrialisation of Japan following the Meiji Restoration of 1868 had greatly increased Japan's prosperity as a nation, but that prosperity had been unequally distributed. In Matsushita's youth, urban poverty and low standards of living had been the norm. Although in his writings he does not explicitly make the link between poverty and early twentieth-century Japanese militarism, the link can be made nonetheless. Japanese expansion into Asia was designed by the country's military rulers in part to take the people's mind off the domestic situation, and partly to create new markets in the occupied territories for Japanese-made goods which would lead to greater prosperity at home. Matsushita, indeed, benefited from this policy for a time in the late 1930s, one of the factors that led to his proscription in 1946.

The war showed the futility of increasing prosperity through military expansion. Instead, said Matsushita, Japan should attempt to become prosperous through internal development of markets and through production of low-cost, high-quality goods that would improve the standard of living for ordinary Japanese. That philosophy can be seen expressed in the range of goods Matsushita produced:

domestic appliances, radios and televisions, and so on. This is sometimes known as the 'tap water philosophy', the belief that consumer goods should be as cheap and readily available as water coming from a tap. Prosperity was best achieved through a spirit of mutual harmony and cooperation, said Matsushita, and in this drive for prosperity, it was up to businessmen and corporations to lead the way. Other industrialists agreed, and the result by the 1980s was a booming economy in which Japanese citizens enjoyed one of the highest standards of living in the world.

Harmony and cooperation were the linchpin of the other half of his philosophy as well. Matsushita had early on developed good relations with his employees, treating them as a family and urging all to pull together for the good of the company. The sense of corporate solidarity so noted by Western observers of Japanese companies in the 1960s through to the 1980s had its origins in part at Matsushita, which was one of the first firms to have its own company song, for example. Matsushita asked for the loyalty of his workers, but gave them his own loyalty in return. He paid high wages and offered good employee benefits, and (not surprising, perhaps, given the events of 1946) supported and encouraged the company union, which he saw not as an opponent but as a vehicle for encouraging worker–manager cooperation.

This approach extended to relationships outside the company as well. Encouraged by the experience of Toyota, Matsushita began developing his own just-in-time supply system in the 1950s. Typically, he did so by forging closer links with his suppliers and asking for their cooperation in order to achieve mutual prosperity, rather than by laying down rules. His strong sense of customer orientation extended to distributors and retailers as well as end consumers, and as early as the 1930s, he had begun laying the groundwork for a complex but highly effective distribution network involving thousands of small retailers across the country. This effective distribution system was one of the company's greatest competitive strengths – as his successors found to their cost when they tried to dismantle it.

Matsushita had many virtues as a manager, including innovation, flexibility, excellent relationship management skills and a fine strategic sense. What was perhaps most impressive about him, however, is that he was able to think about management in a truly holistic way, not just as a series of functions, but as a single integrated activity with an overriding, guiding purpose and social role. He is one of the few thinkers on management whose ideas can truly be said to constitute a philosophy. Early in his career, Matsushita worked out what management was *for*, and used those principles to guide him to his destination: peace and prosperity.

See also: **Bat'a, Fukuzawa, Heinz, Ibuka, Lever, Mooney, Ohmae, Toyoda**

Major works

Matsushita's Peace and Happiness Through Prosperity Institute in Tokyo has produced translations of a number of his writings. The volumes below are nearly all selections from original works, rather than full translations of the originals. They are often hard to find, but are worth reading where they can be found.

Not for Bread Alone, Tokyo: PHP Institute, 1984.
Quest for Prosperity: The Life of a Japanese Industrialist, Tokyo: PHP Institute, 1988.
As I See It, Tokyo: PHP Institute, 1989.
People before Products, Tokyo: PHP Institute, 1992.

Further reading

Gould and Rafferty are both recommended reading. Pascale and Athos helped bring the basics of the Matsushita philosophy to the West: Pascale, a former McKinsey & Co. consultant and now an academic, was an admirer.

Gould, R., *The Matsushita Phenomenon*, Tokyo: Diamond Sha, 1970.
Pascale, R.T. and Athos, A.G., *The Art of Japanese Management*, Harmondsworth: Penguin, 1982.
Rafferty, K., *Inside Japan's Power Houses: The Culture, Mystique and Future of Japan's Greatest Corporations*, London: Weidenfeld and Nicolson.

COSIMO DEI MEDICI (1389–1464)

Cosimo dei Medici created a diversified multinational company and invented the multidivisional form or M-form of business organisation 400 years before it was defined by Alfred **Chandler**. In an age when communications technology was limited to the speed of the fastest horse or ship, Cosimo controlled an organisation with assets across Western Europe and the Middle East, and with trading links as far afield as China and Iceland. He did so by setting up a decentralised organisation with professional management and a system of contractual arrangements which made the restructuring of business units easy and quick to adapt to changing circumstances. Many of the methods of organisation and control used by businesses as late as the twentieth century were pioneered or developed at the Medici Bank.

Cosimo dei Medici was born in Florence on 27 September 1389, the son of Giovanni de Bicci dei Medici, a wealthy merchant and leading citizen of the city. He was educated at the monastery school of Santa Maria degli Angeli where, as well as the basic curriculum, he studied languages including German, French, Greek and Arabic. The education at the monastery was of a strongly humanistic nature, imbued with the ideals of the Italian Renaissance, and Cosimo developed a lifelong interest in philosophy and the arts.

Giovanni de Bicci dei Medici had taken over a small banking and foreign exchange business from his father and had built it up into one of the leading banks in Italy. He had also diversified into textiles production. In 1414, Cosimo joined the business on a full-time basis and was sent first to visit the various banking branch offices in Italy to learn the trade, and later to northern Europe to study the opportunities for business expansion there. After two years of a kind of informal apprenticeship, in 1416 he was appointed general manager of the important Rome branch of the bank, which handled loans to the Papal Curia and other important figures there. In 1419 he was recalled to Florence and made a member of the *maggiori*, the senior partners who controlled the Medici Bank and its subsidiaries. By the early 1420s he was the overall general manager, as his father relinquished many duties and began to retire (Giovanni dei Medici died in 1429).

Under Cosimo's management, the Medici Bank became a truly international business. As well as four branches in Italy – Rome, Milan, Pisa and Venice – branches were opened in Geneva (later transferred to Lyons), Avignon, Bruges and London, and agency relationships were set up in Barcelona, Valencia and several ports in the Eastern Mediterranean, notably Alexandria. Medici agents operated in Scandinavia and Iceland, purchasing furs, fish and tallow. Their network of client relationships was also very strong in the Middle East, expanding up the Spice Road to the Orient with agents in important markets such as Aleppo, Tabriz and Hormuz, and the name of Medici was known to bankers in India and China.

The Medici firm diversified still further, into wool and silk textile manufacturing and especially into the production of alum, a scarce mineral which was used as a fixative in dying cloth and also formed an ingredient in many pharmaceuticals. By the mid-fifteenth century the Medici had organised a cartel which had a virtual monopoly on the mining and production of alum in Europe. They also diversified their banking operations to include not only foreign exchange but also investments and insurance. Their large geographical network allowed them to become involved in international trade, though usually as financiers of shipments rather than as actual transporters, and they were an important element in the growth of international trade between northern and southern Europe in the fifteenth century, particularly in the importation of high-quality English wool into Italy and the export of silks to the north.

In the early 1430s, as the business grew and became more complex, Cosimo restructured it into a form which Raymond de Roover calls a prototypical holding company, but which also bears a strong resemblance to the multi-divisional form (M-form) adopted by early twentieth-century American corporations.[1] The main holding company was the Medici Bank, directed by Cosimo and his general managers. Below this came three semi-independent divisions. Silk manufacturing and woollen cloth manufacturing, which used different processes and had different structures, each had their own divisional structure with their own accountants, production facilities, distribution, and purchasers and sales agents based out of the Medici Bank's foreign branches. Banking and international trade formed the third division; this consisted of the Tavola, the banking head office in Florence, the eight foreign branches and the various agencies. The divisions did interact to some degree (as noted, most branches had on their staff sales and purchasing agents for the manufacturing divisions) but were financially and structurally independent.

The primary device for controlling these various divisions and branches was the partnership. The use of partnerships as a device for managing and organising business ventures had a long history in medieval Italy. It is possible to know a great deal about how these partnerships worked thanks to the survival of many business records from the period, not only those of the Medici but also of many other firms. The most notable archive is that of Francesco Datini (c. 1335–1410), a middle-ranking Florentine merchant whose records and accounts have survived almost intact.[2] Typically, each new business venture would be established as a separate partnership, a method which allowed for flexibility but also limited risk (if one partnership failed, others would be unaffected). Often the same group of partners would found a number of partnerships together, occasionally taking in outsiders who had capital or skills to contribute. Partnerships were of short duration, usually only two years, at which point they were renewed, renegotiated or dissolved at the wish of the partners. Not all the partners contributed capital; each partnership usually had one or more men who were recruited for their technical skills or market knowledge, and who received a share of the partnership in exchange for these skills and knowledge. Viewed from this angle, the large businesses of the Italian Middle Ages and Renaissance resembled not so much the heavily vertically structured corporations of the early twentieth century, but the more flexible network organisations and limited life consortia which had begun to appear at the end of the century.

In the middle of the fifteenth century, the Medici Bank was structured as a cascading series of partnerships. At the top were the *maggiori*, the partners in the 'holding company' who functioned as a kind of board of directors. Most were members of the Medici family. Below these was the central office, with Cosimo himself functioning as an analogue to a modern managing director and a professional, first Antonio Salutati and later the talented Giovanni d'Amerigo Benci, as general manager overseeing operations; then came the various operating divisions. There were then thirteen separate partnership agreements: one with the heads of the silk manufacturing division, Berlinghieri Berlinghieri and Jacopo Tanaglia; two separate partnerships with the joint heads of the wool division, Antonio di Taddeo and Andrea Giuntini; one with Giovanni Ingherhami, the head of the Tavola; one with each of the heads of the eight foreign branches; and finally one with Benci, the general manager at head office. Partnerships normally included only the senior partner or head of each division, though junior partners were sometimes invited in as well, especially in the important branch at Bruges where Angelo Tani and his deputy Tomasso Portinari both held partnerships. Partners normally received from one-eighth to one-sixth of the profits of their own business unit; the case of Benci was special, in that he received a one-eighth share of the profits of the entire Medici Bank. Below these, the operating units could form other partnerships, usually for limited life ventures to fulfil particular projects.

Partners were occasionally junior members of the Medici family or client families like the Portinari, but most were like Benci and Ingherami, men who had worked their way up from office boy and clerk to salaried factor and finally to partner by dint of their own talents and hard work. Part of the strength of the Medici system, as directed by Cosimo, was its ability to spot and reward managerial talent. The career of Giovanni de Benci is a case in point. Five years younger than Cosimo, Benci was born into a middle-class Florentine family in 1394. In 1409, aged fifteen, he was taken on by the firm as an office boy and joined the Rome office. Proving adept at double entry bookkeeping, he had by 1420 risen to be the branch's chief accountant. In 1424, when the Medici made their first expansion north of the Alps, Benci was sent to Geneva to help establish the branch there, and for the first time was taken into a minor partnership. In 1433 he set up a temporary office in Basel to provide financial services for the dignitaries gathered for the Council of Basel, and the success of this venture brought him to the attention of top management. Cosimo dei Medici then brought him back to Rome and into the central office, first as deputy to general manager Salutati and then, after the latter's death in 1443, general manager in his turn. 'A very efficient businessman with an orderly and systematic mind',[3] he helped to engineer the bank's extraordinary expansion and growth across Europe and the Middle East, and was particularly instrumental in setting up agency relationships in Asia and expanding the diversified operations in cloth manufacturing and alum mining. He was eventually appointed to the *maggiori*, and at the time of his death in 1455 was one of the richest men in Florence. How much Cosimo dei Medici owed to this tough, dedicated professional can be seen by the rapidity with which the bank declined when his successors proved less able.

Other professionals abounded throughout the system. Tomasso Portinari at Bruges was unusual in that his family was closely related to the Medici; many other senior managers and partners were promoted on merit alone. The brothers Giovanni and Francesco Ingherami are another case in point. Born in around 1412, Giovanni di Baldino Inghcrami was trained at a *scuole d'abaco*, or book-keeping school (literally, 'abacus school') and then joined the Medici Bank in around 1430. By 1435 he had risen to the post of *fattori* in the Rome office and his salary had increased from the apprentice's starting rate of 5 ducats a year to 80 ducats a year. In 1440 he was called back to Florence and given the general management of the Tavola, which Cosimo was then in the process of decentralising; highly trusted, Ingherami was given the power to make out bills of exchange in the name of the Tavola, a power held until then only by Cosimo and his general managers. Despite this, he was not made a partner until 1445. His younger brother Francesco joined the Tavola shortly after 1440 as a book-keeper and was similarly trusted and promoted, taking over the management of the Tavola after Giovanni's death in 1454. The brothers are good examples of how educated men from the lower middle classes could rise through the organisation's professional ranks on merit alone.

Decentralising the business and handing over responsibility to his professional managers allowed Cosimo to concentrate on another vital task, the management of Florentine and Italian politics. The volatile political situation in fifteenth-century Italy meant that large businesses ignored politics at their peril; only by helping to ensure political stability could they achieve the corresponding economic stability necessary for prosperity. In the early years Cosimo overplayed his hand, with the result that he was briefly exiled from the city in 1433. Thereafter he made sure his influence was never overt, and in public at least, deferred to the city's republican institutions and supported democracy. Behind the scenes, however, he was the acknowledged ruler of Florence. His emphasis on stability and prosperity made him highly popular. He was also a patron of the arts, who founded Florence's Platonic Academy to give a home to refugee scholars from Constantinople and whose patronage was important to the careers of leading humanists such as Poggio Bracciolini and Leonardo Bruni. Likewise he supported artists such as Luca della Robbia, Donatello, Brunelleschi and Ghiberti, whose public works still adorn Florence to this day. When he died in 1464, the Florentine populace voted to give him the title *Pater Patriae* (Father of the Country). His son Piero dei Medici managed the business effectively until his own death in 1469, but thereafter the Medici family became increasingly distant from the management of the company and control passed into the hands of inept general managers. The bank failed in 1494, prompting an urban revolt and the assumption of power in the city by the fundamentalist government of Savonarola.

Cosimo dei Medici was not alone in creating a large multinational business. In the late thirteenth and early fourteenth centuries, the Florentine-based Society of the Bardi had banking and trading links across Western Europe, and in the thirteenth century the Genoese entrepreneur Benedetto Zaccaria had trading interests in Spain, France, Italy, Greece, the Byzantine Empire and the Middle East. Even in Cosimo's later years, the rising Genoa-based Banco di San Giorgio was challenging him for dominance of the European financial markets. But whereas these others were largely family-based organisations with tight personal control, Cosimo was able to use the partnership system, allied to the innovative divisional structure, to effectively decentralise and make the company more flexible. As a business model, this was to endure for centuries; Richard **Arkwright**'s multiple partnerships in the Industrial Revolution were less sophisticated versions of the same principle. Not until the coming of the joint-stock corporation at the end of the nineteenth century did this model lose its appeal. Today, partnership networks between institutions and corporations are becoming an increasingly common way of doing business.

See also: **Arkwright, Chandler, du Pont, Machiavelli**

Major works

Cosimo's written work consists of letters on business transactions and a few papers on philosophy and the arts, nearly all in Latin or Tuscan-Italian. Very little has been translated.

Further reading

De Roover provides an outstanding account of how the Medici Bank was structured and operated. Origo provides a similar account of Datini, particularly in the second half of the book. My own essays on Benci and Ingherami are largely drawn from de Roover.

de Roover, R., *The Rise and Decline of the Medici Bank*, Cambridge, MA: Harvard University Press, 1962.
Origo, I., *The Merchant of Prato*, London: Jonathan Cape, 1957.
Witzel, M., 'Benci, Giovanni d'Amerigo', in M. Witzel (ed.), *Biographical Dictionary of Management*, Bristol: Thoemmes Press, 2001, vol. 1, pp. 71–2.
—— 'Ingherami, Giovanni di Baldino', in M. Witzel (ed.), *Biographical Dictionary of Management*, Bristol: Thoemmes Press, 2001, vol. 1, pp. 474–5.

Notes

1   R. de Roover, *The Rise and Decline of the Medici Bank*, Cambridge, MA: Harvard University Press, 1962. Compare the organisation flowchart de Roover provides for the Medici Bank with the similar flowcharts of the M-form firm shown in Chandler's *The Visible Hand* (1977).
2   The Datini collection is one of the most amazing sets of business records of any age. Preserved in Prato, near Florence, it includes 150,000 letters, 500 account books, 300 deeds of partnership, 400 insurance policies and several thousand other documents, including bills of lading, bills of exchange and cheques.
3   De Roover, *The Rise and Decline of the Medici Bank*, p. 57.

HENRY MINTZBERG (1939–)

Henry Mintzberg is best known as one of the world's leading writers on strategy. Deliberately controversial, he has cast doubt on many of the more mechanistic approaches to strategy, and to management generally, which have been fashionable in Western academia and business over recent decades. To Mintzberg, strategy, and indeed much of management, is *ad hoc* and instinctive rather than structured and planned. His approach favours simplicity over complexity and common sense over rigid principles. Yet unlike other controversialists such as Tom **Peters**,

Mintzberg does not recommend radical change or revolution: whereas Peters urges chaos and deliberate flux, Mintzberg urges creativity and pattern-making. His most famous concept is perhaps the idea of 'emergent strategy', strategy making which is always ongoing as a half-deliberate, half-subconscious process, which shapes itself to changing needs and environments.

Mintzberg was born in Montreal on 2 September 1939. After studying engineering at McGill University and taking a degree in 1961 he joined Canadian National Railways, where he worked in the operations research department for several years before going to the Massachusetts Institute of Technology to take a master's degree in 1965 and then a doctorate in 1968. He then returned to McGill University in Montreal to join the faculty of management and has remained there since, becoming a full professor in 1978. A prolific author, he has received many awards, served as president of the Strategic Management Society, and been elected a fellow of the Royal Society of Canada, the first management academic to be so recognised.

Mintzberg went to MIT, says Stephen Rudman, with an idea of writing a book that would define exactly what it is that managers do in policy terms. Instead, his own studies and research showed him that the nature of the managerial task was nothing like as structured and ordered as most studies assumed it was, and its true nature was in fact quite hard to define. Mintzberg found what he later termed a managerial 'folklore', a body of literature on management studies which considered managers solely as rational beings, whose work day was taken up with 'classic' managerial tasks such as planning, coordinating and controlling. Decisions were made rationally, based on information which was carefully collected and analysed. Mintzberg found that this folklore was not an accurate reflection of reality. His own observations of managers in action found that, rather than being reflective practitioners, most were *ad hoc* respondents to unforeseen situations. Decisions were made quickly, often on the move, and usually based more on intuition and experience than considered analysis. Action was more important than reflection. Of the various tasks performed daily by the CEOs Mintzberg studied, half took less than ten minutes, and only 10 per cent took more than one hour.

The results of Mintzberg's study were published in *The Nature of Managerial Work* (1973), which is still regarded as one of his best books. The portrait of the manager and his task which emerges is one which many managers will recognise immediately as being close to their own: always under pressure of time, always 'firefighting', always working to find not necessarily the best solution but the one that can be implemented given the time and resources available. Mintzberg shows considerable sympathy for managers themselves, and is strongly critical of those who believe that managerial work can be classified and typified. In particular he attacks the notion, derived from **Drucker** (though not wholly supported by the latter's work), that managerial work has broad similarities across organisations. Not so, says Mintzberg; each organisation is as unique as an organism, with its own characteristics, environment, needs and resources.

Drawing heavily on the biological metaphor of organisation, he proposes a typology of organisational 'species', classifying organisations not by things such as size or industry sector, but by coordinating mechanisms, internal structure and the nature of organisational power. In his next major work, *The Structuring of Organizations* (1979), he refers to organisations as 'configurations', reminiscent in some ways of Ronald Coase's much earlier definition of organisations as a nexus of contracts. Organisations, he says, have six component parts. The first three are part of the classic 'line management' model: the operating core or production line, middle management and top management, the 'apex' of the hierarchy. The next two elements are 'staff' standing outside the hierarchy: technical analysts and support staff (such as public relations departments, etc.). The sixth element is intangible: Mintzberg calls this the organisation's 'ideology', the traditions and beliefs that make it individual and give it life, or in other words, its culture. Mintzberg goes on to define six methods of coordination by which organisations are directed and managed: these are mutual adjustment, direct supervision, standardisation of work processes, standardisation of outputs, standardisation of skills and knowledge and standardisation of norms (that is, implementing accepted common beliefs and values across the organisation).

How the organisation is configured and the nature of the coordination mechanisms used determines in turn the 'pulls' to which the organisation's managers respond. Mintzberg defines six 'species' of organisation, each dominated by one of the six elements, and describes the pulls to which each responds:

1   Entrepreneurial organisations: pull provided by strong leaders at the apex of the organisation.
2   Machine organisations: pull provided by the technical staff, with rationalisation the primary goal.
3   Professional organisations: pull provided by the operating core, with improvement of core technical processes the primary goal.

4   Diversified organisations: pull provided by middle management, with leadership provided by the divisional heads rather than head office, which plays only a light coordinating role.
5   Adhocracies: pull provided by the support staff, who play a role in coordinating and collaborating the organisational elements in the absence of a formal bureaucracy.
6   Missionary organisations: pull provided by commonly held ideologies or beliefs.

There is then a seventh type of organisation, the 'political organisation', in which *no* organisational element is dominant, and coordination is either lacking altogether or is exerted through a series of alliances as elements seek to gain power over other elements.

What managers do, then, and how they do it, depends to a large degree on the kind of organisation they are in, the nature of its 'pull' factors and the sources of organisational power. This is particularly important when it comes to strategy, a subject in which Mintzberg became interested early in his career. In the classical conception of managerial work, strategy making was the job of top management. The idea that top management could exist in the kind of Olympian detachment that made considered, analytical strategic planning possible, however, was one that Mintzberg did not believe had much basis in reality. In a typically provocative piece of writing, he compares the 'formal' theory of strategy with creationism and his own view of 'emergent' strategy with Darwinian theories of evolution:

> Man's beginnings were described in the Bible in terms of conscious planning and grand strategy. The opposing theory developed by Darwin suggested that no such grand design existed but that environmental forces gradually shaped man's evolution.[1]

Mintzberg champions the idea of 'emergent strategy', strategy which is formulated as a kind of continuous process in which many people take part, as opposed to 'deliberate strategy' or 'grand designs' formulated by elite and remote teams of strategists. Emergent strategy can be seen as a kind of 'muddling through' (which is, Mintzberg says, what most managers do anyway), but it can also be seen in deeper terms. Elsewhere Mintzberg speaks of 'crafting strategy', a kind of intuitive design in response to the materials the manager has to work with, in which strategy creation and strategy implementation are not separate things but are a continuous process. He compares the art of strategy making to pottery, to the potter sitting at his or her wheel moulding the clay and letting the shape evolve under his or her hands. The metaphor of the potter's wheel for the act of creation is an ancient one, featuring notably in the *Rubaiyat* of Omar Khayyam, for example, and Mintzberg uses it to great effect to show how design and execution should not be seen as separate components, nor even two halves of the same whole, but rather as two intermingled strands.

In his approach to management as an art rather than a science and his promotion of the role of tacit knowledge, Mintzberg resembles **Nonaka**, and even Mary Parker **Follett**. Both are, perhaps, more concerned with formal systems than is Mintzberg, whose argument that the realities and conceptualisation of the managerial task, and especially of strategy making, are far apart has led to criticism. Mintzberg is very good at telling us what management is *not*, say the critics, but he is less good at telling us what it *is*. But is asking what management *is* asking the wrong question? Again, Mintzberg would argue that what managers do and what management is are the same thing; it is impossible to separate the two.

Nor is the criticism an entirely fair one. Mintzberg has no prescriptions because he sees management as an art and not a science, and art is not prescriptive. But he does know what managers need to do and what abilities they require. Knowledge of their own business in all its aspects and all its capabilities and drawbacks is an essential requirement, more important than 'generic' management skills. So too is the ability to manage through discontinuity, to be able to detect changes but also to recognise patterns and focus on those things that do *not* change. Change is rarely all-embracing; as in nature, some elements of the environment change while others are static or dormant, and different elements change at different times. An emergent approach to strategy – and indeed to management – can detect discontinuities and manage with them and through them as a seamless process, obviating the need to go back and 'unpick' the strategy and start over again each time new circumstances arise.

Mintzberg's approach to strategy is considered radical, and in terms of Western business models it is, but other approaches to strategy would seem to confirm his ideas. Eastern ideas of strategy, for example, tend to be much more fluid. Chinese businesses, for example, do not have formal strategy teams and their leaders seldom speak of strategy making in abstract terms; for them, strategy is something they do every day. Military strategy, too, is full of references to change and flux.

The great nineteenth-century Prussian writer Karl von Clausewitz, whose work is still read by army officers around the world, maintained that, although there are simple principles of strategy, putting these into practice is almost impossible: leaders attempting to execute a strategy, says Clausewitz, are constantly beset by 'friction', a concatenation of unforeseen events and influences which will throw even the most carefully designed strategy off course. The good strategist, says Clausewitz, constantly recreates his strategy through the course of the campaign, responding to unforeseen events. He comments that 'in strategy, everything is very simple, but that does not mean that everything is very easy'; a point of view with which Henry Mintzberg would almost certainly agree.

See also: **Argyris, Chandler, Follett, Machiavelli, Morgan, Ohmae, Porter, Simon, Sunzi**

Major works

The Nature of Managerial Work is an important grounding for Mintzberg's later work. *Mintzberg on Management* is an excellent collection of articles, deliberately controversial and highly enjoyable.

The Nature of Managerial Work, New York, Harper & Row, 1973.
The Structuring of Organizations, Englewood Cliffs, NJ: Prentice-Hall, 1979.
Power in and around Organizations, Englewood Cliffs, NJ: Prentice-Hall, 1983.
Mintzberg on Management, New York: Free Press, 1989.
The Rise and Fall of Strategic Planning, New York: Free Press, 1993.

Further reading

Moore, and Pugh and Hickson, provide useful introductions to various aspects of Mintzberg's thought. Rudman provides a good overall introduction.

Moore, J.I. (1992) *Writers on Strategy and Strategic Management*, London: Penguin, 1992.
Pugh, D.S. and Hickson, D.J., *Writers on Organization*, 5th edn, London: Penguin, 1996.
Rudman, S.T., 'Mintzberg, Henry', in M. Witzel (ed.), *Biographical Dictionary of Management*, Bristol: Thoemmes Press, 2001, pp. 684–93.

Note

1   H. Mintzberg, *Mintzberg on Management*, New York: Free Press, 1989, p. 189.

JAMES D. MOONEY (1884–1957)

James Mooney began his career as an engineer and businessman, and later became one of the key members of the senior management team at General Motors, under Pierre du Pont and Alfred P. Sloan. Responsible for GM operations overseas, he helped make the company into the world's leading car maker, expanding from its domestic base to become a global corporation. Regarded as the leading intellectual on GM's board, he was a respected thinker on organisation and strategy. His book *Onward Industry!* (1931), later reprinted as *Principles of Organisation* (1937), established him as a popular management guru. His work on the nature and historical origins of business organisation is becoming increasingly relevant in the modern age of globalisation.

Mooney was born in Cleveland, Ohio on 18 February 1884. He studied science at New York University and then mining and metallurgy at the Case Institute of Technology, going on to work with mining exploration companies in California and Mexico. Moving on from mining, he took a succession of engineering jobs with companies such as Westinghouse, B.F. Goodrich and Hyatt Roller Bearing Company. It is possible to detect a certain amount of restlessness as Mooney, then in his twenties, hopped from job to job looking for something that would give him job satisfaction and exploit his talents more fully. At Hyatt he did particularly well, and was promoted into a management position around the time of the outbreak of the First World War.

When the USA entered the war in 1917, Mooney joined the US Army and was sent with an artillery regiment to France, rising to the rank of captain by war's end. Back in the USA in early 1919, he was demobilised but quickly found a job as president and general manager of Remy Electric Company, a small subsidiary of General Motors. The following year GM's founder and president, the gifted but erratic William C. Durant, was ousted from the board and his position taken over by the majority shareholder, Pierre **du Pont**. In his rapid reorganisation of the company, du Pont combed its ranks for managerial talent. Mooney, already known as an intelligent and perceptive man and an original thinker, was promoted quickly. In 1922, aged thirty-eight, he was appointed vice-president of GM and president of GM Overseas, in charge of all operations outside the USA. Over the next fifteen years Mooney expanded this division enormously, setting up operations in more than 100 countries and helping to make GM the world's largest multinational. Always aware of local cultural sensitivities, Mooney adapted US working practices and ideas where necessary to fit in with local markets. As the executive in charge of all General Motors plants and service outlets outside North America, Mooney travelled widely and became acquainted with many heads of state and senior government officials, and there seems little doubt that it was his ambassadorship for the company that allowed General Motors to expand its overseas business so dramatically during the 1920s and 1930s.

Mooney became an important figure in General Motors; Pierre du Pont respected him and du Pont's successor Alfred Sloan relied upon him to a large extent. Mooney is sometimes referred to as Sloan's *eminence grise*, the deep thinker on the General Motors board whose ideas on strategy and organisation were highly important to the corporation's development. His ideas on management and especially on organisation theory were among the most advanced of their time, and as well as commanding the respect of heads of state and government, Mooney was also on friendly terms with many of the leading management intelligentsia including Luther Gulick, Lyndall **Urwick** and Mary Parker **Follett**.

One of GM's most important markets in the 1930s was Germany, and the company had several subsidiaries there. Mooney visited Germany a number of times and was familiar with many senior officials in the German government. He regarded the outbreak of the Second World War with personal dismay, and was convinced that the war could be ended if a neutral third party was prepared to mediate between the belligerents in Europe. He had little faith that the war could be solved diplomatically, and believed that the diplomats were treating the war as a strategic contest with little thought for the lives of those involved on either side. Quixotically, he volunteered to undertake the task himself, using his personal knowledge of the leaders on both sides to give him access. In December 1939 and January 1940 Mooney met with President Franklin D. Roosevelt and made his offer to serve as a mediator. Roosevelt granted permission for Mooney to hold exploratory talks with the German and Italian governments, and Mooney accordingly flew to Germany. His contacts in German industrial circles and on the staff of Reichsmarshal Hermann Goering were able to arrange meetings for him, and Mooney met with Adolf Hitler on 4 March 1940, and with Goering a few days later. He then travelled to Italy to confer with Benito Mussolini. But although he was received amicably and was able to present his views, he received no concessions and no further meetings were held.

In retrospect, Mooney's mission looks incredibly naive. It is astonishing that he could have been so close to affairs in Germany and yet not have realised the true nature of the Nazi regime; but it seems this was so. His efforts, though made in good faith, were kept secret at first, but eventually news leaked out and in the summer of 1940 *PM* magazine in the USA ran a series of articles accusing Mooney of Nazi sympathies and linking his meeting with Hitler to his earlier receipt of the German Order of Merit for services to industry in 1938. Mooney sued the magazine and won, but he never again attempted to intervene in affairs of state. Resigned to the inevitability of war, he left General Motors Overseas and set up a group of directors to begin planning the conversion of the corporation's facilities to wartime production. Already an officer in the US Naval Reserve, Mooney was called up once the USA entered the war in 1941. He served with the Bureau of Aeronautics, then in staff posts in Europe, and finally on the staff of the Chief of Naval Operations, finishing the war with the rank of captain in the navy. After the war he returned only briefly to General Motors, leaving in 1946 to become chairman and president of Willys Overland.[1] He later retired from this post and set up a consulting firm, J.D. Mooney Associates, in New York, working with this firm until the time of his death.

Mooney wrote a number of essays and articles, but it is *Onward Industry!* (1931) that best sums up his ideas and management philosophy. He begins by stating his view that organisation is a constant: 'Organization is as old as human society itself.'[2] This was not an entirely original view: the academic Edward D. Jones had used almost the same words fifteen years earlier. Mooney is particularly influenced here by the lawyer and historian John Davis, whose *Corporations* (1905) had likewise described organisation as an essential part of human activity. Davis believed that corporations were primarily social instruments, established by society in order to undertake a particular task. The ecclesiastical corporations (the Catholic church and the monastic orders) were set up to expand and regulate religious worship; the medieval guilds and city corporations were established to support craft production; the educational corporations (the universities) came to provide education, and finally the joint-stock corporations arrived at a time when there was a need to finance and expand industrial production and commerce.

Mooney follows Davis in believing that 'organization is the form of every human association for the attainment of a common purpose'.[3] This does not mean that all organisations are alike; in fact, there are as many different types of organisation as there are purposes for them to achieve. However, underlying all types of organisation there are basic or first principles, concepts to which all successful organisations adhere, and it is these that he sets out to identify.

Again like Davis, Mooney's approach to organisation is historical. He sees the roots of modern business organisation in two previous organisational types: the medieval monastic orders, and eighteenth- and nineteenth-century professional military organisations such as standing armies. He describes in some detail how and why both these organisational forms emerged and the principles on which they are based. Through these descriptions he highlights many similarities with modern business organisations, most notably the simultaneous need for coordination and control and the links between successful achievement of purpose, strong leadership and sound organisational structure.

Mooney also takes a holistic view of organisation, and makes reference to the biological metaphor which had been developed by Harrington **Emerson**, Herbert **Casson**, Charles Knoeppel and others. He criticises some writers (but does not name them) who see organisation as merely the framework or skeletal outline of the business. This, he says,

> implies that organization refers only to the differentiation and definition of individual duties, as set forth in the familiar organization charts. But duties must relate to procedure, and it is here that we find the real dynamics of organization, the motive power through which it moves to its determined objects. Organization, therefore, refers to more than the frame or skeleton of the industrial edifice. It refers to the completed body, with all of its correlated functions. And it refers to these functions as they appear in action, the very pulse and heart beats, the circulation, the respiration, the vital movement, so to speak, of the organized unit.[4]

He goes on to draw a distinction between the terms 'organization' and 'management'. If organisation is the body as described above, then management is the 'vital spark' that animates it and moves it; he likens management to a 'psychic force':

> The technique of management, in its human relationships, can be best described as the technique of handling or managing people, which should be based on a deep and enlightened

human understanding. The technique of organization may be described as that of relating specific duties or functions in a completely coordinated scheme. This statement of the difference between managing and organizing clearly shows their intimate relationship. It also shows, which is our present purpose, that the technique of organizing is inferior, in logical order, to that of management. It is true that a sound organizer may, because of temperamental failings, be a poor manager, but on the other hand it is inconceivable that a poor organizer may ever make a good manager ... The prime necessity in all organization is harmonious relationships based on integrated interests, and, to this end, the first essential is an integrated and harmonious relationship in the duties, considered in themselves.[5]

Mooney is an advocate of the line and staff principle of management first developed by Harrington Emerson. In his view, an effective organisation requires both 'line' or functional departments involved in production, supply, marketing and so on, and a staff, a corps of advisory managers engaged in planning, analysis, monitoring and coordinating activities, and generally supporting the board and top management. Line management is about achieving targets; staff management is about deciding what the targets are to be and setting them. But Mooney does not fall into the trap common to other writers of the period in thinking that the staff in some way governs or controls the line. On the contrary:

the line not merely dominates but includes and contains the staff ... They must not be thought of as segregated functions. The idea of a staff that simply recommends, or of a line that simply does what the staff recommends, would be an absurdity in organization.[6]

Line managers are not only more important than staff managers, as it is on their shoulders that the productivity and profitability of the firm rests, but they also have more knowledge; in their own specialised departments, they are far more knowledgeable and skilled than the staff. The ultimate purpose of the staff is to *transmit knowledge*, to ensure that the specialised knowledge which accumulates in the departments is shared out through the organisation and, most importantly, reaches the highest levels of the organisation where it can be used to assist in analysis and decision making.

Coordination is an ever-present problem in organisations, and here Mooney's views more nearly resemble those of Mary Parker Follett. Control should be decentralised as far as possible, as tightly centralised control is not efficient; but at the same time, too much decentralisation and independence leads to divisions wandering off on their own and failing to work towards the overall goal. In his professional life Mooney often saw this in practice as General Motors, a sometimes unstable coalition of formerly competing car firms, often had difficulty in persuading refractory division chiefs to pull together. Only the strong leadership of Alfred Sloan and his successors could achieve this, and Mooney duly devotes considerable attention in *Onward Industry!* to the need for leadership to overcome the problems of coordination. In a later article, Mooney argued that good leadership establishes authority without imposing it:

> Here we come to what I conceive to be a vital distinction; that between authority as such, and the form of authority that projects itself through leadership. The difference may be seen in their relation to the organization itself. It takes supreme co-ordinating authority to create an organization; leadership, on the other hand, always presupposes the organization. I would define leadership as the form in organization through which authority enters into process; which means, of course, that there must be leadership as the necessary directive of the entire organized movement.
>
> We know how leadership functions in the direction of this movement, and we are all familiar with the structural form through which it operates. We call it delegation of duties, but few realize how absolutely necessary to an orderly and efficient procedure is a sound application of this delegating principle.[7]

There is one organisational principle more important than all others, however. All organisations have a goal, and every organisation's sole purpose is the achievement of that goal. It is imperative, Mooney says, to focus on the goal, and not to confuse the goal itself with the means required to meet it. Despite being a supporter of scientific management and the efficiency movement, Mooney expresses some concern with what he sees as a growing trend towards seeing these as ends in themselves. Efficiency, says Mooney, is never more than a means to meeting a goal:

Worthiness in the industrial sphere can have reference to one thing only, namely the contribution of industry to the sum total of human welfare. On this basis only must industry and all its works finally be judged ... The lessons of history teach us that no efficiency of procedure will save from ultimate extinction those organizations that pursue a false objective; on the other hand, without such efficient procedure, all human group effort becomes relatively futile.[8]

Very popular in his day, Mooney is now only read by management historians, among whom his reputation remains very high. In organisation theory, he was a populariser and synthesiser rather than a wholly original thinker, but he commands respect for the position he held and the ways in which he and his organisation so obviously tried to put these principles into practice – and by and large succeeded. New developments in organisational theory and practice have moved away from hierarchical organisations, but if anything they have made Mooney's views seem even more valid. The need to maintain focus on organisational goals and to see organisation as an end to meeting that goal was confirmed by Chandler's theory that structure follows strategy. The need for coordination from the centre rather than control from above, though derived from Follett, is very germane to modern management, as is the need for effective leadership if decentralised organisations are to function efficiently and effectively. And finally, the stress on business corporations as social constructs which exist because society requires them to meet its needs is one that has important resonances for business ethics and corporate governance, especially in the wake of the Enron disaster of 2001.

See also: **Chandler, du Pont, Emerson, Follett, Ford, Machiavelli, Urwick**

Major works

Onward Industry! remains Mooney's masterwork. *Principles of Organization* is an updated edition with no major changes. The 1937 essay is an accessible abbreviated version of his views.

(With A.C. Reilley) *Onward Industry! The Principles of Organization and Their Significance to Modern Industry*, New York: Harper and Bros, 1931.
'The Principles of Organization', in L.F. Urwick and L.H. Gulick (eds), *Papers on the Science of Administration*, New York: Institute of Public Administration, 1937, pp. 91–8.
Principles of Organization, New York: Harper and Bros, 1941.

Further reading

Sloan and Drucker are the main authorities on General Motors during Mooney's period. Davis is essential reading for anyone interested in the history of the theory of organisation and corporate governance, as is Jones's article in *Engineering Magazine*.

Davis, J.P., *Corporations*, New York: G.P. Putnam's Sons, 1905, 2 vols.

Drucker, P., *Concept of the Corporation*, New York: The John Day Company, 1946.

Jones, E.D., 'Military History and the Science of Administration', *Engineering Magazine* 44 (1912): 1–6, 185–90 and 321–6.

Sloan, A.P., *My Years with General Motors*, New York: Doubleday, 1964.

Notes

1   He took over this post from Charles Sorenson, who had been head of production at Ford before the war.
2   J.D. Mooney and A.C. Reilley, *Onward Industry!*, New York: Harper and Bros, 1931, p. xiii.
3   *Ibid.*, p. 10.
4   *Ibid.*, pp. 12–13.
5   *Ibid.*, pp. 14–15.
6   *Ibid.*, p. 494.
7   J.D. Mooney, 'The Principles of Organization', in L.H. Gulick and L.F. Urwick (eds), *Papers on the Science of Administration*, New York: Institute of Public Administration, 1937, p. 93.
8   *Ibid.*, pp. 97–8.

GARETH MORGAN (1943–)

Gareth Morgan is best known as the creator of the concept of 'organisational metaphors' as a management tool. His greatest insight has been to determine that, while there is no one model of organisation that can entirely capture the essence of organisation, it is possible by means of metaphors to look at organisations from different angles and see different facets. Similarly, as no one single metaphor is adequate to explain the nature and behaviour of organisations, it is necessary to use multiple metaphors in combination to get closer to the reality. Morgan's eight metaphors of organisations, first set out in his 1986 book *Images of Organization*, are one of the most powerful concepts in organisation theory today. He has gone on to argue that managers should be less bound by methodology and rules of procedure, and became more reflective, creative and intuitive in their thinking.

Morgan was born in Wales on 22 December 1943. He took a BSc in economics at the London School of Economics in 1965, going on to work for several years in local government. He then attended the

University of Texas, taking a master's degree in public administration in 1970. Back in Britain, he took up a teaching post at the University of Lancaster, where he also received his PhD in organisation theory in 1980. He currently lives in Toronto, where he is professor of administrative studies at York University.

According to Charles Hampden-Turner (1998), author of one of the best analyses of Morgan's career, Morgan began his interest in the problems of organisation and management while at Lancaster. In the course of research for his PhD, he came to the realisation that there is no real agreement, either in business and management literature or elsewhere, as to what an organisation is. Different authors down through the years have used a variety of different methods or metaphors to describe organisation, but these are all dependent in some way on the authors' own backgrounds, training and personal agendas; in other words, views on the definition of organisation are strongly conditioned by the authors' own social and professional backgrounds. This theme is touched on in *Sociological Paradigms and Organizational Analyses* (1979), which Morgan co-authored. In a later work, *Beyond Method* (1983), Morgan went on to argue that organisations also had widely differing images of themselves and their functions. As Hampden-Turner summarises: 'Accounting, for example, could be a history of transactions, a branch of economics, a form of information, a disciplined control, or a methodology.'[1]

The problem here will be readily apparent. Morgan found that there was no such thing as organisation theory, but rather a lot of different theories of organisation jostling for position. Mechanistic, humanistic, biological and economic theories were all current, and although they overlapped on many points, there were also very many points of discord. In part, this is due to the diverse nature of the origins of management as a discipline. The early twentieth-century theorists on management, both those involved with scientific management and in other fields, borrowed from a wide range of other intellectual activities, including economics, psychology, engineering, mathematics and statistics, military science, sociology, law, politics, philosophy, biology and other natural sciences, and literature and the plastic arts. A huge number of different concepts were fed into the conceptual machine in the course of a relatively short time. Although old as a practice, management is young as a discipline and has not had time to settle down and agree on basic principles.

And, as Morgan rightly points out, everyone who looks at management is conditioned by their own background, training and personal outlook (indeed, in *Beyond Method* he makes it clear that this is true of all the social sciences). This can easily be demonstrated by some of the examples in this book. Frederick **Taylor** saw organisations as machine-like because he was an engineer. **Emerson** was impressed by his experiences as a youth in the Franco-Prussian war and adopted a military model. **Maslow**, a psychologist, used psychological theories to develop his views on motivation in organisation. **Follett**, a political scientist and sociologist, developed a relational theory of organisation behaviour; and so on.

In his next book, the best-selling *Images of Organization* (1986), Morgan attempts to draw all these views and many others together and create not a synthesis – he rightly judges this to be impossible, at least at the present time – but a model by which each metaphor or model can be used either individually or in combination to help explain what goes on inside organisations. Unlike many other organisation theorists, who attempt to explain away paradoxical behaviour – why organisations sometimes behave in a fashion that is not in the best interests of themselves or their members, for example – Morgan accepts paradox as a natural part of human life. It is possible to have two seemingly conflicting images of a subject such as organisation, both of which in fact make sense. As Hampden-Turner comments, 'Metaphors are contingent on particular circumstances: the more images we have, the more versatile are our ways of understanding both organization and action. Tension between metaphors creates flux, flow, transformation, renewal, loops and self-renewal.'[2]

At the heart of Morgan's work lie the eight metaphors of organisation, summarised in *Images of Organization*. In describing these, Morgan, like his predecessors, often goes outside the literature of management to borrow concepts from many other fields. The eight metaphors are:

1   organisations as machines;
2   organisations as biological organisms;
3   organisations as brains;
4   organisations as cultures;
5   organisations as political systems;
6   organisations as psychic prisons;
7   organisations as flux and transformation;
8   organisations as instruments of domination.

The metaphor of organisations as machines is perhaps a natural outcome of industrialisation and mechanisation. The German sociologist Max Weber was the first to note how industrialisation and bureaucratisation seemed to go hand in hand; expansion of the production process led to increasing hierarchy and more functional administration. This can be seen in the ideas on chain of command and scalar hierarchy promoted in the administration theory of Henri **Fayol**, but even more so in the writers on and practitioners of scientific management, where the machine metaphor was consciously adopted as a means of making organisations more machine-like and efficient. The machine metaphor sees an organisation as an agglomeration of components, all of which have been fashioned to work together for a common purpose. This is a very powerful and popular image, but it has its faults; machines tend to be rigid, inflexible and slow to adapt, and so too do mechanistic organisations.

An alternative view is to see organisations as composed primarily of living beings and therefore to compare organisations with biological organisms. Emerson, and after him, **Casson**, were among the first to articulate this approach, comparing the organisation to the human body; this idea also had its proponents among the human relations school of the 1920s and 1930s. Later, organisational psychologists such as Douglas McGregor would stress the relationship between personality and organisation, and Henry **Mintzberg** has developed the idea of organisations as 'species' existing in an environment and dependent on that environment for survival. The organisation metaphor stresses the interdependence of the parts – the individuals – and the whole – the organisation – and concludes that the whole is in some way greater than the sum of its parts. It tends to emphasise fluid systems and coordination rather than rigid systems and control. The ability to link organisations to their environment is a powerful feature of this metaphor, but on the flip side it tends to place too much emphasis on the whole and not enough on the parts, subsuming individual personality and needs into the embrace of the organisation.

The brain metaphor has its origins in cybernetic theory, notably the work of Norbert Wiener and also Herbert **Simon**, and is currently very popular in theories such as the learning organisation. This metaphor has a strong focus on information and knowledge, and sees the organisation as in effect a single brain working constantly to process information that passes through it. Feedback loops and knowledge management are seen as key elements here: **Nonaka**'s 'hypertext organisation' is another example of the type. Though similar to the organism metaphor, this model focuses on an organisation's ability to be self-aware and self-organising, and particularly on how organisations process information and use knowledge. However, there can be problems in overemphasising the value of learning: organisations must spend at least some of their time producing and selling, as well as learning, if they are to be profitable.

The culture metaphor focuses on organisations as social systems, looking not only at how they are structured and how they use knowledge but also at the various customs and rituals that all organisations seem to embed within themselves, even after only a fairly short period of time. Values, rather than knowledge, are the dominant feature here. The idea of culture is important in that it can help to account for differences between organisations, both in terms of external cultural influences and internal patterns of behaviour, rituals, etc. that are built up over time. The culture metaphor, however, is hard to sustain on its own, as it takes little or no account of features such as the distribution of power within the organisation, a feature that is not necessarily linked to culture at all.

This leads on to organisations as political systems. In this view, organisations are like states or armies, competing for control of resources and markets; and knowledge. Power, however, has replaced both knowledge and values as the dominant feature. Such competition goes on within the organisation as well. **Machiavelli** is an important thinker in this tradition, as are those early writers who drew on military science for their theories of organisation.

One of the most powerful metaphors is that of the organisation as a psychic prison, which focuses on the subconscious process at work in organisations. The image comes from Plato's *Republic*:

> The allegory pictures an underground cave with its mouth open toward the light of a glazing fire. Within the cave are people chained so they cannot move. They can see only the cave wall directly in front of them. This is illuminated by the light of the fire, which throes shadows of people and objects onto the wall. The cave dwellers equate the shadows with reality ... Truth and reality for the prisoners rest in this shadowy world, because they have no knowledge of any other.[3]

Morgan suggests that people respond to the psychic prison in one of two ways:

> People in everyday life are trapped by illusions, hence the way they understand reality is limited and flawed. By appreciating this, and by making a determined effort to see beyond the

superficial, people have an ability to free themselves from imperfect ways of seeing. However, as the allegory suggests, many of us often resist or ridicule efforts at enlightenment, preferring to remain in the dark rather than risk exposure to a new world and its threat to the old ways.[4]

The metaphor of organisations as flux and transformation is drawn from Greek philosophy as well, this time from Heraclitus, who held that the universe is self-generating and in a state of constant transformation. Morgan uses this metaphor to show the dynamic nature of organisations and to describe their constant, sometimes apparently random transformations and changes (more recent attempts to understand organisations in terms of chaos theory and particle physics also fall into this category). How firms choose to deal with change affects how they function. Morgan suggests that their ability to manage change and flux is related to their internal ability to cope with and manage through paradox; random change will inevitably throw up paradoxical situations, in which previously held ideas will no longer be valid; compare this to Andrew **Grove**'s notion of change coming through strategic inflection points.

Finally, there is the metaphor of organisations as instruments of domination, in which organisations seek power not for any particular end or goal, but simply for its own sake. This describes organisations which have perhaps lost their way; the original vision of the founders has disappeared or is no longer valid, and the only alternative to seeking and holding power is decline and dissolution. Even goals such as seeking percentage growth or share price increase could fall into this category, as organisations setting these goals are doing nothing beyond increasing their own power and domination. Whether they are serving the ends of their stakeholders is a moot point; it is possible that they are not.

As Hampden-Turner comments, 'Morgan's view is that there is no one right metaphor; all organizations partake to some degree of all these metaphors, and all allow access to greater understanding of organizations and how they function.'[5] Each metaphor allows us to look at one facet of a complex subject, one that we find difficult to grasp in the round. As Morgan says, 'We use metaphor whenever we attempt to understand one element of experience in terms of another.' He goes on to explain:

> Organizations are complex and paradoxical phenomena that can be understood in many different ways. Many of our

taken-for-granted ideas about organizations are metaphorical, even though we may not recognize them as such. For example, we frequently talk about organizations *as if* they were machines designed to achieve predetermined goals and objectives, and which should operate smoothly and efficiently. And as a result of this kind of thinking, we often attempt to organize and manage them in a mechanistic way, forcing their human qualities into a background role. By using different metaphors to understand the complex and paradoxical character of organizational life, we are able to manage and design organizations in ways that we may not have thought possible before.[6]

We can use metaphor constructively to reconceptualise ourselves and our surroundings. Morgan calls this process 'imaginization', and says that, by using metaphors as instruments of understanding, we can break out of our own psychic prisons and free our minds for developing new ways of thinking and doing things. However, the use of metaphor in this way means that we need to become familiar with managing paradox; we need to understand that the apparent contradictions between metaphors are in fact no more than different manifestations of the same entity. Much of Morgan's later work, notably *Creative Organization Theory* (1989) and *Imaginization* (1993), is devoted to pushing forward the concept of imaginization and teaching the skills of managing by metaphor.

Morgan's theories are of course important for organisation theory, but they have important implications for theories of management more generally. In particular, the management of paradox is a theme that is becoming ever more important. It is also not a long distance from the discussion of multiple metaphors of organisation and the ability these have to generate additional learning to later theories of knowledge management which stress the need to acquire a rich diversity of knowledge from multiple sources.

Morgan's arguments are surely a death knell for the 'one best way' school of management which began with scientific management and has continued through later trends such as re-engineering. His use of metaphor shows that there can be multiple ends to the same goal. It also reminds us that management as a discipline and set of practices is still very much in its infancy, and that there are many competing schools of thought. It is possible that in future the discipline may 'bed down' and it may be possible to come up with a consensual theory of organisation that really does work; but that time has not yet come. Too many things are still unknown. It may be, as both Peter **Drucker** and Charles **Handy** point out, that organisation is itself no more than a tool, constantly evolving and changing in the face of organisational needs and social pressures. In this case, the ability to manage by metaphor will become more important than ever.

See also: **Argyris, Burnham, Chandler, Drucker, Emerson, Fayol, Follett, Forrester, Grove, Handy, Hofstede, Machiavelli, Mintzberg, Mooney, Nonaka, Simon**

Major works

Images of Organization is Morgan's major work. *Imaginization* is a further development of his ideas which shows practitioners how to 'manage by metaphor'.

(With G. Burrell) *Sociological Paradigms and Organizational Analyses*, London: Heinemann, 1979.
Beyond Method: Strategies for Social Research, Newbury Park, CA: Sage, 1983.
Images of Organization, Newbury Park, CA: Sage, 1986.
Creative Organization Theory, Newbury Park, CA: Sage, 1989.
Imaginization: The Art of Creative Management, Newbury Park, CA: Sage, 1993.

Further reading

Hampden-Turner's essay is a deep examination of the subject by a respected authority on organisation cultures.

Hampden-Turner, C., 'Morgan, Gareth', in M. Warner (ed.), *Handbook of Management Thinking*, London: International Thomson Business Press, 1998, pp. 470–5.

Notes

1 C. Hampden-Turner, 'Morgan, Gareth', in M. Warner (ed.), *Handbook of Management Thinking*, London: International Thomson Business Press, 1998, p. 471.
2 *Ibid.*
3 G. Morgan, *Images of Organization*, Newbury Park, CA: Sage, 1986, p. 199.
4 *Ibid.*, p. 200.
5 Hampden-Turner, 'Morgan, Gareth', p. 474.
6 Morgan, *Images of Organization*, p. 13.

J.P. MORGAN (1837–1913)

J.P. Morgan was a banker and financier who, dismayed by the chaos he saw around him in late nineteenth-century America, took it upon himself to regulate and consolidate a number of important industries, including the railways and the steel industry. Morgan hated the idea of competition, which he believed was wasteful and ruinous and ultimately to the detriment of the public interest. Instead, he used his financial clout to merge entire industries into giant combines, or trusts. This provoked a popular reaction as the American public, previously very pro-big business, began to believe that Morgan and the other big industrialists were a threat to democracy. The debate, which raged for several decades, did much to shape modern attitudes to corporate governance, business ethics, managerial responsibility, and market regulation and competition. The environment in which we do business today was shaped in almost equal measure by Morgan and by his opponents.

John Pierpont Morgan was born on 17 April 1837 in Hartford, Connecticut. He was born, in the saying of the time, with a silver spoon in his mouth: his father, Junius Morgan, was a prosperous merchant who later moved the family to Boston. In 1854 Junius Morgan joined the London-based banking firm George Peabody and Company, and the Morgans emigrated to the UK; J.P. Morgan finished his education at a Swiss finishing school and then studied at the University of Göttingen. In 1857 he took a job with the Peabody bank's New York agents and returned to the USA to begin his own career in banking.

Following his apprenticeship with the New York agents, in 1860 Morgan, again with his father's support, set up his own bank, J.P. Morgan and Company, conducting business on his own account and acting as his father's agent in the USA (the transatlantic partnership with Junius Morgan lasted until the 1890s). The Civil War made J.P. Morgan's first fortune as he both financed commodity deals and dealt directly in commodities such as grain, wood and coal; according to some accounts, by stimulating the Northern economy and ensuring the flow of raw materials to its war machine, he played no small part in ensuring the North's victory in the war. Morgan's real rise to power, however, came in the railway boom of the 1870s and 1880s. This was the era of the robber barons, Jay Gould, Jim Fisk, Daniel Drew and Cornelius Vanderbilt, when fierce competition between railway owners was matched by equally fierce speculation in the stock markets. The stockbroker W.W. Fowler, in his *Twenty Years inside Life in Wall Street* (1880), describes some of the practices of the day: insider dealing, watered stock, collusion, rate-fixing and more. This was an era when there were few rules governing conduct in the business world, and what rules there were could not be enforced.

As the railway market reached saturation, the industry was plunged into a series of damaging rate wars which at some points threatened the entire industry. Morgan, who had merged with several other firms and whose new bank was now called Drexel, Morgan and Company, allied with one of the largest railway barons, William Vanderbilt, son of Cornelius. A man of a different stamp from his father, William Vanderbilt saw the rate wars as damaging both in terms of prosperity and publicity. With Vanderbilt as an ally and a seat on the board of the latter's company, New York Central, Morgan proceeded to intervene in the industry on a massive scale. Struggling railway lines were bought up, their directors replaced by Morgan nominees and their finances returned to order. Railway barons who continued to indulge in rate wars were brought to order. In 1889 he set up the Western Traffic Association, in effect a cartel in which the railway operators agreed to fix rates at a reasonable level and not to engage in unrestricted competition. If any failed to sign up, Morgan and his allies in the banking community threatened to withdraw financial support. The federal government, alarmed at this concentration of power, dissolved the Western Traffic Association in 1897, but by then Morgan and his allies, Edward Harriman and Jim Hill, were consolidating ownership of the main rail lines, buying out competitors and ensuring the industry was dominated by just a few big firms.

Other consolidations followed. In meat-packing, mining and smelting, oil, distilling, tobacco, public utilities and many other industries, Morgan and his allies put together financial packages that brought the major companies of each industry together under one roof. The first device used was the trust, a legal entity whereby shareholders assigned control of their shares to a board of trustees. The trust-builders persuaded – and sometimes intimidated – major shareholders to come in with them, and bought up the minor shareholders on the open market. In this way, in a relatively short space of time, control over an entire industry could be gathered into a few hands.

Again, the US government was alarmed at the threat this posed, not least to its own power, and the Sherman Anti-Trust Act broke up many of the larger trusts. Undeterred, Morgan converted most of these into joint-stock corporations, with control still vested in the original circle through the distribution of ordinary (voting) and preference (non-voting) shares. In one famous incident, the Industrial Rayon Corporation issued 500,000 shares; 498,000 non-voting shares for sale to the public, and 2,000 voting shares reserved for the directors.

Morgan also continued his campaign of consolidation. Most famously, United States Steel Corporation was created by a merger of Andrew Carnegie's steel company with a number of other producers to form the world's largest corporation. Daniel Guggenheim agreed to sell his mining and smelting interests on condition that he was made head of the resulting monopoly, ASARCO, and given a major stake in it. AT&T was created from the old Bell company as a monopoly of the emerging telephone and telegraph industry. American Tobacco Company succeeded the former Tobacco Trust with barely a ripple of disturbance in the industry. Morgan also moved into shipping, persuading British and American shipowners to form a transatlantic combine, International Mercantile Marine (IMM); here he was less successful when two leading British shipping lines, Cunard and Furness Withy, refused to join. As these two firms controlled about a third of transatlantic freight and passenger traffic, IMM was never really successful and ultimately dissolved itself.

There were others who rebelled too. Some openly defied the trusts and monopolies, like Charles M. Schwab in the steel industry who carried on down his own independent path outside US Steel. Some joined reluctantly and then tried to sabotage the system from within, like R.J. Reynolds inside American Tobacco. Others tried to save their independence but failed.

Morgan was, and still is, widely perceived as acting for motives of personal aggrandisement. He was the world's richest man; in 1894 he had personally saved the US government from bankruptcy, and he possessed the financial clout to intervene anywhere to any effect he desired. There is little doubt that he saw the acquisition and centralisation of power as a central goal. His motives, however, are more complex. His biographer Jean Strouse, who freely admits that when she set out to research her subject she did so with a strong sense of antipathy towards him, nevertheless became convinced that Morgan was acting for the large part out of a sense of duty. He was, in American terms, an aristocrat, with a responsibility to society. He believed that competition was inherently wasteful, and that unrestrained competition was ultimately ruinous. Competition meant that companies spent money competing with each other, when they could be spending that money to improve product quality or offer goods and services to customers at cheaper prices. The elimination of competition, Morgan argued, meant that goods could be produced more cheaply and with less waste. It also meant that goods production could be regulated to meet demand, thus eliminating the need to compete; if supply could be made to exactly match demand, then there would be enough for all and the motive to compete would be eliminated. It is worth noting that in nearly all the cartels, trusts and corporations that Morgan and his allies set up, the restriction of production was a major feature.

Before condemning this outright, it is worth noting that this view still holds good in certain industries. Cartels in oil have been omnipresent; the Achnacarry agreement in the 1930s between the three world giants, Shell, British Petroleum and Standard Oil, set the standard for future negotiations. Today, the Organisation of Petroleum-Exporting Countries (OPEC), one of the most powerful cartels the world has seen, still argues for its own existence on exactly these grounds. Overproduction in the oil industry, it is claimed, is in no one's best interests: falling prices would hurt producers, lead to waste competition and possibly even military conflict between producing states, and cheap oil would also lead to overconsumption, increased environmental pollution and rapid depletion of a non-renewable resource. Even today, with our strong free market ethic in the West, we are able to accept the need for cartels in some cases.

And there were plenty of people at the time who agreed with Morgan. Industrialists agreed with him because, contrary to modern popular belief, businesses do not enter into competition for its own sake; they do so in order to secure their own position and their own markets. If they can do so without head-to-head competition, then this is clearly in their own best interests. Today, the idea of market alliances and cooperation between firms for mutual advantage, especially in complex global markets, is increasingly coming back on the agenda, and is causing predictable alarm among regulators. And many economists agreed with Morgan too, even if they often condemned his methods. In particular, they believed that the costs of competition, especially of marketing and advertising, were wasteful and were actually increasing the price of goods sold to the public. Although they called for voluntary agreements between firms to restrict competition rather than outright consolidation, there was still plenty of sympathy for Morgan's point of view.

There was revolt brewing, however. In 1905, the lawyer and historian John Davis published his book *Corporations* in which he argued that business corporations were in effect servants of the public good; when they failed to meet that good, they had outlived their usefulness and deserved to be replaced. Free market economists, arguing that the system of regulating production was not working and prices to the consumer were rising, reinforced this point of view. The flamboyant Harvard economist William Zebina Ripley was already leading the way in this direction, and his *Trusts, Pools and Corporations*

(1902) was an attack on both the methods and the motives of the big combines. But the major point of contention was different in nature, though perhaps even more predictable: the trusts and corporations concentrated too much power in too few hands, and the potential for corruption and abuse was glaringly obvious. In January 1903 *McClure's* magazine carried an editorial by its owner and editor calling the American people to arms against the corruption of big business and big government in the following words:

> Capitalists, workingmen, politicians, citizens – all breaking the law, or letting it be broken. Who is left to uphold it? The lawyers? Some of the best lawyers in this country are hired, not to go into court to defend cases, but to advise corporations and business firms how they can get around the law without too great a risk of punishment. The judges? Too many of them so respect the law that for some 'error' or quibble they restore to office and liberty men convicted on evidence overwhelmingly convincing to common men. The churches? We know of one, an ancient and wealthy establishment, which had to be compelled by a Tammany hold-over health officer to put its tenements in sanitary condition. The colleges? They do not understand.
>
> There is no one left; none but us all. Capital is learning (with indignation at labor's unlawful acts) that its rival's contempt of law is a menace to property. Labor has shrieked the belief that the illegal power of capital is a menace to the worker. These two are drawing together. Last November, when a strike was threatened by the yard-men on all the railroads centering on Chicago, the men got together and settled by raising wages, and raising freight rates too. They made the public pay. We all are doing our worst and making the public pay. The public is the people. We forget that we all are the people; that while each of us in his group can shove off on the rest the bill of to-day, the debt is only postponed; the rest are passing it back on us. We have to pay in the end, every one of us. And in the end the sum total of the debt will be our liberty.[1]

That issue of *McClure's* carried three articles: 'The Right to Work' by Ray Stannard Baker about labour disputes in the Pennsylvania coalfields; 'The Shame of Minneapolis', by Lincoln Steffens, about American municipal corruption; and 'The Oil War of 1872' by Ida

Minerva Tarbell, the first of a series of assaults on one of the largest and most powerful monopolies: John D. Rockefeller's Standard Oil. This was the beginning of the movement known as the 'Muck Rakers', crusading journalists who attacked corruption in business and political life, and also the institutions that, as they saw it, spawned corruption. Tarbell, whose monumental *History of the Standard Oil Company* was published in the following year, 1904, attacked not only the company itself but the society which had spawned its existence, and echoed McClure's call for change:

> There is something alarming to those who believe that commerce should be a peaceful pursuit, and who believe that moral law holds good throughout the entire range of human relations, in knowing that so large a body of young men in this country are consciously or unconsciously growing up with the idea that business is war and that morals have nothing to do with its practice.
>
> And what are we going to do about it? For it is *our* business. We, the people of the United States, and nobody else, must cure whatever is wrong in the industrial situation, typified by this narrative of the growth of the Standard Oil Company.[2]

In 1906, President Theodore Roosevelt initiated an anti-trust suit against Standard Oil, which was broken up in 1909. Other suits followed against other companies. Still other corporations broke up of their own accord, as individual members rebelled; R.J. Reynolds, judging that American Tobacco would not dare to prosecute in the current climate, simply broke his contract and began acting independently. More legislation and regulation was passed. Popular opinion, which had once admired Morgan and others like him as talented business leaders, now swung sharply and suspicion of big business became an important and enduring trait in many parts of American society. In 1912 Morgan himself was called before a US Congressional Committee investigating abuses of corporate power. He left the USA shortly thereafter, and died in Rome on 31 March 1913.

J.P. Morgan's legacy for management is the climate in which businesses operate and popular attitudes to management. Through the nineteenth century, the major issue confronting business was the relationship between capital and labour. By the time Morgan was done with reshaping the American economy, that issue, though still important, was no longer paramount. The new dialectic was the relationship between business and society. What role should business play? What was its responsibility to society, and vice versa? Morgan and his circle believed that government was weak, and that ultimately business had to play a leading role. It could play that role best by curbing its own abuses through concentration and monopoly, eliminating wasteful competition and production and using resources effectively. Their opponents argued that business was *not* an effective regulator, and that regulation had to come from outside: partly from governments, but also from society and the people themselves. Often overlooked is the plea by the Muck Rakers for the population as a whole to think again about the values and ethics of business and what its purpose really was. By blindly following the lead set by either business or government the people were, in the words of Ripley, selling their birthright for a mess of pottage.

The argument is far from over. For a time, during the 1920s and 1930s in America, the regulationists had the upper hand, but in the 1950s a swing back towards business began. The end of Bretton Woods and international currency regulation was a major step forward. So was the increasing strength and power of the global economy, described by **Ohmae** Kenichi in the 1980s and given a tremendous boost by advances in information technology in the 1990s. Global mergers such as Daimler with Chrysler or Renault with Nissan are raising the prospect of many industries such as cars being concentrated in the hands of just a few companies. Concentration, it is argued, gives economies of scale and is the only way that companies can stay afloat in the face of increasing competition; the alternative is business failures with massive job losses and blows to national prosperity. Opponents still argue that concentration is both harmful to consumer interests and a threat to personal freedom. As the pace of globalisation and the rate of concentration in major industries both grow, the debate will become even more intense.

Morgan's career raises major issues not just in economics but also in corporate governance and business ethics. He makes us think about what management is, what it is for, and what purpose it should serve. Are they primarily profit maximisers, or is their main function the production of goods and services which the community needs? Today, we are still pondering the puzzles he set before us.

See also: **Burnham, Fukuzawa, Handy, Machiavelli, Mooney, Ohmae**

Major works

Morgan himself wrote little, and destroyed his own personal papers before his death.

Further reading

Morgan is one of the more controversial figures in US history, and opinions on him tend to be extreme. The biographies given below are comparatively objective, especially Strouse, and all give useful details of Morgan's ideas on business and the role of management. Tarbell is the best and most intelligent of the writers who opposed Morgan and the industrialists; Ripley is entertaining reading and was very influential.

Chernow, R., *The House of Morgan*, New York: Atlantic Monthly Press, 1990.
Fowler, W.W., *Twenty Years inside Life in Wall Street*, New York: Orange Judd, 1880.
Ripley, W.Z., *Trusts, Pools and Corporations*, Boston, MA: Ginn & Co., 1902.
Sinclair, A., *Corsair: The Life of J. Pierpoint Morgan*, Boston, MA: Little, Brown and Company, 1981.
Strouse, J., *Morgan, American Financier*, New York: Random House, 1999.
Tarbell, I.M., *The History of the Standard Oil Company*, New York: McClure, Phillips and Co., 1904, 2 vols.

Notes

1   Quoted in D.M. Chalmers, *The Muck Rake Years*, New York: Van Nostrand, 1974, pp. 82–3.
2   I.M. Tarbell, *The History of the Standard Oil Company*, New York: McClure, Phillips and Co., 1904, vol. 2, pp. 292.

NONAKA IKUJIRO (1935–)

Nonaka Ikujiro has won a worldwide reputation for his work on knowledge management and creation. His book *The Knowledge-Creating Company* (1995) (published in Japan as *Chishiki Sozo Kigyo*), co-written with Takeuchi Hirotaka, was an international best-seller and received a number of major awards. Although his work only came to Western attention with this publication in 1995, Nonaka had for many years been studying how successful Japanese companies create and use knowledge as a source of competitive advantage. His concept of the 'hypertext organisation' was seen as an important model comparable to the 'learning organisation' of Arie **de Geus** and Peter Senge. He is one of Japan's foremost management scholars, and along with **Ohmae** Kenichi is one of the Japanese writers on management most widely read in the West.

Nonaka was born in Tokyo on 19 May 1935. After taking a degree in politics and economics from Waseda University, he spent ten years in industry working with Fuji Electric Company. From 1967 to 1972 he studied at the University of California at Berkeley, taking an MBA degree in 1968 and then a PhD. Returning to Japan, he joined the faculty of business administration at Nanzan University in Nagoya, and was made a professor in 1978. Since 1982 he has held a professorship at the Institute of Business Research at Hitotsubashi University; he also holds a professorship at Berkeley. From 1991 to 1995 he was research director of the Tokyo-based National Institute of Science and Technology Policy.

Pitkethly, in his summary of Nonaka's work (1998), divides his academic career into three phases: (1) that which is concerned with the study of strategy and organisation, in the 1970s and early 1980s; (2) that which is concerned with the study of organisational self-renewal and organisation in the later 1980s; and (3) the phase concerned with the study of organisational knowledge, from about 1990 up to the present. This schema is useful so far as it goes, but it should be made clear that Nonaka sees all three subjects as being tightly linked. Following the standard idea that structure follows strategy, Nonaka sees a corporation's organisational form as being defined by its strategic needs. Strategy, in turn, is a long-term proposition in which the ability to innovate is central to sustained competitiveness. Innovation, in its turn, requires the generation and use of organisational knowledge. That in turn has implications for organisation, as companies need to structure themselves so as to use and generate knowledge effectively. This circular process is a theme which appears several times in Nonaka's later work and contributes to a balanced view of organisation rather than one dominated by a particular function or process.

In the late 1980s, Nonaka developed a theory that innovation and organisational self-renewal are linked. Organisations that do not change stagnate and die; those that survive are constantly evolving and changing, recruiting new talent, setting up new teams and bringing in new knowledge. This theory has echoes of Tom **Peters**, but is even more reminiscent of the Japanese entrepreneur **Ibuka** Masaru, founder of Sony, who believed that continuous innovation was required to not only keep a company ahead of its competitors but to maintain internal organisational vitality. The key common factor in both renewal and innovation was knowledge: knowledge acquisition was the purpose of the first activity, and knowledge use was the function of the second.

Nonaka next set out to construct a theory of organisational knowledge in Japanese firms. In the opening chapters of *The Knowledge-Creating Company*, he is at pains to point out that the system he describes in Japan is different from that of the West, and he offers his description of the Japanese model of organisational knowledge as an explanatory factor for Japan's rapid rise to economic prosperity and success against Western competitors on world markets. The differences extend to concepts as fundamental as the definition of knowledge itself: in Western philosophy, he says, it is generally accepted that knowledge is 'justified true belief', eternal truths and verities that exist primarily as mental constructs. Japanese philosophy, on the other hand, regards knowledge as inherent not in universals but in the interaction between body and mind, and in ourselves and other things: 'the ultimate reality for Japanese lies in the delicate, transitional process of permanent flux, and in visible and concrete matter, rather than in eternal, unchanging, invisible, and abstract entity'.[1]

Accepting that knowledge in Japan is concrete and relational rather than abstract and static offers the first step to understanding Nonaka's theory of organisational knowledge. The second is his division of knowledge into two classes, tacit and explicit. Interestingly, this division is derived from a Western philosopher, Michael Polanyi, whose *Personal Knowledge* (1958) is a strong influence on Nonaka's thinking here. Explicit knowledge is formal, easily codifiable and easy to transmit and understand; tacit knowledge is implicit, hard to grasp and hard to express. Western cultures, says Nonaka, tend to privilege explicit knowledge over tacit knowledge; in Japan, it is the other way around, and tacit knowledge is seen as the most valuable.

There are, he goes on, two important kinds of tacit knowledge: the technical dimension, 'which encompasses the kind of informal and hard-to-pin-down skills or crafts captured in the term "know-how"', and the cognitive dimension, consisting of 'schemata, mental models, beliefs and perceptions so ingrained that we take them for granted'.[2] Nonaka is strongly critical of the early Western approach to management, the scientific management of Frederick W. **Taylor** and his colleagues. Taylor, says, Nonaka, ignored or dismissed the cognitive dimension; and indeed, in the works of many writers on scientific management there is a strong argument against any form of mental model which cannot be supported by scientific proof. At the same time, they took the technical dimension and tried to make it explicit by analysing the elements of skills and tasks and codifying them so as to make them easier to understand. In doing so, says Nonaka, they destroyed much of the value inherent in that knowledge.

Nonaka goes so far as to question the Western belief that knowledge is best passed on through education and training. He cites the example of a famous Japanese baseball player who, although a master of his game, was unable to express either visually or verbally the basics of his skills. Nonaka, here echoing Mary **Follett**, believes that the most important knowledge, tacit knowledge, comes from experience. Hence the Japanese emphasis on the importance of learning from failure: failure constitutes experience, every bit as much as does success, and can be even more important as a source of learning. Tacit knowledge is highly personal and cannot be passed on *en bloc*, it has to be formulated slowly and carefully.

And there, says Nonaka, is the secret of the Japanese approach to knowledge. The most important knowledge is not derived from rote study and learning; it does not come through 'brainstorming' sessions that set out to 'create' knowledge, nor from benchmarking against others. The most important knowledge is that which we develop for ourselves, and is therefore unique and valuable:

> Once the importance of tacit knowledge is realized, then one begins to think about innovation in a whole new way. It is not just about putting together diverse bits of data and informa- tion. It is a highly individual process of personal and organizational self-renewal. The personal commitment of the employees and their identity with the company and its mission become indispensable. In this respect, the creation of new knowledge is as much about ideals as it is about ideas. And that fact fuels innovation. The essence of innovation is to re-create the world according to a particular ideal or vision.[3]

This passage could easily describe the approach to innovation of many of Japan's leading companies, such as Sony and Matsushita (and Nonaka devotes an entire chapter to the successful creation of knowledge at Matsushita, which has a very strong guiding philosophy and ideal). He goes on to state that knowledge and innovation are 'not the responsibility of a selected few – a specialist in research and development, strategic planning, or marketing – but that of everyone in the organisation'.[4] This idea that innovation and knowledge creation are the responsibility of everyone in the organisation is one that Nonaka returns to repeatedly. He is sharply critical of American reorganisational tactics such as delayering, very popular in the 1980s and 1990s, which followed the advice of Tom Peters to get rid of middle management 'dead wood' and make the organisation more creative and more flexible. To Nonaka, this is tantamount to ripping the heart out of the organisation: middle managers have a vital role to play not only in creating knowledge, but also in holding the organisation together and transmitting knowledge through its various units and teams.

The bulk of *The Knowledge-Creating Company* is taken up with showing how this system works in practice. Nonaka uses case studies, not only of Matsushita but also of Honda, Canon, NEC and Fuji-Xerox, among others, to great effect; as he says, the book demonstrates to Western managers at least some of the keys to Japanese competitive success. He is on less sure ground when he proposes a synthesis aiming for the best of both worlds. He suggests, for example, that the distinction between tacit and explicit knowledge is a false dichotomy, which at once raises a logical problem: if tacit and explicit knowledge are in fact of equal value, why should Western companies give up on their long-cherished attachment to the latter? In fact, Nonaka continues to make clear the idea that tacit knowledge is the superior form. He proposes a form of matrix organisation which he calls the 'hypertext organisation' which uses technology to enable the rapid transmission of both forms of knowledge between elements of the organisation. One of the strengths of the hypertext organisation is that it allows everyone and every team and department in the organisation to use the IT network to 'buy into' the organisation at an equal level; everyone's knowledge is valued equally and has an equal impact on organisational learning.

Unlike other concepts of learning organisations, Nonaka puts the emphasis on internally generated learning, tacit knowledge acquired through experience and practice rather than scanned from the environment or learned through formal systems. He makes explicit the link between knowledge, innovation, organisation and renewal in a way that few other writers have done. He urges Western companies to follow the Japanese lead in this field. In fact, some have done so. In the early twentieth century the firm of Cadbury Brothers in Britain adopted a kind of hypertext organisation without the technology, using committee systems and employee suggestions schemes to generate internal knowledge, with such success that one observer, Herbert **Casson**, commented, 'At Cadbury, everyone thinks.' But such examples are rare, and the question needs to be asked: can Western companies overcome the 'handicap' that training and education, rather than experience and reflection, are the best ways to generate knowledge? Certainly there are powerful epistemological, social and even institutional reasons why this will not happen quickly: it is hard to imagine Western business schools, for example, agreeing to abolish themselves on the grounds that explicit knowledge is no longer needed.

Nonaka's importance to modern management is twofold. First, he is one of the world's leading thinkers and writers on knowledge management, and his work informs nearly every aspect of this emerging discipline. Second, he is one of the leading interpreters of Japanese management methods and techniques for Western audiences. Like Ohmae, he has striven to bring Eastern and Western managers closer together, and has provided much food for thought on the lessons to be learned by comparing management cultures.

See also: **Argyris, Boisot, Drucker, Follett, Fukuzawa, Hofstede, Ibuka, Ohmae, Peters, Toyoda**

Major works

Only two of Nonaka's major works have appeared in English; his earlier books remain to be translated. He has however authored and co-authored a number of influential English-language journal articles.

Soshiki to Shijyo: Soshiki no Kankyou Tekigou Riron (Organization and Market: A Contingency Theory), Tokyo: Chikura Shobo, 1974.
Shippai no Honshitsu (Essentials of Failure), Tokyo: Diamond Sha, 1984.
Chishiki Sozo no Keiei (The Management of Knowledge Creation), Tokyo: Nihon Keizai Shinbun Sha, 1990.
(With H. Takeuchi) *The Knowledge-Creating Company*, New York: Oxford University Press, 1995; published in Japan as *Chishiki Sozo Kigyo*.
(ed.) *Strategic vs. Evolutionary Management: A US–Japan Comparison of Strategy and Organization*, Amsterdam: North Holland, 1995.

Further reading

Pitkethly's short essay is a useful introduction to Nonaka, particularly in charting the evolution of his ideas. Polanyi, as noted, is an important influence and a seminal work for knowledge management in any case.

Pitkethly, R., 'Nonaka, Ikujiro', in M. Warner (ed.), *Handbook of Management Thinking*, London: International Thomson Business Press, 1998, pp. 482–7.
Polanyi, M., *Personal Knowledge*, Chicago: University of Chicago Press, 1958.

Notes

1 I. Nonaka and H. Takeuchi, *The Knowledge-Creating Company*, New York: Oxford University Press, 1995, pp. 31–2.
2 *Ibid.*, p. 8.
3 *Ibid.*, p. 10.
4 *Ibid.*

OHMAE KENICHI (1943–)

Ohmae Kenichi is one of Japan's most prominent business writers and consultants, known in Japan as 'Mr Strategy'. He first came to the attention of the West with his book *The Mind of the Strategist* in 1982. His work was at first seen as a description of how Japanese firms do strategy, but his ideas have since had a growing acceptance among Western firms as well. His later work on globalisation has set many of the parameters of the current debate. In the 1980s, Ohmae was seen as the apostle of an approach to management which was regarded by many as the best in the world, the Japanese system with its emphases on knowledge, innovation, quality and marketing. Today, he is seen as more of a world figure, forecasting the rise and triumph of a technology-enabled globalisation.

Ohmae was born on 21 February 1943 in the city of Kita-Kyushu in southern Japan. He attended Waseda University, taking an undergraduate degree in chemistry in 1966 and an MA in nuclear physics in 1968. He then went to the USA, where he took a PhD in nuclear engineering at the Massachusetts Institute of Technology. He had also studied music in Japan, and was for a time a flautist with a symphony orchestra. From 1970–2 he worked with Hitachi Nuclear Power as an engineer on the company's fast breeder reactor programme. He then joined the US consulting firm McKinsey & Co., and in 1979 was appointed general manager of the company's Tokyo office; in 1989 he was named chairman and general manager of McKinsey Japan. He has held many other posts, including that of advisor to several Japanese prime ministers, and in 1993 established the Heisei Policy Research Institute for studies in policy planning. He has also been active in politics, founding his own political party in 1992 with the aim of reforming Japanese political life, and has stood as a candidate for Mayor of Tokyo and for a seat in the House of Representatives – unsuccessfully in both cases. He is a prolific writer and columnist, and his work has appeared in newspapers and journals in Japan, the USA and Europe. He lives in Yokohama.

Ohmae's interest in strategy began with his early years at McKinsey, and he had already published on the subject in Japan before *The Mind of the Strategist* brought him to the attention of the outside world. Ohmae was stimulated to write the book, he tells us, by the frequent enquiries he received from Western managers and consultants as to the secret of Japanese business success. Most of his Western contacts, he said, believed that there had to be more to the Japanese recipe for success than 'consensus decision making, company songs and quality circles'.[1] Ohmae agrees, and says that the principal ingredient in the Japanese success story from the 1950s through to the 1980s was the ability of Japanese senior managers to think strategically. Unlike their Western counterparts, Japanese firms do not tend to have separate strategy departments or formal strategy making processes. Instead, there is often one person (or sometimes a group) who has a brilliant, part-intuitive grasp of strategy and who is constantly engaged in the process of strategy making.

Like Henry **Mintzberg**, Ohmae does not see strategy as a set of formal steps and processes, and tends to view strategy as art rather than science:

> successful business strategies result not from rigorous analysis but from a particular state of mind. In what I call the mind of the strategist, insight and a consequent drive for achievement, often amounting to a sense of mission, fuel a thought process which is basically creative and intuitive rather than rational. Strategists do not reject analysis. Indeed they can hardly do without it. But they use it only to stimulate the creative process, to test the ideas that emerge, to work out their strategic implications, or to ensure successful execution of high-potential 'wild' ideas that might otherwise never be implemented properly. Great strategies, like great works of art or great scientific discoveries, call for technical mastery in the working out but originate in insights that are beyond the reach of conscious analysis.[2]

During the rise of corporate Japan the role of brilliant intuitive strategist was often fulfilled by the founder or CEO. But by the 1970s most big Japanese corporations were well established and firmly institutionalised, with strong hierarchies and systems of promotion by seniority. How then did strategy manage to flourish? Ohmae says that, as Japanese companies mature, the creation of strategy becomes the province of talented creative groups of younger managers – he calls them *samurai* – who, though not hierarchically senior, are given the freedom to create and to almost literally dream the company's future. In this way, there is a constant process of renewal of ideas and values coming from below.

This theme of renewal is often found in Ohmae's work, and was at the centre of his political activities as well. The first stage in renewal is to determine the critical factors that require analysis. Here, he says, many companies go wrong by identifying the wrong critical factors. For example, in a company where overtime work is rising and is increasing the wage bill, it is possible to view the problem in several ways. Are workers working hard enough during their regular hours? Are they taking excessively long breaks, or spending time on private matters during regular hours? It takes an extra creative leap, says Ohmae, to go beyond these ideas, which look only at the symptoms of the problem, and look instead at the cause: is the company's workforce large enough for the tasks in front of it? Another important pre-requisite is to have identified the key factors for success (KFS) in a given industry. These will vary, and are not always immediately obvious. In the steel industry, for example, the key factor for success may be the ability to produce high quality steel at a low cost; in breweries, the key factor may be in distribution, reaching the maximum number of high volume customers.

Like Michael **Porter**, Ohmae offers four generic strategic routes which any company can follow. One option that he rules out is head-to-head competition, in the same market with the same products: this can only end in a price war, which is damaging to everyone. His four recommendations are:

1   Compete in the same market but concentrate on strengthening KFS so as to create differential advantage.
2   Emphasise products and services for which there is no direct competition so as to create relative superiority in the market.
3   Look to change the rules of the game, putting your competitors at a disadvantage and competing on the basis of 'aggressive initiatives'.
4   Innovate and create new products and services which your competitors cannot match, and compete on the basis of 'strategic degrees of freedom'.

This is in fact quite a tough approach to strategy, much more so than Porter's relatively simple fourfold typology which requires just two basic decisions. The Ohmae model cannot really be approached unless the manager or team has sufficient vision and courage to consider all four options, and the risks they may involve. It is for this reason that Ohmae stresses over and over again the idea of the mind of the strategist. Those who are practised in strategic thinking will be able to master these concepts and view the alternatives clearly and in a creative manner. Above all, they are able to avoid the obvious traps:

> Strategic thinking in business must break out of the limited
> scope of vision that entraps deer on the highway. It must be
> backed by the daily use of imagination and by constant
> training in logical thought processes. Success must be
> summoned: it will not come unbidden or unplanned ...
> To become an effective strategist requires constant practice in
> strategic thinking. It is a daily discipline, not a resource that
> can be left dormant in normal times and then tapped at will in
> an emergency.[3]

All strategic thinking, says Ohmae, operates under three constraints. He names these – with a McKinsey consultant's typical love of alliteration – reality, ripeness and resources. *Reality* refers to the need to focus on concepts that are actually relevant to the company's needs; innovating new products that will hurt the company's existing markets without providing a corresponding new market are an example of the need for realism. *Ripeness*, or timeliness, refers to whether the strategy is right for the time. Many strategic options are chosen prematurely; he cites the introduction of dishwashers to Japan in the 1970s, at a time when most kitchens were still too small to accommodate them. Finally, *resources* reflects whether the company's resources are adequate to implementing the strategy. This, says Ohmae, is an aspect that many strategists often overlook, and is a reason why so many diversifications fail: the distiller Suntory, for example, developed a successful product in Kirin beer but lacked the experience and resources to distribute beer effectively and had corresponding difficulties in the market. Recognising these constraints and managing them is a key attribute of successful strategic thinkers.

In the later 1980s Ohmae turned his attention to the onset of globalisation. *Triad Power*, published in 1985, noted the increasing concentration of economic power in three areas: Western Europe, the USA and Japan. Ohmae noted too how these three regions were becoming increasingly economically interdependent. Often taken as a prediction of the future, in fact *Triad Power* was a description of what was going on at the time in the mid-1980s. Ohmae believed that the economic power of the triad members would allow them to defend their economic supremacy against the rest of the world for the foreseeable future; in this he may have been premature, failing to foresee the rise of China in particular as a coming economic superpower. *Triad Power* caused a minor sensation among left-wing politicians and groups around the world, who were arguing against precisely this concentration of economic power.

More recently, *The Borderless World* (1990) has stressed the theme of interdependence and noted how virtually every company today is competing in a global market, whether it knows it or not; even if its primary market is local and domestic, it is vulnerable to foreign competition. Ohmae argued that international trade was breaking down not only economic barriers but also political ones, and that nation-states were fast becoming irrelevant. Globalisation was not only an economic force, but also a technological and cultural one, and he believed that the emergence of global communications networks such as the Internet would create new economic, political and cultural realities. He urged companies to begin planning for the new economy and to help bring it to pass. Again, there is the theme of renewal: Ohmae believed that the old world order was stagnant and out of date and a new one was waiting to be ushered in.

The dotcom collapse of 2001 and the ensuing wave of scepticism about the new economy has made many see Ohmae's ideas as ahead of their time, at the very least. More seriously, the work of **Hofstede** and his successors on cross-cultural management has shown how enduring and resilient the barriers of culture, in particular, can be. The nation-state, too, is not going to go down before the forces of globalisation without a struggle. It is far too soon to say whether Ohmae's vision will, or will not, come to pass. But his ideas on globalisation, and on strategy, are too powerful to be ignored.

See also: **Chandler, Fukuzawa, Hofstede, Machiavelli, Mintzberg, Nonaka, Porter**

Major works

The Mind of the Strategist, New York: McGraw-Hill, 1982.
Triad Power: The Coming Shape of Global Competition, New York: The Free Press, 1985.
The Borderless World: Power and Strategy in the Interlinked Economy, New York: Collins, 1990.

Further reading

Ohmae's approach to strategy should be compared to Nonaka on knowledge management: there are many points of common ground. Porter's approach to strategy is in contrast to that of the West, while Mintzberg manages to partake of both yet agree with neither.

Mintzberg, H., *The Rise and Fall of Strategic Planning*, New York: The Free Press, 1993.
Nonaka, I. and Takeuchi, H., *The Knowledge-Creating Company*, New York: Oxford University Press, 1995.

Porter, M., *Competitive Strategy: Techniques for Analyzing Industries and Competitors*, New York: The Free Press, 1980.

Notes

1   K. Ohmae, *The Mind of the Strategist*, New York: McGraw-Hill, 1982, p. 1.
2   *Ibid.*, p. 4
3   *Ibid.*, p. 78.

ROBERT OWEN (1771–1858)

Robert Owen was an entrepreneur who became one of Britain's most successful business leaders during the Industrial Revolution. Paradoxically, he was also one of the most important figures in modern socialism, who helped to found the trade union movement and the cooperative movement. His utopian views of economics and society were falling into disrepute even in his own lifetime, but his successes as a manager remain outstanding. His methods of personnel management were nearly a century ahead of their time, and in the early twentieth century both British and American management writers saw him as a major influence and role model for leadership. His views on business ethics, concerning both the relationship between employers and workers and the relationship between business and society, remain of primary importance.

Owen was born in Newtown, Montgomeryshire, Wales on 14 May 1771 into a fairly humble family; his father was an ironmonger and saddle maker. The youngest of seven children, he was largely self-educated, but was assisted by a quick and retentive memory and a love of reading. He later described as his two formative influences Defoe's novel *Robinson Crusoe*, which taught him self-reliance, and the Methodist tracts handed out by the local ladies, which he said turned him into an atheist by the age of ten. In 1781 he left home to live and work with his elder brother in London; a year later, aged eleven, he was apprenticed to a draper in Stamford, Lincolnshire. Here he learned, among other things, how to gauge the quality of cloth, and he also continued his self-education, reading voraciously before and after work.

Owen completed his apprenticeship at age fifteen and moved back to London, taking a job as a shop assistant. Disliking the work, he went north to Manchester and took work as an assistant in a haberdashery. This was the most important move of his life so far. Manchester was prospering as new factories were being built and the Industrial

Revolution was in full swing. Richard **Arkwright** was then at the height of his success and other entrepreneurs such as Samuel Oldknow and David Dale were also on the rise. Quickly seeing where the opportunities lay, Owen quit his job and set up a partnership with a mechanic named John Jones to make and sell spinning mules, a relatively new piece of technology designed by Samuel Crompton in 1779. Jones made the machines, while Owen sold them, handled the finances and managed the firm's forty workmen. His almost total lack of technical knowledge at the outset of the venture never proved a hindrance, and the partnership prospered. The relationship between Jones and himself did not last, however, and Owen sold his share and used the profits to buy three spinning mules, with which he set up a small workshop and began spinning and selling high-quality yarn. By 1790 he was earning profits of around £6 a week.

The next turning point in his career came when a local mill owner, Peter Drinkwater, advertised for a mill manager. Owen applied for the post. When asked what salary he expected, he asked for £300 per year. When Drinkwater pointed out that this was double what any other candidate had asked, Owen responded by saying that he was already earning this much in his own business and would not be interested in working for less. When he showed Drinkwater his books and his workshop, the latter was so impressed that he offered Owen the job of managing a modern factory employing over 500 people. Owen was then nineteen years old.

His appointment had been greeted with disbelief by the Manchester mill-owning community, who declared that Drinkwater had lost his senses. But Owen, although still short on technical experience, was emerging as a born manager of people. He introduced new working methods and found new sources of high-quality cotton from North America, and his skilful management improved quality and nearly trebled productivity in the first two years. Drinkwater, who clearly believed in the separation of ownership and control – Owen says he visited his mill just three times in four years – rewarded Owen with a partnership and a free hand in managing the business. The partnership came to an end, however, when the ambitious young mill owner Samuel Oldknow, Drinkwater's son-in-law, persuaded the latter to dissolve the partnership and hand the mill over to himself. Owen was offered the job of mill manager at any wage he cared to name, but he seems to have disliked Oldknow and was in any case anxious to strike out on his own.

In 1795, now aged twenty-four, he founded the Chorlton Twist Company in Manchester, overseeing the building of the new mill and then managing the business once it was in operation. He was now quite prosperous and a man of affairs in Manchester. He became a member of the Literary and Philosophical Society of Manchester and gave several papers before it, and numbered among his friends scholars and scientists such as Robert Fulton, to whose plans for canal-building Owen gave encouragement. Owen's new business took him frequently to Glasgow, where he met David Dale, owner of New Lanark, one of the largest and most prosperous mills in Scotland. He also met and fell in love with Dale's daughter Caroline. There was, however, a major obstacle to their marrying: the Dales were devoutly religious, while Owen was an atheist. To smooth the path of romance, Owen offered to buy New Lanark for the colossal sum of £60,000, to be paid in instalments. Dale agreed, and the purchase and marriage both went ahead.

Owen took over New Lanark in 1800, and managed it for the next twenty-eight years. Under his guidance, New Lanark was not only hugely profitable but a model of enlightened capitalism. The patience, attention to detail and people management skills that he had developed in Manchester now came fully into their own. New Lanark was a much larger establishment than the Drinkwater mill or his own Chorlton Twist Company; in addition, it was located some way out of Glasgow, and most of the workers lived on site. The problems of management were correspondingly more complex.

Some mill owners in the Industrial Revolution did make attempts to look after their employees both in and out of the workplace; others did not, and many mills were dangerous, unsanitary places with illness and accidents taking a heavy toll among the workers, many of whom were women and children. Owen was from the beginning opposed to child labour, and later strongly supported legislation prohibiting the practice. In his own mill he immediately raised the minimum working age from ten to twelve, and later to fourteen; he also stopped the previous practice of taking in pauper children as workers. Instead of working, children were given an education in the mill school. For all workers, Owen cut the working day from fourteen hours to ten and three-quarter hours – still long by modern standards, but a radical step for the time – and provision was made for meals and adequate rest breaks. Owen ensured his mill was clean and as safe as possible given the technology he was using, and in particular made sure that there were adequate sanitary facilities.

Rather than driving his workers, Owen chose to motivate them. Contrary to Owen's own later utopian socialist beliefs, discipline and control were strong in New Lanark, and there was a hierarchy of supervision; drunkenness was not tolerated and workers whose conduct was persistently poor were liable to be dismissed. One of the more interesting pieces of motivational psychology that Owen used was the so-called 'silent monitor', a coloured symbol which was placed over each worker's station to denote his or her conduct and performance at work the preceding day. If the worker's conduct had been poor, the symbol was black; if merely indifferent it was blue; good conduct was rewarded by a yellow symbol, and excellent conduct by a white one. Records were kept of what symbols had been awarded over time, similar, said Owen, to the recording angel marking down the good and bad deeds of the human character. The task of handing out the symbols was carried out by the superintendents, but any worker who felt he or she had been unjustly treated could appeal to Owen in person.

This right of appeal was in fact an important element in Owen's system of discipline. In particular, he kept a watchful eye on his managers and superintendents, ensuring that they did not abuse their powers over the workers. He perceived that the key to good discipline was equity and fairness; in a system where all were perceived to be treated fairly and according to merit, no one would complain if they were punished for a genuine transgression (and even if they did, they would get little support from their co-workers).

Owen believed that, by improving the quality of life and the physical conditions of work for his workmen and their families, not only would he be contributing to the good of society, but also happier, healthier workers would be more efficient and productivity and quality would improve. He had already tried some limited experiments of this sort while in Manchester, and on coming to New Lanark resolved to attempt widespread reforms. As he later wrote:

> My intention was not to be a mere manager of cotton mills as such mills were at this time being managed – but to introduce principles in the conduct of the people which I had successfully commenced with the work-people at Mr. Drinkwater's factory, and to change the conditions of the people who, I saw, were surrounded by circumstances having an injurious influence upon the character of the entire population of New Lanark. I had now, by a course of events, got under control the groundwork on which to try the experiments long wished for, but little expected ever to be in my power to carry into execution.[1]

The houses of the factory workers at New Lanark were cleaned and enlarged, and new accommodation was built; systems were installed for proper drainage and sanitation. Health care was provided free from the beginning. The private shops which had been overcharging workers had their leases terminated, and Owen established company-owned shops which offered good quality goods at fair prices; interestingly, while many other model communities of the nineteenth century were strictly teetotal, Owen's shops sold beer and spirits at cost price.

Another important aspect of the New Lanark model community was education. There had been education at New Lanark under Dale, but it had been mostly religious in nature. Owen, unsurprisingly, abolished this and instituted a secular education programme, first for children and then later for adults as well. There has in the past been much debate as to whether Owen's reforms were motivated by genuine social concern or for the advancement of his enterprise's profit, and in fact, at least during the New Lanark period, it is difficult to disentangle the two motives. The economist G.D.H. Cole was later to note that

> The basis of Owenism was his theory of education, as a means to the formation of character and the possession of happiness. First and foremost Owen believed in the power of education, rightly directed, to turn the world's affairs into a prosperous course ... Without it, error and disunity were bound to persist; by its means the vast productive powers known to science would be unloosed for the common good of all.[2]

The success of the management reforms and the model community was such that New Lanark prospered: Owen paid off the debt to his father-in-law ahead of schedule and went on to become a rich man. By 1820, he was a hero to many in Britain, and his name was becoming known overseas as well. As many as two thousand visitors a year came to see New Lanark, including personalities as various as the abolitionist William Wilberforce, the future US president John Quincy Adams and the Russian Grand Duke Nikolai, later Tsar Nicholas I. Economists and philosophers including Jeremy Bentham, James Mill and Thomas Malthus were also among the visitors, and Bentham was so impressed that he bought a one-sixth partnership in the business. Owen, believing that his system could easily be replicated, appealed to other industrialists to follow his lead:

He went on to say that every manufacturer realised the need for getting the best machinery and taking the greatest care of it. 'If, then, due care as to the state of your inanimate machines can produce such beneficial results, what may not be expected if you devote equal care to your more vital machines, which are far more wonderfully constructed?' At New Lanark, he pointed out, he had done his best to care for the minds and bodies of the workers, and 'the time and money so spent, even while such improvements are in progress only, and but half their beneficial results obtained, are now producing a return exceeding 50 per cent., and will shortly create profits equal to cent. per cent. on the original capital expended in these mental improvements'.[3]

Yet there is evidence that Owen himself was growing increasingly disenchanted with the system of which he himself was a part, and in 1815, in his *Observations on the Effect of the Manufacturing System*, he stated his belief that managers who managed solely for pecuniary gain were destructive to the happiness of the nation and of society. He began considering how to propagate the New Lanark model more directly, and became involved with various other communities who attempted to work on his model, even giving financial support to some; unfortunately, many of these communities were run by visionary utopians or downright cranks, and most failed. Famously, Owen tried to establish a community of his own in the USA at New Harmony, Indiana between 1825–8, but gave up after finding it impossible to persuade the community to stick to his principles; this failure is often put down to rugged Yankee individualism being ill suited to the needs of communal life, but is more likely due to the fact that Owen tried to manage this community from a distance, remaining at New Lanark and only visiting the colony on a few occasions.

More practical achievements and dissemination of his views came in two other directions. Realising that many mill owners would never see that proper treatment of their workers was not only good for society but good for themselves, Owen decided that the workers would need to organise in order to press for their rights, and set about reorganising the fledgling trade union movement. In 1833–4 he engineered the creation of the Grand National Consolidated Trades Union with half a million members. This organisation did not last long, but it did give rise to the Chartist movement and later organised labour bodies such as the Trades Union Congress in Britain. Owen also supported the cooperative movement, which he saw as embodying many of his principles of communal working, solidarity and improving prosperity and living conditions for all. Here, Owen the atheist found willing allies among the churches, particularly the dissenting faiths. By 1830 the cooperative movement numbered more than 300 societies throughout the UK and was spreading to the continent. Owen was quick to perceive the opportunities the movement offered for worker management, which he believed would give workers still more control over their lives and greater prosperity.

Owen's influence has been widespread. In the UK, he became the archetypal social capitalist, a man who showed how a successful business could be an ethically sound one: Titus Salt, George and Edward **Cadbury**, Benjamin Seebohm Rowntree and William **Lever** all knew his ideas, and the model villages at Saltaire, Bournville and Port Sunlight are all heirs to his work. In the mid-twentieth century there was renewed interest in his personnel management methods and he has been described as one of the founders of modern management by no lesser authorities than Lyndall **Urwick** and Edward Brech.

Comparison is sometimes made between Owen and one of the founders of modern communism, Friedrich Engels. Inheriting ownership of a Manchester mill from his father, Engels, while he was collaborating with Marx, was at the same time a successful business man with considerable personal wealth and a pair of mistresses (sisters, as it happens) and an enthusiastic member of his local fox hunt. Engels's argument, however, was a pragmatic one: the workers' revolution would one day overthrow the capitalist system, but that day had not yet come, and so in the mean time he had a responsibility to his employees and their families to run an efficient business and keep them in work. (The need to provide funds to support his indigent colleague Karl Marx may also have played a role in his decision.) Owen took a different view. To him, running a successful business and the egalitarian principles of socialism were not incompatible or mutually exclusive. Rather, business was necessary to create prosperity, while a socialist system was indispensable to its just distribution.

Ian Donnachie, author of the best recent biography of Owen, says that his thinking was often woolly at best; as an economist he was second-rate, and he was so impressed by the potential shown in New Lanark and some of the other successful communities with which he was associated that he believed this potential stemmed entirely from the character of the people who lived and worked there. He failed to understand that a large portion of the success of these communities was due to himself, to his vision and leadership and his ability to manage people. It is this, say Urwick and Brech, that accounts for his success at Drinkwater, Chorlton and New Lanark:

> his success came from a different source, an inherent executive ability, an intuitive grasp of the principles of sound management and of the methods of applying them effectively. Above all, he knew how to handle his people, how to weld them into a team and to secure from them a degree of co-operation and achievement to which only the real leader can aspire.[4]

See also: **Arkwright, Cadbury, Handy, Heinz, Lever, Urwick**

Major works

Owen was a prolific writer, especially in his later years, but most of his works are socialist or other political tracts. *A Statement Regarding the New Lanark Establishment* is his appeal to other manufacturers to follow his lead. *Observations on the Effect of the Manufacturing System* was written in support of the movement to reform factory working conditions, and is a widely cited condemnation of the practices of many of his fellow mill owners.

A Statement Regarding the New Lanark Establishment, Edinburgh, 1812.
Observations on the Effect of the Manufacturing System, London, 1815.
Two Memorials on Behalf of the Working Classes, London, 1818.

Further reading

Owen's career and ideas remain highly contentious, and most attention focuses on his economics and utopian beliefs. Urwick and Brech provide the best summary of his management methods, and Pollard helps to set him in context. Cole is a good overall assessment of his life and works. Donnachie is the most recent biography, and also gives some attention to Owen's management style.

Cole, G.D.H., *The Life of Robert Owen*, London: Macmillan, 1930.
Donnachie, I., *Robert Owen*, East Linton: Tuckwell Press, 2000.
Pollard, S., *The Genesis of Modern Management*, London: Edward Arnold, 1965.
Urwick, L.F. and Brech, E.F.L., *The Making of Scientific Management*, vol. 2, *Management in British Industry*, London: Management Publications Trust, 1949.

Notes

1 Quoted in L.F. Urwick and E.F.L. Brech, *The Making of Scientific Management*, vol. 2, *Management in British Industry*, London: Management Publications Trust, 1949, p. 49.
2 G.D.H. Cole, *The Life of Robert Owen*, London: Macmillan, 1930, p. 126.
3 *Ibid.*, p. 138.
4 Urwick and Brech, *The Making of Scientific Management*, p. 55.

TOM PETERS (1942–)

Tom Peters was one of the most popular and widely read management gurus of the 1980s and 1990s. A consultant by training rather than an academic, he has drawn on his own business experiences and his understandings of the causes behind business successes and failures to present a compelling picture of American business and management culture; and to argue for revolutionary changes in that culture. He believes that many of the fundamental principles on which American management is based are outmoded, outdated and wrong. In his later works he speaks of the need for 'liberation' from the values of the past, especially away from the overly mechanistic approach to management and organisation which developed from scientific management, and a move towards flatter hierarchies, decentralisation, creativity and freedom of action for managers and workers alike.

Thomas J. Peters was born in Baltimore, Maryland on 7 November 1942. After taking a bachelor's degree from Cornell University, he served in the US Navy from 1966 to 1970, seeing action in the Vietnam War. Leaving the navy, he joined the consulting firm Peate Marwick Mitchell, also taking an MBA from Stanford University in 1972. In 1973 he joined the US Government Office of Management and Budget in Washington, DC, first as director of a cabinet committee on international narcotics control, and then as assistant to the director for federal drug abuse policy. In 1974 he moved to San Francisco and joined the international management consultants McKinsey & Co.

At McKinsey, Peters became interested in the concepts of organisational effectiveness and excellence. He had previously served in two highly ineffective organisations: the US armed forces, trying and failing to win the war in Vietnam, and the US federal administration, trying and failing to win the war on drugs. The highly 'rationalist' and bureaucratic approach of both organisations seemed to be a contributing factor in these failures, and Peters began developing ideas for an alternative way. He became known as a highly effective consultant, writer and speaker, and by 1976 had become McKinsey's principal practice leader on organisational effectiveness, working with other McKinsey 'stars' of the 1970s such as Richard Pascale and Robert Waterman, with whom he developed the now famous 7S model of organisational variables: structure, strategy, systems, skills, staff, style and shared values.

It was with Bob Waterman, again, that Peters produced what is still his most famous and widely read book, *In Search of Excellence*, in 1982.

This sold over a million copies worldwide and became one of the most popular management books of all time. Shortly before its publication, Peters left McKinsey to set up his own firm, the Tom Peters Group, through which he continues to undertake consulting programmes and organise seminars. He became known as a pundit: his media credits include a weekly column syndicated in US and some foreign newspapers, and a television series on the PBS network. Later books, especially *Thriving on Chaos* (1987) and *Liberation Management* (1992), have also been extremely popular.

In *In Search of Excellence*, Peters asks what it is that companies can do to achieve excellence. He chooses to examine the subject not by using academic models, but by using his own experiences and those of his colleagues, selecting real-life examples of companies which have achieved excellence and then seeking common factors. He develops here the idea of the 7S model referred to above, and makes it clear that of the seven elements it is the final one, shared values, which is most important. In his view, excellence is a cultural factor, with companies working hard to make sure employees buy into that culture. He quotes the psychologist Ernest Becker to the effect that people are driven by two apparently contradictory factors: a need to conform, and a simultaneous need to be seen as individuals (fuller explanation of this idea can be seen in Abraham **Maslow**'s concept of the hierarchy of needs). Companies which achieve excellence will have to meet both these needs. Peters accepts that this is a paradox, and continues: 'If there is one striking feature of the excellent companies, it is this ability to manage ambiguity and paradox. What our rational economist friends tell us ought not to be possible the excellent companies do routinely.'[1]

Peters then brings in what he calls the eight attributes of an 'excellent' company. These are:

1   A bias for action (taking the initiative).
2   Close to the customer.
3   Autonomy and entrepreneurship.
4   Productivity through people.
5   Hands-on, value driven leadership.
6   Stick to the knitting (stay close to the business you know).
7   Simple form, lean staff.
8   Simultaneous tight-loose properties (central core values combined with decentralised organisation).[2]

Quality and customer orientation are also important hallmarks, but Peters puts very strong emphasis on streamlining and simplifying organisations. *In Search of Excellence* claimed that excellent companies were those which were 'brilliant on basics'; 'Tools didn't substitute for thinking ... those companies worked hard to keep things simple in a complex world.'[3] His later books take up this theme even more strongly. In *Thriving on Chaos*, for example, he attacks the cult of 'giantism' and, by implication, Taylorism and the whole concept of the division of labour, calling for greater empowerment of employees and fewer controls. In *Liberation Management* he cites the German *mittelstand* system which encourages many small and mid-sized companies to establish themselves in niche markets, limiting growth but managing innovation and customer service through small, focused units. He has consistently attacked large, inflexible organisations and called for delayering and cutting down of hierarchy in order to bring top management closer to the workforce: in *Liberation Management*, in an obvious attack on the **Chandler**-inspired view of professional management being the backbone of the American industrial system, he claimed that 'middle management, as we have known it since the railroads invented it right after the Civil War, is dead'.[4]

The idea of a 'revolution' in outlook on the part of management, which became a running theme in Peters's later work, is present here as well. He believes that the notion of management as a science has come close to eclipsing the notion of management as an art and that:

> Professionalism in management is regularly equated with hard-headed rationality. ... The numerative, rationalist approach to management dominates the business schools. It teaches us that well-trained professional managers can manage anything. It seeks detached, analytical justification for all decisions. It is right enough to be dangerously wrong, and it has arguably led us seriously astray.[5]

He attacks concepts such as economy of scale and low-cost production which are often believed to be the only ways to success: 'The numerative, analytical component has an in-built conservative bias. Cost reduction becomes priority number one and revenue enhancement takes a back seat.'[6] He encourages 'overspending' on product development, quality control and customer service, arguing that even if these do not yield value for money in the classical sense, encouraging innovation and focusing on customers are powerful marketing tools and will help the company achieve excellence.

Running throughout *In Search of Excellence* is a sense of urgency: unless American industry begins to adapt its thinking and ideas, it will be unable to compete with more efficient, more flexible and more customer-centred competitors coming in from abroad, especially Japan. The early 1980s was a time when American business, and some other segments of society as well, finally woke up to the competitive threat posed by Japan. In some circles the response bordered on near-paranoia, with Michael Crichton's novel *Rising Sun*, for example, suggesting that the Japanese competitive assault posed a threat to the American way of life. There were frantic searches for the secrets of Japanese success, and a sudden revival of interest in the work of American quality gurus such as W. Edwards **Deming**. Peters paid full tribute to the success of the Japanese firms, especially their ability to manage knowledge – he uses the concept 'learning organisation' here – but like another American guru, Rosabeth Moss Kanter, he also believes that American companies have to tap into their own inner cultural strengths: freedom, democracy, creativity and innovation, in other words, the things that made America great in the first place.

The ideas introduced in *In Search of Excellence* were developed and drawn out in Peters's later works, sometimes to extreme lengths. In *Thriving on Chaos*, he warned that the recommendations spelled out in *In Search of Excellence* were no longer 'nice-to-do' but were now 'must-do' concepts. In *Liberation Management* he describes in more detail his concept of a management revolution, the principles of which are a complete rethinking of organisational scale and control, with a greater emphasis on decentralised units and flexibility. The concept of managing ambiguity, which he discusses as a key feature of managerial excellence in *In Search of Excellence*, is now a major theme running through all his work. He continues his assault on bureaucracy, taking this to at times extreme lengths and urging organisations to scrap all hierarchy; control is the enemy of entrepreneurship, and the latter must be promoted at all costs. In a world of globalisation and rapid technological change, Peters sees change moving at such a rate that it amounts almost to chaos. Instead of trying to defend against change, however, organisations should embrace and even create change. He is in favour of 'stirring the pot', shaking up organisations and people so as to stimulate them and encourage new ideas. He attacks any notion that successful systems should be left well enough alone, as exemplified in the old American saying, 'if it ain't broke, don't fix it'; Peters's response is, 'if it's not broke, it's because you haven't looked hard enough. Fix it anyway.' Organisations should never be allowed to settle, never be given time enough to build up defensive routines.

Only through this constant process of change and regeneration can businesses survive.

Peters's ideas have attracted much criticism. The concept of management chaos conflicts with a basic human need for stability, which is shared by most workers and most managers in most organisations; the bitter hostility to the wave of corporate downsizings in the USA, which was inspired in part by Peters, showed graphically how few companies could actually live up to his revolutionary ideas in practice. His early recipes for success have also been criticised, with critics pointing gleefully to the fact that many of the 'excellent' companies profiled in 1982 did not manage to survive into the 1990s. The increasingly radical tone of his books has offended many academics, and his criticisms of business schools and their apparent dedication to excessive rationality have also won him few friends. One criticism of Peters's work is that it is too superficial, concentrating on a handful of examples and lacking academic rigour. But Peters himself is strongly influenced by academic thinking; his comment that 'organization falls out of strategy' is drawn from Chandler, and his theories on organisational culture owe something to the work of Mayo and Barnard at Harvard Business School in the 1930s. In *Liberation Management* Peters acknowledges the influence of Charles **Handy**.

His ideas admittedly have their weaknesses, but Peters did achieve a revolution of sorts: he startled American management into life. By 1980, depressed by two oil price shocks and wavering in the face of aggressive foreign competition, American management had become almost bankrupt of new ideas. Peters made it clear that change was not only possible but desirable, and in doing so opened the door for other gurus such as Rosabeth Moss Kanter, Warren Bennis and, especially, Gary Hamel. Thanks to his immense popularity and easy writing style, his works became highly popular; he still has an immense following, at times approaching cult status. Ironically, given his views on middle managers, his greatest audience is among middle managers. Baffled, he wrote in 1992:

> Am I a middle management basher? Yes. Are most of the people who come to my seminars middle managers? Yes. Why do they come? Beats me.[7]

But middle managers follow Peters because, in an era when the role and value of the middle manager are increasingly uncertain, he offers them a chance to at least discuss how they might make a greater contribution. His books and ideas have given many managers greater enthusiasm for and interest in the complexities and ambiguities of their jobs, and have made them more interested in the fundamentals of excellence. Most of all, Peters has helped to overturn the notion of the rationalistic, 'one best way' of management, and made managers aware that managing in a world of paradox and ambiguity offers not only dynamic problems but also dynamic solutions.

See also: **Casson, Drucker, Handy, Ibuka, Mintzberg, Porter, Simon**

Major works

In Search of Excellence remains Peters's most important book, but *Thriving on Chaos* and *Liberation Management* are good guides to his later ideas.

(With R.H. Waterman) *In Search of Excellence: Lessons from America's Best-Run Companies*, New York: Harper and Row, 1982.
(With N. Austin) *A Passion for Excellence: The Leadership Difference*, New York: Random House, 1985.
Thriving on Chaos: Handbook for a Management Revolution, New York: Knopf, 1987.
Liberation Management: Necessary Disorganization for the Nanosecond Nineties, New York: Knopf, 1992.
The Pursuit of Wow! Every Person's Guide to Topsy-Turvy Times, New York: Vintage, 1994.

Further reading

It is useful to compare Peters with several of the other leading contemporary American gurus, whose works are given below.

Bennis, W.G. and Nanus, B., *Leaders*, Reading, MA: Addison-Wesley, 1985.
Hamel, G. and Prahalad, C.K., *Competing for the Future*, Boston, MA: Harvard Business School Press, 1994.
Kanter, R.M., *The Change Masters: Innovation for Productivity in the American Corporation*, New York: Simon and Schuster, 1983.
Porter, M., *Competitive Advantage: Creating and Sustaining Superior Performance*, New York: The Free Press, 1985.

Notes

1   T.J. Peters and R.H. Waterman, *In Search of Excellence: Lessons from America's Best-Run Companies*, New York: Harper and Row, 1982, p. xxiv. Throughout this chapter I refer to Peters's ideas in *In Search of Excellence*. This is not to deny the important of Waterman's contribution; but as many of these ideas appear in Peters's later works, it seems safe to ascribe them to him here as well. They are Peters's ideas; they are, perhaps, not his alone.
2   *Ibid.*, pp. 13–16.
3   *Ibid.*, p. 13.

4   T.J. Peters, *Liberation Management: Necessary Disorganization for the Nanosecond Nineties*, New York: Knopf, 1992, p. 758.
5   Peters and Waterman, *In Search of Excellence*, p. 29.
6   *Ibid.*, p. 44.
7   Peters, *Liberation Management*, p. 715.

MICHAEL PORTER (1947–)

Michael Porter is one of the world's leading writers on strategy. His approach is to describe the building blocks of strategy, notably the determinants of competitive advantage on which successful strategies can be built. His concept of strategy is built on a few simple but effective tools, notably the famous 'five forces' model, the value chain and the fourfold typology of generic strategies. All of these are now widely used in strategic thinking by businesses around the world. More recently he has looked at broader issues such as how nations and regions can seek and maintain competitive advantage in the global economy.

Porter was born in Ann Arbor, Michigan on 23 May 1947, the son of an army officer. After taking an undergraduate degree at Princeton University, he took an MBA and then a PhD from Harvard University, winning honours and distinctions at every step. Soon after completing his PhD he was offered an academic post at Harvard; in 1981, at the age of thirty-four, he was made a full professor. He has remained at Harvard ever since. He is also an important and highly respected consultant, who has worked with many of the world's top companies including Royal Dutch/Shell, Procter and Gamble and Du Pont. In 1983 he was asked by US president Ronald Reagan to serve on the President's Commission on Industrial Competitiveness, and he continues to advise the US federal government in a number of capacities. He has also worked with the government of the state of Massachusetts, setting up and chairing its Council on Economic Growth and Technology. He also served as an advisor on national competitiveness to the governments of Sweden, Canada and New Zealand. One of his most recent books, *Can Japan Compete?* (2000), was widely seen as a prescription for the recovery of the beleaguered Japanese economy.

Porter's greatest achievement has been to relate business strategy to applied microeconomics, two fields of study which had previously been considered independently, and build a set of models and tools for analysis. His first major book, *Competitive Strategy* (1980), revolutionised approaches to business strategy; his second, *Competitive Advantage*

(1985), extended his thinking from analysing competition to creating sustainable creative advantage. More recently, Porter has concentrated on global applications of his strategic principles, including the nature of global competition and national determinants of competitive force; his major work in this field, *The Competitive Advantage of Nations* (1990), was an international best-seller and was read by business men, economists and politicians alike.

Competitive Strategy uses this link between microeconomics and strategic thinking to show that there are generic principles of strategy, which can be applied not only to individual companies but also to entire industrial sectors. Looking at the strategic requirements of different sectors, Porter detected a number of common features. This led him to the development of the first of his series of important models, the five forces. These are: (1) the threat of new entrants and the appearance of new competitors; (2) the degree of rivalry among existing competitors in the market; (3) the bargaining power of buyers; (4) the bargaining power of suppliers; and (5) the threat of substitute products or services which could shrink the market. The strength of each of these forces varies from industry to industry, but taken together they determine long-term profitability. They help to shape the prices firms can charge, the costs they must pay for resources and the level of investment that will be needed to compete. The threat of new entrants limits market share and profit; powerful buyers or suppliers, using their superior bargaining power, can drive down prices or push costs up, eroding margins, and so on. The strength of each of the five forces is a function of what Porter calls 'industry structure', which is also defined as 'the underlying economic and technical characteristics of an industry'.[1]

Next, Porter develops what he calls 'generic strategies' for responding to the pressure of the five forces. In any given situation, he says, companies have four primary strategic options. In order to determine which of these they will pursue, they need to make two choices. First, they need to determine competitive scope: will they seek a broad market, or target specific niches? Second, they need to determine which element they will rely on to seek competitive advantage: cost advantages over competitors, or differentiation from competitors. Depending on the outcome of these two divisions, the company will then pursue one of the following strategic options:

1   Cost leadership, based on pursuing lower costs in a broad target market.
2   Differentiation, based on differentiated products or services in a broad target market.

3   Cost focus, based on low costs and targeting of specific niches or segments.
4   Focused differentiation, based on differentiated products or services aimed at specific niches or segments.

Porter makes it clear that he is offering these as strategic options: there is no one best strategy for any company or industry, and strategic needs will change over time as the balance between the five forces changes.

Finally, Porter introduces the concept of the value chain. When producing a product and delivering it to the consumer, firms add value to the original product through a variety of supporting activities beyond the basic function of production and distribution. These support activities can add value directly (for example, developing and adding new technology features to a product) or indirectly, through measures that allow the firm to become more efficient. The value chain is crucial, says Porter, because it demonstrates that the firm is more than just the sum of its parts and activities; all activities are connected by linkages, and the product uses these linkages to follow a critical path through the firm from its first inception to its delivery as a finished good. The firm needs to examine all of its value-adding activities and decide which ones to optimise in order to meet industry competitive pressures and achieve competitive goals. The influence of this concept can be seen in many later business concepts, notably business process re-engineering (BPR), one of the great management fads of the 1990s.

Porter followed up the ideas of *Competitive Strategy* with *Competitive Advantage* in 1985, exploring further the concept of creating sustainable competitive advantage. This search for sustainable advantage was taken up in other quarters as well, and led to Arie **de Geus**'s famous statement in 1989 that a company's only sustainable competitive advantage may be its ability to learn. Porter, meanwhile, began broadening his horizons and looking at competition as a global issue. In *Competition in Global Industries* (1986), he set out to apply his principles of competitive strategy to global markets. Again using industry analysis as his framework, Porter defined two types of international competition: (1) multi-domestic industries, in which competition occurs on a country-by-country basis (consumer banking, for example); and (2) global industries, which he defines as industries 'in which a firm's competitive position in one country is significantly affected by its position in other countries'.[2] The car industry is an example of a global industry. The difference between multi-domestic and global industries is that international competition in multi-domestic industries is discretionary: companies can choose whether to compete or to withdraw from the market in any one country. In global industries, however, competition is compulsory, as what happens in every country affects other countries.

In global competition, value chain activities are spread over a number of different countries: in the car industry, for example, parts makers and suppliers may be in many different countries other than the one where the final assembly takes place, and assembly itself can happen in many different countries. Therefore, as well as choosing competitive scope and competitive advantage as in the original fourfold generic strategies model, companies can choose strategic options based on the *configuration* of value chain activities (by geographic concentration, determining where these will take place) and *coordination* of value chain activities (how closely they are linked with one another). Again, Porter offers four options:

1   High concentration, high coordination: a simple global strategy in which value chain activities are based in one region or country and are centralised.
2   High concentration, low coordination: an export strategy with production activities concentrated but marketing decentralised.
3   Low concentration, high coordination: a foreign investment strategy, with operations geographically dispersed but closely coordinated from the centre.
4   Low concentration, low coordination: a country-centred strategy in which subsidiaries are decentralised and free to focus on their own markets with only light guidance from the centre.

Once again, Porter says, there is no one best strategy. All these options have their applications, depending on time and circumstances. The pressures of the five forces will be the most important determinants in choosing which strategy is the right one for the place and moment, but as circumstances change, strategic options can change as well. He argues against excessive concentration on geographical location, pointing out that it is more important to focus on *how* value chain activities are carried out rather than on *where*.

In his best-known book, *The Competitive Advantage of Nations*, Porter goes on to look at the determinants of national rather than industrial competition, and applies the same principles to the guidance of national economic policy. Believing that 'ultimately nations succeed in particular industries because their home environment is the most dynamic and most challenging, and stimulates and prods firms to upgrade and widen their advantage over time',[3] he sets out to find the fundamental determinants of competitive forces in countries. He lists four key determinants that can be applied to each industry in each nation:

1 Factor conditions: the availability of factor inputs such as skilled labour or infrastructure.
2 Demand conditions: the nature of the market demand for that industry's products or services.
3 The presence of related and supporting industries such as suppliers and distributors.
4 The nature of corporate structures and competition, as well as organisational and managerial cultures.

These determinants serve as the background for competitive forces in each industry. Porter notes how the differing nature of competitive advantage between nations often leads to clustering, either in industries (such as heavy machinery in Germany or electronics in Japan), or geographically within a region, such as the concentration of German industry in the Rhineland and Bavaria, or Italian industries in the Po valley. In some cases there are concentrations that are both industrial and geographical, such as Silicon Valley, the French aerospace cluster around Toulouse, or the German car cluster around Munich.

Whether discussing the individual competitiveness of firms or the national competitiveness of states, Porter continuously points out that there is no 'best' strategic option. The option chosen must always reflect circumstances, and it is for this reason that he repeatedly stresses environment factors such as the five forces and the determinants of national competitive advantage listed above, and also the firm's internal capabilities as represented by the value chain. Previous approaches to strategy had tended to present options as black and white, 'either/or' choices. Porter's approach has resulted in the definition of a much broader range of strategic options, giving decision makers more freedom of manoeuvre.

Porter's system has been criticised for being overly simplistic. His fourfold schemas are sometimes considered to be too limiting, not allowing for enough options, and the boundaries between classifications as too rigid. Real-life strategy making, as Porter's contemporary Henry **Mintzberg** has frequently pointed out, is often fuzzy and partakes of elements that are not easily categorised. On the other hand, the simplicity of Porter's models means they are easy to understand and use. If they are regarded as tools to enable strategic thinking rather than a cookbook of recipes for strategic success, then their value can be understood for what they are: highly flexible tools of analysis which can clarify situations and help define strategic direction, especially in international strategy.

See also: **Chandler, Drucker, Mintzberg, Ohmae**

Major works

Competitive Strategy sets out the basics of the Porter system, while *Competitive Advantage* expands on these. *The Competitive Advantage of Nations* is an important text for modern theories of globalisation.

Competitive Strategy: Techniques for Analyzing Industries and Competitors, New York: The Free Press, 1980.
Competitive Advantage: Creating and Sustaining Superior Performance, New York: The Free Press, 1985.
(ed.) *Competition in Global Industries*, Boston, MA: Harvard Business School Press, 1986.
The Competitive Advantage of Nations, New York: Macmillan, 1990.
(With H. Takeuchi and M. Sakakibara) *Can Japan Compete?*, Tokyo: Diamond and New York: Basic Books, 2000.
(With S. Stern and J.L. Ferman) *The Determinants of National Innovative Capacity*, New York: National Bureau of Economic Research, 2000.

Further reading

Rohani's article is one of the few detailed treatments of Porter's ideas and impact.

Rohani, K., 'Porter, Michael E.', in M. Witzel (ed.), *Biographical Dictionary of Management*, Bristol: Thoemmes Press, 2001, vol. 2, pp. 821–5.

Notes

1   M.E. Porter, *Competitive Strategy: Techniques for Analyzing Industries and Competitors*, New York: The Free Press, 1980, p. 35.
2   M.E. Porter (ed.), *Competition in Global Industries*, Boston, MA: Harvard Business School Press, 1986.
3   M.E. Porter, *The Competitive Advantage of Nations*, New York: Macmillan, 1990, p. 71.

HERBERT SIMON (1916–2001)

Economist, psychologist and computer scientist, Herbert Simon demolished the concept of the business organisation as a rational entity and introduced a behavioural theory of the firm which put the human element squarely at the centre of issues such as strategic thinking, decision making and organisational relationships. He introduced the concepts of 'bounded rationality', arguing that managers are rarely if ever in possession of complete sets of information, and accordingly engage in 'satisficing', seeking to make not the best decision *per se*, but the best decision possible given limited information. His work lies at the basis of most modern ideas about organisation and managerial behaviour. He has won many awards, including the Turing Award for his work with computer models in 1975 and the Nobel Prize for Economics in 1978.

Simon was born in Milwaukee on 15 June 1916. He took a BA in political science at the University of Chicago in 1936, where he also studied psychology, economics and mathematics, and studied the positivist philosophy of Rudolf Carnap. He then joined the Bureau of Public Administration at the University of California at Berkeley, where from 1939 to 1942 he worked on research in municipal administration; this gave him the chance to put his learning into practice and to develop and test many of his early ideas. While working at Berkeley, Simon also completed his PhD with the University of Chicago in 1942; his dissertation on decision making in organisations was later published as *Administrative Behaviour* (1947), his first and arguably his most important book.

From 1943 to 1949 Simon taught political science at the Illinois Institute of Technology in Chicago, and also served on the Cowles Commission for Research in Economics, where he became interested in game theory and other rational choice models of decision making. Although he found these initially interesting, he quickly reacted against the fundamental assumptions of these models about how humans make choices, in particular the notion that people make choices based on full possession and analysis of all relevant information. In practice, Simon argued, this almost never happens. It was during this period that he first developed his ideas on bounded rationality.

In 1949 Simon moved to Pittsburgh and joined the Graduate School of Industrial Administration at the Carnegie Institute of Technology, later to evolve into Carnegie-Mellon University. Here he became part of a highly important group of economists and organisation theorists, including Franco Modigliani, James March and Richard Cyert, among others, who together founded what is now known as the behavioural theory of the firm, sometimes also known as the Carnegie theory. Simon also met and began to work with Allen

Newell, then at the RAND Corporation, and began to explore the possibilities for using computer simulations to model human decision making in dynamic environments. Newell later joined the faculty at Carnegie, and he and Simon worked closely together on decision making and problem solving through into the early 1960s. In 1965 Simon was appointed professor of computer science and psychology, a unique post which reflected his broad interests and his co-mingling of technical and human problems and issues. In all he wrote or co-wrote fifteen books and over 500 articles. He died in Pittsburgh on 8 February 2001.

Much of Simon's career and the majority of his publications were dedicated to decision making and problem solving, looking at how the human mind processes information and arrives at conclusions. This attempt to apply computer technology to problem solving was revolutionary for its time. Working with Allen Newell, Simon attempted to create computer models that could simulate human mental activity, in particular when solving problems. By treating the mind as basically an information-processing machine, Simon and Newell effectively rewrote the book on how we acquire, assess and use information in complex situations. *Human Problem Solving* (1972), their most important work together, became the basis for much further research in this field by Simon and many others, and led directly to his nomination for the Turing Award.

Compared to his research and output on problem solving, Simon's interest in organisation and administration lasted only a short time. In that period, however, he evolved two of the most important concepts of modern organisation theory, bounded rationality and satisficing, and laid the groundwork for the behavioural theory of the firm.

Administrative Behaviour takes as its starting point Chester Barnard's call for consideration of administration and management to concentrate less on formal structures and concepts and more on interpersonal relationships and coordination. Barnard's own earlier work, *The Functions of the Executive* (1938) had gone some way towards this goal, and had resulted in a rethink in academic circles, at least, of the classical approach to administration found in the work of Henri **Fayol** and Lyndall **Urwick**. The latter had been concerned to find fundamental 'principles' of administration and management which could be uniformly applied across all businesses. Simon believed these principles to be mere proverbs or acts of faith: they lacked any scientific rigour and could not scientifically be proven to be effective. His criticism here may be overly harsh – common sense proverbs can, after all, be very effective guides to daily life – but he was fair to criticise the increasingly rational and mechanistic – and bureaucratic – approach to administration that was beginning to emerge. This approach was greatly strengthened during the Second World War, when the US military and industrial 'machines' proved their ability to raise and arm millions of men, provide them with advanced weapons of war and transport them to fields of battle all around the world. Luther Gulick, head of the Institute of Public Administration in New York and a leading figure in the theory of administration, was particularly impressed by this achievement and argued for a theory of administration that was highly compartmentalised, with planning, research and operations all strongly formalised.

Simon's reaction against this was based on an awareness that the administration theory of the day was overly rational. In particular, it assumed a near omniscience on the part of leaders and decision makers, postulating that managers would be in possession of all relevant information and would be able to analyse it accordingly and reach the 'best' decision, one that maximised utility for all concerned. In practice, Simon argued, this almost never happened. Scientists in the laboratory or the thinktank may have the luxury of collecting all information and validating it before reaching conclusions; managers in their daily lives do not. Like Henry Mintzberg a few decades later, his observations suggested that managers almost always work in situations where the information available to them is incomplete and/or misleading, and there is rarely time enough to analyse it or to look for further information to complete the set. He called this condition 'bounded rationality'.

In order to make decisions, then, managers adopt a pragmatic approach. They set, usually informally, minimum thresholds for information, looking not to acquire and analyse 'all' information but rather 'enough' information. The result, rather than seeking to achieve maximum utility, seeks rather to achieve a utility that is adequate to the situation and will lead to an outcome that, if less than perfect, is still satisfactory. For this behaviour Simon coined the term 'satisficing', and showed how managers use satisficing in their everyday work to achieve results that are 'good enough' rather than completely 'good'. Later, researchers in marketing would also note that consumers use satisficing when making purchases, often seeking products that are 'good enough' to satisfy most needs rather than the perfect product to satisfy every need.

Simon goes on to suggest that the nature of the organisation itself serves as a boundary to rationality. Information in organisation consists of two kinds: facts, verifiable by recourse to data, and values, which are mental approaches and mindsets that are embedded in the organisation's culture and how it does things. We make compromises then, not only to deal with a lack of information but also to 'fit in' with the cultures of the organisations to which we belong. In his later work with James March, Simon argues that this feature of organisations as a limit to rationality is in fact an important and necessary one. Organisations serve to channel thinking and decision making along pre-set lines which serve to concentrate and focus thought and action on their own goals. An organisation in which all managers stopped to consider every available option in every situation would be unworkable. Early in the organisation's life, decisions are made on issues such as its purpose, its goals, its target market, and so on. It is right that the outcomes of these decisions should be examined from time to time, but to stop and consider the option of 'should we dissolve ourselves and go out of business', for example, at every board meeting is ludicrous.

This idea that organisations serve to limit or channel thinking has met with some hostility, as has Simon's dualistic distinction between facts and values; it has been correctly pointed out that some information partakes of both categories. But Simon did succeed in helping to orient thinking about organisations and their functions away from rationalistic models and towards more human-centred ones. The transformation, which had begun with the human relations school of personnel management some years earlier, was completed with 1980s and 1990s thinking about the role of knowledge in organisations and the movement of knowledge from being a peripheral asset to a central organisational function in its own right. The idea that organisations have a 'behaviour' which can be observed and which is not always rational is now a central part of management thought. Simon's most important contribution has been to bring the importance of human motivation and behaviour to the forefront of management science, and to bring the latter closer to actual managerial practice.

See also: **Argyris, de Geus, Forrester, Maslow, Mintzberg**

Major works

Not all of Simon's later works on problem solving have been included here. *Administrative Behaviour* is an important foundation work, while *Organizations* is probably the core text of the behavioural theory of the firm along with the work of Cyert and March given below.

Administrative Behavior, New York: Macmillan, 1947.
(With J.G. March and H. Guetzkow) *Organizations*, New York: Wiley, 1958.

The New Science of Management Decision, Evanston, IL: Harper & Row, 1960.
(With A. Newell) *Human Problem Solving*, Englewood Cliffs, NJ: Prentice-Hall,
1972.

Further reading

Barnard was an important influence on Simon. Cyert and March is the other
classic text on the behavioral theory of the firm. Crowther-Heyck's essay is based
on his PhD on Simon and is a concise summary of Simon's career and ideas; I have
drawn most of my details on Simon's career and background from this source.

Barnard, C.A., *The Functions of the Executive*, Cambridge, MA: Harvard University
Press, 1938.
Crowther-Heyck, H., 'Simon, Herbert Alexander', in M. Witzel (ed.),
Biographical Dictionary of Management, Bristol: Thoemmes Press, 2001, vol. 2,
pp. 917–23.
Cyert, R.M. and March, J.G., *A Behavioural Theory of the Firm*, New York:
Prentice Hall, 1963.

SUNZI (SUN TZU) (*c.* 4th century BC)

Sunzi, or Sun Tzu,[1] is the attributed author of a book usually known
as *The Art of War*, which is one of the most famous books on strategy
of all time. Although it is concerned with military strategy, the book
has been widely read by business leaders and managers in both the
East and the West. In China and Japan, the book has been studied as
a source of strategic thinking; in the West, it has most often been
used as a means of understanding the mindset of the East, but
increasingly Westerners too have tried to use *The Art of War* as a
source of personal inspiration. Sunzi's influence has gone beyond
management; in 2001, the Australian cricket team were given
extracts from *The Art of War* to read before going out to play against
England.

Sunzi's identity remains uncertain. Traditional Chinese sources
identify him with Sun Wu, who rose to chief minister and general of
the state of Wu in north China in the sixth century BC, near the end of
the Spring and Autumn period. However, the American military
historian General Samuel B. Griffiths, in his study of the book,
detected a number of anachronisms: the book refers to the use of
crossbows, for example, which were not introduced until the Warring
States period some two centuries later. Sunzi (Master Sun) must
therefore have lived during this period. Further scholarship suggests
the book was not entirely the hand of one author in any case but, as
was common in China at the time, was a syncretic building up of

material over a long period, perhaps several centuries. The version we know today was edited and partly rewritten by the general Cao Cao in the Three Kingdoms period during the second and third centuries AD, who seems to have used it as a manual of strategy, and encouraged his officers to read it.

Along with other works such as *The Thirty-Six Stratagems* and the much later *Romance of Three Kingdoms*, *The Art of War* became one of the foundational texts of later Chinese strategic thinking. In the twentieth century it was studied closely by both Chiang Kai-shek and Mao Zedong. Sunzi was also studied extensively by Japanese military leaders, and has been translated into many Western languages and is taught at most military academies. Along with Miyamoto Musashi's *Book of Five Rings*, a study of the methods of the *samurai* warrior, and *On War* by Karl von Clausewitz, a Prussian staff officer who served in the wars against Napoleon, it has also crossed over into business strategy and a number of popular versions have been produced for the guidance of business leaders in both Asia and the West.

One of the enduring appeals of this book is that it reduces warfare to a set of general principles which can be easily learned and followed. Sunzi starts from five fundamentals:

> The art of war, then, is governed by five constant factors, to be taken into account in one's deliberations, when seeking to determine the conditions obtaining in the field. These are: (1) The Moral Law; (2) Heaven; (3) Earth; (4) The Commander; (5) Method and discipline. The Moral Law causes the people to be in complete accord with their ruler, so that they will follow him regardless of their lives, undismayed by any danger. Heaven signifies night and day, cold and heat, times and seasons. Earth comprises distances, great and small; danger and security; open ground and narrow passes; the chances of life and death. The Commander stands for the virtues of wisdom, sincerity, benevolence, courage and strictness. By method and discipline are to be understood the marshaling of the army in its proper subdivisions, the graduations of rank among the officers, the maintenance of roads by which supplies may reach the army, and the control of military expenditure. These five heads should be familiar to every general: he who knows them will be victorious; he who knows them not will fail.
>
> (Chapter 1, §§3–11)[2]

All warfare requires, first and foremost, careful preparation and analysis:

> Now the general who wins a battle makes many calculations in his temple ere the battle is fought. The general who loses a battle makes but few calculations beforehand. Thus do many calculations lead to victory, and few calculations to defeat: how much more no calculation at all! It is by attention to this point that I can foresee who is likely to win or lose.
>
> (Chapter 1, §26)

Elsewhere, Sunzi argues that the decision to go to war in the first place is one that requires extreme caution and much contemplation; one should never compete with an enemy unless the need is paramount and unless one is fully prepared to do so. Once preparation has been completed, however, the general should strike quickly and hard; there is no efficiency to be gained through delay. The commander should keep his mind focused at all times, on the ultimate goal, victory over the enemy, and not be sidetracked into other activities. It is also critical, says Sunzi, to remain flexible and adaptable, and to change one's plans as may be necessary in the face of changing circumstances. The aim of warfare, he says, is victory, and that is best achieved by striking swiftly and overwhelming the enemy; prolonged wars are rarely successful.

Sunzi advocates the use of stratagem and deception wherever possible. He emphasises that the aim of warfare is not to fight battles: it is to force the enemy to your own will:

> Thus the highest form of generalship is to balk the enemy's plans; the next best is to prevent the junction of the enemy's forces; the next in order is to attack the enemy's army in the field; and the worst policy of all is to besiege walled cities.
>
> (Chapter 3, §3)

He later comments that 'the clever combatant imposes his will on the enemy, but does not allow the enemy's will to be imposed on him' (Chapter 6, §2). He then goes on to describe what he says are the five essentials for victory:

> Thus we may know that there are five essentials for victory:
> (1) He will win who knows when to fight and when not to

fight. (2) He will win who knows how to handle both superior and inferior forces. (3) He will win whose army is animated by the same spirit throughout all its ranks. (4) He will win who, prepared himself, waits to take the enemy unprepared. (5) He will win who has military capacity and is not interfered with by the sovereign. Hence the saying: If you know the enemy and know yourself, you need not fear the result of a hundred battles. If you know yourself but not the enemy, for every victory gained you will also suffer a defeat. If you know neither the enemy nor yourself, you will succumb in every battle.

(Chapter 3, §17)

How important is Sunzi to the modern reader? Certainly much of the book is specific to the military systems of the time, and the passages on the usage of crossbowmen and the speed of march of chariot armies, while perhaps interesting, are at best of limited utility in modern business. But the passages wherein Sunzi discusses the elements of strategy, particularly in the earlier chapters, remain remarkably fresh to the modern eye.

Many see him as expressing no more than good common sense, and the fact that his approach to strategy is not so much different to those of **Machiavelli**, Clausewitz or von Moltke might seem to confirm that. That surely is an argument in favour of his utility, however. Henry **Mintzberg** has pointed out that much of the theory of strategy making in modern business is overly formal and not relevant to what goes on in everyday business life. A dose of common sense might be seen as useful.

Often overlooked in readings of Sunzi is the emphasis on fundamentals and on an attitude of mind, which is outlined in the passages quoted above. His emphasis on analysis and preparation strongly foreshadows the similar emphasis on fundamental analysis by the founders of scientific management; his stress on the need to know one's own capacities, not just those of the opposition or competition, has implications not only for strategy but also for organisation and general management. Most of all, however, he gives us insight into the art of strategic thinking. **Ohmae** Kenichi argues that the best strategy comes from insights which are developed in a mind which is trained to think strategically, rather than from formal systems and principles. Sunzi gives us a glimpse into such a mind (or minds) and its patterns and thought processes. His lasting legacy lies not so much in his principles of strategy, but in showing us how to think about it.

See also: **Chandler, Laozi, Machiavelli, Mintzberg, Ohmae, Porter**

Major works

Sunzu Bingfa (The Military Methods of Master Sun), ed. and trans. L. Giles, *Sun Tzu on the Art of War*, London, 1910; ed. S.B. Griffiths, *The Art of War*, Oxford: Oxford University Press, 1963.

Further reading

Wee *et al.* remains probably the best analysis of the relevance of Sunzi to modern management. Clausewitz and Miyamoto are two other works on strategy with wide diffusion in management circles.

Clausewitz, K. von, *Vom Kriege*, ed. and trans. M. Howard and P. Paret, *On War*, Princeton, NJ: Princeton University Press, 1984.
Miyamoto, M., *Gorin-no-Sho* (Five-Ring Book), revised and annotated by Watanabe Ichiro, *Miyamoto Musashi*, Tokyo: Iwanami Shoten, 1977.
Wee, C.H, Lee, K.S. and Hidajat, B.W., *Sun Tzu: War and Management*, Singapore: Addison-Wesley, 1991.

Notes

1   Sun Tzu is the presentation of his name in the older Wade-Giles romanisation of Chinese; the modern *pinyin* version, Sunzi, is preferred here.
2   Quotations in this entry are taken from the Giles translation of *The Art of War*.

FREDERICK WINSLOW TAYLOR (1856–1915)

Frederick Winslow Taylor is best known as the founding father of scientific management. In his own time, and for several decades after his death, he was the world's most famous management guru, his ideas discussed and implemented not only in the USA and Western Europe but also in many other countries. At the same time, his approach to management has been violently criticised as dehumanising and deskilling, and political economists from the 1950s onwards virtually demonised Taylor for this. More recently a reappraisal of Taylor has begun which emphasises the human elements of scientific management and shifts part of the blame for the faults of his system onto those who implemented it. Though it has been discredited as a total system, many elements of scientific management remain visible in practice to this day.

Taylor was born in Germanstown, Pennsylvania on 20 March 1856. His father, a lawyer, came from an old and prosperous Pennsylvania Quaker family, and Taylor was educated at a series of good schools, including a three-year stint in Europe. He was a keen athlete, and excelled particularly at tennis; in 1881 he and his brother-in-law won the first doubles championship of the US Lawn Tennis Association. He also invented improved models of tennis racket and an improved golf putter. However, while still in his teens Taylor began to suffer from ill health, including migraines and sight impairment, and these ultimately prevented him from taking up his place at Harvard. Instead, he apprenticed as a machinist at the Enterprise Hydraulic Works in Philadelphia from 1874 to 1878, and on completing his apprenticeship, took a job at the Midvale Steel Company, also in Philadelphia. Beginning as a machinist, Taylor was promoted to foreman and then chief engineer. He also took a degree in mechanical engineering from the Stevens Institute of Technology in 1883, and by the mid-1880s was a highly qualified and very experienced engineer with a considerable amount of management experience under his belt as well. It was at Midvale that Taylor first developed the principles of what would later be described as scientific management, described in more detail below.

Taylor had hopes of promotion to senior management, but in 1886 Midvale was sold to new owners who themselves took over most of the senior management spots. He resigned from the company and moved to Maine, where he was for several years general manager of a pulp and paper company. This job too was unsatisfactory and Taylor returned to Philadelphia, this time to set up an independent engineering practice with the aim of further refining and developing the techniques he had experimented with at Midvale. In 1895 Taylor presented a paper on piece-rate systems to the American Society of Mechanical Engineers, which won him considerable attention.

In 1898 Taylor was contacted by the Bethlehem Steel Company, which employed his services over the next three years. His work at Bethlehem saw the Taylor system developed to its fullest extent, and remains a landmark in American industrial history. During this period also, Taylor gathered around him many of the team that would further develop and propagate his ideas, including the engineer Henry L. Gantt and the Norwegian-born mathematician Carl Barth. The work at Bethlehem became the basis of Taylor's book *Shop Management*, published in 1903. However, his own employment by the company had terminated in 1901 when Taylor himself fell out with the owners;

the plant was sold to the steel entrepreneur Charles M. Schwab later that year, and Gantt and most of Taylor's other associates then left as well.

Shop Management was a huge success, and helped to propagate Taylor's doctrines across America and around the world. The consulting firms of Taylor and his associates, who now included such notable names as Morris Cooke, Sanford Thompson and Horace Hathaway, implemented his system in some 180 factories in the USA and more in Europe. Japanese engineers such as Takeo Toshisuke and Araki Toichiro took elements of the system back to Japan. In France, Henri Le Chatelier read *Shop Management* and became a convert, as later did Charles de Fréminville; later, during the First World War, his ideas came to the attention of Lyndall **Urwick**, who worked to introduce a modified version of Taylorism to the UK. In Brazil, the engineer Roberto Simonsen adopted Taylorist methods in his own business and urged his fellow engineers and industrialists to do likewise. In Poland and Russia the mining engineer Karel Adamiecki, who had independently developed his own 'theory of harmonisation' which used many of the same techniques for measurement and statistical control as Taylor's system, helped propagate the system still further.

The term 'scientific management', used to describe the entire system of analysis, control and re-engineering developed by Taylor, was coined at a meeting of some of the leading members of the circle at Henry Gantt's New York apartment in 1911. Taylor himself was not present, but he clearly had no objection as he used the term for the title of his book later that year. *The Principles of Scientific Management* (1911) was the fullest summary of Taylor's ideas, presenting them not merely as techniques for control and production but as a unified philosophy of management. But for Taylor himself, this was almost the last chapter of his involvement with the movement he had created. Never an easy man to work with in any case, his own health was now deteriorating badly, and he fell out with many of his allies and supporters, including the **Gilbreths** and Henry Gantt. There were quarrels between his own followers and those of the Gilbreths as to who should claim credit for certain elements of the system. Taylor's wife's health was also worsening, and he resigned from business to spend the last three years of his life caring for her. He died of pneumonia in Philadelphia on 21 March 1915.

In order to fully understand Taylor's system, it is necessary to consider both the background within which he worked and his own mental approach. American industry in the 1880s and 1890s was far from a picture of efficiency. As David Sicilia comments in his introduction to a recent re-issue (1993) of *The Principles of Scientific Management*, American factory managers 'struggled to match the relentless pace of spinning and weaving with the irregular work patterns common among workers'.[1] Not only did few factories achieve optimum efficiency, but there were rarely even systems of measurement for determining what optimum efficiency might be, let alone whether it was being achieved. Most factory owners only noticed inefficiencies when their profits began to decline; and their usual response in such cases was simply to cut wages rather than investigating the underlying causes of the problem. Such practices, especially in the boom-and-bust economy of the late nineteenth century in America, provoked serious labour unrest, with many violent and bloody strikes.

Wiser heads felt that there had to be a solution to the problems of industrial efficiency and labour unrest, and sought it in new methods of management. In 1886, the engineer Henry Towne had presented a paper to the American Society of Mechanical Engineers calling for new approaches to engineering shop management, and in particular for new ways of managing workers. Three years later, when president of the Society, Towne presented his paper on 'gain sharing' (effectively a form of profit sharing as then commonly practised in the UK and Europe) as a motivational plan for increasing worker output. This was followed in 1891 by Frederick Halsey's premium plan, a modified form of piecework. Both these systems attracted much attention, and the Halsey system was implemented with some success. However, both plans also had their problems. Taylor, studying the situation while still at Midvale, developed an amended piece-rate system or 'differential rate system', a bonus system which offered higher wages to men who exceeded quotas for work completed within a given time. In his 1895 paper to the Society, Taylor explained the system as follows:

> The differential rate system of piece-work consists briefly in offering two different rates for the same job: a high price per piece, in case the work is finished in the shortest time possible and in perfect condition, and a low price, if it takes a longer time to do the job, or if there are any imperfections in the work. (The high rate should be such that the workman can earn more per day than is usually paid in similar establishments.) This is directly the opposite of the ordinary plan of piece-work, in which the wages of the workmen are reduced when they increase their productivity.[2]

The differential rate plan would, Taylor believed, improve productivity by giving workers an incentive to increase output. It would also eliminate 'soldiering', 'goldbricking' and other practices whereby workers deliberately slowed their pace of work to a level that suited themselves. He believed that, if given a choice of idleness and an average wage or working hard and a good wage, most good workers would choose the latter. Taylor developed something of an obsession with soldiering, which he had first encountered at Midvale and which he saw as a problem that needed to be eliminated in many industrial enterprises.

In the question and answer session that followed the paper, Taylor accepted that, to be effective, a differential piece-rate system such as he proposed would require workmen to be highly skilled, trained and motivated. He admitted that it was probably beyond the ability of the average untrained worker to reach the productivity levels he considered satisfactory. Perhaps the most perceptive comment from the audience was that made by Henry Gantt, who said that for the system to work, the man setting the piece rate would have to be a manager of exceptional skill and judgement.[3]

What had been a problem of labour, then, was now a problem of management: how to create conditions in which the workforce would perform with maximum efficiency. In the years between 1895 and 1903, notably in the three crucial years at Bethlehem, Taylor worked to solve it. His approach was to divide labour as far as possible, breaking down every work function into its smallest divisible part. The concentration on the task function lies at the heart of Taylor's philosophy. Here is how he explains the approach in *The Principles of Scientific Management*:

Perhaps the most prominent single element in modern scientific management is the task idea. The work of every workman is fully planned out by the management at least one day in advance, and each man receives in most cases complete written instructions, describing in detail the task which he is to accomplish, as well as the means to be used in doing the work. And the work planned in advance in this way constitutes a task which is to be solved, as explained above, not by the workman alone, but in almost all cases by the joint effort of the workman and the management. This task specifies not only what is to be done but how it is to be done and the exact time allowed for doing it. And whenever the workman succeeds in doing his task right, and within the time limit specified, he receives an addition of from 30 per cent. to 100 per cent. to his ordinary wages. These tasks are carefully planned, so that both good and careful work are called for in their performance, but it is distinctly to be understood that no workman is to be called upon to work at a pace which would be injurious to his health. The task is always so regulated that the man who is well suited to his job will thrive while working at this rate during a long term of years and will grow happier and more prosperous, instead of being overworked. Scientific management consists very largely in preparing for and carrying out these tasks.[4]

To implement a scientific management system, three stages were required. First, it was necessary to study the production process intensely and divide each process into its component tasks; in more complex processes, there could be hundreds of tasks. Next, each task was observed in its performance, often many times over, and the duration of the task was timed using stopwatches. This element was known as the 'time study'. From the observed times, Taylor and his engineers then calculated the optimum time required to perform a task. The piece rate for the work was then set using these optimum times as the standard that all workers should be able to achieve. To quote Sicilia again, 'the task was re-engineered for maximum efficiency, with the smallest details accounted for, including the number, interval and duration of rest periods'.[5]

This system, where it could be implemented successfully, produced results. Productivity rose, as did workers' take-home pay. Yet in practice there were many problems. Taylor accepted early on that his system could only work if the shopfloor workers were willing to cooperate; in *Shop Management*, he argued that the best systems of management are those in which the interests of employee and employer are so mutually intertwined that they cannot be separated. Scientific management required intensive training if workers were to perform at optimum efficiency levels, and only an elite workforce could make the system work. His blind spots were twofold. First, the benefits of the system were so self-evident to him that he could not understand why they were not similarly evident to the workers. Second, being a Quaker and a highly moral man himself, he failed to appreciate that one of the key elements of the system, a fair setting of the piece rates, was open to abuse.

Both these problems plagued scientific management from the outset. At Midvale, and especially at Bethlehem, there was sporadic resistance to the measuring teams and objections to the rates being set. Unions saw in scientific management a plot to force their members to work harder for the same pay, rather than being fully rewarded for their extra effort. And indeed, less enlightened employers often took this tack. After bringing production up to the desired rate, they then proceeded to sporadically cut the piece rate, ensuring that if workers wanted to maintain the same take-home pay they would have to work harder. Workers retaliated by a variety of means, falsifying data and sabotaging the system. The British efficiency engineer Frank Watts described instances in the 1920s of men working deliberately slowly when under observation by the time-study engineers in order to give a misleading impression of the time required for a task, and of equipment such as stopwatches being stolen and even of engineers being intimidated into falsifying records.

Nor did Taylor himself always do his ideas justice. *The Principles of Scientific Management*, his last important work, was written when he was already very ill and in the midst of bitter quarrels with colleagues; undoubtedly his cast of mind was now darker. Whereas in *Shop Management* he argues that his system will provide workers with a fair day's wage for a fair day's work, eight years later his attitude to workers is at best condescending. In a famous example, cited by both supporters and opponents, Taylor describes the work of a steelworker named Schultz (his real name was Henry Knoll) who was carrying an average of 12.5 tons of pig iron a day. After Taylor's engineers had re-designed his work, he was able to carry 47 tons a day. To Taylor in 1911, this increase in productivity was all that mattered: the impact of the additional work on Schultz was unimportant. Taylor always believed that workers should be encouraged to work hard; brought up in a strict work ethic himself, he believed that others should conform to the same rules and had little patience with those who would not.

The Schultz case shows, certainly, how the Taylor process could be dehumanising. Taylor's methods, like those of Henry **Ford**, were widely copied in the Soviet Union, where in 1935 a coal miner named Aleksei Stakhanov and his team, using Taylor methods, reportedly produced 105 tons of coal in a six-hour shift, fourteen times the normal output. This phenomenal result gave rise to the Stakhanovtsy movement, which claimed that if properly motivated and trained, all workers could increase production far beyond current levels, and which spread throughout Soviet industry and became the dominant management phenomenon of the late 1930s and 1940s. In fact, the movement became a cruel sham. Equipment and training were rarely forthcoming except at a few showpiece work sites, and workers were expected to achieve superhuman performance targets often with only the crudest of tools; coal miners equipped only with picks and shovels were expected to achieve the same target as Stakhanov's original team, with workers and their families threatened with the Gulag or worse if they failed.[6] From a system designed to improve efficiency and prosperity, Taylorism had descended into crude quota setting backed up by terror.

But for all its faults, scientific management also had many strengths. The methodical study of how tasks were performed and at what speed taught managers – and workers – many things they did not know about the nature of their work. Taylor's time studies, allied to the system of motion studies developed by the Gilbreths, became the time and motion study, an essential tool in job design for many decades thereafter and still widely used today. The relationship between work, motivation and reward also came under proper scrutiny for the first time, and as time passed, more human-centred methods of personnel management were developed. Most important of all, there emerged for the first time the idea that management could be treated as a discipline, with its own set of principles based on science and exact study, rather than rule of thumb and guesswork. Sixty years before Taylor read his paper on piece work to the Society of Mechanical Engineers, the British mathematician Charles **Babbage** had called for just such an application of the principles of science to business.

There is no doubt that, when properly implemented, scientific management can increase efficiency, often manyfold. The fault of Taylor's system was that it failed to build in mechanisms to temper efficiency with humanity. It was left to later management theorists to attempt to remedy that defect. In the meantime, large enterprises continue to use Taylorist methods to maintain efficient production and service on a mass-production basis. Perhaps the most famous Taylorist institution is one which is also synonymous with the American way of life today: McDonald's.[7]

See also: **Babbage, Emerson, Follett, Ford, Gilbreth, Simon**

Major works

Shop Management is an earlier work which emphasises the human benefits of the system: *The Principles of Scientific Management* is later, more rationalistic and darker.

A Piece Rate System, New York: American Society of Mechanical Engineers, 1895; repr. Bristol: Thoemmes Press, 2000.
Shop Management, New York: Harper and Row, 1903.
The Principles of Scientific Management, New York: Harper and Row, 1911; repr. Norwalk, CT: The Easton Press, 1993, with foreword by D.B. Sicilia.

Further reading

Drury and Hoxie are contemporary assessments of the Taylor system and its impacts. Kanigel is a good example of a modern critic. Warner and Wrege and Greenwood are more dispassionate, pointing out the system's virtues and flaws.

Drury, H.B., *Scientific Management*, New York: Longmans Green, 1915.
Hoxie, R.F., *Scientific Management and Labor*, New York: D. Appleton & Co, 1915.
Kanigel, R., *The One Best Way*, New York: Viking, 1997.
Warner, M., 'Taylor, Frederick Winslow', in M. Warner (ed.), *Handbook of Management Thinking*, London: International Thomson Business Press, 1998, pp. 656–60.
Wrege, C.D. and Greenwood, R., *Frederick W. Taylor, the Father of Scientific Management: Myth and Reality*, Homewood, IL: Business One Irwin, 1991.

Notes

1 D.B. Sicilia, 'Foreword', in F.W. Taylor, *The Principles of Scientific Management*, Norwalk, CT: The Easton Press, 1993, p. viii.
2 F.W. Taylor, *A Piece Rate System*, New York: American Society of Mechancial Engineers, 1895, p. 35.
3 *Ibid.*; the full text of the question and answer session was printed along with the original paper.
4 F.W. Taylor, *The Principles of Scientific Management*, New York: Harper and Row, 1911, p. 39.
5 Sicilia, 'Foreword', p. 9.
6 In 1988, an investigation by Russian journalists revealed that the entire movement had been based on fraud; Stakhanov had added together the production of several other teams to achieve his phenomenal 'result'.
7 Or so says George Ritzer in *The McDonaldization of Society* (Newbury Park, CA: Sage, 1996). Ritzer links Taylorism to Max Weber's concept of machine bureaucracy and argues that McDonald's is the ultimate example of both. Whether this is a good thing or a bad thing ultimately depends upon one's point of view.

TOYODA KIICHIRO (1894–1952)

Toyoda Kiichiro was the founder of the Toyota Motor Company in 1937. His short career with the firm was enough to lay the foundations for its successful later growth into one of the giants of the car industry worldwide. In particular, Toyoda introduced two of the most important elements in what later became known as the Toyota Production System: just-in-time production and *kaizen* or continuous improvement. His influence on production and supply chain management in the years since his death has been immense; probably no other manager since Henry **Ford** has so revolutionised the concepts and processes of manufacturing management.

Toyoda was born on 11 June 1894 in Kosei, near Shizuoka in southern Japan. His father was Toyoda Sakichi, who later founded the Toyota Spinning and Weaving Company, a highly successful textile manufacturer in Japan between the wars. The younger Toyoda studied mechanical engineering at the Imperial University of Tokyo, graduating with a degree in 1929 and then joining his father's firm. Father and son both felt that there was an opening in the market for a domestic car manufacturer, and were determined to diversify. In the late 1920s the car market in Japan was dominated by foreign producers, notably Ford and General Motors, both of which had assembly plants and large distribution networks in place.

Not only did the two US giants seem to have the entire market captured, but the Toyota company had absolutely no experience at making cars. Nevertheless, with the counter-intuitive genius that characterised both men, the Toyodas believed they could take on the Americans and win. Toyoda Kiichiro was put in charge of the project and began in a roped-off corner of the factory floor, first designing and building his own engines and then, in 1935, moving on to a prototype car, the A1. A prototype truck followed the same year. Toyoda spent much of his time recruiting Japanese engineers who had experience of the car industry and bringing them in to create a talent pool. He also recruited the experienced marketer Kamiya Shotaro, who agreed to move from GM Japan to Toyota despite taking an 80 per cent pay cut, because he believed in the need for Japan to have a strong domestic car producer. Many of the others in the company, including Toyoda himself, shared this belief, and it was the Toyota car company's guiding philosophy for many years.

The diversification from textiles into cars was considered too big a stretch for the existing company, and accordingly a new company was set up in 1937. Toyoda Kiichiro was named vice-president of the new Toyota Motor Company and put in charge of production; in 1941 he was promoted to president. The company was a success from the beginning. The G1 1.5 ton truck, the company's first commercial product, sold well both in commercial markets and to the army. When the company launched its first passenger car, Kamiya employed predatory pricing, initially selling at less than production cost so as to undercut Ford and GM. The tactic, which was not illegal then, worked; sales rose quickly and Toyota was able to use economies of scale to bring costs down and begin selling at a profit.

During the Second World War, Toyota went almost entirely over to war production, making trucks for the Imperial Japanese Army. After Japan's defeat in the war, Toyoda Kiichiro began the task of rehabilitating his bomb-damaged factories and offices, and prepared to return to domestic car production. However, the Allied occupation authorities banned all Japanese firms from making cars in 1946, and the company was virtually moribund until 1949 when the ban was lifted. Toyoda, using the slogan 'Catch up with America', again began gearing up to resume production, but the company was then beset with serious labour problems which forced Toyoda himself to resign in 1950. In 1952, as Toyota prepared to resume full production of domestic cars, he was invited to return as president. He died of a brain haemorrhage on 27 March 1952 before he could return to his post. His cousin Toyoda Eiji, who had joined the company when it was established in 1937, now took over. Eiji and Kiichiro's son, Toyoda Shoichiro, built the company into one of the world's largest car makers with a global presence. Much of that success was built on the innovative approach to production pioneered by Kiichiro.

The practice of just-in-time production, in which each component is produced as it is needed and no stocks are held in inventory, stemmed originally from a simple lack of resources. Before the establishment of Toyota Motor Company, Kiichiro was quite literally borrowing space and resources for his car project from the parent weaving company, which could not afford to support him with large investment. There was neither money to acquire nor space to hold large stocks of components. According to legend, Kiichiro hung a large banner reading 'Just In Time' over the shop floor, reminding workers that they must not produce components until the assembly line crews actually asked for them. A card system, known as *kanban*, was introduced to signal when particular parts were required at a workstation. Then, of course, the components had to be produced and delivered at top speed so as to avoid keeping the assembly line crews waiting.

And that, in essence, remains the philosophy behind just-in-time management today. The system helps to eliminate waste and keep down costs by maintaining, in effect, zero inventories. Like many other elements of the Toyota Production System, just-in-time was 'discovered' by the West in the 1980s, where it aroused considerable excitement. Sometimes also known as 'lean production', the name given it by Daniel Jones and James Womack in their 1990 book of that title, just-in-time (JIT) is now widely practised. It is a management method which requires considerable skill, and there are strong elements of risk which are seldom discussed in Western literature. In particular, the lack of parts inventory means that *any* disruption in the supply chain has very swift knock-on effects. In 1998, for example, a strike at two General Motors parts plants in Michigan succeeded in closing all but two of GM's North American assembly plants, causing more than 200,000 workers to be laid off at plants around the world, and delaying production of more than half a million cars; all in under a week. To make JIT work, the producer needs very strong, imperishable links with suppliers, a fact that Toyoda Kiichiro understood very well. Suppliers, in the Toyota system, were treated with equal deference as customers.

The second element was *kaizen*, usually translated as continuous improvement. The central philosophy of this concept was first expressed by Kiichiro's father, Toyoda Sakichi, who declared that no process could ever be declared perfect and that there was always room for improvement. Sakichi was influenced not only by Buddhist philosophy but also by *Self-Help*, the self-improvement manual written by the Victorian entrepreneur Samuel Smiles, which was hugely popular around the world. Both these influences suggested to Sakichi that while perfection would always remain out of reach, in the process of striving for it, considerable good would result.

Kaizen was an important part of Kiichiro's own philosophy as well. Two push factors drove the concept along. First, there was the need to innovate in terms of production processes. As noted above, Japanese car makers such as Toyota lacked the economies of scale afforded to their large American competitors, Ford and General Motors. To compensate for this, they turned to more flexible manufacturing processes in order to drive costs down (indeed, just-in-time can be seen as an innovation in this tradition). Second, and even more importantly, once Toyota began to consider the export market, Japanese goods were perceived in world markets as being shoddy and of inferior quality. Quality improvement was needed if Japanese goods were to compete.

Kaizen, then, was introduced as a driving philosophy behind improvements in both product and process, and ultimately it became embraced within the larger concept of Total Quality Management (TQM). One of the leading exponents of *kaizen* was the engineer Ohno Taiichi, who joined Toyota in 1932 and was responsible for a number of major production innovations, including the *kanban* card system noted above. After the war, Ohno worked with such notable quality gurus as the Japanese engineer Ishikawa Kaoru and the American consultant W. Edwards **Deming**, and the concept of TQM began to emerge more fully, reaching its apogee under Kiichiro's son Toyoda Shoichiro in the 1960s.

In the 1980s, *kaizen* and TQM also exploded onto the world scene, and today they remain widely discussed (if not always very well

understood) production concepts. In a notable development, Tom
Peters and Robert Waterman in their 1982 book *In Search of
Excellence* discussed continuous improvement as a key source of
competitive advantage and linked it directly to knowledge management and the concept of the learning organisation. *Kaizen* became an
important, if indirect, contributor to modern theories of knowledge
management; now more than sixty years old, the concept remains in
fashion.

In just a decade, between 1930 and the outbreak of the Second
World War, Toyoda Kiichiro built up the first domestic car
manufacturer in Japan, and proved it was possible to challenge
entrenched global competitors through attention to quality and
aggressive marketing. He also introduced two management concepts
that continue to be important today, and indeed continue to be widely
discussed as important sources of competitive advantage. Finally, he
laid the groundwork for the Toyota Production System which came to
rival that of Ford in importance. In the 1950s and 1960s the Toyota
system was widely imitated in Japan by firms such as Matsushita; in the
1980s, its influence spread around the world. Few production
managers today do not work with tools and concepts devised and
implemented by Toyoda Kiichiro.

See also: **Bat'a, Deming, Ford, Fukuzawa, Matsushita, Nonaka,
Peters**

Major works

Toyota Kiichiro produced no major works of his own.

Further reading

Toyoda Eiji's autobiography is full of detail on the work of his cousin, and Kamiya
Shotaro's autobiography is likewise highly important. Kimoto includes a number
of minor writings by Kiichiro and his father. Womack *et al.* is the book that
introduced the Toyota system more widely in the West.

Cusumano, M.A., *The Japanese Automobile Industry*, Cambridge, MA: Harvard
    University Press, 1985.
Kamiya, S., *My Life with Toyota*, Nagoya: Toyota Motor Sales, 1976.
Kimoto, S., *Quest for Dawn*, Milwaukee, WI: Dougherty, 1991.
Toyoda, E., *Toyota: Fifty Years in Motion*, New York: Kodansha International, 1987.
Womack, J.P., Jones, D.T. and Roos, D., *The Machine that Changed the World*, New
    York: Macmillan, 1990.

LYNDALL FOWNES URWICK (1891–1983)

Lyndall Urwick is the single most important figure in the development of modern management practices and thought. An original thinker, he also borrowed from many other influences, including the scientific management theories of Frederick **Taylor** and Henry Gantt, the efficiency methods and line and staff organisation of Harrington **Emerson**, the school of administrative management pioneered by Henri **Fayol**, the sociological and psychological approaches of Mary Parker **Follett** and Henry Dennison, and the moral and ethical outlook of British firms such as Cadbury Brothers and Rowntree. Throughout his career, he pushed for greater professionalisation in management and for improvements in management education. His consultancy firm, Urwick Orr and Partners, was enormously influential and was for many years the leading management consultancy in Britain. With his younger colleague Edward Brech, he also began the process of recording the history of the modern management movement, and is regarded as a pioneer management historian.[1]

Urwick was born on 3 March 1891 in Malvern, Worcestershire. He graduated from New College, Oxford with a BA in 1912 and then worked briefly for his family company, Fownes & Co. in Worcester. An officer in the Territorial Army, he was called up in 1914 and served most of the war on the Western Front, first as an infantry company commander, where he was awarded the Military Cross for bravery, and then in a succession of staff appointments, for which he received the OBE. He finished the war with the rank of major (he was later promoted to lieutenant-colonel, and is referred to as 'Colonel Urwick' in many records).

Returning to Fownes & Co., Urwick sought to apply some of the lessons of organisation he had learned during the war to a business setting. During the war he had come across the writings of Frederick Winslow Taylor, and had become a convert to scientific management. Throughout his subsequent career, Urwick continued to admire Taylor, not so much for the details of the scientific management system, but for the methodical approach and scientific discipline with which he approached the task. It was probably during the war also that Urwick came across the ideas of Emerson, and he subsequently developed the line and staff model of organisation still further in his own work. Over the years 1919–21 Urwick slowly developed his own philosophy of management, using scientific management as a basis but adapting and evolving its concepts to suit what he perceived as the specific needs of British industry.

By 1921 Urwick's ideas had come to the attention of Benjamin Seebohm Rowntree, head of the Rowntree chocolate works in York and a fellow convert to scientific management, and Urwick was invited to give a paper at that year's Oxford Management Conference. His subject, 'Is Management a Science?', was electrifying to many in his audience, most of whom had heard of scientific management only vaguely. Rowntree, impressed by the 30-year-old Urwick's ideas, offered him a post with the Rowntree company in York, with the chance to implement his ideas while reorganising the company's sales and administrative offices. Urwick joined Rowntree, where he met and was also greatly influenced by Oliver Sheldon. Sheldon was a remarkable (if now largely forgotten) figure, whose 1923 book *The Philosophy of Management* was a great success at the time and continues to be admired by management historians. Working almost independently, Sheldon had evolved a definition and system of management and administration which both accepted the principles of efficiency and offered a humanist ethic of management that placed issues such as human motivation and personal relationships in organisations at the fore. Sheldon was an early sceptic of the value of scientific management, and thought that human issues were all important:

> Industry is not a machine; it is a complex form of human association. The true reading of its past and present is in terms of human beings – their thoughts, aims and ideals – not in terms of systems or of machinery. The true understanding of industry is to understand the thoughts of those engaged in it. The advance of science and the cult of efficiency have tended to obscure the fundamental humanity of industry. We have paid in largely to our account of applied industrial science, but we are bankrupt of human understanding.[2]

In his four years at Rowntree, Urwick took on board a great deal of this ethos. It was also during this period that he met Mary Parker Follett, who again became a considerable influence on him; he remained an admirer of her ideas long after her death. He also became interested in the problems of marketing, and again was able to learn much from recent US developments in this field. To Urwick goes the credit for the reorganisation of Rowntree's sales department which was of great assistance to the company in its long competition with

Cadbury Brothers, and the influence of Urwick's ideas can be seen in the subsequent 'marketing revolution' at Rowntree in the 1930s.

From 1926 to 1928 Urwick was involved in the establishment of the Management Research Groups. The brainchild of Rowntree, who had seen similar concepts in the USA, these were intended as informal groups of senior managers and directors who would meet periodically to discuss matters of mutual concern and exchange experience in fields such as marketing, production, financial control and other areas of development. The task of setting these up on an experimental basis was given to Urwick, with funding from the Social Research Trust set up by Rowntree's father, Joseph Rowntree. By 1927 four groups had been established, each with 8–10 participating companies. By the end of 1928 the movement was a confirmed success, with more groups being established. Although the initial idea had been Rowntree's, it was Urwick's hard work and management skills that allowed the scheme to come to fruition.

From this success, Urwick moved into international management circles. In 1927 he was a member of the British delegation to the World Economic Conference, and at the end of 1928 he was appointed director of the International Management Institute in Geneva, in which post he served until 1933. During this period he did his best to make British managers more aware of international developments. In this last achievement he was only partially successful; although he succeeded in bringing the International Management Conference to London in 1935, participation by British companies and institutions was lukewarm.

In 1934 Urwick set up a consulting business in London in partnership with the industrial engineer John L. Orr. Orr had formerly been a senior member of the British Bedaux Company, a firm set up to import into Britain the techniques of the consultant Charles Bedaux, based on an amended form of scientific management.[3] Urwick Orr and Partners, the first management consultancy business in the UK, faced the difficulty of persuading traditionalists in British industry to accept this new service, but the company made a steady start and its client list grew. Within five years, thirty consultants were being employed by the company. All had substantial previous management experience and were given additional in-depth training by the two partners. The company described its services as 'consulting specialists in organisation and management', indicating the wide scope of services offered. Within those first five years, specific teams had been developed for providing services in clerical methods and administration, in the effective process of delegation, in sales management and marketing, in the improvement of manufacturing productivity, and in financial planning and control.

In addition to his consulting activities, Urwick worked continually to professionalise management and establish the discipline on a firmer footing. Again he was hampered by resistance in many parts of the British industrial establishment, where the traditional view that management was an innate ability rather than a professional skill that could be learned continued to hold sway; in 1946 Sir Charles Renold, chairman of the British Institute of Management, resigned his post in protest over moves by the BIM to recognise that management was a profession. Nonetheless, Urwick continued to make headway. In 1937 he was a leading force behind the foundation of the British Management Council, and in 1938 he accompanied the British delegation to the International Management Conference in Washington, DC. In 1937 he collaborated with Luther Gulick in editing *Papers on the Science of Administration*, a landmark management publication of the 1930s which included contributions by the two editors, Henri Fayol, Mary Parker Follett, James **Mooney** and John Lee, among others. During the Second World War he was seconded to government service and worked to develop and apply operational improvements in departments and organisations engaged in war work.

Education and training for managers was another of Urwick's abiding interests, and his efforts led in 1945 to his appointment by the Department of Education to chair a departmental committee on education for management. In the face of severe opposition from the establishment, Urwick nevertheless succeeded in creating a consensus regarding the committee's final recommendations. These included a national policy favouring and providing facilities for management studies and examinations covering all aspects and all regions of the country, and an integrated pattern of syllabuses providing for cover of those subjects that were common among different functions and sections of the management process. Both these recommendations were adopted, and the moves Urwick had set afoot eventually led to the creation of the first two modern business schools in Britain, Manchester Business School and London Business School, in the 1960s.

Another aspect of Urwick's professionalisation of management can be seen in his interest in the history of the discipline. Here again it is possible to see the influence of Oliver Sheldon, who had argued in 1923 that:

> Industrial history ... is necessary to place the present in the right focus. History can never act as an infallible guide for the

present. Historical analogy is no proof. Every problem has peculiar features which demand that it shall be treated on its merits. But history gives the necessary background and places events in their true perspective. It gives proportion and a sense of relative values. It shows the forces which have fostered the growth of what to-day are problems ... Management, without a broad knowledge of industrial history, is apt to be impressed only with the vivid colours of the present.[4]

Urwick likewise felt strongly that as a profession, management ought to be aware of its traditions and its heroes; in particular, he believed British managers ought to be proud of the achievements and ideas of men such as Robert **Owen** and Charles **Babbage**, who in many ways had anticipated the ideas of the American scientific management movement by decades. His partner in this endeavour was Edward Brech, who had joined Urwick Orr shortly before the war. Together, Urwick and Brech produced the three-volume *The Making of Scientific Management* (1947–9). Volume I consisted of short biographies of leading figures in international management thought, while Volume II focused on the development of British management from the Industrial Revolution forward. Volume III was an account of the Hawthorne experiments on workplace motivation in the 1920s and 1930s, of which Urwick had been an observer. In 1956 Urwick edited *The Golden Book of Management*, a collection of biographies of pioneers of scientific management which included not only figures from the British and American movements but also otherwise unknown figures such as the Pole Karel Adamiecki and the Brazilian Roberto Simonsen.

Urwick's writings on management covered a broad range of topics, ranging from the principles of organisation to new developments in marketing. Much of his writing consists of explanations of basic principles and techniques. His best general work is *Management of Tomorrow*, written at the depth of the Great Depression and published in 1933. Part expression of personal philosophy, part setting out of a system, part clarion call to British management to come to terms with the new world of business:

Scientific methods of management are in practice the most economical and the most effective. Thus a preparation of minds has been taking place, where such preparation was most important and where, in the long run, it is likely to prove most influential.

303

The necessity for such a development is overwhelming. The paradox presented by the present condition of the world's economic affairs is both unprecedented and intolerable. It is unprecedented because for the first time the world community can produce its requirements. Of that there is no question. It is intolerable because men and women have changed. There are greater general knowledge and wider expectations of life which cynicism may easily ferment into despair and disorder. Broadly speaking, large populations have become at the same time and for the first time intercommunicating and economically conscious.[5]

Here too he offers his own definition of scientific management, reminiscent of **Casson** and Emerson rather than Taylor: 'it is the substitution, as far and to the full extreme which our knowledge allows, of an analysis and a basis of fact for opinion'.[6] Scientific *thinking*, he says, must become the dominant mode of thought for managers. A full chapter is devoted to research, and two more to organisation: not surprisingly, as an ex-army officer, Urwick advocates the 'line and staff' principle of organisation first described by Emerson and introduced into the UK by Casson. In a remarkable chapter which is well in advance of its time, he describes how businesses need to adopt a 'marketing point of view',[7] anticipating the later urging of American writers such as Theodore Levitt and Philip **Kotler** for managers and businesses to become more marketing-oriented. Marketing, says Urwick, is about far more than distribution; it is about finding out what customers want and need, and then providing it for them. He also reiterates his call for more and better training. In the final chapter of the book, Urwick speaks of scientific management as leading to a revolution in the way businesses are organised and governed:

What new forms will be evolved by business and science working in co-operation it is yet too early to say. Knowledge of the facts is insufficient. Thought and experiment are alike hampered by outworn conventions and traditional practices. One thing is certain. They will bear little resemblance either to the forms of the past or to the imaginative structures which theorists have tried to force upon the world. They will be sound and enduring on two conditions only. They must be intellectually consistent with the principles which underlie the achievements of machine production. They must be practically valid, mixed in the crucible of fact and cast in the mould of effective action.[8]

Urwick continued his tireless activities in consulting, writing, training and education until 1965, when he retired, settling in Australia. He died there on 5 December 1983. He remains one of the most important figures in British management history. He saw how to develop on and expand the new ideas coming out of the USA, and adapt them to British culture. He never concentrated on the technical aspects of scientific management, looking instead at the basic principles that he perceived as underlying *all* good management. In an age which perceives management as forever 'new', Urwick had the courage to look back for inspiration to the past, finding confirmation of his own ideas on management in the practice and thought of men such as Owen and Babbage.

See also: **Babbage, Casson, Emerson, Fayol, Follett, Lever, Mooney, Owen, Taylor**

Major works

Urwick was a prolific writer, and what follows is only a small selection of his major works. *Management of Tomorrow* is perhaps the most important of these, but *Patterns of Organization* and *The Elements of Administration* are considered, thoughtful works. As noted, his works on management history are now of great interest.

The Meaning of Rationalization, London: Nisbet, 1929.
Management of Tomorrow, London: Nisbet, 1933.
(With L.H. Gulick) (eds) (1937) *Papers on the Science of Administration*, New York: Institute for Public Administration, 1937.
The Elements of Administration, London: Nisbet, 1944.
Patterns of Organization, London: Nisbet, 1946.
(With E.F.L. Brech) *The Making of Scientific Management*, London: Management Publications Trust, 1947–9, 3 vols; repr. Bristol: Thoemmes Press, 2002.
(ed.) *The Golden Book of Management*, London: Newman Neame, 1956.
Is Management a Profession?, London: Urwick Orr, 1958.

Further reading

Brech's five-volume work has frequent references to Urwick and his achievements, and those of many other pioneers of management in early twentieth-century Britain.

Brech, E.F.L., *The Evolution of Modern Management*, Bristol: Thoemmes Press, 2002, 5 vols.

Notes

1   I am indebted to Edward Brech for much of the material in this chapter. More detail on Urwick's achievements can be found in Dr Brech's monumental work *The Evolution of Modern Management*, Bristol: Thoemmes Press, 2002, 5 vols.

2   O. Sheldon, *The Philosophy of Management*, London: Pitman, 1923, p. 27.

3   Born in France, Bedaux spent much of his working life in America, where he developed an amended version of Taylor's time-study system which also accounted more effectively for worker fatigue and the need for rest. The system was very popular in Britain for a time. Bedaux himself made millions out of the system and returned to France. Right-wing in his views, he collaborated with the Vichy regime and the Nazis during the Second World War, and died in prison while awaiting a trial for treason in 1944.

4   Sheldon, *The Philosophy of Management*, p. 259.

5   L.F. Urwick, *Management of Tomorrow*, London: Nisbet, 1933, p. xv.

6   *Ibid.*, p. 21.

7   *Ibid.*, p. 80.

8   *Ibid.*, p. 201.

JACK WELCH (1935–)

Jack Welch, who retired as head of General Electric late in 2001, was one of the most admired business leaders of the 1990s. Opinion polls of businessmen regularly named him as the most successful CEO in America, or even the world. GE itself was one of the world's most admired companies. Ruthless, talented, ambitious and pragmatic, Welch seemed the archetypal American industrialist. His successes over nearly thirty-five years with the corporation can be ascribed not to a talent for innovation, or to strategic genius – Welch has by common consent neither of these virtues – or even to his own leadership style, but rather are down to simple managerial competence. What Welch did he did well, usually better than his competitors. His career shows us that the ability to focus on basics and work hard may itself be a source of powerful competitive advantage in a world of business dominated by confusion and fad.

John Welch Jr was born in Salem, Massachusetts in 1935, the son of a train conductor. He was the first person in his family to go to university, taking a degree in chemical engineering from the University of Massachusetts and then going on to take a doctorate at the University of Illinois. He then joined a General Electric subsidiary, GE Plastics, as an engineer, but within a year was threatening to quit as he could see no room for promotion in the giant, strongly hierarchical corporation. He was talked out of this move by his boss, who shared many of Welch's frustrations with the GE bureaucracy and who persuaded the corporation to give Welch more scope for his entrepreneurial ideas. Welch stayed, and by 1977 was head of GE Plastics, which he had helped grow into a major business in its own right, with a turnover of more than $1 billion annually. Now recognised as a rising star, he was made a vice-president of GE and given charge of its consumer credit division. In 1981, aged forty-six, he was appointed chairman chief executive of GE after a fierce internal struggle over who should get the job.

Welch continued as he had begun. When he took over GE it was already one of the largest companies in the USA, with profits of around $1.7 billion. He proceeded to develop the company through both acquisition and internal expansion, pushing GE right to the top of the corporate league table; in 2000 profits exceeded $12 billion, and GE's market capitalisation had grown from $12 billion to over $200 billion in twenty years. To some observers, Welch seemed to have the Midas touch; some journals hailed him as the greatest CEO ever. Everything he did seemed to work successfully. Only at the very end of his career was there a sour note; a bid to take over the European electronics firm Honeywell failed when it was vetoed by the European Commission. Welch himself had masterminded the deal, and when it failed, many blamed him personally; in fact, domestic political pressures in the European Union were the likely cause of the veto. In any event, this marked the end of Welch's career and he retired slightly later than planned in late 2001.

The ingredients of the Welch success are few and simple: organisational flexibility, quality products, well-trained and motivated people, and strong leadership from the top. When Welch took over GE it was a bureaucratic nightmare, with a labyrinthine bureaucracy and managers required to follow huge procedures manuals, the Blue Books, for even simple tasks. Welch set about abolishing most of this structure, stripping out layer after layer of management and making nearly a quarter of GE's workforce redundant in a matter of a few years. Unprofitable subsidiaries were sold off or closed down. Welch himself won the nickname 'Neutron Jack', after the neutron bomb which reputedly killed off people while leaving buildings standing intact. But Welch wanted what he got; a much leaner and more flexible organisation which concentrated on its core strengths and markets and could respond quickly to new events. Welch had shown that there was no inherent contradiction between size and flexibility; big organisations did not necessarily have to be bureaucratic. He showed this through a rapid expansion in the company's core markets in the 1980s which saw more than 500 acquisitions or start-ups around the world in the space of a decade.

Welch was an early convert to the quality movement, and an admirer of the quality gurus such as W. Edwards **Deming** and Joseph Juran. He was also probably influenced by another highly successful chief executive and competitor, Robert Galvin at Motorola, who in the 1980s introduced a 'six sigma' quality programme aimed at achieving total quality (i.e. no rejects) in production. Welch introduced his own 'six sigma' programme in 1995, one of the first American companies after Motorola to do so, with the aim of achieving a defect rate of fewer than 3 per million in all the corporation's manufacturing units. By 1997, the programme had yielded costs savings of over $300 million, and was a major factor in GE's rising profitability.

GE's investment in training has been one of the corporation's most remarkable features. By 1998 the centre had trained over 15,000 managers. Welch set up an in-house management training centre in upstate New York and personally oversaw its development. He put in a personal appearance during almost every programme and spoke to the managers involved. By some estimates, GE spends half a billion dollars a year on training, making it one of the largest investors in management training in the USA.

Perhaps the most impressive thing about Welch is his approach to leadership. Unlike many companies that de-layer and strip out their managerial hierarchy, Welch realised from the beginning that this stripping out would have to be counterbalanced and that a new centre of organisational gravity would be required. He believed in devolution of responsibility down the line, and encouraged workers and managers to form teams and come up with ideas, but he knew from the beginning that in an organisation of the size and complexity of GE, departments and divisions could not simply be allowed to wander at will. Some form of coordination mechanism was required. For twenty years, Welch himself was that mechanism. Much of his working life was spent travelling around GE's far-flung operations, meeting managers and workers, learning about and solving their problems, and trying to enthuse them with his own vision of where the company was going. He backed this up with an ability to recruit and place talented younger managers in key subsidiaries – for example, when taking over the failing broadcaster NBC, Welch was able to revive the company by replacing key managers with his own choices, young and energetic managers who transformed NBC in just a few years – but at GE, every manager knew that the buck stopped with Welch himself.

The management historian David Lewis notes that Welch's management philosophy can be summed up in a few key phrases:

- invest in people;
- be number one;
- change is constant;
- speed is everything;
- services are the future;
- a manager is not a dictator;
- communication must be candid;
- strangle bureaucracy or it will strangle you;
- a company can be run just like the corner store.

The keynotes, says Lewis, 'are simplicity, flexibility and focus'.[1] In other words, none of this is managerial rocket science. Welch has not done anything radically new at GE; indeed, in many ways he has not gone as far as the gurus and theorists might like. Ultimately pragmatic, he has recognised what will work and what will not. He has a few basic values – respect, flexibility, openness and hard work – and he has implemented these. In this way, as Lewis fairly says, Welch 'has indeed achieved something remarkable'.[2]

So are the encomiums of Welch justified? Is he really the greatest CEO of all time? Or does his success merely show up the poor quality of corporate leadership in the world around him? If Welch has achieved miracles by merely doing the basics right, what have his competitors and rivals been doing? Much interest is focusing on the performance of Welch's hand-picked successor as CEO at GE, Jeffrey Immelt. If Immelt succeeds to the same extent as Welch, it will be argued that the system of management Welch put into place at GE is an enduring one and there will be a scramble to copy his methods. If, however, GE's fortunes wane, it will be suggested that Welch's successes were due to his own leadership and that he was another 'flash-in-the-pan' leader who could not build an enduring edifice. At the time of writing it is too soon tell which will be the case.

If one looks at Welch's career expecting to find some flash of insight or decisive moment that marks him out for greatness, such as **Ford**'s vision for the Model T or **Matsushita**'s tap water philosophy, then one looks in vain. Welch treated management neither as an art nor a science but as a craft. What he did, he did well: very, very well indeed. If there is a single word which best sums him up, it is probably 'competent'.

In some senses, asking whether Welch was the greatest CEO ever is asking the wrong question. Greatness is a relative term in any field, but never more so than in management, where success is contingent not only on personal qualities but also on economic and market forces outside individual control. What we can say of Welch is that he did what all managers ought to be doing, and he did these things far better than his competitors did them. It may be that successful management amounts, in the end, to just that.

See also: **Arkwright, Bat'a, Ford, Gates, Matsushita, Medici, Toyoda**

Major works

Welch's autobiography, for which he reportedly received a seven-figure advance, is said to be in preparation.

Further reading

Like Bill Gates, Americans tend to either love Jack Welch or hate him. O'Boyle is a harsh critic; Lowe and Slater approach their subject with more reverence.

Lowe, J., *Jack Welch Speaks: Wisdom from the World's Greatest Business Leader*, New York: John Wiley & Sons, 1998.
O'Boyle, T.F., *At Any Cost: Jack Welch, General Electric, and the Pursuit of Profit*, New York: Knopf, 1998.
Slater, R., *Jack Welch and the GE Way: Management Insights and Leadership Secrets of the Legendary CEO*, New York: McGraw-Hill, 1999.

Notes

1 D.C. Lewis, 'The Legacy: How Will General Electric Fare without Jack Welch?', *Mastering Management Online*, August 2001, www.ftmastering.com/mmo
2 *Ibid.*

FURTHER READING

The biographies of managers and management thinkers can be an excellent tool for studying the development of management methods and comparing and evaluating different techniques, as this book hopefully demonstrates. The following may be of use when exploring this field further.

Crainer, S. and Clutterbuck, D., *Makers of Management*, London: Macmillan, 1990. (Very good short assessments of a number of modern figures.)

Davis, W., *The Innovators: The Essential Guide to Business Thinkers*, London: Ebury Press, 1987. (Short and overly fulsome biographical sketches, but includes a number of important figures not often found elsewhere.)

Drury, H.B., *Scientific Management: A History and Criticism*, New York: Columbia University Press, 1915. (Contains some excellent biographies of the principal figures in the field – Taylor, Gantt, Gilbreth and Emerson, plus others – drawn from interviews and personal knowledge.)

Gabor, A., *The Capitalist Philosophers*, New York: Times Business, 1999. (Good profiles of managers and others influential in the business world over the past century.)

Ingham, John N. and Feldman, Lynne B., *African-American Business Leaders: A Biographical Dictionary*, Westport, CT: Greenwood Press, 1994. (An excellent collection of studies of little-known figures.)

Jeremy, D.J. (ed.), *Dictionary of Business Biography*, London: Butterworths, 1984–6, 5 vols. (A massive undertaking, covering many hundreds of British entrepreneurs from the mid-eighteenth century to the 1980s. This work is highly inclusive, and includes studies of all senior figures during this period, not just the 'successes'; an indispensable reference work.)

Leavitt, J.A., *American Women Managers and Administrators: A Selective Biographical Dictionary of Twentieth-Century Leaders*, Westport, CT: Greenwood Press, 1985. (A very important study of an often overlooked group of business leaders and managers.)

Piramal, G., *Business Maharajahs*, New Delhi: Viking, 1996. (Indispensable to anyone studying business in India.)

Tsutsui, W.M., *Manufacturing Ideology: Scientific Management in Twentieth-Century Japan,* Princeton, NJ: Princeton University Press, 1998. (Not biographies as such, but good profiles of leaders and their ideas.)

Urwick, L.F. (ed.), *The Golden Book of Management: A Historical Record of the Life and Work of Seventy Pioneers*, London: Newman Neame, 1956. (Now long out of print, but very useful; rescues from obscurity dozens of otherwise unknown but very important figures.)

Urwick, L.F. and Brech, E.F.L., *The Making of Scientific Management*, London: Management Publications Trust, 1947–9, 3 vols; repr. Bristol: Thoemmes Press, 1994. (Volume 1 includes biographies of thirteen pioneers, including Taylor, Fayol, Follett and Babbage.)

Warner, M. (ed.), *IEBM Handbook of Management Thinking*, London: International Thomson Business Press, 1998. (Around 150 in-depth biographies, focusing mostly on theorists and researchers but with a good selection of practitioners also (Ford, Matsushita, Ibuka, etc.). Recently featured on a *Financial Times* list of the ten most important management books.)

Witzel, M. (ed.), *Biographical Dictionary of Management*, Bristol: Thoemmes Press, 2001, 2 vols. (Over 600 biographies of management thinkers and practitioners from the classical world to the present day, edited by the present writer. Includes many important figures from Europe and East Asia not included in other collections, but omits a number of the theorists included in Warner, above.)

Wren, D. and Greenwood, R.G., *Management Innovators: The People and Ideas That Have Shaped Modern Business*, New York: Oxford University Press, 1998. (Highly important study by two leading US management historians: essential reading, as are all of Wren's other works.)

INDEX

Abbé, Ernst 27
action 53
action research 6
action science 3, 6–8
actionable knowledge 6
Adamiecki, Karel 288, 303
Adams, John Quincy 262
adaptability 159
administration 97–101
advertising 46, 189–191, 195–197
Allen, Paul 129–130
alliances 243
Araki Toichiro 147, 288
architecture 31
Argyris, Chris 3–8, 53, 64, 67, 121
Arizmendiarietta, José Maria 29
Arkwright, Richard 9–16, 67, 218, 259

Babbage, Charles 17–22, 132, 165, 293, 303, 305
Baker, Ray Stannard 244
Barnard, Chester 101, 270, 279
Barnum, P.T. 162
Barrett, Andrew 189
Barth, Carl 139, 287, 290
Bat'a, Jan 25, 28
Bat'a system of management 23
Bat'a, Tomás 23–29, 35, 112
Bat'a, Tomik 25
Becker, Ernest 267
Bedaux, Charles 300
behavioural theory of the firm 278–279
Benci, Giovanni d'Amerigo 216–217
Bennis, Warren 270

Bentham, Jeremy 262
Berle, Adolph 38–39, 59, 74, 78
Berlinghieri, Berlinghieri 216
Bernard, Claude 97
Berners-Lee, Tim 129, 131
Bliss, William 49
Boisot, Max 30–35, 64, 66, 157, 172
Bond, Michael 171
Boulton, Matthew 13
bounded rationality 278, 280–281
branding 164
brands 22
Brech, Edward 22, 105, 264, 303
Brown, Donaldson 82–84
Buckley, William F. 38
Burnham, James 36–42, 59, 74, 200
business, role of 246
business and society 15–16, 78–79, 258
business units 85
Buzzell, Robert 178

Cadbury, Edward 43–47, 264
Cadbury, George 43–44, 191, 264
Cao Cao 283
capital, owners of 38
Carnegie, Andrew 51
Carpenter, Walter 83–84
case study method 140–141
Casson, Herbert 7, 22, 46, 48–55, 64, 77, 89, 94, 228, 235, 251, 304
Chandler, Alfred D. 39, 41, 56–62, 75, 82–83, 85–86, 159, 213, 231, 268
change 152–154, 156, 223, 237, 270
change, resistance to 5
chaos 269
Chen Huan-Chang 186

Cherington, Paul 139–140, 179
Chiang Kai-shek 283
Clark, Fred 179
Clausewitz, Karl von 152, 201, 224, 283, 285
Clements, Joseph 19
clusters 276
Coase, Ronald 221
cognition 195
Colt, Samuel 162
communications 182, 194–198
competence 306
competition 242
computers 17–20, 118–120, 129–132, 198
Comte, Auguste 97
Confucius 186–187
consolidation 192, 241–242
continuous improvement 46, 69, 76, 297, 298
control 4, 76, 105, 107, 228
Cooke, Morris 288
coordination 105–107, 228, 230
Copeland, Melvin 140, 179
corporate governance 246
Couzens, James 111–113
creativity 220
Crichton, Michael 269
Crompton, Samuel 259
Crosby, Philip 72
cultural space (C-space) 34–35
culture 31–32, 34–35, 66, 126, 156–157, 159, 169–173, 196–197, 236, 249, 257, 267
Cunningham, W.J. 139
cybernetics 119
Cyert, Richard 278

Dale, David 259–260
Daoism 184
data 32, 153
Datini, Francesco 215
Davis, John 227–228, 243
de Geus, Arie 63–66, 247, 274
decentralisation 23, 268–269
defensive routines 5
Deming cycle 70
Deming, W. Edwards 8, 66–72, 76, 127, 269, 297, 308
democracy 107

Dennison, Henry 299
Dewey, John 204
disabled workers, employment of 146
dissatisfaction 5
diversification 214
division of labour 15
Dodge, Horace 111
Dodge, John 111
double loop learning 7
Drew, Daniel 240
Drinkwater, Peter 259
Drucker, Peter 53, 73–79, 85, 101, 155, 239
Drury, Horace 94
du Pont, Alfred 81
du Pont, Coleman 81, 84
du Pont, Pierre 56, 58, 75, 81–86, 113, 225–226
Dunham, Russell 82–83
Durant, William C. 75, 84, 111, 225

economies of scale 150, 176
Edison, Thomas 110
efficiency 26, 51–52, 87, 90, 92–94, 148, 289
Eliot, Charles 137, 138
Ellison, Larry 133
Emerson, Harrington 51, 64, 87–94, 100, 127, 228, 234, 235, 299, 304
employee relations 212
Engels, Friedrich 15, 264
Enron 41, 231
entrepreneurship 76, 173
environment 67, 148
ergonomics 144
ethical issues 66
ethics 42, 155, 161, 168, 199–200, 246, 258, 264, 299
excellence 267–268

factory system 12–15
Fayol, Henri 75, 96–101, 235, 279, 299, 302
feedback 7
feedback loops 119, 235
Fisk, Jim 240
five forces 272
Fleming, Sir Ronald 68, 70
flexibility 94, 151, 212, 269, 284, 307
flexible manufacturing 23

flux 237
Follett, Mary Parker 7, 102, 223, 226, 230, 234, 249, 299, 300, 302
Ford, Bill 39
Ford, Clara 114
Ford, Edsel 113
Ford, Henry 25, 45, 84–85, 109–117, 211, 292, 294, 309
Ford, Henry II 114
Forrester, Jay Wright 64, 66, 118–122
Fréminville, Charles de 98, 100, 288
Freud, Sigmund 203
Frick, Henry Clay 51, 163
Friedman, Milton 178
Fukuzawa Yukichi 122–128
Fulton, Robert 81

Galvin, Robert 308
Gantt, Henry 87, 143, 287, 299
Gates, Bill 129–135, 154
Gay, Edwin 57, 136–141
Giddens, Anthony 103
Gilbreth, Frank 87, 100, 127, 142–148, 288
Gilbreth, Lillian 87, 100, 127, 142–148, 288
Giuntini, Andrea 216
globalisation 173, 253, 256–257
goals 230
Goering, Hermann 226
Goldstein, Kurt 204, 206
Gompers, Samuel 49
Gould, Jay 240
Gras, N.S.B. 57
greatness 310
Griffiths, Samuel B. 282
groups 157–158
Grove, Andrew 130, 149–154, 237
Gulick, Luther 100, 105, 226, 280, 302

Halsey, Frederick 289
Hamel, Gary 270
Hampden-Turner, Charles 35
Han Feizi 187
Handy, Charles 8, 66, 155–161, 239, 270
Hardie, Keir 49
Harriman, Edward 241
Haskell, Amery 82, 84–85

Hathaway, Horace 288
Heinz, Henry 22, 138, 162–168, 193
Heinz, Howard 163
Heraclitus 237
heroes 303
Herzberg, Frederick 203, 207
Hibi Osuke 127
hierarchy 59, 62, 187
hierarchy of needs 204–208
Highs, Thomas 11
Hill, Jim 241
Hitler, AdolF 226–227
Hofstede, Geert 35, 157, 169–173, 257
home economics 144
Hoover, Herbert 90, 144
human resources management 169
Huxley, Aldous 109
hypertext organisation 235, 251

Iacocca, Lee 114
Ibuka Masaru 173–176, 210, 248
ideology 221
Immelt, Jeffery 309
industrial democracy 23
information 32
Ingherami, Francesco 217
Ingherami, Giovanni di Baldino 216–217
innovation 76, 134, 173, 175, 212, 248, 306
intellectual property 11
internationalisation 47
intuition 151
Ishikawa Kaoru 297
Iwama Kazuo 173
Iwasaki Yataro 126

James, William 204
Jobs, Steve 131, 133
Jones, Edward D. 227
Juran, Joseph 66, 67, 69–70, 72, 308
just-in-time 212, 296

Kahn, Albert 112
kanban 296
Kanter, Rosabeth Moss 62, 269, 270
Kay, John 11
Kellogg, William K. 140
Kennedy, John F. 57

key factors for success (KFS) 255
Keynes, John Maynard 74
Khayyam, Omar 223
Kierkegaard, Søren 74
King, William Lyon Mackenzie 137
Knoeppel, Charles 54, 90, 228
knowledge 7–8, 21, 32–33, 35, 64–65, 91, 104, 108, 134, 159, 172, 229, 247–252, 281
knowledge, codification and diffusion 33
knowledge management 30, 72, 104
Knudsen, William 85, 112–114
Kobayashi Ichizo 127
Kotler, Philip 177–183, 304
Krupp, Alfred 43

labour relations 21
Lamont, T.W. 140
Laozi 184–188
Larson, Henrietta 57
le Chatelier, Henri 98, 100, 288
leadership 72, 200–201, 306–308
learning organisation 63–65, 251
Lee, John 302
Lenin, Vladimir Ilich 109
Lever, William 22, 43, 188–193, 264
Levitt, Theodore 77, 178, 179, 183, 304
Levy, Sydney 181
Lewis, John 21, 29
Likert, Rensis 203
line and staff 90–91, 229, 299
living company 65
living organisms 64
location 135
Lovelace, Ada, Countess of 19

Machiavelli, Niccolò 38, 199–202, 236, 285
machine bureaucracy 4
Macnamara, Robert 114
Mahin, John Lee 77
Malcolmson, Alexander 110–111
Malthus, Thomas 262
management by objectives 76
management education 136–141, 299, 302, 308
management, principles of 101
management tasks 75, 98

managerial capitalism 60–61
managerial work 220–222
Mao Zedong 283
March, James 278, 281
marketing 54, 77, 134, 138, 162, 164–166, 168, 177–183, 188–191, 207, 304
marketing concept 180
Marx, Karl 15, 22, 264
Maslow, Abraham 147, 203–208, 234
mass marketing 10, 193
mass production 10, 14, 112, 116, 211
Matsunaga Yasuzaemon 127
Matsushita Konosuke 175, 208–213, 309
Mayo, Elton 6, 67, 270
McArthur, General Douglas 209
McCarthy, Jerome 178
McCormick, Cyrus Hall 112
McGowan, Harry 84
McGregor, Douglas 203, 207, 235
McKann, H.K. 51
McLuhan, Marshall 173, 194–198
Means, Gardiner 38–39, 59, 74, 78
media 195–198
Medici, Cosimo dei 200, 213–218
Medici, Giovanni de Bicci dei 214
Medici, Lorenzo dei 200
mental models 120
metaphors 157
Metcalf, Henry 103
Michels, Roberto 38
middle management 268
Mill, James 262
Mill, John Stuart 22
Mintzberg, Henry 8, 219–224, 235, 254, 276, 280, 285
Mitchell, Wesley Clair 140
Miyamoto Musashi 283
Modigliani, Franco 278
Moltke, Helmuth von 88, 91, 285
Mondragón Cooperative Corporation 29
Mony, Stephane 96
Mooney, James D. 75, 84, 113, 225–231, 302
Moore, Gordon 129, 150
Morgan, Gareth 108, 157, 232–239
Morgan, J.P. 81, 192, 239–246
Morgan, Junius 240

Morita Akio 173–176
motion study 142, 144, 147
motivation 72, 88, 158, 207, 260–261
Moxham, Arthur 82–83
Muck Rakers 245–246
multi-divisional form (M-form) 58, 61, 86, 213, 215
Munsey, Frank 50
Mussolini, Benito 226
Muto Sanji 127

Nakamigawa Hikojiro 127
Nasser, Jac 39
Need, Samuel 12
negotiation 152
networks 105
Newell, Allen 279
Nicholas I, Tsar of Russia 262
Nietzsche, Friedrich Wilhelm 117
Noble, L.C. 163
Nonaka Ikujiro 223, 235, 247–252
Northcliffe, Lord 192
Noyce, Robert 129, 149–151
Noyes, Pierrepont 28

Ohmae Kenichi 246, 247, 252, 253–257, 285
Ohno Taiichi 69, 297
Oldknow, Samuel 13, 259
Oneida 28
organic growth 65
organisation behaviour 104
organisation theory 233
organisational 'species' 221
organisations, purpose of 227–228
Orr, John L. 300
Otaguro Jugoro 127
Owen, Robert 16, 43, 258–265, 303, 305
ownership and control, separation of 38–40, 59

paradox, management of 160, 271
Pareto, Vilifredo 38
participation 44, 202
Patterson, John 50
Perry, Commodore Matthew 123
personal capitalism 61
Peter, Laurence 4
Peter Principle 4–5

Peters, Tom 6, 53, 62, 64, 219, 248, 250, 266–271, 298
philanthropy 44
physiocrats 186
piece rates 45, 289
planning 101, 152
Polanyi, Michael 249
Poor, Henry Varnum 56–57
Porter, Michael 8, 172, 255, 272–277
Portinari, Tomasso 216
POSDCORB 98–99, 101
positivism 97
power 41, 187, 237
Procter, William 193
productivity bonuses 45
professional management 216–217
professionalisation of management 40, 59, 302
profit sharing 21, 27, 191–192
promotion 164–166, 182
prosperity 211
psychic prisons 236
psychology 103–104, 142, 146, 203–208
Pulitzer, Joseph 50

quality 15, 22, 67–72, 76, 88, 165–166, 307–308

Rand, Ayn 40
Raskob, John J. 82, 84–85
Rathenau, Walter 38, 74
Reagan, Ronald 38
Reich, Wilhelm 203
relationships 106, 108, 212
Renold, Sir Charles 40, 302
requisite organisation 28, 88
resistance 5, 7
responsibility 75, 78, 264
revolution 268
Reynolds, R.J. 242, 245
Ripley, William Zebina 38–39, 78, 243
Rockefeller, John D. 245
Roethlisberger, Fritz 6, 67
Roosevelt, Franklin D. 38, 86, 114, 226
Roosevelt, Theodore 245

Rowntree, Benjamin Seebohm 46–47, 103, 264, 300
Rowntree, Joseph 46

Salt, Titus 43–44, 264
Salutati, Antonio 216
Samuelson, Paul 178
satisficing 278–280
scale 133
Schön, Donald 3, 6
Schumpeter, Joseph 73–74, 76
Schwab, Charles M. 51, 242, 288
scientific management 22–23, 54, 87, 90–91, 93, 96, 103, 106, 112, 144, 148, 249, 286, 288–293, 299
scientific methods 20
Scott, Walter Dill 179
Senge, Peter M. 63–66, 121, 247
Shaw, Anne 142, 147
Shaw, Arch 140
Sheldon, Oliver 100, 103, 300, 302
Shewhart, Walter 67–69
Shibusawa Eiichi 128
Shingo Shigeo 69
silent monitors 261
Simon, Herbert 122, 147, 235, 277–281
Simonsen, Roberto 288, 303
single loop learning 7
skills 14, 126
Sloan, Alfred P. 59, 75, 84–86, 113, 114, 225–226, 230
Smalley, John 11
Smiles, Samuel 297
Smith, Adam 59, 125, 186
social dimension of work 78
socially responsible business 43
societal marketing 181
society 155, 227
software 130–135
Son Masayoshi 134
Sorel, Georges 38
Sorenson, Charles 112–114
Stakhanov, Aleksei 292–293
standards 88, 91–92
statistical quality control (SQC) 66–68, 70, 72
Steffens, Lincoln 244
stratagems 284
strategic inflection points 153

strategic thinking 285–286
strategy 58, 62, 199, 201, 219, 222–224, 225, 253–256, 272–277, 282–285
structure 75–76, 82
Strutt, Jedediah 12
suggestion schemes 45
Sunzi 282–286
system dynamics 119–122
systems 66

Taddeo, Antonio di 216
Takeo Toshisuke 288
Tanaglia, Jacopo 216
Tani, Angelo 216
tap water philosophy 212
Tarbell, Ida Minerva 245
Taylor, Frederick W. 45, 54, 81, 83, 87, 90, 94, 96, 100, 112, 117, 127, 139, 142–144, 234, 249, 286–293, 299, 304
Tead, Ordway 103
Teagle, Walter 59
technocracy 104
technocrats 40
technological development 13
technology 20–21, 25–26, 28, 173, 195–196
technology diffusion 14
Teece, David 62
therbligs 144
thinking 66
thinking organisation 135
Thompson, Sanford 288
Thornley, David 11
time and motion study 142, 147
total quality management 69–72, 297
Towne, Henry 289
Toyoda Eiji 296
Toyoda Kiichiro 69, 294–298
Toyoda Sakichi 295, 297
Toyoda Shoichiro 296, 297
Toyota Production System 67, 69–71, 294, 296–298
training 152, 249
transaction costs 15
transformation 83
Trompenaars, Fons 35
Trotsky, Leon 37
trusts 241–242

Tsukamoto Tetsuo 173
Turing, Alan 20

Ueno Yoichi 147
Urwick, Lyndall 22, 103, 105, 143, 226, 264, 279, 288, 299–305

value chain 274
Vanderbilt, Cornelius 240
Vanderbilt, William 241
vertical integration 60, 192
virtue 185
'visible hand' 59

Wang An 118, 133
Waterman, Robert 6, 64, 266, 298
Watt, James 13
Watts, Frank 292

Wayland, Francis 125
Weber, Max 235
Welch, Jack 188, 306–310
welfare 44, 128, 191, 261–262
Wellington, Duke of 19
Westinghouse, George 163
Wiener, Norbert 122, 235
Wilberforce, William 262
Willis, Childe Harold 111
Willys, John North 111
Wood, Robert 59
worker relations 112
workplace autonomy 23
works committees 46
wu-wei 184–186

Zaccaria, Benedetto 218
zero defects 69